SOVIET MILITAR

CASS SERIES ON SOVIET MILITARY THEORY AND PRACTICE

Series Editor – David M. Glantz
Ft. Leavenworth, Kansas

This series examines in detail the evolution of Soviet military science and the way the Soviets have translated theoretical concepts for the conduct of war into concrete military practice. Separate volumes focus on how the Soviets have applied and refined theory in combat and on how they have structured their forces to suit the requirement of changing times.

1. David M. Glantz, *Soviet Military Deception in the Second World War*
2. David M. Glantz, *Soviet Military Operational Art: In Pursuit of Deep Battle*
3. David M. Glantz, *Soviet Military Intelligence in War*
4. David M. Glantz, *The Soviet Conduct of Tactical Maneuver: Spearhead of the Offensive*
5. David M. Glantz, *Soviet Air Assault: The Vertical Dimension of Maneuver*

SOVIET MILITARY INTELLIGENCE IN WAR

DAVID M. GLANTZ

FRANK CASS

First published in 1990 in Great Britain by
FRANK CASS & CO. LTD.
Gainsborough House, Gainsborough Road,
London E11 1RS, England

and in the United States of America by
FRANK CASS
c/o International Specialized Book Services, Inc.
5602 N.E. Hassalo Street, Portland, Oregon 97213

Copyright © 1990 David M. Glantz

The views expressed here are those of the author. They
should not necessarily be construed as those of the U.S.
Department of Defense or the United States Army.

British Library Cataloguing in Publication Data

Glantz, David M.
  Soviet military intelligence in war.
  1. Soviet military intelligence services, history
  I. Title
  355.34320947

  ISBN 0-7146-3374-7
  ISBN 0-7146-4076-X pbk

Library of Congress Cataloging-in-Publication Data

Glantz, David M.
  Soviet military intelligence in war / David M. Glantz.
      p.   cm.— (Cass series on Soviet military theory and practice;
  3)
  Includes bibliographical references.
  ISBN 0-7146-3374-7. — ISBN 0-7146-4076-X (pbk.)
  1. World War, 1939–1945—Military intelligence—Soviet Union.
  2. World War, 1939–1945—Campaigns. I. Title. II. Series.
  D810.S7G552 1990
  940.54'8647—dc20   90-33240
                                                                      CIP

Printed in Great Britain by
Antony Rowe Ltd, Chippenham

CONTENTS

LIST OF MAPS

LIST OF FIGURES

ABBREVIATIONS

A	Army
B	Brigade
Bn	Battalion
CC	Cavalry corps
CD	Cavalry division
D	Division
GA	Guards army
GCC	Guards cavalry corps
GCD	Guards cavalry division
Gds	Guards
GMC	Guards mechanized corps
Gp	Group
GRD	Guards rifle division
GTA	Guards tank army
GTB	Guards tank brigade
GTC	Guards tank corps
MC	Mechanized corps
PzA	Panzer army
RB	Rifle brigade
RC	Rifle corps
RD	Rifle division
TA	Tank army
TB	Tank brigade
TC	Tank corps

On maps, numerals with no
abbreviations attached are divisions
(German and Soviet).

PREFACE

Churchill once referred to the conflict on the Eastern Front during the First World War as the *Unknown War*. This would also be a most fitting description for the war between Nazi Germany and the Soviet Union — which, although it has drawn considerable attention in general nevertheless remains obscure in many of its details to those in the West and even to the Russian public. In this volume, Colonel Glantz sheds light on the most hidden dimension of this second unknown war — namely, the role of Soviet intelligence in what the Soviets term their "Great Patriotic War."

Soviet Military Intelligence in War is the second of three volumes written by Colonel Glantz on the contribution of intelligence and deception operations to the Soviet victory over Nazi Germany.[1] These pioneering volumes lay a solid foundation for future research in this field but cannot be considered definitive since few official documents on the role of intelligence have been released by the Soviet Government. Indeed, no other field of research, as shown by Professor Hinsley in his magisterial Official History of *British Intelligence in the Second World War*, suffers from such a critical scarcity of direct documentation. Consequently, Colonel Glantz's work had to be based on fragmentary information gleaned from close scrutiny of Soviet literature on the "Great Patriotic War." In addition to meticulously surveying this literature, Colonel Glantz also gained access to some Soviet classified reports prepared during the war on the performance of their intelligence in support of military operations. Whenever possible, he also relied on a methodologically indirect approach that involved trying to learn as much as possible from German wartime intelligence reports; these reports assessed the collecting methods, organizational structure, procedures, and overall performance of Soviet intelligence.

As Colonel Glantz indicates in the text of this volume, numerous questions related to the performance of Soviet intelligence during the war remain unanswered. Foremost in every reader's mind is the question whether Soviet intelligence succeeded in systematically breaking the higher-level German enigma codes on a scale approaching that of the British and American ULTRA system. It is perhaps wiser to ask *whether* Soviet intelligence managed to develop its own equivalent of the ULTRA system, *when* such a system matured and *how* effectively it was integrated into the formulation of Soviet strategy and the planning of military operations.[2]

There are numerous hints in Colonel Glantz's text that point to the existence of a major Soviet success in the Sigint intelligence war. For example, during the last days of June 1943, what was the nature of the information that finally convinced the ever-suspicious Stalin and the hesitant Stavka that Kursk alone was the main objective of the German offensive "Zitadelle"? There is little doubt that intelligence from multiple sources (e.g., human intelligence; the interrogation of POWs; and air reconnaissance) strongly indicated that Kursk was the designated *Schwerpunkt* of the forthcoming attack. But none of these sources could, by itself, be considered definitive; moreover, Soviet intelligence, much more so than the German Abwehr (*Fremde Heere Ost*), must have been aware of the ease with which human perceptions could be manipulated for the purpose of deception. Yet at the end of June, Stalin and the Stavka were suddenly *certain* that they had the right answer:

> The situation *finally became clear* in the last few days of June, and we realized that the enemy would mount an offensive in the coming days *precisely* here at the Kursk area *and nowhere else*. (See p.198 – Zhukov's words quoted by Glantz [my emphasis])

Although such cryptic statements do not constitute proof, they resemble many similarly veiled references to ULTRA in Western official histories and in the memoirs of some top civilian and military leaders. It therefore appears that a Soviet counterpart of the Allied ULTRA system had finally matured by the end of June 1943. For those aware of how difficult it is for any intelligence organization to pinpoint the axis of an attack, even if the attack is known to be imminent, the unequivocal identification of Kursk as the target of the German offensive is reminiscent of the battles of Midway or Alam Halfa in which the defenders' certainty regarding the place of attack was based on information from unquestionable Sigint sources.

Furthermore, although not known for certain, it can be assumed that like the pre-ULTRA-disclosure literature in the West, many references to the successes of human intelligence or to air reconnaissance actually serve as a cover for successful Sigint operations. In Soviet literature, for example, it is likely that much of the praise heaped upon the achievements of the master spy Richard Sorge is only a convenient cover for Soviet Sigint successes in breaking various Japanese codes. The same is probably true of accounts lauding the spectacular achievements of the "Lucy" ring in penetrating the OKW and passing information on a continuous and near real-time basis to Soviet intelligence. This reminds one of the role of "Boniface" on the Allied side.

In addition, we still know relatively little about the actual contribution of the Soviet equivalent of the British "Y" service to military operations, but what we do know is in this impressive volume. Based on this information, it is quite possible that the Soviet radio *razvedka* played a more important part in the overall Soviet intelligence effort than its counterpart did in that of the West; and that which we attribute to the existence of a Soviet ULTRA system may actually owe more to the Soviet "Y" service. These and many other questions cannot be answered definitively until the Soviet Union opens its archives -- a possibility which appears remote even in the age of glasnost and perestroika.

This book is primarily concerned with the contribution of Soviet military intelligence on the operational and tactical levels of war, and less so with that on the strategic level which he discusses elsewhere in *The Role of Intelligence in Soviet Military Strategy During the Second World War*.

Soviet Military Intelligence in War is dedicated as much to the study of military operations as it is to intelligence. To be more precise, it examines the area where intelligence and operations *overlap*; the nature of coordination between the two; and the support provided by intelligence to operational planning and execution (or the absence of such support). This is not a study of intelligence work as such, but of how intelligence can improve the chances of success on the battlefield by facilitating the more effective and economical use of troops. This book is the first to be published on intelligence and military operations of the Red Army in the Second World War and one of very few on the topic in general.[3]

Since it was both impossible and unnecessary to rewrite the entire history of Soviet military operations in the Second World War, Colonel Glantz has chosen four detailed case studies comprising a representative sample of different periods in the evolution of Soviet military intelligence throughout the war. Each chapter is structured along the following lines:

(1) A detailed summary of the military situation at a given point in time and the operational intelligence problems it creates.

(2) A detailed discussion of the intelligence assets available at the time for the collection and processing of intelligence, including a discussion of the different intelligence organizations, and special intelligence units – ranging from air *razvedka*, artillery *razvedka*, and human intelligence to units specializing in the gathering of intelligence and sabotage behind enemy lines, partisan *razvedka*, and the Special Motorized Rifle Brigade of Special Designations (a cross between the SOE and LRDG). This section also includes a discussion concerning the tasking of the intelligence community by different command levels as well as the coordination efforts among the various intelligence organizations (i.e., NKVD and GRU) and between the intelligence community on all levels and those responsible for the conduct of operations. The coordination of all intelligence work was seen (as in Britain) as *the key* to its contribution to the war effort.

(3) The final section evaluates the contribution of intelligence to the planning, implementation, and follow up on the battlefield of military operations. It is an assessment of the *actual* influence of intelligence on the course of military operations on all levels.

As Colonel Glantz demonstrates, the Soviet military in fact paid much greater attention than most Western military organizations to the role of intelligence before the outbreak of the war, and at least on paper, Russian military intelligence was more advanced than that of most other countries (Chapters 2 and 3). Yet as the first case study reveals, that which appeared satisfactory in theory proved inadequate in practice under conditions of strategic and operational surprise that led to the destruction of the Soviet intelligence infrastructure in 1941 and 1942 (Chapter 4). During the second phase, the Soviet Army regained its equilibrium as the Wehrmacht overextended itself beyond what Clausewitz called the culminating point of the attack and proceeded to rebuild its intelligence infrastructure almost from scratch while slowly learning the lessons of acquiring and using intelligence in modern war.

This arduous trial and error process, which was experienced by all other military organizations during the war (in particular by the Allies) finally culminated in the Stalingrad counter-offensive in the winter of 1942/1943 (Chapter 5). After a series of setbacks during the late winter and spring of 1943, partially as a result of inadequate intelligence, the Russians, while still on the defensive, finally gained the intelligence initiative early in the summer of 1943 immediately preceding the battle of Kursk. This was also the period in which Soviet intelligence matured and made *the most critical contribution* in finally wrenching the initiative from the Wehrmacht. The outstanding quality and success of Soviet intelligence was evidenced by its accomplishment of the very difficult and important task (never achieved by either German or Japanese intelligence) of sounding a clear and timely warning regarding the enemy's offensive plans and intentions (Chapter 6). After that point, although Soviet intelligence had come into its own – its contribution became less pivotal since the balance of power had shifted irreversibly in favor of the Soviet Union. Thereafter on the offensive, the Red Army was capable of winning the war even with imperfect intelligence, while intelligence, in any event, became more difficult to obtain and use on the move (1943–45) (Chapter 7).

The final chapter is dedicated to intelligence lessons learned from the "Great Patriotic War" – the greater Russian awareness of the importance of operational and combat intelligence in the age of high-tech; the increased lethality of precision-guided munitions; and increased speed and mobility – all of which put an even higher premium on the value of intelligence and its real-time integration into the battlefield decision-making process. Colonel Glantz then shows how the Soviet military translated all of these lessons, problems and its understanding of the potential offered by modern technology for the collection and processing of intelligence into specific intelligence procedures and integrated them into the combat doctrine as it evolved in recent years.

Most important, Colonel Glantz argues that these experiences indicate that the quantity of intelligence offers no panaceas for commanders in battle. Rather, it is quality – both in information and most important, analysis – that contributes most to the achievement of victory.

Colonel Glantz's work on Soviet military intelligence reveals a richness of detail that cannot be matched in any other work. Others can now rely on his research as their starting point for addressing a number of more general methodological and comparative questions that the scope of this book does not allow him to raise. For instance, how does the experience of the Soviet military, insofar as intelligence and military operations are concerned, compare with that in the other theaters of war in the Second World

War? How does one tackle the methodological question of identifying (or isolating) the role of intelligence and deception as compared with other factors shaping the outcome of battle?[4] What problems accompany the use of intelligence on the operational level as compared with that on the strategic and tactical levels? Did military leaders take best advantage of the intelligence they were provided with and what factors either limited or enhanced their proper use of intelligence?

Many of Glantz's observations seem to bear out the experience of the British and American military during the war. The simplest yet most important lesson for the future is that no matter how well the intelligence community is *appreciated before* the outbreak of war or how closely *acquainted* senior military leaders are with intelligence work (which normally is not the case), events following the outbreak of war always make the availability and optimal use of intelligence far more difficult than anticipated. As Colonel Glantz concludes, new and unexpected technological developments, communications problems, lack of experience, flawed procedures, and combat conditions in general, necessitate a prolonged learning process to develop not only the intelligence assets but also the understanding of how best to put them to use.

Experience teaches that it is much easier to employ intelligence in defense than in mobile warfare, where the fluid nature of battle renders intelligence less reliable and shortlived. A corollary of this is the fact that intelligence makes its greatest contribution in planning the first or initial phases of a battle, but grows increasingly more difficult to obtain and exploit as the battle progresses and unexpected developments occur. This is why other factors such as military strength, good contingency planning, combat experience, and seasoned leadership must always be present. Even perfect intelligence is therefore only a necessary but not a sufficient condition for achieving victory in war. As Colonel Glantz puts it in his realistic and balanced conclusions: "Although *razvedka* does not guarantee success in battle, its absence can contribute to failure" (see p. 384 below). Neither the Germans nor the Japanese military ever fully grasped this simple lesson during the Second World War.[5] It is precisely the Soviet military's appreciation of the value of intelligence in combination with a powerful military machine that makes it such a formidable opponent.

MICHAEL I. HANDEL
Professor of National Security Affairs
U.S. Army War College, Carlisle Barracks

PREFACE

NOTES

1. The first volume, which must be read alongside this one, is David Glantz, *Soviet Military Deception in the Second World War* (London: Frank Cass, 1989). The third is *The Role of Intelligence in Soviet Military Strategy during the Second World War* (Novato, California: Presidion Press, 1990).
2. For an interesting exchange on this subject see: Geoff Jukes, "The Soviets and Ultra," *Intelligence and National Security*, Vol. 3, No. 2, April 1988, 233–47; P.S. Bitner-Barry, "The Soviets and Ultra: A Comment on Jukes' Hypothesis," *Intelligence and National Security*, Vol. 3, No. 2, April 1988, 248–250; Geoff Jukes, "More on The Soviets and Ultra," *Intelligence and National Security*, Vol. 4, No. 2, April 1989, 374–84; Ralph Erskine, "The Soviets and Naval Enigma: Some Comments," *Intelligence and National Security*, Vol. 4, No. 3, July 1989, pp.503–11; also Timothy Mulligan, "Spies, Cyphers and 'Zitadelle'," *Journal of Contemporary History*, Vol. 22, No. 2, 1988.
3. The number of military histories describing the role of intelligence in support of military operations is still relatively small even when the documents and information are readily available, as evidenced from the rare appearance of the word intelligence (or deception) in the indexes of such books. Among the best of such books are (and they are dedicated more to the role of intelligence than that of operations): Ralph Bennett, *Ultra and Mediterranean Strategy* (New York: William Morrow, 1989); Ralph Bennett, *Ultra in the West* (London: Hutchinson, 1979); Patrick Beesly, *Very Special Intelligence* (London: Hamish Hamilton, 1977); Michael I. Handel (ed.), *Intelligence and Military Operations* (London: Cass, 1990); F.H. Hinsley *et al.*, *British Intelligence in the Second World War*, Vols. 1–4; Ronald Lewin, *Ultra Goes To War* (London: Hutchinson, 1978).
4. On this see: Michael I. Handel (ed.), *Strategic and Operational Deception in the Second World War*, Introductory chapter, pp.58–82.
5. On this see: Handel (ed.), *Intelligence and Military Operations*.

CHAPTER ONE

INTRODUCTION

The term military intelligence normally evokes the image of shadowy wartime schemes, devised at the highest levels of national intelligence, designed to reveal and thwart the strategic military plans of an attacking or defending opponent. This image is replete with agents and spies insinuating themselves into the highest enemy military or political councils of state and brilliant codebreakers eavesdropping on the most sensitive of military secrets. It recalls the feats of a Mata Hari, the impact of a lost operational order falling into the hands of a lucky enemy soldier, and the codebreaking contributions of Ultra. The scarcity and notoriety of these examples prompt us to romanticize them and generalize from them to conclude that such brilliant strokes of intelligence work often determine the course and outcome of war. More importantly, the existence of these popularized cases blinds us to one of the realities of modern combat – that intelligence in war is a mundane, time-consuming, and often frustrating process which frequently confuses, as much as it clarifies, the course of battle and war.

Intelligence, simply defined as knowledge of the enemy and his intentions, is seldom a decisive factor in war. It does not alter such concrete realities of war as the strength of contending armies and the overall war aims of contending states, and it may have only minor effect on the planning and conduct of operations. A force which lacks good intelligence may still succeed because of its strength, sound planning, and military efficiency. Conversely, a force possessing good intelligence may still fail because of weakness, planning failures, and combat inefficiency.

Sound intelligence produced by systematic study of the enemy and terrain conditions can, however, provide a marked advantage over an opposing force. It can even affect a nation's decision to go to war in the first place. Once at war, it can place an enemy in a disadvantageous position by revealing his intentions and his dispositions. Intelligence provides a fundamental foundation for

1

sound planning. If accurate, it can place the enemy at a disadvantage regarding the timing of an attack, concentration of forces, selection of a main attack axis and objectives, and assessing the likely duration of an operation. Intelligence can also validate planning and provide a basis for both conducting and verifying the effects of deception. In essence, intelligence provides leverage with which to accentuate the positive effects of military actions, be they offensive or defensive.

Intelligence collection, analysis, and exploitation is a difficult process, made more so by the very fog of war itself. Chance in war makes its effects even less predictable. Throughout the twentieth century, the growing complexity, scale, and technological level of war have provided greater opportunity for intelligence collection while at the same time complicating the process of analyzing and exploiting its effects. What is certain is that intelligence will remain a difficult and challenging task.

Few nations have developed a healthier respect for the relationship between intelligence and warfare than the Soviet Union. The four years of warfare on the Eastern Front during the Second World War, known by the Soviets as the Great Patriotic War, were unprecedented in scale and intensity. From the commencement of Barbarossa on 22 June 1941 to the end of the European War in May 1945, intelligence played a significant role in the course and outcome of operations. Most Westerners have only a sketchy awareness of that role. The Soviet intelligence failure of June 1941 and the apparent intelligence success at Kursk in 1943 have received attention in numerous works. Yet the appreciation of both has been, at best, superficial, replete with generalizations which have characterized most descriptions of war on the Eastern Front.

This book tests those generalizations by examining intelligence as a system whose maturation occurred over time, beginning in the pre-war years and extending through 1945 into the post-war years. It summarizes the theoretical basis of Soviet intelligence work in the pre-war period and how those theories translated into practice during war-time in what was, in effect, an arduous education conducted during the course of war.

Accurate analysis of the performance of Soviet war intelligence organs throughout the winter of 1942–43 is now possible because some Soviet classified studies are available for that period. Soviet open source literature accurately reflects those studies but contains significantly less detail and candid analysis. For the period after March 1943, little former classified Soviet archival material is

2

available, although Soviet operational accounts, memoirs, and unit histories cover the later period more thoroughly.

Numerous German archival sources, principally from the files of *Fremde Heere Ost* (Foreign Armies East), are available, which cast considerable light on Soviet intelligence operations and their effects. These data, juxtaposed against the actual operations of the Red Army, provide valid grounds for judgements regarding Soviet intelligence capabilities.

Post-war Soviet writings on intelligence operations and declassified and open-source Western assessments permit description of current Soviet intelligence capabilities and intentions. These take on an added dimension when viewed against the panorama of Soviet intelligence operations in the past.

This study, then, provides a baseline from which future historians can analyze more effectively Soviet intelligence operations during and after the Second World War. It is, however, clear that definitive work on Soviet intelligence cannot be completed until more extensive Soviet archival material becomes available to military scholars.

CHAPTER TWO

THE NATURE OF INTELLIGENCE
(RAZVEDKA)

The Soviets use a single generic term – *razvedka* – to describe all actions necessary to achieve a better understanding of their enemy, while the English language applies the distinctive terms "intelligence" and "reconnaissance" to information collection and analysis at various levels. The Soviet and U.S. approaches differ more than just semantically. The Soviets view *razvedka* as a single entity encompassing mundane actions at the lowest combat level as well as highly sophisticated procedures used at the national level to collect and process information on enemies or potential enemies. The term *razvedka* means both intelligence and reconnaissance and, with an appropriate adjectival qualifier, it pertains to every possible means of intelligence collection and analysis.

Soviet *razvedka* treats reconnaissance as a process, and intelligence as the product. The two are closely interrelated and equally important, and only context distinguishes between the two. The Soviets define military *razvedka* as:

> the obtaining, collection, and study of data about military-political conditions in individual countries and in probable or actual enemy coalition nations; their armed forces and military-economic potential; the composition, dispositions, condition, nature of actions, and intentions of groups of forces; and also about the theater of operations.[1]

Razvedka is one of many functions the Soviets include under the rubric protecting combat actions (*obespechenie boevykh deistvii*), which includes other functions, such as defense against weapons of massive destruction (ZOMP), *maskirovka* (deception), engineer protection, troop security, and rear area protection.[2] Collectively, these protective functions preserve the combat readiness of forces and facilitate their successful use in combat while simultaneously reducing the effectiveness of enemy forces. Commanders and staffs at all levels are responsible for conducting *razvedka* at all times, in all situations, and under all circumstances. *Razvedka* can be strategic, operational, and tactical depending on its scale and purpose; and, because activities at all three levels are closely interrelated, success at higher levels depends directly on the efficiency and effectiveness of like measures at lower levels.

At the highest level, strategic *razvedka* examines enemy planning and conduct of operations in a theater of operations or in war as a whole. It arises "simultaneously with armed struggle."[3] The means of conducting strategic *razvedka* have matured in consonance with advancing technology. Whereas in the past nations relied primarily on agents to obtain strategic information, today they rely heavily on aviation, communications, and cosmic *razvedka*. The High Command and national political authorities organize and conduct continuous strategic *razvedka* to determine:

> The composition, condition, and distribution of enemy armed forces in a theater of military operations; views on the nature and means of conducting war; enemy plans for preparing (conducting) war; military-economic potential; the condition and prospective development of arms and military equipment, especially weapons of mass destruction; measures for immediate preparation for unleashing war; and preparation of the theater of military operations.[4]

Today, the primary concern of strategic *razvedka* is determining the likelihood of nuclear war. It focuses on the timely disclosure of enemy concentration of strategic nuclear weapons, determination of enemy preparedness to use those weapons, and judgements concerning the timing of those enemy preparations. All Soviet national *razvedka* assets concentrate on achieving that priority aim. The Soviets believe centralization of strategic *razvedka* assets is an absolute criterion for achieving effective results in a world potentially threatened by nuclear war.

Operational *razvedka* employs "an aggregate of measures for the gathering and study of information about actual or probable enemies in the region of military actions in the interests of preparing and successfully conducting operations."[5] Intelligence collection at the operational (*front* and army) level seeks information concerning: preparations for war; prospects for the use of nuclear weaponry; the grouping and capabilities of forces and weaponry; the probable nature of operations; the presence and location of enemy nuclear weapons, fire support systems, radio-electronic means and control posts; the location and likely actions of aircraft, anti-aircraft, and anti-rocket defenses; the system of rear area support; the political-morale condition of enemy forces; and other information required by the commander. In addition, operational *razvedka* must discern the physical nature of the area of operations, the availability of local resources, and the political sentiments of the local population.

While strategic *razvedka* knows no geographical limits, the scope of operational *razvedka* varies with the size of the theater of military operations (TVD), the size and configuration of the force, and the nature of its assigned missions. Regardless of the dimensions of the TVD, *razvedka* is ubiquitous throughout its depth and breadth, both before and during hostilities. At *front* and army level, as at all other levels, *razvedka* is a command function and responsibility.

Tactical *razvedka* relates to all measures undertaken to obtain and analyze information concerning the enemy in preparing for and conducting battle (*boi*). It is organized at all levels below army and in all types of forces under direct supervision of the commander and his staff. It is "conducted simultaneously on land, in the air, and at sea by specially designated *razvedka* organs, by aircraft (helicopters), and by ships."[6]

Tactical *razvedka* organs are responsible for determining enemy strength, dispositions, combat readiness, manner of operations, and intentions; the presence and location of nuclear weaponry, fire support systems (including high-precision weapons), radio-electronic means, and command and control posts; the location of air defense systems and the basing and operational methods of aviation; and new combat techniques and methods and means of conducting combat actions. In addition, tactical reconnaissance clarifies the physical nature of the area of operations by detecting: the presence of obstacles and ground features which may affect operations; changes in terrain caused by use of nuclear weapons; the trafficability and presence of roads in the region; and enemy barrier systems, enemy engineer fortifications, and areas blocked by rubble. The depth of tactical *razvedka* varies with terrain, the size of the force, and its assigned missions. As is the case at higher command levels, the commander is responsible for its conduct.

The Soviets classify *razvedka* according to type and method of intelligence collection. Distinct types of *razvedka* reflect the specific missions to be accomplished, the force designated to conduct these missions, and how that force conducts its missions.

Types of *razvedka* have multiplied throughout the century and today include: agent (*agenturnaia*), air (*vozdushnaia*), cosmic (*kosmicheskaia*), special (*spetsial'naia*), radio (*radiorazvedka*), radio-technical (*radiotekhnicheskaia*), ship (*korabel'nia*), troop (*voiskovaia*), artillery (*artilleriiskaia*), engineer (*inzhenernaia*), radiological (*radiatsionnaia*), chemical (*khimicheskaia*), biological (*biologicheskaia*), radio-technical (*radio-tekhnicheskaia*), radio-location (*radiolokatsionnaia*), topographical (*topograficheskaia*), mine (*minnaia*), rear area (*tylovaia*), and technical (*tekhnicheskaia*).[7] Although each type is separate and distinct, all are centrally controlled and coordinated at whatever level of command they are employed.

The Soviets also classify *razvedka* functionally by virtue of the method employed to collect intelligence information. These methods today include: combat action of forces, observation (*nabliudenie*), eavesdropping (*podslushivanie*), photography (*fotografirovanie*), interception (*perekhvataia rabota*), direction finding (*pelengatsiia*), radio-electronic means (*radioelektronnye sredstva*), sweeps (*poisk*), raids (*nalet*), ambushes (*zasada*), reconnaissance in force (*razvedka boem*), interrogation of civilians (*opros*), interrogation of prisoners (*dopros*), and study of documents. Newer collection methods include: thermal (*teplovaia*), magnetic-metrical (*magnitometricheskaia*), and radio-thermal (*radioteplovaia*).[8] Closely related to these methods is the Soviet concept of the commander's personal reconnaissance of the battlefield, which they refer to as *rekognotsirovka*.[9]

Although the Soviets catalogue a wide array of *razvedka* types and methods, often employing sophisticated technological equipment, and emphasize the systematic and scientific planning and conduct of *razvedka*, they continually emphasize the human factor as the most critical element. They believe man, using his judgement, is always more important than technology.

Regardless of type and method, the Soviets believe *razvedka* must be continuous; active; timely; authentic; and, above all, organized with a clear goal in mind. Its focus must correspond closely with the overall aim of any strategic, operational, or tactical plan to provide unity of purpose necessary for all intelligence fragments to form a meaningful and useful mosaic of the enemy. The scope of that mosaic and the intelligence effort which produces it varies from operation to operation. The depth of *razvedka* and the amount of data required depend directly on the scale of the military operation, the complexity of a force's combat missions, the nature of the terrain, and the strength and depth of enemy dispositions. While *razvedka* at every level and on every scale must be centrally controlled and focused on a single set of aims, it must also be flexible enough to adjust to changing combat conditions. Otherwise, the best *razvedka* plan can become victim of what the Soviets call *shablon* (pattern or stereotype). Stereotypical action defeats the purposes of *razvedka* by conditioning a force to becoming a victim of its own misperceptions.

Razvedka at every level is a command function performed by the commander through his chief of staff and intelligence officer, who also serves as his chief of reconnaissance. Today *razvedka* is controlled throughout the entire Soviet force structure from the top down by the head of the Chief Intelligence Directorate (*Glavnoe razvedyvatel' noe upravlenie* − GRU) of the General Staff. Intelligence work at lower levels is carried out by the intelligence directorate (*razvedyvatel' noe upravlenie* − RU) at TVD and *front* level, by the intelligence department (*razvedyvatel' nyi otdel'* − RO) at army, and by the intelligence officer at divisional, regimental, and battalion levels. At each level, *razvedka* organs perform specific functions which have evolved over time but which, by virtue of centralized control, form a single unified effort.[10] *Razvedka* is the first mechanism in the carefully orchestrated command and control cycle (*upravlencheskii tsikl*). Effective *razvedka* assists the commander in reducing time spent gathering and collecting information on the enemy and, hence, creates conditions conducive to effective planning, smooth conduct of operations, and the achievement of battlefield victory.

CHAPTER THREE

TO 1941

PRE-WORLD WAR ANTECEDENTS

Intelligence methods of the Red Army in the years after the World War and Russian Civil War were shaped in part by pre-war military regulations and by *razvedka* practices of those two wars. The basic regulation (*Ustav*) governing Russian Army intelligence activities before and during the World War was the 1912 *Field Service Regulations* which defined *razvedka* as:

> The gathering of information about the enemy and about the region in which one has to operate. ... *Razvedka* of the enemy consists of investigating and determining the strength, dispositions, and actions of the enemy. *Razvedka* of the region determines [enemy] qualities which may influence the disposition and actions of forces.[1]

The *Ustav* identified reconnaissance units and subunits and aerostatic balloon observation detachments as the principal active means of tactical intelligence collection. Prisoners of war, line crossers, local inhabitants, mail, and telegraph correspondence could provide additional information. Higher level military authorities employed spies and processed documents and papers found on enemy casualties or prisoners. During the approach march to battle or during maneuver battle, cavalry provided the bulk of intelligence by conducting tactical reconnaissance. When forces were operating in close proximity to one another, infantry units performed most combat reconnaissance work while both artillery and engineer troops performed specialized reconnaissance. The 1912 *Ustav* was the first to sketch out a *razvedka* role for aircraft by stating, "Airplanes are most capable of rapid procurement of information, on the basis of frequent but short-term observation."[2]

Pre-war and wartime intelligence was under the centralized control of the General Staff, which had a special department responsible for organizing intelligence in pre-war military districts

9

(*voennyi okrug*) and in the sectors of potential wartime *fronts*. Military districts relied heavily on agent networks organized in potential enemy states (principally Germany, Austria–Hungary, and Turkey).[3]

Before the outbreak of war, the Russians had created *razvedka* units within their force structure including subunits of infantry and cavalry as well as artillery reconnaissance units. In general, however, these units remained too small to operate effectively; and the data they produced was often neglected.

THE WORLD WAR

During the World War, war experience improved the less than satisfactory performance of Russian *razvedka*. Soviet military writers have since cited the case of the 1916 Brusilov offensive as a positive example of *front razvedka* where effective planning and use of a variety of measures paved the way for considerable offensive success.[4] In general, the most effective *razvedka* means the Russians employed throughout the war was troop reconnaissance (*voiskovaia razvedka*) which involved a combination of tactical intelligence gathering measures including observation, seizure of prisoners and documents relating to enemy intentions, and reconnaissance in force. In fluid combat conditions, cavalry played a particularly effective role and was the principal means of strategic (long range) reconnaissance. To supplement troop reconnaissance, the Russians also employed engineer, artillery, air, radio-telegraph, telephone eavesdropping, agent, and photographic *razvedka*, all of which underwent considerable improvement during the war.

The intelligence section (*razvedyvatel' noe otdelenie* – RO) of the staff of the High Command centrally controlled wartime *razvedka* of all operating forces. *Front* and army staffs each had a similar department; and each corps, division, and regiment had a *razvedka* officer with a small staff. Each army also had a chief of artillery *razvedka*, subordinate to the army inspector of artillery, who received his instructions from the army RO. The army operational department controlled aviation reconnaissance through an aviation section.

Wartime experiences with *razvedka* prompted Russian publication in 1917 of *Instructions* on the organization and conduct of *razvedka* in operating armies. These instructions provided intelligence guidelines through the remainder of the World War and during the Civil War period which followed. Its thoroughness earned praise from subsequent Soviet military theorists who claimed it guided subsequent *razvedka* activities for decades and contained provisions which "have not lost their meaning today."[5]

The 1917 *Instructions* advanced the concept of command and staff responsibility for *razvedka* at every level from the High Command to each infantry regiment and artillery battalion and established continuity, timeliness, veracity, and accuracy as the basic requirements for all intelligence collection and analysis. It declared, "*Razvedka* must provide, in timely fashion, exhaustive and fully processed information about the enemy and the terrain he occupies. ..."[6] *Razvedka* was to be active rather than passive at each level and governed by basic principles including: unity of purpose and methods of collection, centralization of collection and processing, cooperation between *razvedka* organs, and their subordination to the special needs of higher intelligence channels to permit achievement of a unified purpose. At the same time other instructions appeared which governed conduct of operational and tactical *razvedka* throughout the military.

The Russian General Staff specified the following missions for strategic *razvedka*:

1. In modern conditions, the preparation and conduct of war requires each nation to study exactly and attentively all forces of its enemy. This study is not only limited to the single realm of military activity of the enemy country but is also directed toward his economic and political existence, and related to study of both the internal as well as the external policy of the given government.

2. Experience shows that very intensive agent activity is also displayed in neutral countries since, on the one hand, they can serve as intermediaries between enemy states and, at the same time, often they can carry out important orders, directly connected with the defense of the investigated states. These and other conditions provide abundant material for the work of agents.

3. Agents are interested in all that the nation considers necessary to maintain secrecy. From that point of view, they display special interest first in the degree of perfection of enemy armed forces and the level of his military-material and military-technical means, and second, in the reciprocal relations of studied countries with other nations.[7]

Despite this broad guidance, an efficient system for coordinating agent activities did not emerge; and separate agencies coordinated military, diplomatic, commercial, industrial, financial, and other agent activities. Thus, by 1917, the vast realm of *razvedka* was well defined, although organs to control such activities were developed only in the military realm.

Throughout the World War, two major trends in *razvedka* appeared which would also continue to develop in the Civil War. First, war experience underscored the importance of intelligence and gave rise to a greater number of technical collection means, including aerial photography, radio-telegraph intercept, and sound ranging. Second, the positional nature of warfare in the World War cast doubt on the reconnaissance utility of cavalry, since cavalry operations were continually thwarted by the crushing effects of firepower from new weaponry.

The war did confirm the growing Russian belief in the necessity of having unified *razvedka* at all levels and, concurrently, it produced a fairly well organized chain of *razvedka* organs working at every level of command. Centralization of all such efforts from the High Command down through army level proved useful. It fostered subsequent identification of more specialized *razvedka* needs which, in turn, prompted the creation of specialized reconnaissance and intelligence units at each level, staffed by specially trained personnel.

Last, and perhaps more important for the future, the linear positional nature of combat in the World War placed a higher premium on the identification and tracking of enemy reserves, particularly those in the operational depth. This increased the importance of, first, visual observation and, later, aerial observation. Wider employment of air reconnaissance in turn required greater reliance on radio-telegraph to transmit aerial intelligence information in more timely fashion.

Russian development of concepts, techniques, and organization for *razvedka* during the World War materially influenced subsequent use of *razvedka* by the fledgling Red Army during operations in the Civil War and shaped Soviet views on intelligence in the 1920s and 30s.

THE CIVIL WAR

Soviet intelligence efforts during the Civil War built upon the legacy of the World War. From the Russian Army, the Red Army inherited its centralized *razvedka* structure unified under the emerging Red

Army High Command and extending through operating forces as they developed. Although, at first, the emergence of a new intelligence collection structure was hindered by the growing pains of the Red Army, ultimately it resembled the earlier World War structure.

The 1917 *Instructions* provided the basis for *razvedka* techniques, but with some important modifications prompted by the very nature of the Civil War. Operations during the Civil War were fluid and conducted across wide areas. Forces moved by rail between theaters of operations to mount new strategic operations or thwart new enemy thrusts. The paucity of modern weaponry, the relatively small size of forces engaged, and the expansive area of operations precluded domination of the battlefield by linear positional combat. In many instances warfare was mobile, and forces operating on horseback or on foot conducted operations to great depths. This placed great value on the conduct of distant reconnaissance and the accuracy of intelligence in the depths. Consequently, the role of cavalry in operations grew as did the role of cavalry *razvedka* in the service of both infantry and cavalry formations of various sizes. Aircraft were particularly well suited for obtaining information about enemy movements and concentrations in depth, and they became the principal means (along with agents) of determining enemy strategic and operational intentions. Ultimately, cavalry and air *razvedka*, often operating in tandem in the service of cavalry armies and corps and rifle armies, emerged as the most attractive form of reconnaissance. These experiences provided the focal point of future study by Soviet theorists, who in the 1920s developed new operational concepts of maneuver war. Side by side with these new mobile *razvedka* concepts, the Soviets retained an appreciation of strategic intelligence employing agents and basic tactical intelligence techniques to serve ground rifle force commanders.

The Red Army intelligence structure patterned itself closely on that of the Russian Army. The High Command centrally controlled *razvedka*, and intelligence departments within *fronts* and armies directed the activities of the chiefs of intelligence within subordinate divisions and brigades. At division and brigade level, the chief of intelligence worked for his respective chief of staff and had small staffs subordinate to him (one to three officer assistants: an interpreter, clerk, and typographer). The air commander at division level also worked for the chief of staff but normally placed part of his assets (one section) at the disposal of the chief of intelligence. Artillery intelligence was also coordinated through the chief of staff.[8]

The chief of intelligence received information from higher head-quarters, neighboring staffs, subordinate tactical units, divisional and brigade artillery, divisional engineers, divisional air units, divisional secret services, and divisional and brigade *razvedka* units directly subordinate to him. Organic intelligence assets and sources included wireless stations, telephone and telegraph monitors, observation posts of subordinate units, captured documents, and interrogation reports from POWs, enemy deserters, partisans, and local inhabitants. The chief of intelligence was responsible for organizing intelligence activities and holding periodic conferences to coordinate with other agencies on *razvedka* matters. He was also responsible for training intelligence personnel from lower tactical units which, in turn, would instruct on intelligence matters at their level. So important was the intelligence function that regulations ordered, "A list of intelligence personnel of a division must be kept separate from the other personnel and no change should take place without the approval of divisional headquarters. ... Lists of intelligence personnel of the division must be submitted monthly to the Chief of the Intelligence Section of the Army Staff."[9]

Army, divisional, and brigade intelligence officers coordinated all peacetime and wartime intelligence collection within their units and prepared periodic reports for their commanders and higher headquarters. Specifically, this included daily reports, weekly intelligence summaries to higher headquarters, twice-monthly situation reports, and maps on the situation in the enemy rear area. In addition, they were required to maintain current enemy order of battle maps and files including enemy strength and dispositions, enemy artillery distribution and activity, location of enemy defenses, and enemy rear area dispositions. The divisional intelligence officer maintained files on aviation reconnaissance and prisoner interrogation reports. Army and higher headquarters maintained similar records regarding agent-generated intelligence information.

The Soviets appreciated the necessity for appointing trained personnel to all intelligence assignments and hence, emphasized appointment of General Staff officers to key intelligence positions throughout the chain of command.

THE 1920s – TOWARD DEEP BATTLE

Building on the existing principles and structure of *razvedka* developed during the World War and Civil War, in the 1920s the

Soviets sought to match intelligence activities to their changing perceptions of the nature of war. During that decade Soviet military theorists studied ways to restore to warfare mobility and maneuver so lacking in the major theaters of the World War. Based on their study, they rejected the older categorization of warfare into strategic and tactical levels and defined a new intermediate level of war which they called operational. They concluded that only by conducting successive operations using operational maneuver could modern armies convert tactical success into strategic victory.

The emergence of new Soviet concepts postulating conduct of operational maneuver to produce, first operational, and then strategic success required creation of forces capable of conducting operational maneuver and new intelligence methods to support that new mobile force. Ultimately, Soviet theorists concluded only a comprehensive mechanization and motorization program would produce a force structure capable of implementing the new maneuver concepts. That necessitated, first, an economic and industrial revolution to create a matériel base required to create such a mobile force and, second, major reforms in the Soviet military machine. Implementation of the five-year plans satisfied the first requirement.

As Soviet industry reformed and produced a technical base necessary to create a new force structure, Soviet military theorists pondered what form that new force would take and what combat role it would play. One of the most significant questions they addressed was, "What *razvedka* capability was required by modern mobile warfare and what form should it take?" Soviet theorists accepted the role of existing intelligence organs but debated what new elements were required to supplement older *razvedka* capabilities to match the requirements of maneuver war. Quite naturally, they began by analyzing the most mobile existing intelligence assets, cavalry and aircraft.

Numerous works appeared throughout the 1920s analyzing the use of cavalry and aviation units, individually or jointly in intelligence collection. A 1926 work on wartime use of cavalry specified intelligence missions for two types of cavalry — army and troop cavalry. It described army cavalry as "an organ of *razvedka*, combat, and pursuit in the service of the High Command. It conducts its work on a strategic scale. ... It includes separate cavalry brigades, cavalry divisions, and cavalry corps."[10] Troop cavalry served a variety of functions including *razvedka* in the service of rifle corps, division, and brigade commanders. "The main mission of troop cavalry is close tactical *razvedka*."[11] The work recognized the necessity for continuous *razvedka*, given the complexity of modern war and stated it "required joint participation in that work of all *razvedka* organs: aviation, army and troop cavalry, infantry *razvedka*, and agents."[12] Further, only aviation in cooperation with strategic cavalry could produce data required by strategic intelligence. The book described *razvedka* forces required at each level, their depth of operations, and measures necessary to coordinate their activities and reiterated the requirement for centralized processing of intelligence information and efficient communications to process the information in timely fashion.

A work by a leading Soviet air theorist, A.N. Lapchinsky, which appeared in 1926, devoted an entire chapter to tactical air *razvedka*. Lapchinsky declared *razvedka* was "the most dangerous and most fascinating work of aviation. At the same time, it provides for the tranquility and security of thousands of foot-slogging soldiers, making them aware of conditions. The responsibility of air scouts is great, and the importance of their work is difficult to over-assess."[13] The mission of air *razvedka* was simple yet fundamental to the achievement of success in combat – to reveal enemy intentions by observation of his dispositions, his movements, and his positions on the ground.

Lapchinsky rejected the older categorization of air *razvedka* by range into "distant" for *front* and army and "close" for corps and division which, in essence, corresponded roughly to strategic and tactical missions. Instead, he recognized the existence of operational *razvedka* and linked *razvedka* to the command level employing it (air *razvedka* of front, army, corps, and division). More important, he tied the range of *razvedka* to the speed at which operations developed. Thus, "the range of *razvedka* is defined not in kilometers, but in kilometers per hour." Lapchinsky assessed the relationship of depth of *razvedka* and the width of the front, to conclude, "The greater the depth of *razvedka*, the wider the occupied front."[14] In short, Lapchinsky argued for greater reliance on creative and imaginative air *razvedka*.

A subsequent work, published in 1928, reiterated the need for joint cavalry–aviation conduct of *razvedka* and expanded on the 1927 Red Army Cavalry Regulation (Ustav), which addressed that issue by stating succinctly that, "Aviation ... is the eyes of cavalry." Therefore, "groups of combat aviation and reconnaissance aviation units must be attached to large cavalry formations" to include reconnaissance squadrons and separate reconnaissance detachments, all coordinated by a single commander (of cavalry).[15] It quoted the regulation, stating, "The participation of the chief of aviation in operational meetings of the senior force commander and command staff and the dispatch to aviation of all orders and operational and reconnaissance reports is mandatory."[16] The work reviewed aircraft capabilities, communications means, and procedures for assigning missions and coordinating aircraft and cavalry reconnaissance activities. "No less important is the agreement of cavalry actions and cooperating aviation" regarding "the concept of the operation, ... the location, ... the time, and the means" of its conduct.[17] The work quoted liberally from other works and regulations, highlighted obstacles to successful operations as well as the benefits, and devoted an entire chapter to the subject of *razvedka*, again citing the basic principles of timeliness, veracity, completeness, and continuity.

These and other writings found full expression in the 1929 *Field Regulations of the Red Army*, which, for the first time, articulated the concept of deep battle (*glubokyi boi*). Deep battle envisioned the use of newly created mechanized and tank units to lead the attack and conduct tactical maneuver through the tactical depths of the enemy defense, a task which heightened the need for accurate pre-combat intelligence.

The 1929 Regulation treated *razvedka* under the rubric of combat security for troop operations. It described *razvedka* as "the gathering of information ... on the enemy, the terrain, the population and local resources" which "is a general duty of all military units, directorates, and individuals in all instances of combat activity."[18] Underscoring the importance of intelligence and the necessity for unified collection efforts, it stated:

> Every commander of a military formation is responsible, without waiting for instructions from above and regardless of whether *razvedka* has been sent out by the superior commander or not, for the gathering of information, for reconnoitering by *razvedka* or specially appointed units, and for conducting reconnaissance continuously throughout the breadth of the zone of operations of the formation and on the flanks.[19]

All intelligence information received, regardless of who obtained it, was to be sent immediately to higher and adjacent headquarters because, "Often the most insignificant information, when juxtaposed against other information, affords an opportunity for drawing correct conclusions."[20]

The scope, breadth, and depth of *razvedka* depended on the force's mission, its operational or combat formation, and the nature of the terrain. Collection means included aircraft (and balloons), cavalry forces, reconnaissance detachments of all types, personal observation, analysis of communications, "political organizers," agents, captured documents and equipment, and interrogation of prisoners and the local populace. Each means was best suited to obtaining different levels of information. Aircraft and agents were the principal sources of strategic *razvedka* data, while the other means contributed to clarification of the operational and tactical situation. The regulation recognized the difficulties inherent in *razvedka* during fluid situations such as pursuit or meeting engagements.

Because *razvedka* was increasingly difficult in mobile war, it had to be focused and well organized to produce accurate data within a cloak of security and secrecy. To provide necessary order to the *razvedka* process, all headquarters were to prepare *razvedka* plans which established "the goals of *razvedka* in accordance with the mission," specific *razvedka* tasks, time requirements, and methods for reporting results. *Razvedka* plans were to be updated constantly to reflect changing conditions. Within these planning constraints, the force chief of staff then issued orders to *razvedka* organs reflecting the requirements of the plan. To insure security, all orders contained the minimum required information and were verbal. Orders included measures for terrain reconnaissance and reconnaissance of the local population and resources in the area of operation.

At higher levels, organic aviation conducted *razvedka* in the enemy's rear area using observation and photography to ascertain his force dispositions to a depth of up to four days' march. The regulation specified that no less than two such sorties be flown per day. Aerial balloon observation supplemented the efforts of aviation at shorter depths. Cavalry and infantry forces carried out ground *razvedka*. Strategic cavalry served armies and corps while small organic cavalry units in squad to platoon strength conducted reconnaissance for divisions and regiments to depths of 30 and 15 kilometers respectively (one half to one day's march). All other forces sent out reconnaissance detachments as required by the situation. Infantry *razvedka* units, however, restricted their range to within a half day's march, primarily conducting raids with artillery support aimed at seizing prisoners.

The regulation ordered commanders to conduct personal reconnaissance to afford "an opportunity for verifying the information that has been obtained on the disposition of the enemy and the terrain, and thereby acquiring for himself the most complete idea of the conditions under which the planned combat will proceed."[21]

Unlike earlier regulations, the 1929 Regulation emphasized new communications *razvedka* methods, including radio location and radio traffic analysis, intercept of enemy radio and telephone communications, and analysis of radio and press traffic. Regarding agent *razvedka*, it stated:

> Agent *razvedka* is the basic means of strategic *razvedka* in the deep rear of the enemy and a most important means of intelligence in the process of individual operations, and an auxiliary means in tactical operations.[22]

Specific procedures for agent *razvedka* were covered by a separate regulation, but the method itself was considered an integral part of the force's *razvedka* plan.

The regulation specified other types of *razvedka*, such as artillery, engineer, and chemical, which were carried out by respective branch representatives but which were also closely coordinated by the force chief of *razvedka* and were included within the overall plan. In addition, the regulation added, "The branches of the army and headquarters immediately and reciprocally exchange information obtained by their *razvedka* which is both of interest and essential to other arms of service."[23]

Another section of the regulation dealt with interrogation and stated, "Interrogation of prisoners and enemy deserters is one of the most basic means of reconnaissance of the disposition, movements, and intentions of the enemy and also the condition of his troops." It also specified rules pertaining to acquiring documents, isolating prisoners from one another, timing of interrogations, the scope of the questioning, and useful approaches for obtaining information. It warned, however, "No information from the interrogation may be taken on trust but must be compared with the data of the interrogation of other prisoners and deserters and with data obtained by other means of *razvedka*."[24]

Thus, the regulation was comprehensive. Building upon principles and techniques espoused in earlier regulations (particularly that of 1917), it incorporated new operational and tactical concerns of the 1920s, and took cognizance of changing technology by incorporating detailed material on future use of air and radio *razvedka* to supplement existing intelligence collection means. It reflected Soviet development of deep battle concepts and paved the way for expanding that concept into the even broader concept of deep operations (*glubokaia operatsiia*), which would dominate Soviet military thought in the 1930s.

THE 1930s – TOWARD DEEP OPERATIONS

During the early 1930s, the Red Army began realizing the promises of the 1929 regulations regarding deep battle. Force structure reforms first created experimental tank forces and then a wide array of mechanized and tank forces for use at every level of combat. By 1934 the Soviets had created mechanized and tank battalions, regiments, and brigades to provide armored support for rifle and cavalry divisions and corps. New mechanized corps furnished a deep maneuver capability to armies, and powerful and varied air force units provided a vertical dimension to the deep maneuvering ground force.

Theoretical work kept pace with technological and force structure changes and, in turn, spurred on further developments in both realms. By 1936 the tactical concept of deep battle had given way to the broader operational concept of deep operations (*glubokaia operatsiia*). Deep operations postulated use of multiple armored echelons, cooperating with infantry and artillery, to penetrate enemy tactical defenses and, thereafter, begin the exploitation into the operational depths. To carry out the new concept, the Soviets created four powerful mechanized corps, increased the number and size of their other mechanized and tank forces, and created airborne brigades to cooperate with ground maneuver forces.

The concept of deep operations and existence of armored and mechanized forces throughout the force structure had a considerable impact on virtually all combat techniques, including the conduct of *razvedka*. Now the Soviets faced two realities, one which offered improved *razvedka* and one which challenged the utility of existing *razvedka* techniques. Cavalry, which for years had been plagued by its fragility in the face of new weaponry, was now supplemented with, or replaced by, armored and mechanized forces which, if they could be sustained, were a far less vulnerable force. At the same time, prospects for more rapid-paced, mobile operations to greater depths over shorter durations placed great strain on the intelligence system. Consequently, intelligence agencies had to increase their range of operations and their ability to respond rapidly to changing conditions. In part, technological changes in intelligence collection systems met this challenge. But these changes themselves generated new challenges regarding how to integrate them into a new system and how to process the increasing volume of often confusing intelligence data collected.

The Soviet 1936 *Field Service Regulation* established a framework within which orderly change could take place. This, and subsequent regulations for armored, mechanized, and artillery forces, defined the concept of deep operations, set forth requirements for all types of forces, and established basic staff procedures for such matters as *razvedka*.

While accepting most of the responsibilities and procedures outlined in the 1929 regulation, the *razvedka* section of the 1936 regulation integrated aviation and mechanized/armored concepts and extended the range of intelligence and reconnaissance activities. The general aims of and responsibilities for *razvedka* remained as before. Commanders were responsible for intelligence work through their chiefs of intelligence and the same hierarchical relationship pertained between intelligence directorates (RU) at the High Command and *fronts*, intelligence departments (RO) within armies, and similar smaller agencies at corps level and below.

The regulation recognized several new *razvedka* methods and elaborated further on other methods. It placed greater emphasis on ground force combat reconnaissance in the belief that such techniques could "supply more authentic and complete information about the enemy."[25] Aerial reconnaissance was designated as "the principal means of the commander for obtaining strategic data ... and the principal means for obtaining tactical information," and all ground observations were to be verified against aerial photographs.[26] A more elaborate approach to communications intelligence emphasized *podslushivanie* (eavesdropping) and use of radio intercepts both to obtain enemy information and to check on the functioning of friendly radio communications.

The regulation, like its predecessor, declared, "*Razvedka* is conducted ceaselessly and without interruption before, during, and after the battle, and during a lull in the fighting," all according to a centralized plan. *Razvedka* planning was more deliberate than before, and each plan had to include:

1. Objective of *razvedka*, information to be gained, and time to be accomplished;
2. Designation and strength of reconnaissance units or

detachments, the objective of each, and precise areas to be reconnoitered;

3. Uniform or clothing to be worn by staff officers;

4. Method of delivery of data obtained (radio, armored car, vehicle, motorcycle, messenger, or message center);

5. Order of relief of reconnaissance units;

6. Reserve equipment and personnel assigned for auxiliary reconnaissance.[27]

In general, *razvedka* missions sought the same type of information designated in the 1929 regulation, only more rapidly.

Unlike the 1929 regulation, that of 1936 stipulated that ground reconnaissance forces operating on principal offensive axes should be reinforced with mechanized troops, artillery, and aviation units. In some circumstances, groups of aircraft could perform the mission in their own right. An expanded section on the role of aviation tasked air *razvedka* forces of corps and armies with obtaining strategic and operational intelligence for fronts, armies, and corps while divisional aviation patrols observed the field of battle and maintained contact between units at altitudes of up to 500 meters but without crossing behind enemy lines. Corps aviation units conducted reconnaissance up to 100 kilometers deep behind enemy lines at altitudes of not less than 1,500 meters.[28]

Ground *razvedka* by divisions, regiments, and battalions also extended to greater depths than before. Divisional reconnaissance battalions conducted both distant and close reconnaissance in their respective sectors. Distant reconnaissance reached out to 25–30 kilometers in advance of the main force. The reconnaissance battalion, operating at that range, in turn sent out patrols with armored cars and mobile observation posts headed by an officer. To cover the operations of distant ground reconnaissance, the divisional chief of staff assigned a staff officer in an aircraft to accompany the force and provided for aerial observation throughout the duration of its actions.

Divisional close reconnaissance by the reconnaissance battalion normally consisted of reconnaissance in force or night raids at shorter depths. Reconnaissance battalions conducting reconnaissance in force were reinforced with artillery and infantry and operated so as to disclose the depth of the enemy's tactical defenses and the disposition of his forces and to seize prisoners for interrogation. To distract the enemy, division artillery conducted demonstrations in other sectors of the front. To capitalize on surprise, divisions conducted night raids without artillery or machine gun preparations.

The regulations also required additional combat *razvedka* to be conducted by selected rifle battalions of first echelon regiments. These so-called "advance" battalions, reinforced by up to two artillery battalions and at least one platoon of tanks, performed tasks similar to those of the reconnaissance battalion. Rifle regiments and rifle battalions used organic reconnaissance means or rifle forces to conduct similar *razvedka* on a smaller scale and to lesser depths.

Newly created mechanized formations used security detachments and specialized reconnaissance subunits and patrols to conduct mounted *razvedka* in reinforced company strength with attached tanks to a depth of 25–35 kilometers.[29] To exploit this expanded reconnaissance capability, commanders used coded radio messages, aircraft, messengers in armored cars, light tanks, or various vehicles. As before, all commanders were responsible for conducting personal visual reconnaissance (*rekognostsirovka*) of their sectors.

Signal *razvedka* also received increased attention in the new regulations as the Soviets delineated what they thought modern communication means could achieve. Specific tasks included:

(a) determining the location of active hostile radio stations and, through it, the location of enemy headquarters and the disposition of hostile forces;
(b) intercepting orders and conversations of the enemy over the radio which may disclose the situation, and intercepting radio press reports of the enemy;
(c) listening in on military conversations and orders of the enemy given over the telephone.[30]

The *razvedka* section of the regulation ended with exhortations for rapid transmission of all information to higher headquarters and between adjacent forces.

The *razvedka* portion of the 1936 regulations was the most comprehensive that had yet appeared. It underscored the importance and complexity of the subject and focused attention on new technical means of *razvedka*, such as aircraft and radio which, operating in tandem, seemed to offer a solution to the dilemma of conducting deep, extensive, and timely intelligence collection in support of deep operations.

This task became even more urgent given Soviet war experience in the late 1930s and the impact this experience had on the theory of deep operations. The military purges, which began in 1937 and ultimately eliminated half the officer corps, including most high-ranking officers, had an obviously adverse effect on Soviet military thought and practice. Compounding that problem, Soviet tank forces fighting in Spain suffered undue losses trying to operate in accordance with the 1936 regulation. Tanks leading the attack were subjected to intense artillery and machine gun fire which stripped away their defending infantry. Subsequently, enemy artillery and antitank fire took a heavy toll of the poorly defended and relatively lightly armored vehicles. As a result, after extensive analysis by military theorists and a vigorous debate in the press and journals throughout 1938, the Soviets modified their concepts of deep battle and deep operations.[31] Henceforth, tanks cooperating closely with infantry and artillery would conduct the penetration operation. Only after the penetration operation had succeeded would larger mobile forces, themselves restructured with a better combined arms mix, begin a slower and more systematic exploitation.

Although the debate over the nature of deep operations focused primarily on the use of tanks, it also highlighted the necessity for more accurate intelligence data prior to and during operations. This, in turn, produced a new series of works on the subject in general, and on the two most promising sub-components of a *razvedka* system – specifically radio-location and the use of air reconnaissance.

Soviet work on radio-location began in the early 1930s in a number of military and non-military scientific institutions. Initially, the Soviets were concerned with its naval application and use in the air defense realm. The first experiments using radio to detect the presence and identity of aircraft took place in 1934. Ultimately research work produced the *Reven'* (rhubarb) apparatus (RUS–1) which was fielded in air defense units of the Kiev, Far East, and Trans-Baikal Military Districts. The system could detect the presence but not the exact range of enemy aircraft. Parallel work on an even more elaborate system ceased in 1938 when its developer, A.I. Sediakin, in the Soviets' words "was unjustly repressed and could not realize his plans."[32] Other scientific work produced a number of systems, few of which achieved major results prior to June 1941.

Similar work with radio *razvedka* went on to serve the needs of the ground forces:

Up to the Second World War, the development of means of waging combat with radio-electronic means occurred along the lines of strengthening *radiorazvedka*, radio disinformation, and radio-electronic suppression. *Radiorazvedka* gathered information only by means of the interception of radiograms and determining, with the help of radio direction finding, the location of working radio stations. It followed, if one could organize transmissions of false reports, that one could disinform the enemy and force him into actions favorable for one's own forces. Thus appeared the second element of radio-electronic combat – radio disinformation.[33]

The first operational success with radio disinformation occurred in August 1939 when a Soviet force commanded by G.K. Zhukov used radio disinformation and successful deception against Japanese forces at Khalkhin-Gol.[34]

By 1940 communications *razvedka*, at least in theory, was a major weapon in the Red Army's arsenal of intelligence means. A major work published that year by N.I. Gapich delineated in detail the missions and functions of communications chiefs in all branches of the forces. Among the many tasks performed by the chief of communications at each level of command was "organizing communications with *razvedka* [organs], while paying special attention to the timely receipt in the staff of that intelligence data."[35] In his planning, the communications chief was to study enemy communications systems to determine enemy dispositions and find "the weakest places in the enemy command and control system" in order to determine "what measures it is necessary to conduct, in order to disrupt the work of enemy means of communications and at the same time facilitate the victory of one's own forces."[36]

Gapich wrote extensively on eavesdropping (*podslushivanie*) on both enemy wire and radio communications, in both a defensive and an offensive sense. He emphasized the importance and utility of radio listening on the offensive, when the fluidity of the situation would force the enemy to rely heavily on radio transmissions to command and control his forces. "This must permanently benefit communications units of the attacking side to organize eavesdropping on his [the enemy's] transmissions."[37]

Of equal importance was the matter of organizing communications for friendly *razvedka* units operating in the air, on the ground, or in the security area forward of main units' positions. Here "the main communications means of the division staff with ground *razvedka* organs are radio and mobile means of communications (motorcycles, vehicles, armored cars, tankettes, etc.)," all of which must be accurate and timely.[38] In any case, the operational range of *razvedka* forces determined the means of communication employed. In general, radio was used for transmissions of more than 20 kilometers. All communications were carefully planned and based on use of signals tables and reporting formats which permitted rapid transmission of precise data. Transmissions of less than 20–30 seconds could provide necessary data while foiling enemy radio direction finding and interception. For longer transmissions, coded messages were employed. To assist in longer distance transmissions, the Soviets established radio-reception posts at varying distances to collect and relay transmissions. Aircraft were also tied in by radio to intelligence collection points and division staffs. Gapich's detailed account demonstrated the degree to which *razvedka* organizations were interwoven into the fabric of force communications and demonstrated Soviet concern for both offensive and defensive aspects of communications *razvedka*.

Other works stressed the growing importance of air *razvedka*. A 1938 article by I. Kovalev in the General Staff journal *Voennaia mysl'* (Military thought) thoroughly reviewed the missions of reconnaissance aviation in the initial period of war and in subsequent operations, paying particular attention to the role of aircraft in support of motor-mechanized units.[39] Among the prominent objectives of air *razvedka*, he added: rail lines, major roads and airdromes, the observation of which could help determine enemy disposition and intentions. Kovalev concluded that it was necessary to use all aviation forces for reconnaissance because of the growing demands of *razvedka* in modern war. Above all, all reconnaissance activities had to be centralized according to a unified plan. At the highest level, "*razvedka* aviation of the high command and air armies must extend for 1,000 kilometers."[40] Further down the chain of command, *front razvedka* extended to more than 600 kilometers, army to up to 300 kilometers, and force *razvedka* from 100 to 125 kilometers.

Razvedka was organized within the limits of the zone of operations of specific ground force units and required extensive resources, in particular to cover adequately the growing network of highways and roads. In addition, the complexity of air *razvedka* required less reliance on visual observation and more reliance on use of photography and photographically based schemes to assist officers conducting visual *razvedka*. Finally, Kovalev recognized that the enemy was likely to use night to cover concentration and regrouping of his forces. Therefore, "Night aviation *razvedka* acquires no less important meaning than daytime."[41]

In 1940 Major General of Aviation B.L. Teplinsky, in a work on air force tactics, reiterated the increased importance of aviation *razvedka*, stating, "Combat aviation independent of the actions of troop, army, and *front* reconnaissance aviation is to organize *razvedka* in the interests of its own work or so-called self-*razvedka*."[42] He characterized self-*razvedka* as: preliminary, focused on the enemy's depth; immediate, during actual combat operations; and special, involving pursuit of the enemy to his home airdromes. He argued that *razvedka* could supplement and materially assist the success of the overall aviation intelligence effort.

The same year M.D. Smirnov published a major book on troop aviation which surveyed in detail all aspects of air operations, including *razvedka*. After extensively reviewing the history of air *razvedka* of all nations, he analyzed the experiences in the World War, Civil War, and more recent wars, and pondered technological changes which permitted construction of a comprehensive modern view on the use of aviation in an intelligence role:

> According to our field regulations, aviation is considered as the chief means of operational *razvedka* and as one of the means of tactical *razvedka*. From this, it follows that troop aviation, while serving the tactical interests of troop formations ... is one of the chief means of tactical *razvedka*.[43]

Before and during combat, troop aviation forces performed special reconnaissance for tank, artillery, and other forces and observed the field of battle to detect shifts in enemy dispositions and to correct artillery fire. Moderate bad weather could protect air reconnaissance; and darkness was to be exploited whenever possible, although at that time the Soviets' photographic capability was limited to daylight operations. Use of illumination flares and bombs and moonlight periods were means of carrying out night observation.

Aviation fell into two principal categories: army and corps (troop). At times army assets could be assigned to corps for specific missions under the chief of staff or chief of artillery. The chief task of corps aviation was *razvedka* (tactical and battlefield) on behalf of the corps and division commanders. Corps aviation assets performed reconnaissance for the chief of artillery and for army cavalry forces, which themselves conducted reconnaissance for army and *front*. All assigned *razvedka* missions were integrated into the overall corps operational plan by means of a special aircraft utilization table (see Figure 1). Aircraft performed similar missions throughout the duration of both offensive and defensive combat.

Ориентировочный расчет расхода мото - и энергетического ресурсов 5 КАЧ

Этап	День, число	Задачи	Колич. самоле-тов	Колич. выле-тов	Продолж. полета в часах	Общее количество самоле-то-часов
I	5	Разведка выдвижения противника из района .	1	2	2	1/4
		Резервные вылеты'. .	2	2	2	2/4
	6	Фоторазведка укреп-ленного рубежа	3	1	2	3/6
		Разведка района . . .	1	2	3	1/4
		Резервные вылеты . .	2	2	2	2/4
		Итого . . .				9/22
II	7—8	Наблюдение поля боя				6/12
		Обслуживание артил-лерии				5/10
		Разведка				3/6
		Итого . .				14/28
III	9—10	Разведка отходящего противника				5/10
		Всего . . .				28/60
		Остаток .				

Примечания. 1. В числителе — количество самолетов, в знаменателе — количество моточасов.
2. На первые дни производится возможно точный подсчет, на последующие этапы — ориентировочно.

Fig. 1. Aircraft utilization table

Smirnov then specified technical requirements for aircraft carrying out reconnaissance, including radius of action (up to 200 kilometers), working ceiling (1,500–3,000 meters), speed (from 450–500 to 150–160 kilometers/hour), aircraft construction, engine type, and equipment (including cameras).

Aviation could play an important role in meeting engagements as well:

Information received from army reconnaissance aviation occupied in a given period with studying the deep enemy rear has a huge importance. This information concerns the general grouping of the enemy and in spite of its general nature, this very information, received from army reconnaissance aviation, can be sent to higher commands and commands of troop aviation since they may "aim" the basic work of corps aviation to permit it to decide "where to look and what to look for."[44]

Troop reconnaissance aviation was directly subordinate to the rifle corps through the intelligence department and the corps chief of staff. The corps chief of staff personally assigned all tasks to troop aviation, but all detailed orders regarding reconnaissance came from the chief of intelligence and intelligence department. Normally, tasks and missions corresponded to the planned phases of combat, and preparation of the actual *razvedka* plan was the responsibility of the intelligence department. The basic plan included mission, means of accomplishing the mission, and the period within which it was to be accomplished (see Figure 2). The army staff then coordinated the efforts of its aviation with corps aviation forces.

Smirnov enunciated the following principles of effective reconnaissance work: planned nature (*planovost'*), flexibility of maneuver means during changing conditions, economy of means; subordination of *razvedka* missions to the interests of combat; cunning (*khitrost'*) and avoidance of preconceived judgements about enemy intentions. He then related detailed means of controlling the many *razvedka* missions of troop aviation and discussed the proper format for *razvedka* orders (Figures 3–4).

As evidenced by the work of Smirnov and others, by 1940 the Soviets had a sound understanding of the goals of *razvedka* and a developing appreciation of the intricacies of those processes necessary to achieve those goals. Unfortunately, theory was often difficult to transform into practice.

The most articulate Soviet description of the nature and importance of operational *razvedka* appeared in a 1939 General Staff journal article by A. Starunin which surveyed the entire spectrum of intelligence operations to provide a context for operational *razvedka*.[45] Noting the sweeping technological changes that had occurred in modern armies, Starunin emphasized the critical role of intelligence:

Таблица расчета потребности в самолетах

Наименование соединения	Вид боя	Задачи	Количество потребных самолетов	Обоснование расчета
Стрелковый корпус	Наступательный бой	*До боя*		
		Фотографирование оборонительной полосы противника	17	Масштаб аэрофотосъемки — 1 : 4000. При 50% перекрытия (при $f = 21$ *см*) между маршрутами длинная сторона пластинки снимает $40 \times 9 = 360$ *м*, при двух заходах самолет снимает полосу шириной по фронту $360 \times 2 = 720$ *м*. Корпус нуждается в съемке полосы по фронту до 12 *км*. Для одновременной съемки потребуется 12000:720=17 самолето-вылетов
		Тактическая разведка	3	Не менее 2 самолето-вылетов днем и 1 — ночью
		Всего . . .	20	
		В бою		
		Обслуживание артиллерии ДД	4—8	Корпус имеет артгруппу ДД не более 2 артполков. Один самолет будет обслуживать не более 2 дивизионов. Продолжительность артподготовки до 1—1,5 часа, отсюда и потребность от 4 до 8 самолетов
		Наведение танков на цель . . .	1	Продолжительность работы не более 1 — 2 часов. На группу надо 1 самолет
		Обслуживание наблюдением поля боя	3	Из расчета 1 самолет на дивизию, в 2 смены. При насыщении стрелкового корпуса танками оборонительная полоса будет прорвана не более как через 2 — 3 часа. В результате двух самолето-вылетов на дивизию вполне достаточно

Fig. 2. Air *razvedka* plan

Information about the enemy is among the chief data, on the basis of which commanders make their decisions. Without knowledge of the enemy, his actions, technical equipment, and political-morale condition, it is impossible to count on victory. Even if it is insufficient for the achievement of final

Fig. 2 (continued)

Наименование соединения	Вид боя	З а д а ч и	Количество потребных самолетов	Обоснование расчета
Стрелковый корпус	Наступательный бой	Наблюдение за подходящими резервами противника из глубины на день боя	2—3[1]	Первый вылет — в момент начала наступления. Второй вылет—к началу подготовки атаки тыловой оборонительной полосы. Третий вылет — при переходе к преследованию
		Всего . . .	10—15	
		Всего в условиях наступительного боя	20	
Стрелковый корпус	Оборонительный бой	*До боя* Наблюдение за противником, подходящим к нашей оборонительной полосе	8—12	Ширина фронта обороны стрелкового корпуса 40—60 *км.* Полоса наблюдения 1 самолета 10 *км.* Отсюда и потребность — 4—6 самолетов. В день 2 вылетов вполне достаточно; 4 × 2 = 8, или 6 × 2 = 12 самолетов
		Проверка маскировки своих войск Связь, обслуживание ОЗ[2] дивизии Ночная разведка	1 3 4	Одного самолета будет вполне достаточно По одному на дивизию Свободу маневра в смысле изменения направления главного удара противник сохраняет в пределах удаления до 15 *км* от линии фронта. Чтобы установить начало и направление движения основной группировки противника, идущего полковыми колоннами (берется наиболее благоприятный для противника случай), потребуется летать не реже как через 2 часа (иначе колонны уйдут незамеченными)
		Всего . . .	16—20	

[1] Могут быть использованы самолеты, до этого обслуживавшие артиллерию.
[2] ОЗ — отряды заграждения.

victory, this information is necessary in every instance and for all levels of command.[46]

While tactical intelligence could be obtained during battle by air and ground reconnaissance, operational intelligence, especially in an initial period of war, was inadequate. Periodic peacetime assess-

Fig. 2 (continued)

Наименование соединения	Вид боя	З а д а ч и	Количество потребных самолетов	Обоснование расчета
Стрелковый корпус	Оборонительный бой	*В бою* Наблюдение поля боя стрелковой дивизии и обслуживающей артиллерии	6	На дивизию надо 2 самолета, так как потребуются более частые вылеты для освещения глубины боевого расположения противника, чем это имеет место в наступательном бою
		Наблюдение за направлением движения эшелонов, развитие успеха (войск преследования)	3	Эти эшелоны, надо полагать, будут прикрыты истребителями, поэтому нет уверенности, что каждый высланный самолет вернется назад; для страховки надо иметь по крайней мере 2 самолета в резерве у командира корпуса
		Выход из боя Наблюдение за частями противника на внутренних флангах наших отходящих войск .	3—6	Командиру корпуса необходимо знать положение на участках дивизий. Эти сведения могут дать быстро и достаточно точно только самолеты. Надо минимум по 1 самолету на дивизию, лучше два, так как напряжение будет большое и отход по времени займет 6—8 часов, что потребует минимум трех вылетов
		Всего в бою .	12—15	
		Всего в условиях обороны . . .	16—20	
Кавалерийский корпус	В условиях преследования противника	*До боя* Наблюдение за объектом, которому конница должна отрезать пути отхода	6	При полосе действия кавалерийского корпуса 20 км. один вылет требует 20 : 10 = 2 самолетов. Объект на глубине 50 км — 7-8 часов хода конницы. Частота вылетов - через 2 часа, минимум 3 вылета

ments were poor sources of information upon which to base actual war plans. Instead, commanders had to have information regarding "what will be the enemy strength during the upcoming operation."[47] Starunin argued that modern commanders must use all advanced technical means and all types of forces (infantry, aviation, and

95. ПРИКАЗАНИЕ
КОМАНДИРУ АВИАЧАСТИ
ПО РАЗВЕДКЕ

Серия Г

Кому: КОМАНДИРУ 3 врэ

Приказание по разведке № 118. Штакор 3 Сорни. 15.8.40 20.00. Карта 50 000—38 г.

Противник обороняется на рубеже В . . . . . ., М . . . . . . , Г . . . . .

2. 3 врэ в течение 16.8 и 17.8:

а) установить наличие и систему заграждений противника в полосе обеспечения, в границах справа . . . . . . , слева . . . . и позицию боевого охранения на линии . . . . Особое внимание Н . . . . и К . . . . ;

б) произвести плановое фотографирование главной полосы сопротивления в границах Ш . . . . , К . . . . , О . . . . с целью определения характера оборонительных сооружений, расположения огневых позиций артиллерии и резервов; масштаб съемки —6 000; повторное фотографирование этого же участка произвести в период с 8.00 до 11.00 17.8;

в) установить наличие, состав и место расположения дивизионных резервов противника в районе М . . . . . , В . . . . , а также подход резервов ко второй оборонительной полосе со стороны В . . . . . , Л . . . . . . и из района Т . . . .

Напряжение: на 16.8—три эскадрилье-вылета, на 17.8—два эскадрилье-вылета. В моем резерве на эти дни иметь по два самолета.

Fig. 3. *Razvedka* order to an aviation squadron

motor-mechanized) in order to establish a useful intelligence picture. In short:

Operational *razvedka* on army scale must provide the commander with necessary information to make a decision corres-

Fig. 3. (continued)

3. 20 нап одной эскадрильей обеспечивает фотографирование по вашим заявкам.

10 шап по вашей заявке подавляет ЗА противника в районе фотографирования.

4. Граница с армейской воздушной разведкой В . . . . . , Л . . . . , И . . . .

5. Для связи с ВВС: пароль самолетов — горка и серия красных ракет; отзыв 3 ск — 123, 10 сд — 124, 11 сд —125.

6. Фотосхему отпечатать в . . . 7 . . . экземплярах.

Первый экземпляр доставить в штакор к 18.00 16.8, остальные — к 22.00 16.8.40.

7. Донесения о результатах разведки — вымпелом в штакор 3 к 6.00, 9.00, 12.00, 16.00 16.8.40.

Начальник штаба	Военный комиссар
. . . .	штаба . . . .
(звание и подпись)	(звание и подпись)

Начальник разведывательного отдела . . . .
(звание и подпись)

Отпечатано в 2 экз.

Экз. № 1 получен лично командиром ВРЭ.

Экз. № 2 в деле. ₃

ПНР . . . .
(зтание и подпись)

ponding to conditions, faultless and timely information about the enemy; it must provide his forces freedom of maneuver and forewarn them in time about an unexpected enemy blow.[48]

To forestall a surprise attack and subsequent defeat, the commander required a minimum of information about the enemy, the theater of operations, and the population. Initially, this included intelligence about enemy concentrations; deployments by rail; unloading regions; location of airfields; and the location, speed, and

96. ПРИКАЗАНИЕ ДИВИЗИИ ПО РАЗВЕДКЕ

Серия Б

НАШТАДИВ 1, 2 и 3

Приказание по разведке № 107. Штакор 7 Лесанка. 15.8.41 15.00. Карта 50 000—39 г.

1. Взять контрольных пленных на участках: 1 сд . . . . ; 2 сд . . . . ; 3 сд . . . .

2. Уточнить передний край, развитие и характер препятотвий и укреплений на участках: 1 сд . . . . ; 2 сд . . . . ; 3 сд . . . .

3. Особая разведывательная задача 2 сд — определить, не являются ли оборонительные постройки на линии . . . . ложным передним краем.

Наштакор   Военный комиссар штаба

. . . .

(звание и подпись)   (звание и подпись)

Начразведотдела . . . .

(звание и подпись)

Отпечатано в . . . . . экз.
Разослано по списку № . . . .
Экз. № . . . .
Отправлено . . . .
Получено . . . .

ПНР . . . .
(звание и подпись)

Fig. 4. *Razvedka* orders to division and *razvedka* request to higher headquarters

duration of movement of enemy vehicular columns on the army's front. Army *razvedka* assets could then verify this information during the approach to the enemy. All this added up to the questions, "Where is the enemy, and what is he doing?"[49]

Long-range reconnaissance, principally aviation and radio,

Fig. 4 (continued)

97. ЗАПРОС
В ВЫСШИЙ ШТАБ
НА АВИАРАЗВЕДКУ

Серия Г

Кому: НАШТАКОР 2

Время отправления: 21. 5. 39 21.05

Откуда: ИЗ ШТАДИВА 4 ПЕТРОВО № 8

1. Прошу авиаразведкой установить:

а) время выступления противника из районов
. . . ., группировку и
направление движения его колонн;

б) время подхода колонн противника к рубежу
. . . . ;

в) время появления противника на стыке 4 сд
и 2 кд.

2. Командир 4 сд просит сообщить данные
разведки вымпелом к 5.00 22.5 в . . . . ;
в дальнейшем до 8.15 22.5 в . . . . ; после
8.15 — по пути следования . . . .
. . . .

Наштадив 4 . . . . Военкомдив . . . . :
    (звание и подпись)   (звание и подпись)

Отпечатан в 2 экз.
Экз. № 1 — наштакор 2,
Экз. № 2 — в дело.

ПНР . . . .
    (звание и подпись)

obtained basic information about the enemy as specified by the
1936 regulation. Thereafter army commanders employed reconnaissance units of large mechanized and cavalry formations to verify
this data. Night reconnaissance was especially critical in the light of
enemy use of night force movement and concentration. As the
enemy neared friendly positions, special observation units, and

radio/telephone intercept units would lend their efforts to clarifying the enemy intelligence picture.

The complexity involved in coordinating *razvedka* measures required that all measures be carefully planned according to time and phase of operation. Starunin warned, however, that planning itself must avoid the arch danger of stereotyping the enemy:

> Often that system [of organizing *razvedka*] turns into a habitual scheme-pattern which we try to apply to any situation, and it leads to misfortune. Therefore, one must not prescribe any such scheme or pattern regarding required organization of *razvedka* in a given operation. Each operation is distinctive from other operations by virtue of conditions, and *razvedka* must arise from those conditions.[50]

All *razvedka* planning began first with a clear aim and concept regarding how that aim was to be achieved. Planners had to avoid any sort of preconception regarding what the enemy intended to do or how he would do it. Information received by various branches of *razvedka* had to be well organized to form a complete mosaic and had to be timely. "In order to secure required time for the command, *razvedka* by army means must be conducted: in the absence of contact with the enemy at a depth of from 100–150 kilometers to 250–300 kilometers; and during contact with the enemy at a depth of up to 100–150 kilometers."[51]

Long-range reconnaissance aviation focused its efforts on rail lines and highways to determine enemy strength and movements. Night reconnaissance was particularly difficult, and Starunin reminded readers that mobile columns could move up to 100–150 kilometers at night virtually unobserved. Thus, it was important for day reconnaissance to determine direction of movement so that detected forces could be found the following day. Once enemy forces were detected from 50 to 100 kilometers deep, cavalry and mechanized force reconnaissance would begin to play a significant role.

Army *razvedka* operated in an army sector 90 to 100 kilometers wide. Rifle corps each covered a 12 to 15 kilometer main sector or a 20 to 25 kilometer secondary sector with reconnaissance assets focused on the 15 to 20 march routes in each sector. Since aircraft could observe across a 10 kilometer front, eight to ten aircraft were required for simultaneous observation of the entire army front. Starunin reiterated that *razvedka* had to be "purposeful, timely, continuous, and in consonance with the army mission and conditions."[52] Purposeful meant concentrating intelligence assets on answering the most critical questions and avoiding the scattering of *razvedka* means. Timeliness and continuousness were critical in the light of the increased mobility and maneuverability of modern forces.

In Starunin's view, only well-synthesized intelligence data could produce "conclusions and suppositions upon which one could make a decision and effectively command and control an operation. Analysis of intelligence data was the highest form of processing and using collected information and was, at the same time, the most difficult matter for the intelligence department of the army staff."[53] He reiterated the contents of the 1936 regulation regarding the analysis of intelligence data and emphasized the necessity for verifying all information received. It was especially critical to be aware of possible enemy disinformation, "Therefore one must treat very carefully facts which, at first, appear correct."[54]

In summary, he added:

> The continuously growing quantity and variety of *razvedka* organs in wartime bears witness to the importance of *razvedka* in modern battle. Very often strategic and operational mistakes on the field of battle are the result of mistaken, partial, and tardy intelligence data. Knowledge of the techniques of gathering intelligence data, skill in organizing it quickly and accurately, skill in processing received data and using it expediently, are all the basic prerequisites for the precise work of commanders and intelligence officers.[55]

CONCLUSIONS

By 1941 Soviet military theorists had developed a thorough understanding of the importance of intelligence and its critical role in the conduct of operations at every level of war. Intensive study of the subject and detailed analysis of earlier experiences with *razvedka* produced sound and detailed concepts for its future use, which found expression in the 1936 and 1941 *Field Service Regulations* and in a host of other books and journal articles. Superb Soviet analysis of German operations in Poland and France further illustrated the remarkable Soviet grasp of what had to be done in the *razvedka* field. A series of articles published in *Voennaia mysl'* (*Military thought*) and *Voenno-istoricheskii zhurnal* (*Military historical journal*) reached sound conclusions regarding German use of intelligence, deception, and, ultimately, deep operations.[56] The Soviets saw the Germans doing all that they had wished to do in war; moreover, doing it effectively.

There was, however, a contradiction between Soviet appreciation of and theoretical concepts for *razvedka* and their ability to convert theory into practice. Hence, Soviet war experiences prior to 1941 were replete with failures in a whole host of realms, including intelligence.

In the Soviet–Finnish War of 1939, hasty Soviet war preparations and an almost cavalier attitude toward planning led to numerous initial battlefield disasters across the breadth of the front. Inadequate preparations, including almost total lack of sound intelligence, caused Soviet forces to go into battle virtually blind, with predictable negative results. Only after extensive preparations in a more sober atmosphere did the Soviets prevail during the second phase of the war. Many of the same faults marred Soviet participation in the military dismemberment of Poland. Only at Khalkhin-Gol, in the Far East, did Soviet forces operate with requisite efficiency.

Soviet failures resulted, in part, from an absence of capable leadership in the aftermath of the 1937 purges which had liquidated the most experienced and thoughtful senior commanders. The failures were a consequence also of the poor level of training of junior commanders now suddenly propelled to higher command and of individual soldiers serving in the drastically expanded Red Army. Compounding these difficulties were technical problems experienced by a nation simultaneously trying to expand its force structure, modernize its technological base, and assimilate a host of new technological means into its operating techniques. By trying to do too much too fast, the Red Army failed to achieve most of its goals. When war broke out in June 1941, the Red Army mechanized forces were not ready, nor was the Red Army air force. Advanced equipment was just beginning to be fielded and had yet to be fully tested. The logistical and technical support systems for the Red Army and Air Force were equally unprepared. Training, equipment, and leadership problems all underscored the fact that the Red Army was not prepared for war. This applied also to *razvedka*.

CHAPTER FOUR

THE FIRST PERIOD OF WAR

CONTEXT

The first period of war, by Soviet definition, encompassed the period from 22 June 1941, the day Operation Barbarossa began, to 19 November 1942, the day the Soviet Stalingrad counteroffensive commenced. Throughout this period the Germans maintained the strategic initiative, except during the period December 1941–February 1942 when Soviet forces conducted the Moscow counteroffensive and temporarily forced German forces on to the defense. The period was also marked by the near destruction of the Soviet pre-war army, severe alterations of the Soviet force structure to accommodate it to the demands of war, and serious testing of Soviet pre-war operational concepts, which had proven difficult, if not impossible, to implement in wartime.

Marked weaknesses in Soviet force structure and doctrine, so apparent in combat late in the pre-war years, were also strikingly evident in the initial period of war. The surprise German offensive, which wrought havoc on the Red Army and ultimately threatened its destruction, accentuated those weaknesses. Throughout the summer of 1941 and into the fall of that year, the Soviets sought, at huge cost, to slow and halt the German offensive. Ultimately, in late fall, assisted by deteriorating weather and the over-extended state of German forces, they were able to do so successfully. In November and December, first on the flanks (Tikhvin and Rostov) and then in the center (Moscow), the Red Army launched counteroffensives which halted or threw back German forces (see Map 1). These hastily planned and conducted counteroffensives surprised the Germans, made limited gains on the flanks, and threw German forces back from the immediate environs of Moscow.

As fighting waned and the front stabilized, both contending High Commands planned for a resumption of combat in the spring. The Germans postured to resume the attack on Moscow but actually

1. The Winter Campaign, December 1941–April 1942

prepared for a strategic offensive across southern Russia, while the
Soviets took the bait and prepared for a strategic defense in the
Moscow region. To supplement that defense, the Soviet High
Command planned offensives in the south, near Khar'kov and
Kerch, to distract German attention and forces from the critical
Moscow axis. In May 1942 German forces, secretly concentrated for
the strategic drive in the south, thwarted these Soviet offensives.

2. The Summer–Fall Campaign, May–November 1942

After inflicting heavy losses on the Soviets in the Khar'kov and
Kerch operations, German Army Group South commenced an
offensive into the Donbas and toward the Don River (see Map 2).
By mid-fall, after a series of unsuccessful Soviet counterattacks,
German forces had plunged into the Stalingrad and Caucasus region
while the Soviets strained to halt the advance and prepare a counter-
stroke of their own. All the while, during the summer and fall,
Soviet forces to the north, in the Leningrad and Moscow regions,

postured for or launched limited offensives to weaken the German southern thrust. By November 1942 the momentum of the German drive had ebbed, establishing favorable conditions for a Soviet counteroffensive.

INTELLIGENCE SITUATION IN 1941

The strength and vigor of the initial German attack in June 1941 staggered Soviet forces and almost paralyzed them. The ensuing chaotic situation made Soviet intelligence collection difficult, if not impossible. Initial Soviet difficulties associated with the surprise German attack were exacerbated by pre-war Soviet estimates that any invading force would concentrate its efforts on the Ukraine (where German forces had focused their efforts in the First World War). The Soviets had deployed their forces accordingly. Ironically, there were strong indications that Soviet strategic intelligence and collection at lower levels were not entirely remiss in the period prior to the outbreak of war. Soviet suspicions about German strategic intentions were sufficient for the High Command (Stalin) to begin, in April 1941, deploying strategic reserve armies forward into positions in eastern Belorussia and eastern Ukraine. In accordance with pre-war planning assumptions, the bulk of these reserves were concentrated in the south. In fact, by 22 June four armies (16th, 19th, 21st, 22d) had deployed into position along the Dnepr River line from Veliki Luki southward to the Zhitomir and Cherkassy regions. Another army (20th) assembled in the Moscow region. Within thirty days of hostilities commencing, when the Soviets had correctly perceived the direction of the main German thrust, ten additional armies (24th, 28th, 29th, 30th, 31st, 32d, 33d, 34th, 43d, 48th) formed two new strategic defense lines west of Moscow.[1]

In addition, close investigation and comparison of actual Soviet force dispositions along the border and in the depths with German intelligence assessments reveal some interesting facets. The Soviets deployed their forces in depth with weak rifle forces disposed along the border, backed up by echeloned rifle forces and echeloned mechanized corps. The heaviest force concentrations were astride the Rovno–Kiev axis in the Ukraine, where the Soviets assumed the main German thrust would occur.[2] Consequently, Soviet defenses in the Ukraine consisted of separate consecutive lines of rifle forces and mechanized corps from the border eastward to the Korosten–Zhitomir area. Presumably forces deployed forward along the border sacrificially were to produce attrition of advancing German forces. Subsequently, other defending echelons would erode German strength further and halt their advance somewhere west of Kiev, where yet another echelon of Soviet forces would counterattack to destroy the invader and expel him from Soviet territory.

Across the breadth of the front, German intelligence overassessed Soviet rifle forces deployed in close proximity to the border by between 30 and 50 percent. Conversely, German intelligence failed to detect the presence of most Soviet mechanized corps along the border and, to a greater degree, in the depths of the border military districts.[3] Comparison of German intelligence data and actual Soviet dispositions strongly suggests the existence of a Soviet deception (*maskirovka*) plan. The plan seems to have had the dual objective of portraying greater defensive strength along the border (possibly to deter or force German commitment of more forces than otherwise required) and hiding the dispositions of the most critical offensive or counteroffensive force of the Red Army, the mechanized corps.[4]

It was clear that Soviet intelligence organizations had more than just minimal warning of the impending German assault, in particular at army level and below. Evidence of German preparation mounted across the breadth of the front in the days prior to the attack. General A.M. Vasilevsky, then serving on the General Staff, noted:

> In June 1941, the General Staff had been continuously receiving alarming reports from operations departments of western districts and armies. The Germans had completed the concentration of forces by our borders. In a number of places they had started dismantling their own wire entanglements and making passes in their minefields, clearly preparing ways of access to our positions. Large panzer groups had been brought up in the areas of departure, the roar of their engines distinct at night.[5]

Hundreds of Soviet memoirs and a few studies document the accuracy of Vasilevsky's statement.

Political considerations, however, clouded the picture, making it almost impossible for Stalin to accept the fact that an attack was looming, and precluded Soviet commanders from reacting to that intelligence. Vasilevsky noted, "The political and state leaders in the country saw war coming and exerted maximum efforts to delay the Soviet Union's entry into it." In trying to deter the outbreak of war, Vasilevsky concluded Stalin "overestimated the possibilities of diplomacy in resolving the issue." In essence, when faced with a decision of acting or not acting, "Stalin was unable to make that decision at the right time, and that remains his most serious political mistake."[6]

General G.K. Zhukov, Chief of the General Staff, in his memoirs, substantiates Vasilevsky's judgement and underscores the intelligence failure by citing a March 1941 assessment by General F.I. Golikov, Chief of the Intelligence Division of the General Staff, which correctly noted the possible variations and overall intent of a German offensive thrust. Golikov's conclusions, however, "nullified its importance and misled Stalin" by stating an offensive was not likely to occur before the fall of England and by attributing reports concerning the imminence of war in the East to English or German disinformation.[7] Vasilevsky also criticized military intelligence assessments and national level assessments as well, which he claimed were often not coordinated with those of their military counterparts:

> ... the isolation of the intelligence agency from the General Staff apparently played a part here. The head of intelligence, being also the Deputy Defense Commissar, preferred to make his reports directly to Stalin without conferring with the Chief of the General Staff. If Zhukov had been conversant with all the vital intelligence information. ... I am sure he could have made more precise conclusions from it and put them to Stalin in a more authoritative way.[8]

Thus, despite numerous indicators and warnings, the German offensive achieved strategic, operational, and tactical surprise and benefited from its consequences. The motivation of the Soviet government (Stalin) in making the political decision to ignore indicators of the impending offensive remains unclear and controversial.

Once the German offensive had materialized, the Soviet intelligence system at all levels collapsed under the weight of combat realities. The circumstances of a rapidly collapsing front, exacerbated by the almost total disruption of communications and destruction of the Red Army air force on the ground, made systematic intelligence collection impossible.

Zhukov noted the information vacuum within the General Staff early on 22 June, stating, "The General Staff was unable to obtain credible information from district headquarters and field commands, and this, naturally, placed the High Command and the General Staff in a very awkward situation."[9] The situation did not appreciably improve by day's end. "By the end of 22 June, despite vigorous measures, the General Staff had failed to receive accurate information about our forces and the enemy from *front*, army, and air force headquarters. The information on the depth of enemy penetrations was contradictory."[10]

What information did arrive concerning the enemy was derived from scattered unit contact reports (where communications existed) and from those few air reconnaissance units which had escaped destruction in the early fighting. These survivors reported, "Battles were being fought in our fortified zones and partially 15–20 km inside our territory."[11] In the absence of any other reports from *fronts*, armies, or separate corps, these fragmentary bits of information and intuition itself governed General Staff planning. General S.M. Shtemenko described the chaotic situation and one technique used to remedy it:

> It was not our fault [General Staff] that we did not always have sufficient detailed information about the positions of our troops. But it was a great misfortune. Incidentally, it was no easier to obtain information about the enemy. What tricks we resorted to! I remember one occasion when we just could not find out the position of the sides on a certain sector of the Western Front. The field telephone line was damaged, so one of the operations officers decided to put an ordinary call through to one of the village Soviets in the area that interested us. The call was answered by the chairman of the Soviet. We asked whether there were any of our troops in the village. "No," he said, there were not. What about the Germans? There were no Germans there either, but they had captured some villages close by, and the chairman mentioned which. The result was that our operational maps acquired what was later confirmed as a quite reliable picture of the positions of the two sides in this area.[12]

The almost total lack of precise intelligence data continued throughout the first few weeks of war. Zhukov noted in retrospect, "In those days neither the Front commands, nor the High Command, nor the General Staff had complete enough information about the enemy forces deployed against our Fronts. The General Staff was receiving plainly exaggerated intelligence from the Fronts about the enemy panzers, air, and motorized units."[13] The intelligence picture, of

46

course, varied from *front* to *front*. Generally, where German forward progress was more rapid, intelligence was the weakest. In the Northwestern Front area, German Army Group North advanced rapidly into the Baltic States against the Soviet Northwestern Front. "In all this time, the General Staff had received no clear and exhaustive dispatches from the staff of the North-western Front as to the position of its troops, the deployment of the enemy, or the location of its panzer and motorized forces." Hence, the General Staff "had to judge the developments by conjecture – a method which is no guarantee against mistakes."[14]

The intelligence situation was no better in the critical Western Front sector covering the important Bialystok, Minsk, Smolensk axis. There the rapid German advance and their diversionary activity severed *front* communications with the High Command and its subordinate armies. Consequently, "the decisions of the *front* commander, made in those days, emanated from such assessments [false] of the situation. Because of an absence of data, he could not see the threat hanging over the forces on his left wing. All measures were directed basically at localizing the enemy penetration on the right wing of the *front*."[15] To restore communications with 10th Army on the right flank, the *front* commander sent his deputy, General I. V. Boldin, to clarify the situation and organize a counterstroke. Boldin's memoirs remain vivid testimony to the confusion which reigned during those days regarding the enemy situation.

In the south, where the Southwestern Front prepared to deal with what the High Command assessed to be the major German effort, the higher density of Soviet forces somewhat alleviated the intelligence situation, but not entirely. The *front* chief of staff, General I. Kh. Bagramian, commenting on the effects of the German attack on the critical 5th and 6th Army sectors between Vladimir–Volynsk and L'vov, stated:

> It was natural that, in these conditions, neither the chief of intelligence nor I could present the commander with such information that could have satisfied him. ... Our reconnaissance forces did not possess any concrete information about the quantity and make-up of enemy forces invading our land and about the direction of his main blow.[16]

In effect, the combat situation in the Southwestern Front sector, as was the case elsewhere, became clearer only as combat operations unfolded. As unit contact reports came in to higher headquarters, a picture of the operational situation slowly emerged, only too late for Soviet commanders to remedy the numerous looming disasters. Across the entire front, the Soviet High Command was condemned to a reactive stance which persisted well into July. Since, at least initially, the Soviet High Command was not able to anticipate German actions, German armored columns across the breadth of the Eastern Front advanced rapidly and penetrated deeply to produce numerous encirclements of Soviet forces, some of strategic proportions.

During this initial period of war, spanning late June and July, most Soviet intelligence data came from unit contact reports and visual ground observation of German forces as they advanced. By early July this information was supplemented by some information obtained from visual air reconnaissance units which could detect enemy concentrations and movements but could not precisely identify enemy units. In time, an accurate mosaic of German intentions emerged, but primarily only as a result of ongoing German operations. The blue arrows spreading across Soviet operational maps provided a crude basis upon which Soviet commanders could begin to adopt sounder countermeasures. It would be months, however, before intelligence would be able to provide a more refined view of what was actually occurring.

At the strategic level, German plans to advance along all three critical strategic axes (toward Leningrad, Moscow, and Kiev) ultimately eased Soviet intelligence tasks, for the Soviets had no choice but to contest the Germans' advance in all three axes. The Soviet High Command could decide along which axis to concentrate its efforts. At this stage of the war, a phenomenon appeared which persisted until the summer of 1943. In the absence of accurate intelligence delineating German priorities, the Soviets created and employed strategic reserves to cover virtually all potential German strategic axes of advance.

Since Soviet strategic intelligence regarding German intentions was weak and Soviet reserves were deployed in dispersed fashion across a wide front to thwart whatever German thrusts occurred, the Soviets soon faced several crises produced by faulty intelligence collection or assessments. The most notable and costly of these failures occurred in August 1941, when the Germans shifted the focus of Army Group Center's advance southward in order to encircle Soviet forces in the Kiev region, and in October 1941 when the Germans finally resumed their drive on Moscow.

In August 1941 the German High Command decided to halt its drive on Moscow, and instead turned Guderian's Second Panzer

Group southward into the region east of Kiev. This created an immediate crisis for the Soviets and considerable controversy thereafter. Stalin, firm in his belief that the German thrust toward Moscow would continue, deployed his force accordingly. He created the Briansk Front under command of General A.I. Eremenko and ordered Eremenko to deal with the southern wing of the projected German advance, which he assessed would be Guderian's Second Panzer Group. Meanwhile Zhukov, Vasilevsky, and others on the General Staff warned of a possible German advance southward into the rear of the Soviet Southwestern Front defending Kiev and urged Stalin to withdraw that *front*'s forces eastward across the Dnepr River. Stalin, however, resisted the advice, feeling that Eremenko's *front* could deal with Guderian's panzer group and maintain communications with the Southwestern Front.

Zhukov noted in his memoirs:

> In the second half of August, having analyzed the strategic situation and the nature of enemy action on the Western direction again and again, I became even more convinced that my forecast of possible actions by the Nazi Command in the nearest future set forth in the report to Stalin on July 29 was correct. ... My certainty was strengthened by information obtained from prisoners-of-war captured on our front that Army Group Center was passing over to a temporary defensive on the Moscow sector.[17]

Zhukov reiterated his views in a telegraph to Stalin on 19 August:

> The enemy has temporarily abandoned the idea of an assault on Moscow and, passing over to an active defense against the Western and Reserve Fronts, has thrown all his mobile and panzer shock units against the Central, Southwestern, and Southern Fronts. The possible enemy plan: to crush the Central Front and, reaching the Chernigov–Kornotop–Priluki area, to smash the armies of the Southwestern Front with a strike from the rear.[18]

Consequently, Stalin ordered the Briansk Front to deal with Guderian's force but still prohibited Soviet forces from abandoning Kiev.

Vasilevsky echoed Zhukov's view, writing:

> Right up to 17 September, he [Stalin] refused even seriously to consider, let alone accept, the proposals he was receiving

from the commander-in-chief of this direction, GHQ member Zhukov, the South-Western Front military council and the leadership of the General Staff. This is explained, in my view, by the fact that he underestimated the threat of encirclement of the Front's main forces, he overestimated the Front's potential in eliminating the threat on its own and even more he overestimated the offensive undertaken by the Western, Reserve, and Briansk Fronts toward the flank and rear of the enemy's powerful grouping, which was engaged in striking along the northern flank of our South-Western Front.[19]

For his resistance to Stalin's view, Zhukov was removed from his post and transferred to a new posting at Leningrad.

A.I. Eremenko also noted the tenuous intelligence data upon which these fundamental decisions were based. He stated, "Up to 16 August the grouping of the enemy, expected in this sector of front, had still not been established." Consequently, when the groupings did not materialize in the expected manner, "All commanders and staffs were ordered to conduct *razvedka* to establish the enemy grouping of forces." On 23 August a German prisoner revealed that his division (3d Panzer) and 4th Panzer Division had orders to advance south. Two days later *front* aviation units confirmed the POW report when it observed, "A motor-mechanized column of the enemy (more than 500 vehicles) moving along the road Unecha–Starodub and further south."[20] Eremenko forwarded this information to the General Staff the following day. Shortly thereafter, heavy German attacks on Eremenko's left flank confirmed the validity of intelligence information.

At first Eremenko and the General Staff believed the Germans were pressing to seize Briansk. "The *STAVKA* of the High Command, failing to discover this strategic maneuver of the enemy, oriented us on the fact that the main group of Guderian was aimed at the right (northern) wing of the Briansk Front." Eremenko concluded from these and other exchanges with the *STAVKA* that, "the *STAVKA* did not know about conditions in the *fronts* and accepted the dissolution of the Central Front, defending that sector, upon which the enemy was striking his main blow." Neither Eremenko nor the *STAVKA* "knew about the fundamental changes in enemy intentions."[21] Weak *razvedka* was, in Eremenko's view, a chief reason for the intelligence failure.

Although the High Command had *razvedka* assets and information available upon which to base a judgement regarding German intentions, they misjudged the information received. Lieutenant General K.S. Moskalenko, 40th Army Commander, noted:

> On the night of 11 September the chief of the General Staff declared that, according to his information, "Aviation reconnaissance discovered at 1325 and 1425 [10 September] the approach of two columns of vehicles with tanks and a gathering of tanks and vehicles at the village of Zhitnoe, north of Romny … judging by the length of the columns, there were small units here, of no more than 30–40 tanks. …" From this the chief of the General Staff concluded, "All this information does not provide a basis for accepting that fundamental decision, about which you request, namely – about withdrawal of the *front* to the east."[22]

Moskalenko wryly added, "But those enemy units which the chief of the General Staff considered 'oozing' into the Romny region in reality represented the advanced force of 2d Panzer Group." In Moskalenko's view, "He [Stalin] clearly underestimated the danger hanging over the forces of the Southwestern Front."[23]

By the end of September, the Germans had completed the destruction of Soviet forces in the Kiev region and were ready to resume the advance on Moscow. Soviet intelligence was able to discern overall German intentions from the general situation but did not possess refined enough intelligence to act to prevent another series of initial disasters similar to those experienced at Kiev in September. To prepare defenses along the Moscow axis, the High Command deployed three *fronts* (Western, Reserve, and Briansk) along the western approaches to the capital. "Having revealed by means of agents and air reconnaissance preparations of enemy forces for an offensive on Moscow, the *STAVKA* on 27 September ordered forces of these *fronts* to undertake a rigorous and stubborn defense along the entire front."[24] Simultaneously, the *STAVKA* ordered its remaining strategic reserves to deploy throughout the depths of the defense.

While correctly assessing the German strategic intention to move on Moscow, the *STAVKA* and *fronts* had less success in determining precise German operational and tactical intentions. In ensuing operations, the Germans penetrated Soviet defenses in several sectors, encircled 19th, 20th, 24th, and 32d Armies near Viaz'ma, pushed 22d, 29th, and 31st Armies back to Ostashkov and Sychevka, and thereafter shattered the defenses of the Briansk Front and encircled large segments of its forces as well.

Vasilevsky noted, "The setback in the Viaz'ma area was largely due both to the enemy's superiority in men and matériel and our lack of reserves, and to the GHQ's and General Staff's wrong gauging of the enemy's main thrust and, therefore, to mistakes in the structure of the defense."[25] Eremenko faulted the Briansk Front's reconnaissance effort, which had failed to reveal German intentions and attack locations. The Chief of Staff of Soviet 4th Army, Colonel L.M. Sandalov, described a meeting of the Briansk Front military council on 28 September. Eremenko asked his Chief of Intelligence whether enemy attack indicators were apparent. The Chief of Intelligence responded:

> Judging from prisoners taken in the last two days and by documents taken from dead Germans, two new infantry divisions of Second Army have appeared on the approaches to Briansk. The enemy has filled out his forces in front of the left flank of 13th Army, where radio *razvedka* had noted the staff of a new army corps.
> — Today, in the second half of the day, aviation reconnaissance revealed intensive movement of auto-transport from the southwest on Glukhov and Shostka, — received new information about the enemy from General Polynin. — Our aircraft bombed one column of up to 300 vehicles.[26]

Despite these indicators, the Briansk Front failed to detect the presence of German XXXXVII Motorized Corps and did not appreciate that the Glukhov, Shostka area was the best route for an advance on Orel and Tula. According to Sandalov, "However, the commander and staff of the Briansk Front could not decipher that easy code. They underestimated the concentrated force of the enemy and overestimated the forces of Ermakov [defending Briansk]."[27] Consequently, within two days of the beginning of his assault, Guderian's forces had cut a 60-kilometer swath through Eremenko's defenses to a depth of 100 kilometers into the Soviet rear.

The Soviet intelligence failure in October 1941 was followed by the two-phase German offensive which propelled German forces to the very gates of Moscow by early December. Once the enemy offensive had fully developed, Soviet intelligence kept better track of its progress and was able to discern where the German armored spearheads were aimed. Zhukov, restored to Western Front command after his relief and transfer to Leningrad in late August, stated, "The important thing is that at the beginning of November the concentrations of the enemy striking forces on our *front*'s flanks had been detected in good time, which allowed us to anticipate correctly the directions of the enemy's main effort."[28]

By late November, with German forces worn down in incessant and ever more bitter fighting, Stalin and the *STAVKA* began planning for a counteroffensive, spearheaded by several new armies deployed forward from the strategic reserve. This offensive, launched on 5 December, ended a long string of difficult Soviet defensive operations, which extended back almost to the beginning of the war. Throughout that period the Soviets had experienced severe problems with both operational and tactical *razvedka*, which, in turn, had serious implications for Soviet prospects of halting the German thrust. Soviet *razvedka* procedures were uneven, and reconnaissance forces either did not exist or were used with mixed effectiveness. Consequently, Soviet *front* and army commanders often operated blindly and compensated for their blindness by deploying their forces on wide frontages to counter any contingency and by launching broad front counterattacks without paying sufficient attention to either reconnaissance or concentration. Although Soviet tactical and operational *razvedka* procedures and forces had improved somewhat by late 1941, serious deficiencies with *razvedka* at all levels persisted well into 1942. Only then, after the Soviets devoted greater attention to the problems, did *razvedka* begin to improve.

One circumstance, unfortunate in the main, did contribute to future improvements in *razvedka*, in particular at the strategic level. A sizeable minority of the several million Soviet forces encircled and bypassed in the massive German encirclement operations of 1941, escaped destruction and survived behind German lines. These forces joined with elements of the local population to form partisan units which, over time, were organized into a military hierarchy and slowly integrated into the *STAVKA* command structure. Ultimately, this partisan structure served High Command needs by conducting *razvedka* and diversionary operations in the German rear, increasingly on a planned basis.

By late summer the High Command began dispatching intelligence and saboteur teams, which had been specially trained by the GRU, into the German rear, often to cooperate with partisan units. Zhukov referred to one such team:

> In early July, when the enemy had occupied Minsk, and enemy troops were streaming toward the Berezina River, an intelli-

gence and saboteur group was to be sent behind the enemy lines in the Minsk area. It was made up of two girls and two boys, all of them members of the Komsomol, who had a good command of the German language. If my memory serves me well, the girls had been students of the Institute of Foreign Languages.[29]

Throughout the summer, German operational situation maps attested to Soviet reconnaissance and diversionary activities in the German rear area by displaying numerous small parachute symbols on the maps, each indicating the supposed location of a Soviet airborne insertion of such a team.

During the summer the Soviets employed a portion of their regular airborne force in a reconnaissance-diversionary role. For example, the 214th Airborne Brigade spent most of three months (July–September) engaged in such work around Minsk. During July the 204th Airborne Brigade of 1st Airborne Corps also conducted more than ten airdrops of teams in the Ukraine to conduct diversionary and intelligence operations.

Soviet use of agents, partisans, and airborne forces to conduct intelligence and diversionary operations in the German rear was haphazard and random and, consequently, had only minimal effect on *razvedka* efforts during the summer. After August 1941, when the High Command formed more highly specialized intelligence and diversionary forces and when partisan organizations became more highly structured, this dimension of *razvedka* would grow in importance and, by 1943, become one of the most important means of strategic and operational intelligence.

By the time of the 5 December 1941 Moscow counteroffensive, the Soviet High Command and subordinate headquarters had taken some steps to implement sound *razvedka* procedures in accordance with the recommendations of pre-war regulations. Based on early war experiences, on 18 September 1941, the People's Commissariat of Defense issued Order No. 308 governing the conduct of operational and tactical *razvedka*.[30] This was soon expanded upon by other General Staff directives. The order required all units to conduct systematic *razvedka* before beginning an offensive. Among its specific recommendations, it required commanders to perform personal visual reconnaissance of the enemy and terrain over which their units would operate. Despite the order, few units employed reconnaissance in force or troop reconnaissance to the extent required.

Armed with considerable experience, much of it unpleasant,

and new orders regarding *razvedka*, on 5 December the Soviet High Command began the Moscow counteroffensive, an operation which endured through several stages until late February 1942, when it expired in exhaustion short of its goals. The Moscow counteroffensive itself evidenced mixed motives on the part of the Soviets, driven as it was by a mixture of desperation and optimism. The desperation resulted from the Soviets' need to expel the Germans from the close approaches to Moscow before one last desperate German lunge carried into or around the city. The optimism reflected Soviet faith that German forces were near the end of their tether and their belief that the commitment of new reserve armies could produce a German collapse.

Soviet attack dispositions mirrored uncertainty over exact German dispositions. Soviet armies attacked in timed sequence and in almost uniform sectors along a broad front extending from Kalinin in the north to Elets in the south. Ultimately the attack encompassed virtually every possible offensive axis. All available aviation assets supported the effort and, at the height of the offensive, the Soviets dropped numerous reconnaissance-diversionary teams in the German rear to monitor troop movements, detect German force dispositions, and disrupt command and control and logistics networks. The lack of focus of the Soviet offensive and the fragility of Soviet forces, especially when they had penetrated into the German rear, by February had created a crazy patchwork quilt of overlapping German and Soviet positions and left several large Soviet troop concentrations isolated in the German rear. During the course of the offensive, several penetrating Soviet forces (e.g. 33d Army) were cut off and destroyed by counterattacking German reserves. At least part of the explanation as to why the Soviets failed to achieve their full offensive aim (the destruction of German Army Group Center) rests in the spotty nature of Soviet intelligence at this stage of the war.

A few examples of that intelligence will suffice, drawn from the Moscow operation and from other sectors of the front where supporting offensives occurred. On 8 January 1942, the second phase of the Moscow counteroffensive began as the Kalinin and Western Fronts sought to envelop Army Group Center by an attack toward Smolensk. On the right flank of the Kalinin Front, Eremenko's newly formed 4th Shock Army had the mission of attacking via Toropets through the forests toward Smolensk from the north. This was one of the first occasions when the Soviets used deception successfully and achieved surprise, for the Germans failed to detect the Soviet force concentration before Soviet forces were well into their rear area.

Despite the deception success, the Soviets did not fully realize how well their plan had succeeded. The 249th Rifle Division, whose mission was to cover the secret forward deployment of 4th Shock Army, performed well because it was composed of former border guards forces who knew how to conduct reconnaissance. Therefore, the Soviets had a fair picture of the German forward defensive positions. The same, however, was initially not true regarding deeper reconnaissance. According to Eremenko:

> Information about the enemy, which I received in the *front* headquarters, unfortunately did not at all correspond with reality. Thus, for example, the second defensive belt which, according to the information of the *front* staff, was supposedly created along Lakes Sterzh and Vselug and had a system of strongpoints, pill-boxes and barbed wire entanglements, did not turn out to be so. In the *front* staff I received information that an enemy tank division was concentrated in the Selzhanov region. That was also not confirmed. The *front* staff affirmed that the axis Ostashkov–Andreapol' was unfavorable for the offensive. However, I treated them critically, since, in the course of two months, the *front* staff had not had one prisoner in that sector.[31]

Consequently, Eremenko ordered the 249th Rifle Division to seize prisoners on all critical axes and conduct deeper reconnaissance. Within five days 4th Shock Army possessed a complete picture of German dispositions and finally determined there was no second defensive line 15–20 kilometers behind the forward defenses. During 4th Shock Army's successful operation, the Soviets relied heavily on agents, small intelligence groups dropped from aircraft in the enemy rear, and long-range ski patrols to collect intelligence. The use of ski units proved especially useful and was highlighted in subsequent Soviet critiques of *razvedka* during the winter campaign.

Further south, in the Elets sector, where 13th and 38th Armies conducted an offensive operation in December, enemy documents captured by reconnaissance units materially contributed to Soviet success. According to Moskalenko of 38th Army:

> On the day that General Kostenko's group [mobile group] began its offensive, prisoners were taken at the village of

Zamaraika, among whom was an officer from the 95th Infantry Division staff. A combat order of 5 December 1941 turned up on him. From this document it was apparent that even the division commander, General Arnim, did not suspect the concentration of the front cavalry-mechanized group against his units. Conversely, he wrote in his order, "The enemy in front of the 95th Infantry Division have weak covering detachments only in separate places, which in the event of energetic attacks, will withdraw to the east and not accept battle."

Thus, the command of the German-fascist group, being persuaded that there were no Soviet forces on the right flank, threw large forces to the north of Yelets where they were pinned down by our cavalry-mechanized group. So we were better able to strike a flank attack with our *front* group against the unsuspecting enemy.[32]

Later in January in the Donets Basin, the Southwestern and Southern Front launched an offensive across the Northern Donets River against German Army Group South. Before the attack the Soviets collected intelligence from the *STAVKA*, from agents operating with partisans, and from combat units, which formed an accurate picture of German dispositions. Southwestern Front chief of staff Bagramian noted:

> To everyone it was clear that the precious information about the grouping of enemy forces was not simple to obtain. Besides troop and aviation *razvedka*, it was obtained by hundreds of people, risking their lives in the enemy rear.[33]

The *front* chief of intelligence, Colonel I. V. Vinogradov, helped prepare a plan to take advantage of the intelligence picture. In the subsequent Lozovaia–Barvenkovo operation, the Soviets took advantage of accurate intelligence to conduct a surprise offensive and seize a sizeable bridgehead on the south bank of the Northern Donets River.

During the same time frame, Soviet intelligence used different methods to assess the nature of German positions in the Demiansk region where German forces had been isolated in a pocket during the Soviet January offensive. There the German Sixteenth Army had established a strong defense based on extensive dug-in fortifications. It was the Northwestern Front's task to first analyze and then overcome the defense. Here, for the first time, the Soviets attempted to use aerial photography to decipher the defense. The

6th Air Army's reconnaissance aviation units used aerial photography to conduct a survey of German positions. The photographs were deciphered by the 21st Motorized Topographical Detachment of the *front*'s topographic section. The results were recorded on 1:25,000 and 1:50,000 scale maps and analyzed by *front* cartographers. Later, the results were verified by ground reconnaissance. The accuracy of the photographic plots ranged from 80–100 percent for firing points, trenches, and pillboxes; 75 percent for artillery fire positions; and 30–50 percent for individual machine guns, mortars, and antiaircraft gun positions. A Soviet after-action report concluded, "Aerial photography is a most effective means of revealing the actual outline of enemy defenses. The results of deciphering, assisted by ground reconnaissance, provide, in the final analysis, exhaustive information about the enemy's defense."[34]

A negative example of *razvedka* work occurred during preparations for the Soviet amphibious assault at Kerch in the Crimea in late December 1941. Although the Soviets successfully seized a foothold in the Crimea, Soviet critiques of the operations faulted the intelligence effort:

> Cooperation of fleet, army, and air force *razvedka* forces and means was weak. *Razvedka* work was passive: there was no systematic reconnaissance of the forward area or depth of the enemy defense in places and regions of assault landings and an absence of study of tactical positions and technical means of the enemy. As a rule, with a few exceptions, there was no *razvedka* of the landing areas by special groups from submarines, cutters, and aircraft; or by means of seizing prisoners, interrogation of the local population, aerial photography, demonstrative reconnaissance actions, disinformation, use of radio, light, and sound *razvedka*.[35]

Consequently, the forces landed "blindly" without knowing much about potential enemy opposition. Although these deficiencies did not abort the Kerch effort, the report noted similar problems had produced earlier failures (e.g. at Shlissel'berg near Leningrad in September 1941).

ASSESSMENTS OF RAZVEDKA: 1941–WINTER 1942

The Soviets intensively analyzed the results of past operations through the winter of 1942, first at the *front* level, and later, when the *STAVKA* became disillusioned with the uneven quality of analysis at *front* level, at the General Staff level. The first of these reports appeared in early 1942 and others were published late in the year. Collectively they reveal the nature of *razvedka* in the first 18 months of war and indicate the direction of future improvements.

One major study focused on Soviet performance in the winter campaign of 1941–42. While praising the achievements of the Red Army, it recognized the many problems which limited Soviet success, problems which would have to be overcome in the future. In general, the report highlighted the inexperience of Soviet officers and units, apparent training deficiencies, and resulting weaknesses in combat techniques which, taken together, produced "an inability to carry through to conclusion major operations resulting in the full defeat of the enemy on the field of battle due to insufficient capabilities."[36] Among the noted weaknesses was *razvedka* at every level of command.

The study declared that command *razvedka* by all forces was necessary to determine the nature and characteristics of the defense. During winter, terrain reconnaissance was "particularly important." It cited a failure of 4th Shock Army to judge correctly the terrain in front of one of its divisions (360th Rifle Division). There reconnaissance had assessed the presence of roads where there were none. Consequently, planning for the movement of artillery and tanks had to be altered once the operation had begun.[37] But 4th Shock Army received high praise for its use of ski troops to conduct *razvedka*, particularly at night, using either infiltration techniques or deep thrusts into the enemy rear. Ski troops determined enemy dispositions, reported on movement of enemy reserves, and conducted diversionary operations as well. It was, however, judged particularly important to allocate sufficient time for ski units to conduct their work.

Razvedka was also important during the pursuit phase of the operation when "it is essential to keep up continuous reconnaissance out ahead as well as on the flanks." Reconnaissance units determined the direction of withdrawal, dealt with obstacles, and, at times, hindered enemy withdrawal by conducting small scale attacks. The report recommended that reconnaissance units, whenever possible, engage and destroy enemy command and control points and logistical facilities.

When cross-country movement was difficult due to deep snow, ski units were particularly valuable. Ski battalions, detachments, and other units crossed the terrain easily and revealed antitank obstacles and other defensive features. "Notwithstanding the difficulties surrounding reconnaissance in winter, there is no excuse for leaving any sector of the front unreconnoitered."[38] For example, the Northwestern Front failed to reconnoiter a swampy, forested area on its right flank and subsequently allocated its forces improperly. In general, better reconnaissance would have provided for more efficient deployment and use of forces throughout the *front* sector.

The report cited proper use by 1st Guards Rifle Corps of its two ski battalions in the Mtsensk operation which produced more effective intelligence and greater operational success. Other positive examples occurred in the Leningrad and Volkhov Front sectors. From their study of these detailed examples, the Soviets concluded that ski battalions could conduct operational reconnaissance to a depth of 100 kilometers over a lengthy period of time. The Soviet report ended with a veiled threat that, "The mistakes which have been made in the past cannot be tolerated."[39]

Soviet analysis of artillery *razvedka* experiences also surfaced some major problems. For example:

> The artillery staff of 5th Army, in preparation for the March offensive, had far from adequate information concerning the enemy on which to plan its work. Only the enemy's MLR [main line of resistance] fire system had been reconnoitered; the tactical depth of the enemy defense had not been examined at all by our reconnaissance elements. Lack of full data concerning the enemy made it impossible for the army artillery staff to make the right decisions as to grouping of its artillery resources, the expected rates of ammunition consumption, and artillery targets and missions at the various phases of the operation.[40]

Commanders' reconnaissances were also often done only "on the map" rather than by actual visual observation of the terrain. This contributed to inaccurate delivery of fires as well.

The study cited a positive case of artillery *razvedka* in the Briansk Front sector where a ten-day reconnaissance preceded an operation in the Bolkov region. "As a result of this thorough artillery program, the artillery chiefs of divisons, the staffs of artillery groups, and the army artillery staff all had a clear and accurate idea of the disposition of the enemy and his fire system in the forward edge of his defense and in his immediate tactical depth."[41] Likewise the artillery staff of the Western Front conducted thorough reconnaissance for its February 1942 operation and incorporated reconnaissance measures into all *front* and army plans.

The report on artillery *razvedka* concluded by detailing those measures all artillery staffs were to observe in the future, including the organization of observation post (OP) systems, liaison between artillery and infantry personnel, inclusion of artillery representatives in infantry reconnaissance patrols, the dispatch of special artillery reconnaissance groups (6–10 men) into the depths of the enemy defenses, and the organization of sound and flash observation to determine enemy targets. Sound ranging procedures, hitherto used only in High Command artillery units, were also to be employed in the future by army artillery. The report cited excellent air reconnaissance and aerial photography work in the Leningrad and Western Fronts sectors and mandated use of these practices in other *fronts*. Above all, it ordered the integration of air and ground *razvedka* efforts and improvements in communicating the results of reconnaissance to planning and operational staffs.

In short, Soviet analysis of *razvedka* in 1941 and early 1942 demonstrated what could be achieved in all aspects of air and ground reconnaissance, even in more technologically sophisticated realms. As a result of this analysis, the *STAVKA* ordered all commands to capitalize on these experiences. Meanwhile the General Staff worked on orders and instructions which specifically addressed *razvedka* issues. One such order, issued on 5 April 1942 and entitled *Instruction on the Reconnoitering of Field Reference Positions*, laid out specific requirements for on-site personal reconnaissance by all commanders and staffs.[42] *Front* and General Staff analysis in the winter and spring of 1942 was designed to provide a sound basis for Red Army performance in the critical operations planned for the spring and summer of 1942.

THE INTELLIGENCE SITUATION: TO NOVEMBER 1942

During preparations for military operations in the spring and summer of 1942, Soviet strategic *razvedka* suffered a major setback when it fell victim to German strategic deception. As spring approached on the Eastern Front, both sides sought to seize the initiative and achieve strategic goals unrealized in 1941. Hitler decided Germany would resume the strategic offensive in early summer but, unlike the offensive of 1941 which had developed along three strategic axes, the 1942 thrust would cross southern Russia into the Caucasus region. The strategic drive, codenamed

Operation Blau, would be accompanied by a major strategic deception designed to convince the Soviets that the focus of German strategic concern would be the Moscow region.

The Soviet High Command permitted the Moscow axis to dominate its attentions and plans for 1942 operations. Zhukov later wrote:

> The Supreme Commander assumed that in the summer of 1942 the Germans would be capable of waging major offensive operations simultaneously in two strategic directions — most likely the Moscow and the southern. ... Of the two sectors in which Stalin expected strategic offensive operations, he was most concerned about the Moscow sector where the Germans had assembled more than 70 divisions.[43]

While Chief of the General Staff General B.M. Shaposhnikov argued for the cautious conduct of a strategic defensive, Stalin demanded the Red Army undertake active limited offensive operations to pre-empt German action or distract the Germans from their principal aim. Meanwhile, Stalin concentrated the bulk of Soviet strategic reserves in the Orel–Kursk sector to defend the southwestern approaches to Moscow.

The then chief of the operations department of the General Staff, Vasilevsky, recalled:

> The biggest enemy grouping (over 70 divisions) was located on the Moscow approaches. This gave the GHQ and General Staff grounds for believing that the enemy would try to make a decisive attack on the Central direction with the start of the summer season. This opinion, as I know very well, was shared by the command on most *fronts*.[44]

By 15 March, the *STAVKA* concept for operations in 1942 was complete. It called for conduct of an active strategic defense, a build-up of reserves, and then a resumption of offensive operations on the Moscow–Smolensk axis. Over Zhukov's objections, the *STAVKA* planned supporting offensives in the north, near Leningrad, and at Khar'kov and in the Crimea in the south to distract German attention from the Moscow area. According to Vasilevsky, "Stalin gave his permission [for the Khar'kov offensive] and ordered the General Staff to consider the operation the internal affair of the sector and not interfere in any matters concerned with it."[45]

By 10 April 1942 the Southwestern Direction command, led by

Marshal S.K. Timoshenko, formulated a plan for the Khar'kov operation which included a major deception operation to conceal Soviet force concentrations and offensive intent. While the deception worked to a certain extent, poor Soviet intelligence work ultimately spelled doom for the operation. Success in the Khar'kov operation was based on the premise that Soviet forces could attack from bridgeheads across the Northern Donets River north and south of Khar'kov and subsequently exploit and encircle German Sixth Army in the Khar'kov region *without* interference from German reserves. Thus, it was essential for the Soviets to determine accurately German strength in the Khar'kov area and to ensure no German forces could threaten the operation from the south. This was the task of *razvedka*.

Timoshenko's chief of staff, Bagramian, has written extensively about Soviet intelligence assessments during this period. He noted it was particularly difficult to determine what additional forces German Army Group South had received from other sectors.

> To elucidate this question we did not have much important information. We did not know even the most general outline such as the human and material-technical resources at the disposal in the rear of Fascist Germany and her allies to create new troop formations ... and the degree to which they had succeeded in filling the combat losses in personnel and weapons, lost during the winter campaign.[46]

To answer those questions, the Soviet Southwestern Direction command used all available intelligence, including reports from neighboring *fronts*. However, Bagramian admitted, "Our progress was based more on conjecture than on real information."[47] He claimed intelligence had "rather convincing information" that the main attack would be along the Moscow axis. Specifically, "according to information from agents and testimony of prisoners, the enemy is concentrating large reserves with a considerable quantity of tanks east of Gomel' and in the Kremenchug–Kirovograd and Dnepropetrovsk regions – evidently with the aim of undertaking decisive action in the spring."[48] Bagramian admitted it was impossible to tell for sure where they would be employed. For his part, he believed the main offensive would be toward Moscow with a secondary thrust between the Northern Donets River and Taganrog. The offensives would begin, he thought, after the middle of May. Later he added, "Personally, I also firmly supported that [the *STAVKA*'s] opinion, which turned out mistaken."[49]

Acting on these beliefs, the Southwestern Direction planned its Khar'kov offensive. "Our *razvedka* took some pains to reveal conditions on the enemy side. Furthermore, our actions during the Barvenkovo operation [January 1942] also brought us fully trustworthy and extensive information about the state of German defenses."[50] This, however, applied primarily to its tactical depths.

The Soviet offensive commenced on 12 May and continued through 16 May. During this period, according to Bagramian:

> Our *razvedka* opportunely revealed the whereabouts of enemy tactical reserves. The matter of exposing operational reserves developed poorly. Nevertheless, aviation detected the accumulation of enemy forces on the left flank of the [northern] shock group. True, they reported only about two tank divisions. The arrival there of three infantry regiments was reported later.[51]

These reports affirmed the earlier Soviet assumption that the principal German concern was to defend Khar'kov, in particular against the northern Soviet shock group. On 14 May another serious indicator appeared when the Germans gained air superiority over the region, which should have indicated the concentration of a larger German force in the area than originally assessed. Later the Soviets realized the German Fourth Air Fleet had been transferred to the region. At the same time, Soviet air reconnaissance detected new German troop movements from the Belgorod region in the north which threatened the northern shock group. On 16 May, when Bagramian questioned the Southern Front about conditions in its area, he received a comforting response, "Kleist [Col. Gen. Ewald von Kleist, commander of German First Panzer Army] is motionless." In fact, according to Bagramian, "In these days the command and staff of the Southern Front, in their reports and dispatches, provided no kind of alarming news, which would provide a basis to assume the possibility of the enemy resuming an offensive against its right flank armies."[52]

The next day, a major German counteroffensive suddenly began against the Southern Front's quiet right flanks, and within six days German Army Group South encircled and destroyed virtually the entire Soviet southern attack force. Soviet authors have since asked, "How could that have happened?" Bagramian cryptically explained that the Southern Front made some mistakes, the most serious of which related to a total lack of intelligence regarding German forces or intentions. Simply stated, "The Southern Front staff did not devote required attention to *razvedka* and could not correctly evaluate the enemy groupings and their intentions."[53]

By the evening of 17 May, indicators clearly evidenced a strong German counterstroke was underway. By then, however, it had become a matter of convincing Timoshenko and Stalin to call off the offensive in order to deal with the new threat. That took another three days, by which time the fate of the Soviet offensive and its attacking forces were sealed. Zhukov, from his vantage point in Moscow, confirmed Bagramian's explanation, adding:

> If one analyzes the course of the Khar'kov operation, it is not difficult to see that the main reason for our defeat lay in the underestimation of the serious threat posed by the South-Western strategic direction, where the necessary Supreme Command reserves had not been concentrated.[54]

Vasilevsky placed even greater blame on the General Staff, stating, "The preconceived, mistaken opinion that in the summer the main enemy blow would be delivered along the central direction prevailed within the High Command right up to July."[55]

Soviet intelligence failures at Khar'kov extended from the strategic-operational realm into the tactical realm as well. Uncertainty over German tactical dispositions led Timoshenko to procrastinate and fail to commit his powerful mobile reserves for a drive on Khar'kov until it was too late for them to do any good. One major legacy of the Khar'kov operation, which would be reinforced by events late in the winter of 1942–43, was a growing tendency of the *STAVKA* to take a more prudent view of enemy intentions – that is, to be sure to cover all eventualities in case assessments, in particular strategic ones, turned out to be erroneous.

The disaster at Khar'kov marked an inauspicious beginning for Soviet operations in 1942. After this defeat, the initiative fell firmly into German hands. In June the Germans began Operation Blau, and the Soviets could only react to forestall even greater disaster. As had been the case in 1941, however, the single German thrust across southern Russia ultimately eased the job of Soviet intelligence. Unlike 1941, in 1942 Soviet armies more nimbly dodged the German thrusts and avoided wholesale encirclement. By early July any doubts within the *STAVKA* concerning the direction of the German thrust were dispelled. From that point on to mid-fall, the Soviets simultaneously sought to slow or stop the German offensive in the south, mount offensives elsewhere along the front to distract the Germans, and marshal reserves with which to mount a new strategic counteroffensive.

The new strategic duel began in late June when German forces initiated Operation Blau with attacks across a broad front from Kursk to the Northern Donets River. As had been the case in May, *STAVKA* assessments that a Moscow thrust was imminent clouded Soviet judgements regarding German intentions; and again the Soviets fell victim to an intelligence failure. Soviet misjudgements, in part, can be attributed to a major German deception plan called Operation Kreml which portrayed false German intent to strike along the Moscow axis.[56]

While the *STAVKA* mistakenly operated on the assumption that the Germans would attack toward Moscow, the Southwestern Direction also misassessed where the main German blow would fall. In late May air reconnaissance and prisoner interrogations detected a major German buildup in the Chuguev bridgehead opposite 38th Army.[57] This area, which the Germans had held so tightly during the May battles, was a natural launching pad for new German attacks in the south. Based on this intelligence, improved German air capability, and report of new German units arriving from the west, the Southwestern Front staff assessed the Germans would attack from the Chuguev area toward Kupiansk.

On 29 May the Southwestern Direction used this and other intelligence information to formulate a new estimate of German dispositions and intentions based on the following assessment of German strength:

Sector	Strength
Oboian–Khar'kov	7 infantry divisions
Pechenegi–Izium	14 infantry divisions
(Chuguev)	6 panzer divisions
	1–2 motorized divisions
Izium–Lisichansk	7 infantry divisions
Lisichansk–Taganrog	16 infantry divisions
En route from Crimea	5–6 infantry divisions
	2 panzer divisions[58]

While the correlation of forces was favorable for defense in three of these sectors, in the fourth, that of Chuguev, it was markedly unfavorable. Consequently, the Southwestern Direction assessed a high likelihood of a German advance in that sector toward Kupiansk during the next five to ten days with a secondary thrust occurring from Izium toward Starobel'sk.[59] Repeated Southwestern Direction attempts to wring new reserves from the *STAVKA* failed in the light of the perceived threat to Moscow. However, even the Southwestern Direction considered its estimates as only short-term and also believed the main attack would occur at Moscow. In short, they were convinced the German concentration in the south was for a secondary attack.

Amidst the confusion of conflicting estimates, a fortuitous event occurred which, if interpreted properly, could have resolved the entire matter. In Moskalenko's words:

> On 19 June 1942 soldiers of one of the subunits of 21st Army's 76th Rifle Division shot down a fascist "Frischer Storch" aircraft near the village of Belianka. On one of the dead crewmembers, who turned out to have been Major Reichel, chief of the operations department of 23d Panzer Division, documents were taken relating to Operation Blau. From these, the Soviet High Command learned of the preparation, concept, and operational aims of the German-Fascist command. It was revealed that one of the blows would be conducted in the 21st Army sector by the forces of Sixth Army and XXXX Panzer Corps, and another — to the north, in the 40th Army's sector of the Briansk Front by the forces of Fourth Panzer Army. The aim of the offensive was the encirclement of Soviet forces west of Staryi Oskol.[60]

A dilemma now arose for the Soviets concerning whether the documents were accurate or merely a case of disinformation. Moskalenko stated, "The trustworthiness of the documents was subjected to aviation and radio *razvedka*. Although the date of the beginning of the enemy operation remained unknown, it was clear that it could be expected in the near future. The staffs of our forces were then warned about this."[61]

Shtemenko noted the receipt of these documents by the General Staff, stating, "This caused much excitement ... for such things rarely happened. ... We now had in our possession a map with the objectives of the 40th Panzer Corps and the 4th Panzer Army and many other documents, including some in code. These did not take long to decipher."[62] Timoshenko reportedly believed the documents and passed them to Vasilevsky who, in turn, brought them to Stalin. Transfixed by his earlier estimates, "Stalin suspected that they might have been fed to us deliberately in order to throw a veil over the true intentions of the German command." Consequently, "Stalin demanded that everything about the plans of the German command should be kept secret," while assuaging Timoshenko's concern by promising to pay closer attention to all threatened sectors.[63] The following day, 21 June, the *STAVKA* abolished the Southwestern Direction command and assigned Timoshenko to command only the Southwestern Front.

On 28 June the German offensive began when Army Detachment Weichs struck the joined flanks of the Briansk Front's 13th and 40th Armies east of Kursk. Two days later German Sixth Army and XXXX Panzer Corps launched their attack (as indicated in the captured orders) against the Southwestern Front's 21st and 28th Armies. The two German thrusts penetrated deeply toward Voronezh and Ostrogoshsk and threatened to encircle Soviet 21st and 40th Armies. In essence, the German assaults capitalized on the confusion in Soviet intelligence circles. Vasilevsky has answered these charges from the perspective of the General Staff, stating, "An opinion is now voiced sometimes that the main reason for the defeat of our troops in the Briansk Front in July 1942 was that the GHQ and the General Staff had underestimated the Kursk– Voronezh direction. I do not share that opinion. Nor is it true that the GHQ and the General Staff had not expected the attack."[64]

Vasilevsky admitted the General Staff expected the German attack to occur in the central sector rather than in the south. But in planning for the defense of Moscow, he claimed the *STAVKA* had reinforced the Briansk Front with a considerable number of reserves including the newly formed 5th Tank Army. Vasilevsky attributed Briansk Front problems to a failure on the part of the *front* to organize its defense properly and mount a coordinated counterattack with its sizeable reserves.

Despite the *ex-post-facto* arguments, two facts were clear by early July. The Soviet High Command had seriously misassessed German force dispositions and intentions; and, because of this misassessment, German forces had crushed Soviet defenses and had begun a major advance across southern Russia toward the Don River. Intelligence and *razvedka* failures had contributed in a major way to the military disaster. If further disaster was to be averted, Soviet intelligence would have to do better in the future.

The German offensive across southern Russia carried German forces to the Don River near Voronezh and then southeastward along the southern bank of the Don River toward Millerovo. As German forces in the Donbas joined the attack, the entire mass of

German Army Group South pressed Soviet forces back toward the Don River and Stalingrad beyond. From July to November 1942, combat took on a dual nature within the context of the German strategic offensive. First, the Soviets sought to stabilize the front in the south by launching counterattacks to slow and channelize the progress of German forces and by conducting defensive operations to halt the Germans and create conditions suitable for the conduct of a counteroffensive. Second, in other sectors of the front, but primarily in the central sector, the Soviets mounted limited objective offensives to distract German attention and forces from the threatened southern flank.

From late July to late September, in bitter, often confused fighting, Soviet forces used delaying tactics, occasional counterattacks, and terrain to shape and ultimately limit German forward progress. By mid-fall, the Don and Volga Rivers and the Caucasus Mountains delineated the extremities of the German advance. As German forces became transfixed by the battle for Stalingrad itself, by means of counterattacks and localized combat, the Soviets jockeyed for suitable positions from which they could launch a counteroffensive.

Throughout the three-month German advance, the Soviets mobilized all intelligence means at their disposal to better ascertain the objectives of the German offensive. The fluidity of the combat situation at first hindered this effort. Despite the confusing situation, it was relatively easy to discern overall German strategic intent, just as German intent had become very apparent the year before. Moreover, by July the German plan captured on 19 June had become more credible and, hence, revealed to the Soviets the outline of actual German strategic aims. The truth of the document dawned slowly on the Soviets throughout late June and early July. Shtemenko noted that even after German forces had reached the Don River near Voronezh, "Stalin then concentrated his attention on the Voronezh area. Possibly he assumed that, if the German forces broke through there, they would force the Don and begin an encircling movement in the rear of Moscow."[65] Consequently, Stalin dispatched three reserve armies (renamed 60th, 6th, and 63d) to the threatened sector and ordered newly formed 5th Tank Army to conduct a counterstroke. Due to the army's complex make-up (infantry, tank, and cavalry units), inexperienced command leadership, and poor intelligence, 5th Tank Army's July counterattack aborted almost from the start.

Operationally and tactically, the Soviets had difficulty pinning down precise German intent and dispositions. Despite this, Soviet forces displayed an agility absent in 1941, and most forces parried the German thrusts and were able to withdraw without falling victim to significant encirclements and ensuing catastrophic losses. Symptomatic of the cloudy intelligence picture was Shtemenko's description of one instance during the early stages of the Soviet withdrawal:

> At the crucial moment of withdrawal [early July], the General Staff stopped receiving reports on the situation from the Southwestern Front. There was nothing for 24 hours. And by this time the enemy was attacking near Rossosh, where our forces were trying to organize the defense along the southern bank of the River Chernaya Kalitva. The General Staff operations officers were at their wits' end and trying to discover whether the enemy had been halted. ... Naturally, the uncertainty was extremely worrying to those in charge of strategy.[66]

Other Soviet forces, like the hastily assembled 1st and 4th Tank Armies, went into combat on the approaches to Stalingrad with an obviously unclear understanding of where German units were located or what they intended to do. In reality, however, the results would probably have been no better had the Soviets possessed accurate intelligence data. In spite of these complexities and problems, the failed counterattacks exacted a toll on the advancing Germans, slowed the German advance, and ultimately led to stalemate in the Stalingrad area. Through judicious use of field and air *razvedka*, German intentions finally became clear. By mid-July, "it became clear that the enemy's main efforts were aimed at piercing the junction between our South-western and Southern Fronts and also outflanking from the north the densely populated industrial areas of the Donets Basin. ... Now the concept of the Nazi command had revealed itself to the full."[67]

This impression soon evolved into a firm Soviet belief that the Germans would focus their attention on the Stalingrad area, a view confirmed as operations on the close approaches to Stalingrad unfolded. "With relative accuracy the Soviet General Staff had foreseen how, where, and why Paulus's army would advance. Analysis of the engagement fought by the German forward detachments [on the distant approaches to Stalingrad] and their subsequent combat operations had shown that the enemy intended to break through to the Volga."[68]

Throughout the period of German advance toward Stalingrad

and the Caucasus and particularly during the defensive fighting and Soviet counterattacks of August and September 1942, Soviet participants in the operations repeatedly stressed the positive role of air *razvedka* in determining the operational dispositions and directions of advance of German forces. Although air *razvedka* functioned well, the Soviets had continual and persistent problems with tactical *razvedka*. Inability to detect the precise composition, identification, and tactical disposition of German forces limited the effectiveness of Soviet counterattacks and persisted even into November when the Soviets launched their major counter-offensive.

Operations conducted elsewhere across the front during the summer illustrated the problems faced by Soviet forces when they attempted to conduct operational and tactical *razvedka*. From June to August 1942, the High Command planned a series of operations to distract German attention and forces from operations in the south. The largest scale operations took place in the Bolkhov–Kozel'sk sector of the Briansk Front and the Rzhev–Sychevka sectors of the Kalinin and Western Fronts. Soviet after-action reports concerning action at Kozel'sk underscored *razvedka* problems there and elsewhere during 1942.

The Soviets conducted two major offensives in the Bolkhov and Kozel'sk regions. From 5 to 12 July 1942, the 16th and 61st Armies on the left flank of the Western Front launched an offensive in support of the Briansk Front which was then being pressed back by the northern wing of German forces attacking into southern Russia. The two Soviet armies attacked against a strong sector of the German defenses which were organized in depth. Two tank corps were tasked with exploiting the success of the penetration operation. Soviet preparation for the attack included extensive reconnoitering by commanders at all levels during four days preceding the attack and aviation *razvedka* over a more extended period.

Razvedka organs painted an accurate picture of German dispositions and identified most defending units. They did not, however, do as thorough a job on analyzing terrain or detecting changing conditions during the attack. The Soviets conducted a "weak study of the enemy during the preparatory period of the operation, in spite of the direct contact with them over a long period of time. For example, in some sectors, the combat outposts were taken as forward area of the main defensive zone (16th Army)."[69] Throughout the operation intelligence agencies collected information but did

71

not convey that information to operational organs. Consequently, "weak enemy sectors, discovered during the first day of battle, were not considered for the expansion of further success." As the operation developed the tank corps were committed to battle on the evening of 7 July. "As a result of poor terrain reconnaissance, the first echelon became bogged down in swamps. All the night of 7 to 8 July was used for the extraction of the machines." Poor route reconnaissance, among many other reasons, rendered the tank corps' operations ineffective.[70]

In August 1942 the Kalinin and Western Fronts achieved limited success in the Pogoreloe–Gorodishche operation against German forces defending the Rzhev–Sychevka sector west of Moscow. *Razvedka* was more effective in this operation. For example, 31st Army employed extensive ground *razvedka* (observation, sweeps, ambushes, combat patrols, and artillery) and air *razvedka* as well. The *razvedka* plan of 1st Air Army used its assets and those of the army aviation regiment to conduct aviation reconnaissance to a depth of from 50–80 kilometers into the enemy's rear area. Ground *razvedka* sought to cover areas closer to the front.[71] Soon after these operations had ended, on 15 August German forces took advantage of the action to the north by launching an attack in the Kozel'sk sector. After halting the attack, the Soviets planned a counterthrust by 16th and 61st Armies reinforced by 3d Tank Army. Soviet air and ground *razvedka* developed an accurate estimate of enemy positions and were able to detect German reserve groups to the rear among which it identified elements of 25th Panzer Grenadier Division. Based on intelligence information, the Soviets assessed a favorable correlation of forces of about 2:1.

The ensuing operation, which lasted from 22 to 28 August, failed to achieve significant results, primarily because of the ineffective employment of the tank army's three corps. Soviet assessments did not criticize the preliminary reconnaissance activity for, in fact, the intelligence picture was fairly clear. However, as had been the case in July, advanced reconnaissance and route reconnaissance conducted during the operation, especially in support of the armored forces, was weak. Again the tank corps stumbled into obstacles or became bogged down on impassable routes. As a result of these and other more serious problems, the offensive aborted without achieving its aims.[72] The Bolkhov and Kozel'sk experiences typified Soviet offensive efforts in 1942, at least up to November.

ASSESSMENTS OF RAZVEDKA: TO NOVEMBER 1942

Despite the strategic intelligence failures in the spring of 1942, the Soviet High Command continued to improve its procedures for conducting *razvedka* at all levels. Armed with sound theoretical guidance from the 1930s, a new mid- and high-level leadership emerged which was more capable of implementing those procedures than their predecessors of 1941. Combat experience contributed to their education by vividly revealing both what was possible and what was necessary. It was the task of these officers to manage the art of the possible by implementing the means and procedures whereby intelligence could be collected, processed, and harnessed to the needs of planners and operators. War gave shape, definition, and impetus to the evolving process. War experience studies and actual Soviet combat performance evidenced progress made and regulations codified and generalized *razvedka* procedures and processes for the benefit of the Red Army as a whole.

Combat in 1942 indicated in gross terms the strengths and weaknesses of Red Army *razvedka*. Soviet strategic intelligence was still frail, the victim of the limited range and fragile nature of long range collection means. Air *razvedka*, although more effective than it had been in 1941, still suffered from German dominance of the skies. As the Germans lost that dominance, however, it would become even more effective. Soviet air *razvedka* could detect heightened German activity and major troop concentrations. However, it was less able to identify precise units and keep track of those concentrations for other than short periods.

The fledgling agent, partisan, and reconnaissance-diversionary activities in the German rear, of limited effectiveness in 1941, took on greater importance in 1942, fueled by the infusion of new Soviet units in the German rear (particularly in the center) and by the emergence of a partisan network (particularly in the center and north) with links to field commands of the Red Army (the so-called Big land – *Bol'shaia zemliia*). Supplementing air and agent *razvedka* were early attempts at radio interception organized at *front* level and within the air warning system (VNOS) of air defense forces. These three means of strategic *razvedka* were still in their infancy, being slender reeds upon which to base sound strategic assessments. In the last analysis, Soviet planners were forced to rely on their understanding of the flow of combat and their perceptions of German future intent. This "intangible" system worked poorly at the onset of operations, particularly when the Germans employed active deception as in early summer 1942. It fared better after offensives had unfolded and, in particular, when time and distance had taken their toll on German force maneuver capabilities.

Operationally and tactically, Soviet intelligence improved, prompted in part by stability along major sectors of the front and, in part, by the improving quantity, range, and coordination of Soviet *razvedka* means. Often, however, strategic perceptions overruled judgements based on sound information (Khar'kov 1942). Intelligence worked best in stable situations, when the Soviets were planning offensives or while German offensive drives were grinding to a halt. It was less effective in fluid periods when rapidly changing conditions challenged Soviet collection means and overburdened evolving Soviet communications systems and staffs.

Tactically, more effective short-range aviation and radio *razvedka*; more systematic observation; and more refined search, ambush, and patrol techniques permitted identification of opposing German units, particularly in sectors where these units were on the defensive. Active and passive German concealment and deception still confounded Soviet *razvedka*, and Soviet study of the terrain was weak. Tactically, Soviet units on the move, in particular mobile forces being committed to combat, were unable to gather enough intelligence to react effectively to changing conditions. The Soviets highlighted all these tendencies in critiques of their own operations. Subsequently, new Soviet orders, instructions, and regulations issued in 1942 acknowledged these problems and proposed solutions to them.

Throughout 1942, extensive Soviet analysis of successful and unsuccessful cases of *razvedka* provided a wealth of information regarding its organization and conduct. In general, this analysis focused on the lowest level of combat and worked upward, based on the assumption that intelligence operations formed a continuum. The validity of strategic and operational assessments and the completeness of higher level intelligence pictures rested firmly on the quantity and quality of tactical intelligence data. This applied particularly to offensive or counteroffensive operations where success depended first and foremost on the conduct of an effective penetration operation, without which no exploitation could occur. This emphasis produced predictable results. Soviet tactical intelligence improved the most, while operational level efforts continued to lag. The logical battlefield consequence was that Soviet forces could penetrate defenses successfully only to confront unexpected situations in the enemy's depths. Operational intelligence collection was a shared responsibility of army, *front*, and High Command, where longer range intelligence gathering means were located. Strategic *razvedka* remained within the purview of *front* and the High Command. Because of the difficulty and complexity of collection, improvements occurred more slowly in this realm.

An extensive classified Soviet critical analysis of *razvedka* appeared in March 1943, which derived lessons from study of 1942 operations. It accurately reflected the state of Soviet *razvedka* and provided much of the material upon which the Soviets based their judgements on *razvedka* contained in the 1942 *Field Service Regulations*. It also shaped how the Soviets organized *razvedka* assets in headquarters at every level and coordinated information-sharing between headquarters up and down the chain of command.

Characteristically, war experience critiques at first focused on *razvedka* techniques at the lowest level within army, division, regiment, and battalion. Through analysis of selected attempts by armies to organize combat *razvedka* throughout the tactical depth of enemy defenses, the Soviets concluded that, often "lack of control and direction over reconnaissance work and reconnaissance organs can create a false intelligence picture or a hastily conjured up one full of error."[73] Lack of control permitted laxness, and some *razvedka* units simply did not bother to perform their assigned missions, but sent back fictitious reports instead. This was also true of reconnaissance unit commanders throughout the chain of command up to army level. Consequently, the analysis stated, "They [commanders], and the intelligence officers of their staffs, should exercise control firmly, particularly since many of the reconnaissance unit commanders lack experience themselves."[74]

The Soviets criticized the role of *front* and army staffs in *razvedka* planning, noting their role "has often been limited simply to drawing up and distributing plans and directives" when they, in fact, should have been taking an active role in training *razvedka* units. In short, "The sooner commanders and staffs of formations at all levels get away from directing *razvedka* by paper and by remote control and get down to direct personal contact with the men who are going to do the job on the ground, the sooner we will get worthwhile results."[75] Regarding planning, critiques stated that, "*Razvedka* should be fitted into a well-regulated plan, and it should be active and continuous." The chief of intelligence, in accordance with the orders of the commander and chief of staff, was to prepare the *razvedka* plan as a basic working document. The plan designated specific missions for subordinate units employing specific *razvedka* assets to obtain specific data on the enemy. Every distinct piece of data had its unique place in the resulting mosaic. By comparing this ideal with reality, the analysis then focused on specific deficiencies experienced in 1942. In some cases units had no *razvedka* plan at all, and, in other instances, they simply copied the plan of higher headquarters and mechanically sent it to subordinate units. At the other extreme, "some army intelligence sections planned everything in such minute detail that it robbed the divisional intelligence sections of any initiative."[76] The same occurred at lower levels. This had been particularly harmful in periods of rapidly changing conditions as witnessed in the Southwestern and Briansk Fronts in the summer of 1942.

On the basis of experience, the study noted:

> In a relatively stabilized situation, the intelligence staff of a *front* can plan generally the intelligence work of the subordinate armies for a period of not more than two weeks; if the situation is more fluid, the *front* intelligence staff should not plan more than 6 to 8 days ahead. A division or brigade receives from the army (or corps) staff its general *razvedka* mission covering a period of 8 to 10 days if the situation is stabilized, while it plans the *razvedka* missions of its regiments for a period of not more than three days in a stabilized situation.[77]

Failure to organize *razvedka* in timely fashion inevitably produced "negligible" results.

Further:

> Reconnissance men often fail to understand, and their leaders do not explain to them, that a *razvedka* plan is a working document, that it "lives," develops, and changes as the actual combat situation develops and changes. But, even in a stable situation, the size of the units involved, the terrain conditions, the enemy dispositions, and the strength and resources at hand always determine the character of the *razvedka* mission and the way it will be carried out.[78]

Consequently, the chief of staff and the commander were ordered to provide personal guidance and direction. "The commander himself or his chief of staff must personally prepare the *razvedka* order. It is absolutely inexcusable to delegate the function to an insufficiently trained or inexperienced person."[79]

While recounting the means for obtaining intelligence, the

critique pointed out that reconnaissance in force (*razvedka boem*) "provides the fullest detail concerning the enemy." It was also the weakest link in troop *razvedka* in 1942. Reconnaissance in force ideally had to provide exhaustive details of enemy strength and dispositions, particularly if combined with attempts to seize enemy prisoners and documents. It required assignment of sufficient forces and resources integrated by a detailed and realistic plan designating "who, what, where, and how" to conduct *razvedka*. Flexibility and imagination on the part of commanders was necessary to adjust reconnaissance in force to suit local conditions. This required on the part of commanders a willingness and capacity for altering *razvedka* missions quickly and for preparing new reconnaissance efforts to supplement those already planned.

The critiques recommended use of other specific types of troop *razvedka*, including night raids, hunter groups (*komandy okhotnikov*), and ambushes, and provided detailed advice on how to carry out each function. In each case, it was important to avoid adhering to stereotypical actions (*shablon*) if the technique was to achieve requisite results. The analysis considered hunter groups to be the best means of capturing important prisoners (officers) and documents. These groups were formed to operate throughout the depth of the enemy's tactical defense with their efforts focused on depths of up to 15 kilometers. Each group consisted of from 6 to 12 men operating under control of the divisional intelligence chief.

Ambushes involved up to 12 men each with three to four men involved in the actual ambush and the remainder observing from a distance. Ambush parties oriented on enemy command posts (CPs), observation posts (OPs), or patrol routes. Both the hunter groups and ambushes were specifically ordered to avoid contact or combat with larger enemy forces. Regardless of what method of troop *razvedka* was being used, it was essential for commanders and staffs to institute extensive training programs for *razvedka* officers and personnel. That training, which was seldom conducted in 1942, was now the responsibility of all headquarters from *front* down to regiment.

Another deficiency identified by the analysis was the improper use of intelligence officers at all levels, a practice which produced high casualties among those officers and inhibited intelligence collection as well. The use of intelligence officers as line unit commanders and reconnaissance units as combat units was widespread. For example, "during the period from January to March, the divisional intelligence officers of one of the shock armies were relieved on an average of two to three times, mostly as a result of wounds." Other intelligence chiefs were used as morale officers, billeting officers, and for other non-intelligence-related tasks. Consequently, the critique warned, "this type of misuse of specially trained personnel and units cannot be tolerated, for it can lead to a failure of *razvedka*, which is a very important element in the security of commands at all levels."[80]

The study ended with a series of conclusions, most of which were converted into orders or directives by late 1942. It emphasized the importance of intelligence and drove the point home, stating, "A good *razvedka* man ... is a hunter. The fascist is the beast he is stalking. He must learn the habits of the beast, so that he can kill him or take him alive."[81]

To accomplish these missions, *razvedka* men and units had to be well trained, protected, and used in a focused manner. Above all, they had to be rewarded for successful service. Commanders and staff were personally responsible for effective performance of *razvedka* within their units to include all aspects of training, planning, and conducting *razvedka*. Planning had to be continuous, realistic, detailed, and coordinated at all levels of command, both on the defense and on the offense. Specifically, "in organizing an offensive, the army staff must distribute down to subordinate units (down to and including battalions), not later than two days before the offensive, thoroughly worked-out maps or overlays showing in detail all the available data concerning the enemy. The maps should be on as large a scale as practicable." During the conduct of an offensive, "special *razvedka* groups should be attached to the forward units; their mission being to infiltrate into the enemy defense positions and discover the system and lay-out of the defense, in depth."[82] To ensure that intelligence information reached appropriate headquarters, sufficient radio, telephone, and pyrotechnical equipment was necessary in each *razvedka* unit or team. Without this communications equipment, even the best *razvedka* plan was condemned to failure.

This detailed critique of *razvedka* found more concrete expression in the *Red Army Field Service Regulation* of 1942 published late in the year.[83] In the expanded *razvedka* section, the regulation stated:

> One of the main duties of headquarters is to organize *razvedka* and compile all the data it provides. The Commander will tell the Chief of Staff what data he requires, when he requires it,

and what forces and means may be used to conduct *razvedka*. In the absence of such instructions from the Commander, the Chief of Staff himself must organize *razvedka* at the proper time.[84]

The chief of staff then "personally assigns to the Chief of Intelligence Branch the main *razvedka* tasks and sets the time limits for reporting the information gained."[85] Throughout the process, all actions had to be coordinated with the efforts and needs of higher headquarters. Thus, *razvedka* was to form a continuum throughout the entire chain of command. Responding to critiques of earlier failures, the assignment of non-intelligence tasks to intelligence officers was categorically forbidden.

The regulation required *razvedka* to be focused and continuous, and enjoined commanders to allocate adequate resources to perform the mission. It specified in detail the purposes and contents of *razvedka* plans and stipulated that reserve *razvedka* assets be maintained to ensure the plan could be carried out effectively. The plan was "an operational document of headquarters...approved by the Chief of Staff." For security's sake, it "has no circulation." Its content and form varied with time available for its preparation; but, in no case, would it consist of less than "notes on the map and in the field book of the Chief of the Intelligence Branch."[86]

The plan incorporated air, artillery, and ground *razvedka*. Air *razvedka*, normally under army or *front* control, focused on clarifying the ground situation through use of visual and photographic techniques. It was particularly important to conduct multiple (redundant) air *razvedka* and, if possible, verify findings by ground *razvedka*. All results of air and artillery *razvedka* were coordinated centrally through the army intelligence branch to insure unity of effort and analysis. The regulation stressed the importance of obtaining and interrogating prisoners and provided detailed instructions for the conduct of interrogations. Interrogations provided a means for double-checking other means of *razvedka*, and all interrogation reports were passed on to and consolidated at higher headquarters, as were all captured enemy documents.

Analysis of collected information was extremely important both as a source of data and as a basis for planning subsequent *razvedka*. Verification of data was especially necessary regarding reports from agents, deserters, or interrogation of the populace. All data was to be rated according to reliability and value. Information regarding the presence of new enemy units was particularly sensitive and had to be immediately forwarded to the commander, the chief of staff, and higher headquarters. "When a new enemy unit appears on the front, the Intelligence Branch organizes a systematic study of its condition. Corps headquarters, and sometimes also divisional headquarters, maintain a 'field chart of enemy forces' on which all information on the battle composition of enemy troops is entered."[87] In addition, the Intelligence Branch was to prepare working maps and periodic charts on the enemy.

To close the gap between intelligence and operations organs

> All information about the enemy is to be sent immediately by intelligence to operations; similarly, all such information received from the troops by operations and other branches of headquarters is immediately communicated to Intelligence. A periodic exchange of fresh data between the Chiefs of Operations and Intelligence Branches is necessary to keep both parties well-informed.[88]

Finally, the regulation provided detailed instructions regarding the integration of all types of observation posts into the intelligence collection system. This fostered closer links between troop units and intelligence. Accordingly, all troop units were to maintain "observation journals," which themselves became intelligence documents.

By late 1942, army and *front* headquarters began organizing their efforts in accordance with the new directives and regulations. The case of 61st Army (Briansk Front) illustrated how the process worked.[89] The army commander determined intelligence objectives, specific targets, required information, and time constraints and often personally assigned missions to the intelligence-gathering unit. The army chief of staff analyzed missions from *front* and army commanders, established the sequence of their execution, determined concentration of efforts, resources to be committed to collection, and units and reserves which would conduct reconnaissances in force — just then beginning to be employed.

The intelligence chief and his section officers executed the missions. They drew up draft intelligence plans and orders; verified execution of tasks; collected, processed, and synthesized intelligence data, prepared reports and summaries for army and *front* headquarters, passed intelligence to neighboring units; and worked with translators to interrogate prisoners and process captured enemy documents. Pre-war exercises had indicated that army commanders required intelligence reports two to three times a day and division commanders the same reports every three to four hours. The first two years of experience, however, showed this system was inadequate. Instead, the army commander received reports every two to three hours and division commanders every one to two hours, particularly during fluid operations.

The army intelligence chief personally prepared the combat intelligence plan, which was then approved by the chief of staff. Planning for defensive operations covered 10–15 day periods while offensive plans encompassed the entire operation. Plans corresponded to the stages of the operation and were more detailed for the preparatory stage and for execution of the first day's intermediate mission. Thereafter, less detailed plans focused on the principal concentration areas and army offensive or defensive axes. It also included intelligence coverage of main partisan activities in support of the offensive. The plan specified *razvedka* objectives, missions, areas of concentration of intelligence efforts, assignment of specific tasks and equipment, timetables for mission execution, and sequencing and timing of intelligence reporting. A map on a scale of 1:100,000 or 1:200,000 with graphic representation of intelligence measures appended the plan.

Combat intelligence orders, required by the plan, were drafted for rifle corps, separate divisions, and chiefs of arms and services (such as artillery and engineers). Requests for air *razvedka* assistance went to *front* headquarters, and instructions were drafted designating tasks for partisan detachments to perform. The intelligence section cooperated with the operations section to arrange for reconnaissance in force by combat units. Orders described opposing forces, intelligence missions, timetables for execution, and reporting procedures. Missions to arms and services were assigned orally. Requests for *front* air *razvedka* support specified areas and axes for the conduct of visual reconnaissance; zones, scale, and timetable for photographic reconnaissance, and the quantity and timetable for preparing photographic terrain mosaics, if available.[90]

The army relied for its own intelligence collection on reconnaissance units of subordinate headquarters (division reconnaissance companies and regimental reconnaissance platoons). On occasion, combat subunits assisted by conducting reconnaissance in force, although this did not become standard practice until late in 1942. Since the army and subordinate corps had no organic intelligence-gathering personnel or facilities, it relied on *front* for specialized support from air, agent, and reconnaissance-diversionary organs.

Links with partisan units provided the army with its deepest intelligence gathering asset. Otherwise, the army collection effort generally ranged to a depth of up to 15 kilometers and relied primarily on observation; night and day raids; ambushes; radio and telephone eavesdropping; and, by late 1942, reconnaissance in force. After 1942 the army began employing long-range intelligence-reconnaissance detachments, often parachuted into the operational depths of the enemy rear.

The experiences of 61st Army were fairly typical for 1942, although certain armies developed particular talents for specific types of *razvedka*. By November 1942, principles of intelligence collection, processing, and analysis had emerged; and the Soviets had created a logical system for the conduct of *razvedka*. Success, however, depended in large part on the efficiency of each collection means, on the creation of reliable communications means, and on efficient staff operations required to convert raw data into meaningful estimates which could be acted upon. In the first two years of war, collection problems associated with each means often frustrated these ends.

SOURCES OF INTELLIGENCE: 1941–1942

When war began, the Soviets were familiar, at least in principle, with the wide range of intelligence collection means available to modern armies. Their task was to convert these theoretical sources into real producers of accurate intelligence so that the intelligence system could make sense of the data. Because of the variety, complexity, and range of collection systems, in time they were subordinated to the level of command best able to manage them and exploit the information they produced. In general, *fronts* and the High Command maintained control over long range, experimental, or highly sensitive *razvedka* assets. This included air *razvedka*, use of agents or reconnaissance-diversionary forces, employment of partisan *razvedka*, and more sophisticated types of radio intercept means. Armies conducted some radio *razvedka* and exploited links with partisan detachments. Most army intelligence data, however, came from troop *razvedka* and artillery and engineer *razvedka*. In essence, collection responsibilities coincided with the types of missions which forces generally performed (strategic *razvedka* under the High Command, operational in *fronts* and at army level, and tactical within armies).

Air Razvedka

Pre-war military theory postulated a major intelligence collection role for aircraft, at virtually every depth on the battlefield. As was the case in other areas, however, on the eve of war, reality did not match theory. The German surprise attack devastated Soviet air forces and made it impossible to implement prewar *razvedka* theory without a significant reconstruction period.

> Because reconnaissance units had not been completely staffed at the beginning of the war, because there were no special reconnaissance aircraft, and because of losses in the first days of the war, the commanders of the Front air forces had to employ considerable numbers of aircraft from regular units for aerial reconnaissance.[91]

Although all aircraft were responsible for reporting enemy force dispositions, between 10 and 13 percent of aircraft sorties were dedicated to reconnaissance missions only. Most missions employed visual reconnaissance, primarily at tactical depths, for photographic capabilities were limited in 1941 and developed very slowly after the outbreak of war. When equipment became available, photographic missions primarily concentrated on objectives deep in the enemy rear area and, later, on specific penetration sectors. Photographic missions made up 3.2 percent of the sorties during the Moscow defensive operation and 10.2 percent during the battles on the distant approaches to Stalingrad.[92] Later in the war, this index expanded to over 40 percent. Air *razvedka* units, when available, conducted daily observation of the enemy to detect and observe major troop concentrations and airfields at tactical (30–60 kilometers), operational (250–300 kilometers), and strategic (500 kilometers) depths. Air *razvedka* units conducted their reconnaissance missions in distinct sectors.

At the outbreak of war, the Soviet Air Force contained ten separate reconnaissance regiments subordinated to military districts.[93] After July 1941 the decimated Soviet Air Force contained hardly any units which could be called reconnaissance. In effect, all remaining aircraft were to perform the mission, but few qualified as legitimate reconnaissance aircraft. In any event, German air superiority made the task risky at best.

To compensate for the shortage of reconnaissance aircraft, the Soviet High Command enlisted the services of its subordinate Long-

Range Aviation forces which ostensibly were dedicated to long-range bombing. Their principal missions in 1941 and 1942 were to detect German rail movements and then disrupt those movements. The first significant operation occurred at Moscow in December 1941, and thereafter the High Command strove to improve air *razvedka* in general.[94] In April 1942 it created a training course for reconnaissance fliers; and, the following month it began forming reconnaissance air regiments in all armies.[95] This materially improved tactical and operational reconnaissance throughout 1942, although German air dominance continued to hinder Soviet efforts. In 1941 a total of 2,741 such sorties were conducted, followed in 1942 by 10,054. Daylight missions were flown at heights of up to 8,000 meters and night time missions below 1,500 meters.

Visual reconnaissance was further hindered by lack of reliable radio communications, since the Soviets only began to use air-ground radio extensively in the summer of 1942. Until that period, all intelligence reports were sent by phone or radio to headquarters after pilots had returned to their bases.

The first Soviet photographic reconnaissance unit (15th Separate Reserve Reconnaissance Regiment) was formed in November 1941 equipped with small Pe-2 aircraft. During November and December this unit trained crews for an additional two regiments and six separate squadrons. Simultaneously, several schools trained photo interpreters who, after their graduation in April 1942, were assigned as photographic engineer-inspectors in all *front* air forces. However, shortages in such personnel remained. Further organizational changes in early 1942 created aerial photographic sections in reconnaissance aviation units and a photographic section and a separate aerial photographic service company directly subordinate to the Chief of Front air forces' (later air armies') aerial photographic service. The first solid work by these units paved the way for the Stalingrad counteroffensive. Simultaneously, photographic interpretation sections in *front* headquarters developed techniques to use aerial photographs to form aerial mosaics (maps) of large areas. An experiment in the Demiansk area in 1941 and at Leningrad in 1942 highlighted problems in photography and in the mosaic's intelligence use and thus paved the way for future improvements.[96]

The Soviet air defense (PVO) system air-warning radio system (VNOS) played a tangential role in air *razvedka*. This radio system was responsible for warning of enemy air strikes against population centers and for exposing false enemy reports of impending air attacks. The *VNOS* of *PVO Strany* (National air defense around major cities under control of the High Command) cooperated closely with the *VNOS* of *PVO Voisk* (air defense of operating forces) which maintained air warning systems at *front* and army headquarters. Soviet assessments noted:

> VNOS is valuable not only as a system for air warning, but also as a means of ground *razvedka* concerning the enemy. Thus, during the defense of Moscow, the *front* command and supreme command [*STAVKA*] both received frequent and useful reports concerning the enemy ground forces from VNOS elements in the Tula, Kashira, Klin, and other areas. This was equally true of VNOS of *PVO Voisk* and *PVO Strany*.[97]

Air *razvedka* made few positive contributions to Soviet intelligence capabilities in 1941. The paucity of aircraft and trained crews, the fluid situation, and German air superiority limited air reconnaissance activity. Where it existed, it was weak; and the resulting reports were fragmentary. In 1942, however, an organizational structure for air *razvedka* began to emerge, and the number of missions flown rose somewhat. The intelligence these missions obtained was of a general nature and was not timely. Often intelligence organs ignored or misinterpreted the data. By the fall of 1942, however, the situation had improved, as new air *razvedka* units appeared, subordinate to armies, *fronts*, and the High Command. By late fall they contributed to Soviet success at Stalingrad, by assisting in tactical *razvedka* and by providing general information regarding movement of German operational reserves.

Agent and Reconnaissance-diversionary Razvedka

An important potential source of strategic and operational intelligence was a category of intelligence known today as human intelligence (HUMINT). This often gray area of intelligence collection involved the use of a variety of human collectors operating throughout the enemy rear. HUMINT resources included: agents under control of national intelligence organs (NKVD and the GRU); specially created *razvedka* detachments of various sizes inserted into the enemy rear; and intelligence organs of partisan detachments formed at varying depths in the enemy rear. The first two years were formative ones for these intelligence elements, for organization was required for them to realize their full potential, and organization required time and careful planning. It is clear that by late 1942, these HUMINT sources were providing valuable intelligence to the *fronts* and High Command at depths where other collection means were unable to operate.

Agent *razvedka* was under the control of the NKVD, which had general responsibility for the conduct of strategic intelligence collection and for counter-intelligence to combat clandestine operations of enemy agents in the Soviet rear area. The struggle between the NKVD counter-intelligence organ "Smersh" and German Abwehr units is beyond the scope of this book. However, it mirrored a similar struggle going on behind German lines. A system of Soviet agents abroad existed before June 1941, and this system certainly provided intelligence regarding German intentions. An official history of the NKVD stated:

> From Soviet intelligence and from other sources came considerable information about the threatening concentration of German-Fascist forces on our western border and even about the time of Hitler's invasion of the Soviet Union. However, J.V. Stalin, in several instances, did not devote enough attention to that information, considering it to be the fruits of German disinformation.[98]

The external agent network of the NKVD continued to work outside the Soviet borders throughout the war, exemplified by such famous figures as Victor Sorge and more shadowy figures purported to have worked inside the German army structure. The NKVD and GRU also coordinated the activities of various "spy rings" such as "Dora." Although much has been written about each ring or figure, the accounts are journalistic in nature, undocumented, and incomplete. The rings certainly existed, and numerous accounts attest to materials sent to the Soviets. Exact information on the quantity and quality of this intelligence will become clear only if, and when, Soviet archives are open. The Soviets have written about the "Dora" ring operating in Switzerland, but the accounts are general in nature. The agent, codenamed "Dora" was actually the Hungarian-born Alexander Rado, who operated a network of agents throughout Switzerland and probably elsewhere in Europe.[99] One of his agents, Rudolph Rossler, codenamed "Lucy," was reported to have access to key German intelligence figures, one of whom was designated "Werther." Other accounts described Rossler as a conduit by which the British were able to pass Ultra-derived information to the Soviets without revealing the source of the information. The official history of British intelligence, however, categorically rejects this claim.[100] The network of "Dora," "Lucy," and "Werther" was known to the Germans as the "Rote Drei" (the Red Three). It, in turn, fits into a larger European spy network labeled the "Red Orchestra."

The existence of this and other agent networks is less important than the question of the value and timeliness of the information these rings provided to Moscow. The Soviets clearly obtained information from the network during 1941 and 1942 and into the spring and summer of 1943. Whatever information was provided to the NKVD or GRU during the first two years of war did not prevent, and perhaps even contributed to, the intelligence failures of September and October 1941 and May and June 1942. At the least, it could not have contributed to a growth of Moscow's faith in the veracity or accuracy of the sources. Later, in the winter of 1943, agent information from Swiss circles contributed to yet another operational disaster in the Donbas. It was no wonder that, during preparations for the Kursk operation in spring 1943, Moscow still treated agent information skeptically and established its defenses accordingly. After Kursk, agents continued providing information to Moscow, but it was of reduced value. In late 1943 the "Dora" ring began dissolving when, in October, Rado was forced into hiding. Later, in spring 1944, Rossler and other members of the ring were arrested.

German radio intercepts provide one means for assessing the nature and value of "Rote Drei" intelligence operations. About 440 messages were intercepted by German or Swiss authorities which represented only about eight percent of the total, of which nearly half were via "Lucy." References to "Werther" began in December 1942, after the Soviet offensive at Stalingrad. Although the Soviets seemed to praise these reports, they criticized subsequent reports received in February 1943.[101] In any case, the time lag in transmission of agent reports generally spanned several days. While the messages may have been of general assistance, actual Soviet decision-making occurred based on harder intelligence data, from sources more closely attuned to actual German actions.

It is clear that the British did pass Ultra-derived materials to the Soviets through the Military Mission in Moscow as early as July 1941. The British passed intelligence information to the Soviets from the Chief of the Secret Service (CSS) via the British Military Mission in Moscow, all under the guise of information received from "well-placed" or "reliable" sources in Berlin. Initial British willingness to share intelligence data soon waned as the Soviets failed to reciprocate in kind.

A good deal of operational intelligence was sent through the BMM [British Military Mission] up to the summer of 1942. By the spring of that year, however, the BMM and the British Embassy had become frustrated by the cumbersome liaison protocol which the Russians had insisted on applying to most of their contacts; and though constantly bombarded by Soviet requests for further information about German strengths, dispositions and intentions, they had failed to elicit either a regular intelligence bulletin from the Russians or, even, answers to specific enquiries from the United Kingdom about, for example, unidentified GAF [German Air Force] units and GAF aircraft that were known to have fallen into Russian hands. At the same time, the Service intelligence branches had encountered a wall of resistance to their efforts to exchange intelligence via the Soviet Military Mission in London. They had begun them with instructions to hold discussions on a barter basis about sources, methods, and results. By the beginning of 1942 AI [Air Intelligence] had found the Russians unwilling to exchange even technical intelligence about captured enemy equipment; thereafter, while continuing to supply the Mission unilaterally with regular reports on the order of battle, the operations and the intentions of the GAF on the Russian front, AI confined itself to answering specific Russian questions.[102]

British information was certainly of potential value to the Soviets, if they believed it. For example, in mid-July 1941, British reports provided an estimate of German order of battle and an appreciation of German intentions in the Smolensk and Dnepr regions.[103] In late September, the British warned the Soviets about the impending thrust on Moscow, but apparently provided no details as to how that offensive would develop.[104]

Later, in spring 1942, British reports indicated intense German interest in southern Russia, noting, "Germany's primary objective during 1942 would take the form of an initial attack in the south that would be accompanied by containing operations in the centre and the north."[105] Specific reports to Moscow were as follows:

Between mid-May and mid-June Whitehall sent two series of appreciations to Russia. The first, from MI, culminated on

23 May in the warning that Germany intended to concentrate between 13 and 16 Panzer divisions in a southern army group before launching her main offensive, which would not be possible before June. The second, from AI, concluded with a general assessment of Germany's intentions based on Kursk; she would operate in the direction of Voronezh and towards the Don as soon as the operation against Sevastopol was completed.[106]

Soon, however, the British expressed doubts about German intent, which, in reality, increasingly reflected Soviet belief that the offensive would occur in the center.

In the second week of June the retiring Head of the British Military Mission reported that at the time of his recent departure from Moscow it had still been the Soviet view that the German offensive would be on the southern sector; indeed he felt that the Russian dispositions to meet the southern attack might well induce Germany to switch the attack to the centre. By 8 June, on the other hand, MI 14 had received two reports to the effect that the Russians thought the main offensive was likely to come in the central sector. Nothing is known about the origin or reliability of these two last reports. But whatever the truth may be about the Soviet assessment, MI's treatment of the reports suggests that Whitehall was far from sure that it knew the Soviet mind; since there was no evidence that the Germans were making any preparations north of Kursk, it could not accept the reports unless by "the central sector" the Russians meant the Kursk region.[107]

Finally, on July 14:

Whitehall sent a formal warning to Russia that the German intention was to hold the Soviet forces on the Voronezh front and make the main summer offensive south-eastwards between the Don and the Donets; two Panzer armies would swing south-eastwards east of the Donets while Seventeenth Army would attack eastwards from the Stalino area.[108]

This assessment was certainly of value to the Soviets, for it sketched in outline what subsequent events would bear out regarding German strategic intentions. It was another matter, however, for the Soviets to deal with the offensive until it had run its course.

These July messages were, in fact, part of a vastly reduced

intelligence flow from the British to the Soviets, induced in part by fears of compromise of the critical British source of data and by continued Soviet intransigence over exchanging information.

In these circumstances, and also because it continued to get evidence from the Enigma that Germany was reading Soviet communications, the Y Board decided that the supply of high-grade Sigint via the BMM must cease, or at least be greatly reduced. From the end of June 1942 the telegrams despatched by "C" [CSS] on behalf of AI dwindled to a trickle. On evidence of the total flow of Army and Air Force Enigma decrypts, the MI [Military Intelligence Branch of the War Office] series suffered a similar fate; it is clear that from the middle of 1942 items bearing on the Russian front were commonly not forwarded to Moscow. However, despite the fact that on 15 November the BMM was informed that the service was being discontinued altogether for the time being, it did not cease. It appears that the NID [Naval Intelligence Division] continued to send information from the Enigma to the BMM and the British naval liaison officers in Russia when it was "really important" that the Russians should have it, and it is clear that, particularly during the Soviet counter-offensive at Stalingrad which opened on 19 November 1942, operational intelligence about German Army and Air Force intentions was still passed to Moscow, some of it marked "reports sent by the JIC [Joint Intelligence Subcommittee of the Chiefs of Staff]" and some of it at the Prime Minister's insistence, as a special measure. On 22 November "C" expressed his concern that the Prime Minister was requiring him to forward intelligence derived solely from the Enigma when the Germans were tightening their signals security: "it is for this reason that I am always embarrassed at sending the Russians information only obtainable from this source, owing to the legibility of many Russian cyphers."[109]

Materials passed in late 1942 and 1943 were limited primarily to general German intentions and lacked significant detail.

The usefulness of British intelligence material depended directly on its source. The most valuable and regular of Ultra sources were several German army keys and Air Force Enigma, which consisted of several "broken" keys, including general information from air force liaison officers in the Crimea and Donets regions and from Fliegerkorps I, IV, and VII operating in the south by mid-year. Loss of German Army keys in late 1942 was compensated for by an ability to read German Air Force signal intelligence traffic and, from the spring of 1943, OKH non-morse teleprinter transmissions to Army Group South.[110] The contributions of agent networks and British intelligence information to Soviet military efforts are hard to measure, although one can conclude that their information, however complete, was of a strategic nature and difficult to act upon in a timely manner on the battlefield.

Of far greater use was the agent network of the NKVD, established in the German rear after war had begun. Agent operations were organized and controlled by the Special Departments (*Osobyi otdel'* – *OO*) within *fronts* and armies which were, in turn, responsible to the NKVD. By late 1941 the Special Departments had begun organizing operational *razvedka* in the German rear area which focused on the obtaining of military intelligence data.

> *Razvedchiki* [reconnaissance men] and reconnaissance groups of the Special Departments, dispatched into the disposition of fascist frontal units, fulfilled the missions of close troop reconnaissance and gathered information about the dislocation of staffs, warehouses, and other important German objectives. Often they fulfilled, as well, responsible and dangerous missions for demolition of enemy frontal communications and destruction of large enemy bases and fuel depots and for the seizure of fascist staff officers with operational documents.[111]

At first, due to communications problems, the contributions of *razvedchiki* were limited. As communications links with their parent organs improved, however, the importance of their work increased. Eventually, Special Departments actively sought to penetrate German intelligence organs, in particular Abwehr units themselves.

> Already at the beginning of 1942, *front* Special Departments possessed enough information about their enemy by means of the "secret wire." This provided a possibility for transitioning from defensive tactics to tactics of active offensives on the enemy, to disrupt his planned operations, and to analyze from within the mechanism of German military intelligence.[112]

This activity, designed to penetrate German intelligence, gained momentum in 1943.

Specialized forces, formed by the NKVD shortly after the beginning of war, expanded in size, scope of operations, and importance as the war progressed. From 27 to 29 June 1941 in Moscow, the Central Committee and SOVNARKOM authorized creation by the NKVD of special groups of detachments "designated chiefly to conduct *razvedka* and diversionary operations in the fascist rear."[113] In September 1941 two brigades were formed from the personnel of these detachments. Throughout the war, these brigades performed a variety of missions including: assistance in the development of a massive partisan movement; help to underground partisan organs; deep (strategic) *razvedka*, ascertaining the plans of the German command; assistance to Red Army *razvedka*, diversionary and combat operations; disorganization of the German rear; counter-intelligence operations; and organizing reprisals relating "to Hitlerite executioners and traitors to the Soviet homeland."[114]

In late June 1941, the brigades formed at Dynamo Stadium in Moscow, drawing upon experienced intelligence specialists or *Chekisti* from the NKVD and its several training schools. Over 1,500 men joined the brigade in 1941–42, more than 800 of whom were sportsmen from sports clubs *Dynamo, Spartak,* and *Loko-mativ.* Soon the brigades reorganized into two regiments and then, by year's end, into the Special Motorized Rifle Brigade of Special Designation (OMSBON) NKVD commanded by Col. M.F. Driov. The OMSBON included a staff, two motorized rifle regiments, separate companies (combat security, sapper, and communications), medical and parachute *desant* services, several schools, and an aviation element. Subsequently, the brigade formed independent detachments of from 1,000–1,200 men for front operations and special detachments of from 30–100 men and special groups of 3–10 men for operations in the enemy rear.

The brigade conducted special training in firing, combat tactics, topography, ground navigation, use of mines, parachuting, radio communications, and other technical fields. All were trained to live under austere partisan conditions. The 101st Long Range Aviation Regiment, commanded by V.S. Grizodubov, provided transportation for the brigade, principally into partisan airfields or by air drop. The aviation regiment served as the principal communication means of brigade personnel and its parent organs. Later, trained radio personnel permitted establishment of direct radio contact between brigade units and the "Center."

Combat use of brigade personnel began in August 1941 with the dispatch of several special detachments and groups into the enemy rear. The detachments *Boevoi* (Combat) and *Mitia* operated until January 1942, helping create partisan activity in the Briansk area.

During the defense of Moscow in October 1941, OMSBON's two regiments temporarily assisted in the ground defense of the capital in the Mozhaisk–Naro Fominsk sector. Later in the Moscow defensive operation, and into the period of the counteroffensive, special groups and detachments operated both under NKVD and *front* control fulfilling diverse missions both along the front and in the enemy rear. In the summer and fall of 1942 the brigades traveled to the Northern Caucasus area, where they conducted operations to disrupt German activity there and on the approaches to Stalingrad. Other brigade elements provided support for other *fronts* and also trained cadre for partisan units. For example:

> They created for partisan detachments and specialized groups inserted into the enemy rear 803 radiomen, 534 demolitions experts, 5,255 demolition assistants, 126 vehicle drivers, 107 mortarmen, 350 snipers, and 3,000 parachutists; 212 special detachments and groups numbering a total 7,316 men were directed into the enemy rear to conduct combat and *razvedka* actions.[115]

To supplement the work of the OMSBON's two brigades, in the summer of 1941 the Soviets began forming special "destruction" (*istrebitel' nyi*) battalions and regiments. These forces initially performed the primary mission of "securing the rear from the intrigues of enemy agents," but in accordance with Soviet directives issued in late June 1941, these forces received the additional mission of operating with partisan forces in the German rear.[116] By the end of 1941, about 1,350 destroyer battalions numbering more than 250,000 men operated with the Red Army and in the German rear under control of partisan commands and the NKVD. Destroyer battalions and regiments in the German rear concentrated on fulfilling reconnaissance and diversionary missions.

By the end of 1941, the Soviets had deployed extensively destruction units into the enemy rear. For example, "in the Ukraine, to 1 January 1942 6,236 commanders and soldiers of destroyer battalions were sent into the German rear to bring partisan units up to strength."[117] These forces reinforced the 84 specialized reconnaissance groups totalling 1,189 men, either created in or inserted into the German rear area during 1941 and 1942.[118] Even more extensive deployments of destroyer battalions and regiments occurred in the Belorussian and Pre-Baltic regions. In time these forces were fully integrated into the partisan command and control structure and formed an indispensable link in the *razvedka* chain. By late 1942 this concept had been expanded to include destroyer brigades assigned to Soviet operating *fronts* designated to perform the same basic missions as those operating under NKVD control.

During the Moscow operations, Soviet airborne forces joined in conducting deep reconnaissance missions. Elements of the 250th Airborne Regiment operated in the German rear in November and again in December and January in cooperation with elements of 4th Airborne Corps. In conjunction with a larger airborne operation planned for late January 1942, the Soviets dropped seven small reconnaissance-diversionary groups of 20 to 30 men each into the Viaz'ma area to identify German dispositions and monitor German troop movements in response to the Soviet offensive (since other intelligence information was very poor).[119] Although the results of these missions were marginal, they typified Soviet actions in the future – namely an increasing tendency to employ reconnaissance teams deep in the enemy rear, in particular prior to and during periods of Soviet offensives.

By late 1942 a distinct reconnaissance-diversionary force structure had emerged, centrally controlled by the NKVD, but with field operating forces spread down through *front* commands and the partisan movement. At the national level and within *fronts*, a variety of special purpose units conducted long-range *razvedka* and diversionary operations. The activities of those special groups and detachments were controlled by NKVD "Center" and by the Special Departments of *fronts* and armies. By late 1942 virtually all *fronts* and armies probably possessed destroyer brigades and special detachments or groups. These forces parachuted or infiltrated into the enemy rear wearing enemy uniforms or civilian clothes to conduct reconnaissance and diversionary work and to assist in the formation of partisan forces, or to cooperate with them.

Partisan Razvedka

The growing partisan movement promised to become a major source of intelligence once it could be organized and harnessed in the service of state security forces. Zhukov has cryptically described the contribution of partisan forces in *razvedka*, writing, "We received good intelligence information from my partisan detachments, operating in the enemy rear."[120] In general, "Partisan *razvedka* supplied the Soviet Army command with valuable intelligence information about the nature of enemy defenses and the grouping of his forces, and uncovered *maskirovka* (deception) and other measures of the enemy," particularly before Soviet offensive operations.[121]

The formation of the partisan movement and its exploitation by Soviet intelligence took considerable time to evolve. The groundwork was laid on 29 June 1941 when the People's Commissariat of the USSR and the Communist Party Central Committee issued a directive requiring "the creation of partisan detachments and diversionary groups in regions occupied by the enemy, for a struggle with enemy army units, for unleashing partisan war anywhere and everywhere, for blowing up bridges and roads and damage of telephone and telegraph communications, and the burning of warehouses, etc."[122] The entire party structure focused on the task, drawing upon bypassed Red Army units and the local party infrastructure.

Creation of the partisan movement and control mechanisms for it evolved slowly. On 30 May 1942 the *STAVKA* created the Central Staff of the Partisan Movement (TsShPD) under the Belorussian Communist Party Secretary, P.K. Ponomarenko. By this time, local organs had coalesced into a formal structure including republic, regional (*krai*), and province (*oblast'*) partisan staffs. Refined missions for the partisan movement were included in People's Commissariat of Defense Order of 5 September 1942 entitled "Concerning the Missions of the Partisan Movement."

Partisan military forces formed detachments (*otriad*) which usually consisted of subordinate companies, platoons, and squads. Detachments operated independently or as part of partisan brigades and divisions. Among the many missions these detachments performed was *razvedka* of enemy forces in concert with main Red Army forces either on the defense or on the offense. As such, partisan units performed the normal range of *razvedka* functions to identify enemy units, keep track of troop movements, and seize prisoners and documents. In addition, partisans themselves used agents and local inhabitants to obtain intelligence information.

Planned use of partisan forces began as early as November 1941 when the Northwestern Front incorporated partisan actions into projected December 1941 *front* operations.[123] The Kalinin Front did likewise in the spring of 1942. Larger scale joint action took place during the Rzhev–Viaz'ma operation (8 January–20 April 1942) when partisan organs of the Kalinin, Smolensk, and Orel provinces cooperated with the Western and Kalinin Fronts and NKVD *razvedka* forces. Sixty-eight partisan detachments and 37 diversionary groups totaling 2,205 men took part in the operation under Kalinin Front control while another 67 detachments with 16,000 men operated on the Western Front.[124] The intelligence departments and sections of fronts and armies and NKVD organs coordinated *razvedka* activities.

During the operations, liaison officers, often flying into the German rear, provided communications with the "Center." Later, missions and information passed via radio links. Partisan units provided the Kalinin Front with "information about the movement and regrouping of forces and about the strength of enemy garrisons."[125] In this sense, they were instrumental in Soviet seizure of Usviaty, Surazh, and Velizh. Similar information was passed to the Western Front. By late January *front* headquarters and the NKVD assigned specific intelligence assignments to partisan units, which, by this time, were cooperating closely with special detachments under NKVD control. In addition, partisans cooperated with airborne detachments of the 201st Airborne Brigade (4th Airborne Corps) and 250th Rifle Regiment (parachute delivered), operating under *front* control. In the summer of 1942, partisan detachment "Alesia," operating near Mogilev, seized a key German intelligence figure and obtained from him the names of German operatives, agents, and spies in the region.

Partisan *razvedka* in the first period of war was subject to serious problems, many caused by the initial absence of sound organization. Many partisan units operated *Na sebia* (for themselves) and did not serve the Red Army or party. Partisan units were at first fragmented, and only after they had created links between one another could planned intelligence work go on. Nor did many units have well-developed links with the local population. Most serious was the lack of reliable communications which inhibited passage of vital information to agencies which needed it. After NKVD destroyer detachments had established contacts with partisan detachments, these problems slowly withered away. At the same time, some *front* staffs underestimated the value of partisan *razvedka* and, consequently, were slow to further its development. This applied particularly to areas where the partisan movement was slow in forming (such as the Ukraine). The defense commissariat Orders of 5 September 1942 "Concerning the Missions of the Partisan Movement" spurred on organizational efforts by stipulating the objectives and methods of partisan *razvedka*.[126] This would be developed in a more extensive order of April 1943.

Partisan *razvedka* contributed to the Soviet intelligence effort in the first period of war but only marginally and at specific times regarding specific missions. Their work was particularly valuable in early 1942 around Moscow. At best, the Soviet High Command developed an appreciation for what partisan *razvedka* could do if properly organized and supervised. That organization and supervision would expand markedly in 1943 and geometrically increase the contribution of partisans to the Soviet intelligence effort.

Radio-Electronic Razvedka

In the late 1930s, the field of radio *razvedka*, and communications intelligence in general, had held great promise. Pre-war theory carved out a significant role for signal intelligence, but that role seemed far from realization after the disaster of June 1941. Preoccupied with the even greater problems of fielding radios at critical command nodes throughout the force, initially the Soviets could pay only scant attention to radio *razvedka*. The most immediate Soviet concern was for defense of its own limited radio transmissions through communications security and stricter control over transmissions. Soviet efforts with both measures were poor in 1941, but improved somewhat in 1942.

Only in late 1942 were the Soviets able to field specialized equipment capable of accurate radio-location and jamming. Until that time the Soviets made do with existing equipment and crude procedures. Communications units at all levels had standing instructions to pass on intelligence information monitored on enemy frequencies. Intelligence sections and departments at all levels of command did likewise, but these measures were unsystematic and largely dependent upon chance. Soviet production of radios lagged, and the technological level of sophistication of most radio apparatus was low. Accelerated production and intensive research in late 1941 and 1942 began to bear fruit by year's end when the Soviets were finally able to field units devoted to radio *razvedka*.

Until late 1942, transmission of intelligence information was done by radio (where available), wire, and messenger. While the first means was insecure and plagued by technical difficulties, the latter two were more dependable, relatively secure, but slow. Shortage of radios also hindered transmission of aerial reconnaissance data, for few aircraft were equipped with radios. At the end of the first period of war, all aspects of radio *razvedka* were in their infancy — radio *razvedka*, radio-technical *razvedka*, radio disinformation, and radio-electronic suppression. While some improvements would occur in late 1942, the greatest period of progress would have to wait until the summer of 1943.

Troop Razvedka

While Soviet strategic and deep operational *razvedka* was weak and would remain so until technical means of collecting and communications improved, the Soviets believed they could master tactical and low level operational *razvedka*. Here the chief hurdles to overcome were lack of experience on the part of officers, poor training of units, and the need to establish sound procedures to link together the various means of *razvedka*.

Troop *razvedka* included all those active and passive measures troop units could perform to collect intelligence information on the enemy. Active measures involved a variety of *razvedka* techniques employed by both reconnaissance and line units, including raids, ambushes, and sweeps. Eventually the reconnaissance in force (*razvedka boem*) became the most important measure. Passive measures included observation at all levels of command by varied means and conduct of the commanders' reconnaissance (*recognotsirovka*).

During the first five months of war, because of unfavorable combat circumstances and the inexperience of units and commanders, troop *razvedka* was weak and contributed to Soviet combat difficulties. After analysis of early failures, on 18 September 1941 the Commissariat of Defense issued Order No. 308, which was accompanied by General Staff directives, mandating improvements in intelligence collection.[127] The order prohibited the launching of offensives without full reconnaissance of the terrain and enemy positions by all commanders and required all units to conduct necessary tactical reconnaissance measures.

This high-level attention produced results; and by the time of the Moscow counteroffensive, most units employed a wide range of troop *razvedka* techniques. Employment of the most valuable technique, reconnaissance in force, however, remained the exception. According to Soviet critiques:

> In the first period of war, *razvedka boem* [*reconnaissance in force*] before an offensive was very seldom conducted. Our forces were usually limited to observation and sweeps; and, as a result of this, information about the enemy was far from complete. In many cases, this led to incorrect conclusions regard-

ing the strength and intentions of the enemy, as a consequence of which commanders made unfounded decisions, which, in the final analysis, had a negative effect on the success of our offensives.[128]

Another assessment reinforced this conclusion, stating:

> True, in the first period of war, it [*razvedka boem*] was conducted seldom and episodically. Our forces then obtained information on the basis of observation, sweeps, and air *razvedka*, which could not provide a full notion of the defense, especially about the density of enemy forces and about the disposition of his fire means and reserves. That affected the course of the offensive negatively.[129]

There were several reasons for this failure. Reconnaissance in force was principally offensive in nature, and the Soviets were on the defensive for much of the period. Even when on the offensive, at Moscow and elsewhere, Soviet forces occupied jumping-off positions for the attack a considerable distance from the enemy front lines. Units conducting reconnaissance would inevitably be detected as they approached enemy defenses and hence suffered heavy losses. Soviet forces also attacked across relatively broad fronts in shallow combat formations. In these circumstances, any forces detached to conduct reconnaissance further diluted force concentrations required to achieve success. Finally, and most important, Soviet commanders were too inexperienced to appreciate the positive results which reconnaissance in force could produce.

In the first period of war, there were scattered instances when reconnaissance in force was used to good effect; and these examples provided impetus for generalizing the techniques throughout the force. The 37th Army of the Southern Front employed reconnaissance in force during the Rostov operation of November 1942; and, in January 1942, 20th Army of Zhukov's Western Front conducted reconnaissance in force in some sectors two to three days prior to the offensive.[130] The Western and Briansk Fronts employed the techniques in the summer of 1942 in the Rzhev–Sychevka and Kozel'sk operations, but with only mixed results. The 31st Army organized extensive ground reconnaissance using observation, sweeps, ambushes, and reconnaissance in force. This was integrated with planned air *razvedka* by 1st Air Army and the army air regiment. Army *razvedka* ranged to a depth of 80 kilometers, and the reconnaissance in force, conducted to complete the effort, produced positive results. Conversely, 61st Army conducted its reconnaissance in force several days prior to the attack. The *razvedka* measure, however, alerted the Germans to the impending attack and permitted them to alter their defensive posture by leaving their forward positions unoccupied. After the Soviets had pummeled the vacant positions with their artillery preparation, the Germans reoccupied them and repulsed the ground attack.[131]

Before November 1942, some Soviet units employed reconnaissance in force while on the defense. The 38th Army, defending along the Don River near Voronezh, employed reconnaissance in force to seize prisoners and documents "not only to receive trustworthy information about the enemy but also with the aim of improving the positions of our forces, securing dominant heights and bridgeheads on river lines, exhausting the enemy, and creating constantly strained conditions."[132] By early November enough positive experience with *razvedka boem* had been collected for the Soviets to recommend its more general use throughout the Red Army. This would occur at Stalingrad.

Meanwhile, the Soviets improved other methods of troop *razvedka*. The most important of these was the sweep (*poisk*) aimed at capturing prisoners and documents. The principal objectives of sweeps were enemy firing points, sentries, observation posts, and small groups of enemy deployed in the rear area. Early in the war Soviet forces employed relatively large subunits for sweeps, and most were unsuccessful because they were easily detected and defeated. By 1943 the Soviets began using more numerous, smaller units numbering from six to 16 men each. Most sweeps were conducted at night for security's sake and to take advantage of the fragmented nature of enemy defenses. As German defenses deepened and became more continuous, the Soviets shifted to daytime sweeps. Ambushes designed to capture prisoners also became more numerous as the war progressed as did the number and complexity of observation posts distributed throughout troop units.[133]

During the first period of war, the Soviets improved their procedures for observation and commanders' reconnaissance (*rekognostsirovka*). They were quick to notice initial problems. Commanders, their deputies, responsible staff officers, and visual reconnaissance groups necessary to refine data concerning the enemy and the terrain were often forced by circumstances to leave front line positions. Insufficient time and the complexity of the situation further inhibited the process. As a result, army commanders were often forced to make their decisions on the map without adequate reconnaissance. Nevertheless, some positive examples existed which provided a basis for general improvements throughout the force. The 22d Army, when preparing for an operation in September 1941 in the Andreapol' area, established a *rekognostsirovka* group to validate the commander's plan. The group consisted primarily of engineer officers and was headed by the deputy army commander. In a period of seven days, this group, along with similar groups from the army's divisions, thoroughly analyzed the enemy defenses. On the basis of their work, the commander adjusted his plan; and the offensive developed successfully.[134] In time, the composition of reconnaissance groups became more refined. In March 1942, 21st Army created a group headed by the deputy army commander which included representatives from all army staff sections (operations, intelligence, artillery, communications, etc.). Divisions formed analogous groups; and, as a result, reconnaissance, engineer, security, *maskirovka*, and other areas of planning were more effective.

Based on these experiences, on 5 April 1942, the General Staff issued new instructions to forces specifying how commanders' reconnaissance would be performed in the future. The reconnaissance group was to consist of combined arms commanders, and artillery and engineer representatives. The group was to focus on verifying the commander's preliminary decisions, particularly regarding terrain, enemy troop dispositions, fortifications, and enemy fire systems. The instructions also required the reconnaissance group "during work on the terrain to foresee the possibility of the enemy firing in front of the forward limits of the defense by flank or oblique fire of machine guns, anti-tank or other fire means, as well as additional frontal fire by all types of weapons from the depth of the defense."[135] The *front* or army military council reviewed and approved each group's report.

Later in 1942 the new *Red Army Field Regulation* incorporated the contents of the General Staff instructions. In addition, the regulation required division commanders to conduct personal reconnaissance along with their subordinate regimental and battalion commanders. Each group was to determine the forward edge of enemy main defensive positions, reconnoiter the entire sector, and organize cooperation (*vzaimodeistvie*) "on the ground." Soviet forces began operating according to the new regulations during the Stalingrad counteroffensive. By late 1942 Soviet procedures for tactical troop *razvedka* were well-established through thorough analysis of combat experiences. A number of *fronts* had already implemented the new procedures and tested them in combat. Their effectiveness would be further tested in the first major Soviet offensive operation conducted since the Moscow offensive, the November Stalingrad counteroffensive.

Artillery Razvedka

Artillery *razvedka* was closely associated with troop *razvedka*. The Soviets considered it to be a separate category because of their appreciation of the unique impact of artillery on the outcome of battle. It was, in their view, the most dominant of all factors, particularly during the penetration phases of operations. "The most difficult step of an offensive operation is the penetration of a pre-pared enemy defense. Success in this primarily depends on effective fire suppression of defending enemy forces and his objectives."[136] Soviet suppression of enemy defenses was particularly weak during 1941 operations in part because "little attention was paid to organiz-ing *razvedka* of enemy objectives (targets)."[137]

During the counteroffensive at Moscow and the winter general offensive, German defenses improved in continuity and depth. Only thorough *razvedka* could provide the necessary basis for successfully breaching these defenses. The Soviets relied on a combination of air and artillery *razvedka* measures to determine precise enemy firing and defensive positions. At the beginning of war, the Red Army relied on artillery instrumental *razvedka* (*artilleriiskaia instrumental' naia razvedka – AIR*) to determine the locations of enemy firing systems. In theory, AIR consisted of sound, topographical, photogrammetric, and meteorological measures to locate likely and confirmed enemy weapons loca-tions.[138] Soviet efforts to do so were constrained by the limited equipment available to accomplish that task. Consequently, the first two years of war were a testing period to find requisite solutions to the problem – particularly in the realm of command and control and discovering techniques to solve the problem.

The Soviets conducted sound and optical *razvedka*, using an increasingly complex system of observation and listening posts (OPs and LPs) which, in time, they equipped with sound detecting and optical devices such as stereoscopes. These were supplemented with aerostatic (observation balloon) units and aircraft. For example, the Reserve Front in 1941 used fighter aircraft to identify targets and adjust fire. This expedient worked satisfactorily until German aircraft appeared or enemy antiaircraft units joined the fray. In general, during offensive operations in 1941 and 1942, the Soviets conducted an average of ten reconnaissance aircraft sorties over enemy positions daily to detect enemy firing positions. At this stage of war, these sorties and other observation means identified well under half of the enemy weapons prior to the offensive.[139]

Soon after war began, the Soviets began creating or beefing up dedicated artillery reconnaissance forces. Each military district (*front*) headquarters had specific air units designated to perform *razvedka*, an aerostatic observation battalion (*vozdukhoplavatel'- nyi divizion aerostatov nabliudeniia – VDAN*) consisting of three detachments equipped with observation balloons, and one separate reconnaissance artillery battalion. By the end of 1942, the Soviets had strengthened this structure; and *fronts* contained two to three reconnaissance artillery battalions and one separate aviation correction squadron to assist in adjusting artillery fire.

By early 1943 Soviet artillery *razvedka* techniques had improved sufficiently for the Soviets to institute the concept of the artillery offensive, the planned conduct of fire in three stages throughout the duration of the operation.[140] By then, artillery *razvedka* was a planned component of the artillery offensive. As a former Chief of Artillery wrote, however, "Only from the end of 1942, with the growth of the capability of Soviet artillery and the accumulation of experience, was reconnaissance of enemy batteries successfully conducted."[141]

Engineer Razvedka

Soviet pre-war regulations called for the conduct of engineer *razvedka* principally to assist combat forces in negotiating prepared enemy defensive positions. In theory, engineer, artillery, and troop *razvedka*, taken together, would provide information necessary to plan and conduct a successful penetration operation. When the war began, engineer forces suffered from the same general deficiencies as other forces. Although the theoretical combat use of engineers was well documented, actual capabilities to convert theory into practice lagged significantly.

Engineer *razvedka* was supposed to disclose the nature of enemy engineer organization and, above all, the presence and location of obstacles, the types of mines employed, and their disposition in minefields. To serve this function, the Soviets created engineer observation posts (INP), and reconnaissance and search groups, and assigned combat engineers to line units and other units designated to carry out reconnaissance in force. Engineer *razvedka* was primarily associated with offensive operations, and it focused on "illuminating" the details of defensive positions. In 1941, because German defenses were light and non-continuous, there was little necessity for Soviet commanders to pay great attention to engineer *razvedka*. This changed in 1942 as German defenses stiffened. By late 1942 Soviet forces routinely created search and reconnaissance groups which, in cooperation with aircraft, paid considerably more attention to the study of enemy defenses.

At Moscow in early 1942, the Soviets, for the first time, used engineer clearing detachments on the basis of one or two per division to precede the advance of infantry toward and through enemy defenses.[142] During the first period of war, because the Soviets abolished the rifle corps link in rifle armies, engineer assets were found only within divisions (up to one battalion). This battalion provided the basis for engineer *razvedka* measures. Often, however, combat conditions forced division commanders to use the battalion in combat rather than in its engineer role.

Intelligence and Deception

Soviet military theorists had long argued for the necessity of using deception (*maskirovka*) as an adjunct to combat operations. Deception, if properly employed, could perform the dual function of concealing one's own actions and forcing the enemy to operate on the basis of false information. Advantage would accrue to the side which most effectively employed deception. While good intelligence was not an absolute prerequisite for successful deception, it was an important factor, if for no other reason than that commanders could verify the results of their deceptive measures. It is no coincidence that Soviet deception in 1941 and 1942 was most effective where *razvedka* was most successfully carried out (i.e. Rostov − November 1941, Toropets–Kholm − January 1942). Several examples will suffice.

In May 1942 the Soviets conducted a fairly successful operational level deception prior to the Khar'kov operation. They succeeded in concealing from the Germans their intent to attack and the existence of large tank forces, which were to exploit the attack. However, Soviet intelligence incorrectly assessed German strategic intentions and failed to detect German creation of large operational reserves in close proximity to the sector of the Soviet attack. Consequently, intelligence failures negated the effects of Soviet deception and produced an operational catastrophe.[143]

In August 1942 the Voronezh Front planned a major offensive along the Don River with three armies (60th, 40th, and 38th). The 60th and 40th Armies were to conduct the main attack and 38th Army the supporting attack. For fear that the Germans would conduct a pre-emptive assault, the 60th Army commander employed deception to simulate attack preparations on the boundary between him and 38th Army (the right flank). The deception worked, and the Germans shifted forces into the threatened region. However, neither *front*, 60th, nor 38th Armies' reconnaissance assets detected the German movements. *Front* headquarters and 38th Army were also ignorant of 60th Army's deception plan. Consequently, 38th Army's attack ran into the German reinforcements; and the *front* offensive failed.[144]

The Soviets planned their first significant operational deception to supplement their counteroffensive at Stalingrad. It remained to be seen whether Soviet *razvedka* would support or interfere with the success of that deception plan and the counteroffensive as a whole.

ON THE EVE OF STALINGRAD

Soviet fortunes swung wildly during the first 18 months of war. The Red Army endured the disasters of 1941 at huge cost and stemmed the German offensive tide at Moscow. By Herculean efforts, tinged with a degree of desperation, the Soviets launched the crudely fashioned counteroffensive and prepared optimistically for further strategic success in 1942. When those hopes were dashed, the Soviets stoically and patiently waited for the German offensive momentum to ebb. In November 1942 the Soviets again sought to regain the strategic initiative by striking and destroying German forces in southern Russia.

The Soviet intelligence effort in the first period of war was little short of dismal. Strategically, the High Command utterly and repeatedly failed to discover German intentions. In June 1941 and in May and June 1942, the Soviets paid dearly for these failures. In the end, the flow of combat defined German intentions in time for the Red Army to bring the German offensives to a halt. Operationally, the Soviet High Command, *fronts*, and armies fared no better. Intelligence lost track of German forces as they plunged forward along their strategic axes in 1941. They failed to detect the sudden German turn southward toward Kiev in September and likewise were surprised by the location and ferocity of the October German assault toward Moscow.

In 1942 Soviet intelligence, already mesmerized by phantom German intentions to march on Moscow, misassessed the probable locations of German attacks in the south. Throughout the advance toward Stalingrad and the Caucasus, Soviet forces were constantly off-balance trying to assess where the next blow would fall. Finally, Soviet intelligence misjudged the direction and strength of German efforts into the Caucasus. In the last analysis, the Soviets determined German intentions and dispositions simply by hurling forces into their path. These forces, though roughly handled, took their toll on German strength and, together with the configuration of the terrain in southern Russia and the fortuitous decision of the German Army to challenge the Red Army at Stalingrad, the Red Army finally halted the German drive.

With few exceptions, Soviet tactical intelligence in 1941 was as poor as its operational and strategic counterparts. In addition, operational and strategic mistakes rendered tactical intelligence almost superfluous, even when it was effective. In 1942 Soviet tactical intelligence improved, in particular where the front had stabilized. It was obvious to the Soviet High Command that improvements were necessary lest intelligence errors destroy future offensive opportunities or condition the Red Army for further defeats. It is said that necessity is the mother of invention. The Soviets well understood the necessity of improving *razvedka* and that understanding, combined with a wealth of experience from the first period of war, prompted change and improvement.

Side by side with the record of Soviet intelligence failures was a more positive phenomenon. During 1941, and even more so in 1942, the High Command and the General Staff carefully defined problems and sought corrections to them. Driven by wartime necessity and the specter of potential defeat, the Soviets reviewed the theoretical context for *razvedka*, postulated a new system and means for its conduct, and began a lengthy process of implementing the new system. Shortages of matériel and trained manpower inhibited the process and produced innumerable frustrations. In the absence of requisite forces and matériel, the Soviets, however, demonstrated their forte for *po ruchnoi* (by hand) improvisation of *razvedka* techniques which slowly satisfied the requirements of the system.

By late 1942, after publication of a stream of orders, directives, and regulations, Soviet intelligence had made significant progress, in particular at the tactical level. Troop *razvedka* procedures had been standardized, and use of the reconnaissance in force was now required throughout the force. Waning German air superiority now permitted more extensive use of air *razvedka* at both the tactical and operational levels. A fledgling system of agent and specialized *razvedka*, combined in some sectors of the front with a burgeoning and increasingly well-organized partisan movement, promised to produce greater quantities of human intelligence. Even radio *razvedka* was about to emerge from its crude beginning into an intelligence field of potential value in its own right. Rudimentary procedures for all aspects of intelligence collection, processing, and analysis were in place and ready to be tested and improved in future combat.

Most important for the future success of *razvedka* was the improved level of competency in all ranks of the Red Army. Months of combat had weeded out ineffective commanders and staff officers at higher levels of command. The survivors well understood the nature of the war and what it would take to survive personally, and as an army. They understood, as well, that their future survival depended on their efficient mastery of all aspects of the new systems they had devised. The first great test of their performance began at Stalingrad in November 1942.

CHAPTER FIVE

THE STALINGRAD
COUNTEROFFENSIVE

STRATEGIC AND OPERATIONAL CONTEXT

After enduring 18 months of often unsuccessful combat, in late fall 1942 the Red Army prepared its second strategic counteroffensive designed to seize the strategic initiative from the Germans. Armed with this experience and guided by new regulations which governed virtually every aspect of combat operations, the Soviets had good reason to expect success.

The German summer offensive, which had commenced in late June, first swept eastward to Voronezh on the Don River and then southeastward toward the great bend of the Don. The Red Army resisted the German advance and launched a series of counterattacks in the Voronezh region, along the upper Don River, and in the great bend of the Don. Thereafter German forces simultaneously thrust eastward across the Don toward Stalingrad and southeast toward the Caucasus Mountains. The Soviet High Command adopted a deliberate defensive strategy throughout this period by fighting delaying actions, conducting periodic counterattacks, and systematically withdrawing its forces before they were encircled. Finally, in October, the *STAVKA* consciously decided to conduct a deliberate defense in the city of Stalingrad and along the approaches to the Caucasus Mountains preparatory to launching another strategic counteroffensive. Unlike 1941, in late 1942 the Soviets retained the planning initiative and avoided the hasty, reactive type of planning so prevalent during the Moscow operation. By October 1942 German forces were locked in a bitter and costly struggle for the city of Stalingrad, a struggle which consumed critical German operational reserves. The German decision to conduct simultaneous offensive operations at Stalingrad and deep into the Caucasus region strained German resources to the breaking point and forced the German High Command to deploy extensive but poorly equipped allied forces along the over-extended flanks of the main German shock groups. Those long flanks became a focal point of Soviet planning.

As in 1941, in the summer and fall of 1942 the *STAVKA* carefully marshaled strategic reserves. It formed ten reserve armies and new armored forces (tank armies and mechanized corps) under *STAVKA* control and judiciously used some of these reserves to halt the German drive. Although three of the four new Soviet tank armies created in June 1942 had been expended in defensive fighting on the approaches to Voronezh and Stalingrad, one of the original four remained intact; and a new fifth tank army was formed to increase substantially Soviet mobile reserves. The High Command also made a concerted effort to capitalize on its war experiences through systematic collection and analysis and, on the basis of this analysis, issued orders and directives to correct improper practices in virtually every aspect of military operations.

In early September 1942, the Soviet High Command began planning a major counteroffensive to expel German forces from southern Russia.

> The *STAVKA* considered that the German-Fascist command could not rapidly transfer large strategic reserves to the region from Germany and other theaters of war, since there were none and formation of new forces required considerable time. It ruled out the possibility of the transfer of large forces to the south from the western and northwestern directions of the Soviet–German front. That also required too much time. The presence on these directions [axes] of large groupings of Soviet forces provoked understandable uneasiness on the part of the enemy, who expected an offensive.[1]

The Soviet High Command believed that destruction of German forces in the Stalingrad region would halt the German advance into the Caucasus, win back the economically valuable Don and Kuban regions, and possibly facilitate liberation of the critical Donbas (Donets Basin) region. A successful counteroffensive could smash the armies of Germany's principal allies and significantly weaken the Axis alliance as well.

The projected Soviet counteroffensive at Stalingrad formed the centerpiece of a broader concept for a winter campaign "the strategic aim of which was the destruction of forces of the entire southern wing of German-Fascist forces to secure the strategic initiative and create a turning point in the course of war to the

Soviet Union's benefit."[2] Specifically, the Soviets planned first to concentrate large strategic reserves in the Stalingrad direction and to use those reserves to attack, surround, and destroy German Army Group B around Stalingrad proper. Thereafter, Soviet *fronts* adjacent to the Stalingrad region would join the operation and attack from the middle reaches of the Don River and south of Stalingrad toward Rostov, to isolate remnants of Army Group B, and cut off and destroy German Army Group A, whose forces stretched deep into the Caucasus region. Simultaneously, the *STAVKA* planned a series of limited offensive operations in the Leningrad region and on the Northwestern and Western directions. These offensives, conducted before and during the Stalingrad operation, would fix German forces in those regions and prevent reinforcement of German forces around Stalingrad.

Planning for the Stalingrad operation, which started on 13 September while defensive fighting raged at Stalingrad and intensified throughout October and early November, was far more deliberate than in previous operations. Within the *STAVKA*, Stalin, his deputy, Zhukov, and Chief of the General Staff Vasilevsky, played key roles. After initial discussions in Moscow in mid-September, Zhukov, Vasilevsky, and the Commander of Red Army artillery, Colonel General N. N. Voronov, conducted an inspection tour of the Stalingrad region to assess actual conditions; and, when they returned to Moscow, General Staff planning for the operation commenced in earnest.

Both Zhukov and Vasilevsky were convinced the projected operation would produce positive results. Zhukov later wrote:

> The *STAVKA* and General Staff, in the course of combat operations, carefully studied intelligence information about the enemy received from the *fronts* and forces, analyzed it, and reached conclusions concerning the nature of operations and his forces. They studied the considerations of staffs, *front* commanders, and types and branches of forces; and, while analyzing this data, made this or that decision. Consequently, the plan of conduct of operations on a strategic scale can arise in full scope only as a result of the lengthy creative efforts of all forces, staffs, and commanders. The basic and decisive role in the all-round planning and securing of a large strategic operation unquestionably belongs to the *STAVKA* of the High Command and the General Staff.[3]

Vasilevsky also confirmed *STAVKA* confidence, writing:

It was well known to the Soviet High Command that, as a result of the heroic defense of our forces in regions between the Don and Volga Rivers, 6th and 4th Panzer Armies had been drawn into long, drawn-out, and, as a rule, futile battle in a narrow sector in the immediate vicinity of the city; and the flanks of that grouping were covered by weaker, Rumanian forces, over-burdened by war. The great extent of the Rumanian forces' defense sector and the lack of reserves behind them aggravated the vulnerability of the enemy defense still more.[4]

The *STAVKA* decided to conduct the strategic counteroffensive with the forces of three *fronts*, by exploiting the obvious weakness of Rumanian forces in order to surround and destroy German forces around Stalingrad proper. The *STAVKA* created a new *front* (Southwestern) from new and existing forces and assigned it, and the Don and Stalingrad Fronts, the mission of conducting the operation. It appointed Vasilevsky as *STAVKA* representative to coordinate planning for the operation.

STRATEGIC AND OPERATIONAL PLANNING

Detailed planning for the coming operation began in earnest in early October. Despite the bitter defensive combat at Stalingrad, the *STAVKA* and General Staff patiently assessed the situation and consulted closely with *front* and army commanders and amongst themselves. Vasilevsky spent the first week of October at the front acquainting *front* and army commanders and staffs with the general concept of the operation and seeking their comments. Between 6 and 9 October, the Don and Stalingrad Fronts forwarded staff appreciations to the *STAVKA* along with comments regarding their prospective roles in the offensive. Throughout the process the General Staff refined its concept and assessed all aspects of combined arms support. The long, painstaking process resulted in an offensive plan codenamed "Uranus" (*Uran*).

Operation Uranus called for a group of three *fronts* — Southwestern, Don, and Stalingrad — to conduct a strategic offensive operation to encircle and destroy all German forces in the Stalingrad region. The three *fronts*, advancing along a 400-kilometer front, were to penetrate Axis defenses on the flanks of the great Stalingrad salient, penetrate into the depths 140 kilometers from the north and 100 kilometers from the south, link up, and form inner and outer encirclement lines around the isolated German force (see Map 3). Large armored and mechanized forces, assembled and concentrated opposite Rumanian forces on the flanks of the German forces battling in the Stalingrad region, were to play a key role in the operation. The Southwestern Front's 5th Tank Army, secretly deployed southward from the area east of Orel, formed the northern Soviet shock force, and had the mission of attacking southward out of bridgeheads across the Don River. The 4th Mechanized and 13th Tank Corps of the Stalingrad Front were to attack northwestward from positions south of Stalingrad one day later to link up with 5th Tank Army forces west of Stalingrad and form the inner encirclement line. Cavalry forces, advancing on the flanks of the two shock groups, were to form the outer encirclement line. Within days of the mobile forces linking up, follow-on rifle units would fill in the two encirclement lines and begin the strangulation of German forces.

In every respect, Soviet planners displayed a level of maturity absent in earlier operations. Unlike 1941, they took the necessary time to address every critical question. The *STAVKA* studied the correlation of forces on each axis and regrouped forces to establish requisite superiority. It carefully allocated necessary armored and mechanized forces and supporting arms (artillery, engineers) where they were most needed. It reinforced the four air armies (2d, 8th, 16th, 17th) under *front* control and, most important, allocated *STAVKA* assets to perform specialized missions and strategic reserves to guarantee success. Armed with new guidance contained in the 1942 Regulations and numerous directives and instructions, Soviet forces were now, for the first time, able to draw upon the experiences of the first 18 months of war and begin to correct problems which had plagued earlier operations. That produced a first quantum leap in the level of sophistication of Soviet planning.

Two areas where increased sophistication was evident were in the related areas of deception (*maskirovka*) and intelligence. The Soviets had attempted deception in earlier operations, but with only limited effectiveness and mixed success. At Stalingrad, they sought to employ secret planning and integrated into the strategic plan deception measures to conceal the location and timing of the attack and the scope of offensive preparations.[5]

Within a cloak of Draconian security, the Soviets implemented deception plans to convince the Germans of Soviet intent to launch a major offensive on the Moscow axis while Soviet forces remained on the defensive in the Stalingrad area. While active diversionary measures distracted the Germans, the Soviets secretly assembled

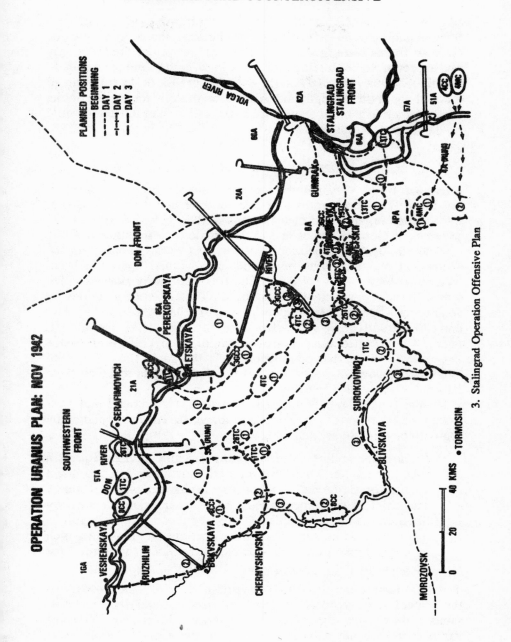

3. Stalingrad Operation Offensive Plan

large forces to conduct the Stalingrad offensive. *Razvedka* performed a simple yet difficult task of checking the degree to which German forces were fooled by the Soviet deception. This was only one aspect of Soviet intelligence work in support of the operation. In addition, Soviet *razvedka* had the even larger task of determining all it could about the strength and disposition of Axis forces lest Soviet forces attack in a blind state, which experience had indicated could be dangerous, if not fatal.

RAZVEDKA PLANNING FOR "URANUS"

Razvedka, by its very nature, was a continuous process. Throughout the defensive operations in late summer and early fall, Soviet intelligence organs used every means at their disposal to track the progress of German forces and to determine their intentions. While routine intelligence collection continued, *razvedka* planning for the Stalingrad operation was integrated into detailed operational and tactical planning at every level. The *front* and army *razvedka* plan was a formal document which focused all intelligence activities by specifying who would conduct it, where, by what means, and to what end. *Front* and army *razvedka* plans included tasks for all air, agent, signal, special, and ground intelligence collection means available to respective commanders. At the same time, the High Command passed down to *front* all intelligence data received from its specialized collection means.

By the time of the Stalingrad operation, a command and staff system had evolved to carry out centralized *razvedka* as specified by regulations, directives, and instructions.

> *Front* commanders, while defining the aim of *razvedka*, as a rule, pointed out what basic strength must be devoted to it and what information and in what time limits it must be obtained. The chief of staff specifies the *razvedka* missions decreed by the commander; establishes the sequence of their fulfillment; and, while specifying the directions (regions) in which to concentrate necessary forces, determines the forces for *razvedka* of the most important objectives.[6]

The intelligence departments (*razvedyvatel'nyi otdelenie – RO*) of the respective *front* staffs organized all *razvedka* activity and maintained links with the Main Intelligence Directorate (*Glavnoe razvedyvatel'noe upravienie – GRU*) of the General Staff from which it received strategic intelligence data. The *front* ROs worked out projects required by the plan, *razvedka* orders for subordinate armies and staffs of subordinate branches and types of forces, and directives for subordinate partisan detachments. Thereafter the ROs supervised collection of intelligence data, processed the materials, prepared necessary reports and estimates, and kept commanders and operations departments informed of the intelligence situation. As the time of the offensive neared, the ROs worked closely with operations departments and operational sections of armies and lower level commands to plan effective combat reconnaissance of enemy tactical defenses (see Figure 5).[7]

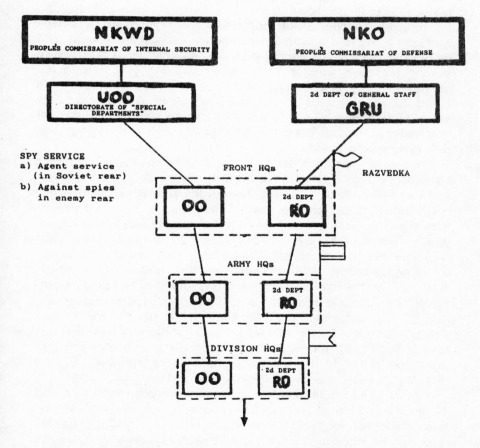

Fig. 5. Soviet intelligence organization to April–May 1943

The *front* intelligence staff planned and organized air, agent, radio, and force *razvedka*, using specialized intelligence subunits under its control and assets of subordinate commands. In addition, *fronts* employed partisan detachments to conduct operational *razvedka* at greater depths in the enemy rear (up to 450 kilometers, but normally 200–250 kilometers). Specialized long-range air reconnaissance units assigned to *front* air armies employed visual and photographic techniques to gather intelligence at strategic and operational depths while army air *razvedka* units used primarily visual observation at tactical and shallow operational depths (50–100 kilometers). Long-range air *razvedka* focused on rail and highway nets in the enemy rear to determine the scale and direction of troop movements. Both long-range and regular air reconnaissance units surveyed tactical and operational assembly areas, and other objectives in the enemy rear, but paid particular attention to principal enemy defense lines, artillery firing positions, headquarters, supply installations, and reserve positions which could affect the development of the Soviet offensive. Air *razvedka* data was passed to the staff which controlled the air assets and, if combat was under way, to all lower headquarters through regiment by clear text radio transmission.

Front headquarters controlled agent *razvedka*, special *razvedka* by reconnaissance-diversionary teams from the *front* destroyer brigade, and partisan *razvedka* through the staff department which had formulated the planned use of each asset. *Front* staff departments processed the intelligence information and, when appropriate, passed it to army headquarters. Specialized radio units at *front* level organized and conducted radio *razvedka* by eavesdropping on enemy radio transmissions, by limited radio location, and occasionally by jamming enemy radio transmissions. Communications units at army and lower level organized eavesdropping activities and, whenever possible, attempted to tap into enemy wire communications. Radio *razvedka*, used extensively for the first time at Stalingrad, sought to obtain information on enemy strength and dispositions, the location of his major force groupings, and the time and place of enemy artillery and air strikes.

Armies and subordinate headquarters conducted ground *razvedka* by means of observation; troop *razvedka*; and, for the first time in the war, large scale conduct of combat *razvedka* – specifically, reconnaissance in force. Ground *razvedka* served primarily to "illuminate" enemy tactical defenses by determining the identity and nature of enemy forces and the location of specific enemy defensive lines and weapons positions. Soviet concern for ground *razvedka* reflected their belief that the first and most important task in any offensive was successful conduct of the penetration phase of the operation, without which all subsequent phases were irrelevant. Consequently, the Soviets paid special attention to refining their ground *razvedka* techniques. Practically speaking, ground *razvedka* was also more "do-able" in late 1942 in terms of force training and equipment availability.

The most basic means of ground *razvedka* was planned observation of enemy defenses. Commanders and staffs at every level organized extensive observation post networks manned by personnel specially trained in observation techniques and equipped with a variety of observation devices. Army first echelon divisions and regiments created the basic observation post (OP) network.

> Constant observation of the *front* sector provided valuable information about the enemy; and its analysis, systematic generalization in comparison with information of other types of *razvedka* permitted in great authenticity the determination of the location, grouping, composition, enumeration, and combat capability of enemy units; the system and nature of their defenses; and by continuous monitoring of the actions and intentions of his groupings as well as the development of his engineer work, to receive necessary information about the terrain.[8]

Ground *razvedka* also included extensive use by armies, divisions, and regiments of small combat groups dispatched into enemy defensive positions to conduct sweeps, ambushes, and raids. In late 1942 these measures were facilitated by the close proximity of opposing force positions and by the vast experience in conducting such operations gained in the first 18 months of war. Small groups of five to eight men conducted sweeps and ambushes to seize prisoners, documents, and enemy weapons. Smaller groups of three to five men conducted diversionary and reconnaissance missions deeper in the enemy rear to perform the same missions and also to locate, reconnoiter, and sometimes destroy enemy command posts, communications facilities, and logistics installations. Divisions and, particularly, armies employed even larger reconnaissance detachments to conduct deeper operations against stronger objectives in the operational depths and to cooperate with partisan detachments. Normally, these larger forces were controlled by the special departments or sections (*osobyi otdel'* − OO) and ROs of armies and *fronts.*[9] In addition, artillery and engineer staffs planned and conducted extensive artillery and engineer *razvedka*, fully integrated with other *razvedka* measures.

At Stalingrad, for the first time, armies planned systematically to conduct combat *razvedka* – reconnaissance in force (*razvedka boem*). Unlike the first period of war, when combat reconnaissance "was conducted most often according to the initiative of the combined arms formation commander and was of a tactical nature ... beginning with the offensive operation at Stalingrad, combat *razvedka* took on an operational nature."[10] *Front* and army staffs planned and conducted reconnaissance in force in the sectors of every army involved in the operation to verify data received from other intelligence sources, to make last minute refinements in the intelligence picture, and to test the durability of enemy defenses. Companies and battalions of forward deployed regiments carried out reconnaissance in force according to plan several days before the offensive to determine the actual forward edge of enemy defensive positions and enemy firing positions (primarily artillery and mortar), to determine the location of enemy tactical reserves, and to provide better data upon which to base planning for the formal artillery and aviation offensive which preceded and accompanied the ground assault.

Zhukov later described the comprehensive planned nature and intent of intelligence preparations at Stalingrad, "When working with the troops, we focused on intelligence bearing on enemy dispositions, the character of the defence efforts, the overall fire system, deployment of antitank weapons and antitank strong points" while working out all other coordination measures for every phase of the operation. "At the same time, we issued practical instructions on how much more intelligence bearing upon enemy positions and movements was required, what additional details might be needed, and what concretely should be done in the field."[11] These new questions, in turn, produced continuous changes and alterations in the *razvedka* plans as overall offensive planning progressed.

Zhukov and other senior commanders themselves participated in *razvedka* to supervise the effort and underscore their concern. On 10 November he visited the command post of 57th Army south of Stalingrad, where he, Vasilevsky, and the 51st and 57th Army commanders personally inspected the terrain across the armies' *fronts.* "We wanted to reinspect the terrain across which we were to develop the offensive of the main forces of the Stalingrad Front."[12]

On the basis of the personal visits, refinements were made regarding subsequent *razvedka* and in the operational plans as a whole. Voronov, both as representative of the *STAVKA* and as the Red Army artillery commander, made similar visits to encourage the developing intelligence effort. While visiting the Southwestern Front headquarters, he impressed Vatutin, its commander, with the importance of thorough artillery *razvedka*:

> With Vatutin, we traveled around the forward observation points in order to inspect the terrain in the sector of the future penetration with our own eyes. During those visits time and time again I called the attention of artillery commanders to the necessity for exactly determining the entire fire system of the enemy and every minute change in it. This data was very important for concrete artillery fire planning during the period of the preparation of the offensive.[13]

The special attention that all high-level commanders paid to intelligence during planning for the Stalingrad operation ensured that adequate consideration was paid to fulfilling the extensive *razvedka* plans. This added ingredient ensured that provisions in regulations and directives regarding intelligence actions would be converted from theory into practice and provided the fundamental basis for all improvements in the intelligence realm during the Stalingrad operation. The scope and effectiveness of Soviet *razvedka* can best be judged by detailed investigation of intelligence practices prior to the offensive and the results they achieved.

PRE-OFFENSIVE CONDUCT OF *RAZVEDKA*

General

Soviet commanders and staff officers at every level now turned their attention to the complex task of implementing plans for the Stalingrad counteroffensive – including the *razvedka* plan which, if effectively implemented, could materially assist in producing victory. In late 1942 the major Soviet means for conducting strategic and operational *razvedka* were air, agent (special), partisan, and radio-electronic *razvedka*. Major improvements had occurred in each field during 1942; and the new regulations, directives, and instructions addressed their potential integrated use. Each, however, was severely limited, principally by technical problems and equipment shortages. Systems had evolved for organizing and employing each means; but, as yet, there was no clear method for integrating the intelligence information they produced. The Stalingrad experience and subsequent experiences throughout the winter of 1943 contributed to the successful creation of such an integrated system. At Stalingrad one can assess how each system functioned in isolation, but not until the summer of 1943 would an overall integrating system be in place and subject to evaluation.

Air Razvedka

Soviet analysis of wartime *razvedka* concluded that by 1942, "in conditions of a rapidly changing situation, air *razvedka* was often the only means of obtaining information about the enemy by combined arms and aviation commands."[14] Since radio intercept was in its infancy, and agent networks were not yet fully operational, in late summer and early fall of 1942 this was certainly the case. By fall, the Soviet High Command had established intelligence collection procedures for all air units and had created specialized air units to serve intelligence staffs at *front* and High Command level. All combat aviation units in *front* air armies performed the auxiliary mission of conducting reconnaissance, and smaller army aviation detachments performed similar missions for army commanders. Within *front* air armies and long range aviation forces subordinate to the High Command, the Soviets created air reconnaissance regiments of four squadrons each to perform air *razvedka*. The former worked under *front* supervision, and the latter performed specialized missions and deep reconnoitering of the rail and highway network in the German rear.

In theory, strategic air *razvedka* extended to depths of up to 500 kilometers, but in actuality few aircraft penetrated more than 450 kilometers; and the average aircraft operating range was 200–250 kilometers. *Front* air *razvedka* units operated at shallower depths of up to 250 kilometers but normally concentrated their efforts on the tactical depths (up to 60 kilometers) and shallow operational depths of the enemy defenses.[15] *Front* and army staffs organized air *razvedka* and prepared the air *razvedka* plan in close cooperation with the *front* intelligence department and other intelligence collecting agencies. Separate aviation reconnaissance regiments and their subordinate squadrons carried out specific tasks required by the plan in timed sequence. Their efforts encompassed 20 percent of reconnaissance sorties. Reconnaissance subunits within bomber, assault, and fighter aviation formations of the air armies assisted by performing the remaining 80 percent of the reconnaissance effort.[16]

During preparation for the offensive, reconnaissance units strove to reconnoiter the entire sector of their parent *fronts*. Seventy to 80 percent of the flights, whether day or night, were concentrated in the depths along principal axes of advance. Night flights concentrated on rail lines and major highways along which the Germans moved their forces. Of the total number of reconnaissance flights, about 70 percent were tactical and the remainder focused on operational targets. This was because most aircraft had limited operating ranges, and the densest array of targets to be reconnoitered tended to be concentrated up to 30–40 kilometers in the enemy rear.[17] This was particularly true at Stalingrad because the over-extended state of Axis forces limited the availability of operational as well as tactical reserves. To improve the quality of *razvedka*, the *front razvedka* plan designated specific belts, in which tactical and operational *razvedka* organs concentrated their efforts. Designated air army air reconnaissance regiments and reconnaissance subunits of other air formations also operated within specific belts and sectors. This division of responsibility permitted air crews to become more familiar with particular terrain features in their sectors and to more easily recognize changes.

The General Staff and Red Army Air Force (VVS) staff employed special long-range reconnaissance regiments and separate crews assigned to Soviet Long-Range Aviation (ADD) to conduct strategic *razvedka* to a depth of up to 450 kilometers.[18] These units concentrated on detecting and monitoring movements of enemy strategic reserves. During the Stalingrad operation, this meant formations moving into the region from the west or from adjacent army group sectors. Analogous activity went on within adjacent *fronts* to detect German troop movements out of sector and verify the efficiency of deception plans (in particular in the Western, Kalinin, and Briansk Front sectors). Information from strategic reconnaissance aviation first went to the *STAVKA* and then to appropriate *fronts* and air armies so that their *razvedka* assets could verify the accuracy of the reports and detect further movement and forward deployment of those strategic reserves.

During preparation for the Stalingrad operation, most reconnaissance aircraft still relied heavily on visual observation, for only 25 percent of the flights were capable of using photography. Poor weather conditions further inhibited the utility of photography. Despite poor conditions, photographic reconnaissance units made significant advances during preparations for the Stalingrad operation. Air reconnaissance units of the three *fronts* accomplished "solid photographic coverage of enemy defenses to the entire tactical depth."[19] Axis defensive positions on planned main attack axes of the Southwestern and Stalingrad Fronts were thoroughly photographed several times. Most photography (80–100 percent), however, occurred during the preparatory period and very little took place thereafter. *Front* topographic sections interpreted air photos and prepared from them reconnaissance maps and overlays. Air force photo interpreters and artillery topographic personnel helped interpret complex photographs and photographic mosaics. The Soviets concluded that trained interpreters "could correctly identify up to 70 percent of the enemy phenomena on them."[20] Tests conducted by Leningrad Front reconnaissance forces during mid-1942 verified the correctness of this judgement.

The increased quantities of radios in aircraft during late 1942 remedied one of the most serious problems evident earlier in the war, that of communicating results back to headquarters. A special radio net provided to air reconnaissance formations speeded the transmission of data to intelligence staffs. The 2d, 8th, 16th, and 17th Air Armies, supporting the three Soviet *fronts*, and the adjacent 4th Air Army operating in the Caucasus controlled air *razvedka* resources for the Stalingrad operation. In addition, at least one air reconnaissance regiment of the High Command's Long Range Aviation also participated as well as small aircraft units assigned to armies. Air reconnaissance assets were not extensive, as indicated by 16th Air Army's strength, of which seven of 342 aircraft were dedicated solely to the reconnaissance mission.[21]

Marshal (then General) K. A. Vershinin, commander of 2d Air Army in the north Caucasus noted:

> I had at my disposal large quantities of various information obtained from aviation *razvedka* in the staff of the air armies and the *front*, but contented myself with only some of it. From 20 September to 5 October enemy aviation groups, numbering up to 175 aircraft each, were discovered on 16 enemy airfields. During the period air reconnaissance discovered that 250 enemy tanks and vehicles approached from the Geogriusk direction; 600 vehicles from Buddeny; that up to one cavalry division was concentrated in the Achukulak–Steponov region; and an infantry formation was located in the Levokumysskoe region.[22]

These and other reports cited by Vershinin led to a correct assessment of German offensive intentions in the Caucasus and provided a basis for subsequent Soviet assessments regarding operations around Stalingrad. Later reconnaissance flights, numbering four to five flights per day during November and December, provided Vershinin with fairly accurate intelligence prior to the general offensive of the North Caucasus Front and detected German movements northward to begin their relief attempt toward Stalingrad.[23]

The 17th Air Army conducted similar missions in accordance with a Southwestern Front order, which read, "Combat aviation conduct reconnaissance to seek enemy objectives (reserves, columns, concentration regions). Be ready to strike massive blows by all aviation means on discovered large enemy reserves, especially enemy tank and motorized divisions."[24] The Southwestern Front's 17th and 2d Air Army, the Don Front's 18th Air Army, and the Stalingrad Front's 8th Air Army each employed its reconnaissance regiment to reconnoiter enemy positions during the preparatory period. The 16th Air Army Commander, General S. I. Rudenko, later recalled, "We paid the most steadfast attention to air *razvedka*. We conducted it continuously in order to know always about enemy intentions and to have exact notions about his dispositions and the displacement of his reserves."[25]

The nature, extent, and effectiveness of Soviet air *razvedka* at Stalingrad can best be judged by contemporary classified Soviet critiques. A critique of operational *razvedka* using fictitious place names and unit nomenclature surveyed *razvedka* techniques employed in the Moscow region during October and November and provided a clear picture of Soviet capabilities. On 10 October the X (probably Western) Front intelligence department issued instructions for air *razvedka* during October as an integral part of the *front* intelligence plan. The instructions required observation of enemy traffic on railroads and main routes and specified reconnaissance aircraft flight routes. Of the ten routes established, army reconnaissance aircraft were to use seven, and *front* assets three. Eight Pe-2, 24 Il-2, and 16 fighter aircraft were to conduct the reconnaissance flights with each crew scheduled to fly two missions per day and four additional crews constantly held in reserve. Army *razvedka* extended to a depth of 75–100 kilometers and *front* from 300 to 450 kilometers.[26] Since the initial instructions proved to be too vague, a few days later *front* headquarters prepared fresh instructions establishing new concrete tasks and setting a five-day limit for their completion. All air missions were closely integrated with agent, radio, and ground *razvedka* measures.

Once initial plans had been carried out, *front* established new plans for the first half of November which were "outstanding in their detailed preparation and clear wording."[27] The October and November *razvedka* plans were associated with general Soviet planning for an offensive in the Rzhev–Sychevka region, west of Moscow. Intelligence sought to detect German redeployments, and new forces moving into the area. During this period air *razvedka*, assisted by other means, detected three new enemy air force divisions, one airborne division, and additional security units, and monitored the internal shifting of four other divisions. Air *razvedka* noted large tank force movements from Maisk to Griboedovsk between 15 and 17 October and, two days later, it detected large convoys east of Leshchyev. These sightings and associated unit identifications indicated the activeness of air *razvedka* and its ability to identify and track the movement of German reserves. The assessment also identified the location of German airfields and the aircraft strength of each, as follows:

Location	Aircraft
Zelenogorsk	70
Petukhov	50
Maisk	60
Snegirevo	50
Urozhai	60
Glukhov	20
Luzhi	12
Radishchev	20[28]

Soviet critiques of air *razvedka* in the Western Front sector match the conclusions of other operational studies and memoir literature. Strategic and operational air *razvedka*, in concert with other reconnaissance measures, kept track of German movements and provided a fairly accurate picture of German operational dispositions. Since this was the case west of Moscow, it is reasonable to assume that similar Soviet techniques employed in the Stalingrad region were at least as effective, for the Soviets committed greater air resources to the Stalingrad effort.

Agent-Diversionary Razvedka

By late 1942 an articulated structure of reconnaissance-diversionary forces existed throughout the higher commands of the Red Army. Controlled by the General Staff's GRU and by the NKVD's special department (*osobyi otdel'*) at *front* and army level, these forces consisted of a separate Motorized Rifle Brigade of Special Designation (OMSBON), which served NKVD "Central" and deployed teams and detachments across the entire *front*; destroyer battalions, regiments, and brigades; and special detachments and groups subordinate to the ROs and special departments of *fronts* and armies. These forces parachuted or infiltrated into the enemy rear to perform specific *razvedka* and diversionary missions as required by the *front razvedka* plan. A history of the NKVD described their function:

> True, the special departments [*osobye otdely*] of *fronts* and armies then began to organize operational work in the enemy rear. However, at first they basically had a military-reconnaissance assignment. *Razvedchiki* [reconnaissance men] and reconnaissance groups of the special departments, dispatched into the dispositions of fascist *front* units, fulfilled the mission of close troop reconnaissance and gathered information about the locations of staffs, warehouses, and other important German objectives. Often they also fulfilled the responsible and dangerous mission of damaging enemy prefrontal communications; destroying large enemy bases and fuel depots; and seizing fascist staff officers with important documents.[29]

During preparations for the Stalingrad operation, the NKVD Special Brigade (*OMSBON*) was dispatched to the central Caucasus region where it operated throughout the fall employing its specialized talents to organize defenses and disrupt German operations.[30] Meanwhile, *front* and army ROs and special departments deployed small detachments and teams from *front* and perhaps army destroyer brigades to support operations around Stalingrad.

Soviet classified after-action reports described the function of these teams:

> Specially selected teams of courageous soldiers and com-

manders, whose task was to penetrate in the course of battle into the rear of enemy positions, were specially trained for the disorganization of the enemy command system, the seizure of his command posts and headquarters, and for the disruption of his lines of communications. Every unit had selected and fully trained special "navigator"-officers whose duty it was to guide at any time, by day or night, a unit (or a subunit) into the area which it was assigned according to plan.[31]

Soviet reconnaissance and diversionary detachments and groups cooperated with NKVD agents already in place and with partisan units, although partisan activity was not well-developed in this region of Russia.

Specific details of reconnaissance-diversionary force operations in support of the three *fronts* are not available. Given Soviet reluctance to write about so highly classified an area, this is understandable. It does not, however, mean those operations were not significant. A glimpse of the importance and scope of such operations is apparent in the critique of operational *razvedka* in the Western Front sector prepared after the Stalingrad operation was over. The critique identified one of the principal sources of operational intelligence as being "special reconnaissance parties capable of penetrating deep into the enemy rear and agent *razvedka*."[32] These parties and agents received specific missions as an integral part of the *front razvedka* plan, the most important of which was the identification of enemy forces occupying the defenses and those transferring into or out of the sector.

One Soviet critique, using fictitious unit identifications, subsequently listed specific intelligence reports received from agents and reconnaissance teams in October and November, which were later confirmed by other sources.[33] These included:

17 October – agent report of the departure of an enemy tank division (10th) between 11 and 14 October. Later correlated with air *razvedka*, radio intercepts, and documents captured by troop *razvedka*.
24 October – agent report of the concentration of another tank division (22d). Later confirmed by POW statements.
29 October – agent reports of a large troop concentration. Confirmed by POW reports and reports of local inhabitants.

This is only a partial listing of accurate intelligence reports received from reconnaissance detachments and agents. Other reports existed of varying accuracy. The entire spectrum of reports evidenced extensive Soviet use of special reconnaissance teams and agents, analogous to the intelligence collection system employed at Stalingrad.

Partisan Razvedka

There is no evidence that partisan operations played a significant role in the Stalingrad operation. Partisan organizations were not active in the Don or Donbas regions because of the rapidity of the German advance and the relatively short-lived nature of the German occupation. It is certain that local inhabitants assisted agents operating in the region and provided some information regarding German troop movements. However, the value of this information paled in comparison with other sources of strategic and operational intelligence.

Radio-Electronic Razvedka

During late 1942 radio *razvedka* began making significant contributions to Soviet intelligence collection efforts. For the first time, the Soviets created specialized radio intercept and jamming units that could focus their attention on German communications. Moreover, regulations and instructions provided necessary structure for these activities and facilitated their interpretation and collation with other intelligence data.

By mid-1942 Soviet communications units at every level routinely monitored German radio transmissions. This activity was best organized at *front* and army level where specific communications units conducted systematic "listening" for the staff intelligence department. In addition, the Soviets began experimenting with radio location, although these early efforts failed to provide accurate enough information for targeting. During the Stalingrad operation the Soviets also attempted radio-suppression (*radio podavlenie*). After encirclement of German forces, the Stalingrad Front created a radio suppression group equipped with several high-powered radio stations subordinate to the 394th Separate Radio Battalion. The *front* also created a series of special radio stations to feed German Sixth Army disinformation.

A major step forward in radio *razvedka* occurred on 17 December 1942 when the High Command began creating special purpose radio battalions (*spetsial'nogo naznacheniia*) tasked with conducting radio-*razvedka* and jamming. Initially, the *STAVKA* formed the 131st and 132d Special Purpose Radio Battalions, and later formed three more (129th, 130th, 228th). Each battalion was subordinate to a *front*, and each was equipped with eight–ten RAF-KV radios mounted on vehicles and designed for jamming, 18–20 "VIRAZH" and "Chaika" reconnaissance receivers, four type 55-PK-3A and "Shtopor" radio-locators, one powerful "Pchela" jammer for use in jamming railroad communications, and a variety of captured enemy radios.[34] These new units contributed to the success of Soviet radio *razvedka* late in the Stalingrad operation.

Meanwhile, during preparations for the offensive, *fronts* employed existing radio assets within their headquarters and those of subordinate armies to perform a variety of functions:

> *Front* radio-*razvedka* revealed the means and system of [enemy] radio communications, and obtained information about the locations of staffs and positions occupied by enemy forces, the regions of concentration of his main forces, and the arrival of new units and reserves. Special attention was paid to interception of transmissions in tank and aviation formations and units, where radio was the principal means of communication.[35]

The Soviets employed crude jamming techniques against German army group command centers, field and panzer armies, army, panzer, and motorized corps and divisions; and also control centers for air force activities. However, since these German units also relied on telegraph and teletype, they avoided the worst consequences of jamming, which was itself in infancy and, hence, only marginally effective.

Soviet critiques of operational *razvedka* primarily cite examples of radio *razvedka* relating to Western Front activities.[36] Extracts from the log of Western Front radio intercepts reveal the scope of these activities:

14 October – radio intercepts indicated transfer of "Grossdeutschland" Motorized Division to a new location. Confirmed on 15 October by a German POW.

27 October – radio intercept located a newly arrived panzer division (10th).

31 October – radio intercepts confirmed location of parent corps

of the panzer division earlier indicated (21 October)
by captured documents.

31 October − radio intercept indicated arrival in region of a new
motorized division (44th) which earlier (3 October)
was confirmed in another area.

All these reports were confirmed as valid by corroborating evidence. Other wireless intercepts monitored data which later turned out to be groundless.

Troop Razvedka

While the Soviets relied on air, agent-diversionary, and radio *razvedka* as principal sources of strategic and operational intelligence, they generated tactical intelligence by thoroughly planned and extensive troop, artillery, and engineer *razvedka*. Only the performance of thousands of mundane and often hazardous tasks associated with these collection methods could reveal the nature of enemy tactical defense sufficiently to permit successful penetration by Soviet forces. From early October to 19 November, Soviet forces designated to participate in the coming offensive, when not engaged in planned combat, undertook constant reconnaissance across their *fronts*.

Front and army *razvedka* plans assigned specific intelligence collection missions to all subordinate units. In addition, subordinate units conducted routine troop reconnaissance in accustomed patterns to conceal Soviet offensive intent. Combat patrols, sweeps, ambushes, and raids occurred regularly across the *front* to determine changes in the defenses and to capture prisoners and documents. Occasionally, these measures produced significant results, such as occurred on 1 October 1942 in the Sadovoe sector of the Stalingrad Front.[37] That day a reconnaissance patrol took from a dead German General Staff officer a map diagraming German offensive plans. The map showed the direction and timetable for the German advance into the Stalingrad region and the Caucasus (like the documents seized on 19 June but not believed by the High Command). Although much of the material on the map was outdated, it vividly showed how far off schedule the German offensive was; and it indicated German order of battle. These documents made it clear how over-extended German forces really were. Without infusion of new German operational reserves into southern Russia, the Soviets could count on success at Stalingrad, if they were able to conduct successfully requisite penetration operations. Although few troop *razvedka* missions produced such valuable information, collectively they provided thousands of bits of data necessary to portray accurately enemy dispositions and future plans.

To verify the data collected by troop *razvedka*, for the first time in the war the *STAVKA* required Soviet forces to conduct systematic reconnaissance in force (*razvedka boem*) across the entire *front*. Zhukov, as *STAVKA* representative, issued orders to that effect in early November. The reconnaissance in force was designed to determine the actual forward area of enemy defenses, the grouping of enemy forces in the immediate tactical depths, the enemy systems of fire, and the nature of engineer preparations of the defense.[38]

To carry out the reconnaissance, first echelon rifle divisions operating on main attack axes formed reconnaissance detachments, normally consisting of reinforced companies or battalions from first echelon regiments, supported by regimental artillery. Sometimes division dispatched several detachments in company strength. The army commander specified the time of the reconnaissance in accordance with the army *razvedka* plan and local conditions. Armies of the Stalingrad, Don, and Southwestern *Fronts* conducted reconnaissance in force from two to ten days prior to the offensive. Typical composition of reconnaissance in force detachments was as follows:

Front	Division and Army	Reconnaissance Detachment(s)
Southwestern	47th Gds RD, 5th TA	1. two reinforced rifle companies, 473d RR 2. reinforced rifle company, 510th RR 3. reinforced rifle company, 437th RR
	119th RD, 5th TA	reinforced rifle battalion
	124th RD, 5th TA	reinforced rifle company, 781st RR
	293d RD, 21st A	reinforced rifle battalion, 1031st RR
Stalingrad	422d RD, 57th A	reinforced rifle battalion
	15th Gds RD, 51st A	reinforced rifle company[39]

The company-size detachments of the 124th and 15th Guards Rifle Division proved too small to be of use, since the enemy dealt with them without having to reveal the dispositions of their artillery and mortars. The battalion-size detachments operated in varied fashion. The 47th Guards, 119th and 124th Rifle Divisions of 5th Tank Army conducted reconnaissance in force on 17 November, only two days before the offensive began: the 293d Rifle Division of 21st Army on 14 November; the 422d Rifle Division of 57th Army on 15 November; and the 15th Guards Rifle Division on 11 November, nine days before the Stalingrad Front's attack. Each reconnaissance in force occurred according to plan which designated parent unit, mission, composition of the reconnaissance detachment, supporting weapons, and timing.

Most reconnaissances began late in the day. The 47th Guards, 119th and 124th Rifle Divisions of 5th Tank Army began operations at 1600 and the 233d Rifle Division of 21st Army at 1700. Detachments took advantage of darkness to complete their operations, but this left inadequate time for main forces to capitalize on any success they achieved. The wide time divergence between each reconnaissance in force also had the adverse effect of permitting the enemy to shift forces and artillery without Soviet detection.

The reconnaissance in force in 5th Tank Army's sector successfully added to the existing intelligence picture formed by prior observation and routine troop *razvedka*. Troop reconnaissance had earlier determined:

> The army had before the *front* the 9th, 14th, and 5th Infantry Divisions (Rumanian), which occupied positions with good engineer installations and a system of company and battalion centers of resistance, its forward edge of defense being on the line Bolshoi, south slope of elevation 220.0 and 210.1, Bazkovsky.
>
> At a distance 2–4 kilometers back from the forward edge, the enemy had a previously prepared second defense line (defense in depth), equipped in the same manner as the first, but weaker in engineer installations. On the line Pronin, Peschany (Ust–Medveditski), Perepazovski, in accordance with reconnaissance data, one assumed the presence of up to two infantry divisions. ...
>
> The total depth of the operational defenses of the enemy was 50 km. The main defense zone had on an average 3–4 earth-and-timber pillboxes of the light type to each kilometer of *front*, was covered by minefields and, in certain sectors, also had barbed-wire entanglements.[40]

Armed with this preliminary assessment, 5th Tank Army intelligence organized a reconnaissance in force which, according to Soviet critiques, fulfilled its mission:

> Hence, for the purpose of finding out the real forward edge of the defense and misleading the enemy as to the scale of the offensive being prepared, we undertook a reconnaissance in force on 17 November with reinforced battalions from each rifle division of the first echelon. Beginning in the morning, we started a methodical processing of targets of the artillery assigned to support the battalions; in the second half of the day, the battalion assumed the offensive, drove away the combat security during the night of 18 November, and advanced to the forward edge of the enemy defenses. In the morning the battalions renewed their offensive; but, upon encountering strong resistance and enemy counterattacks, they began to dig in on the lines reached.
>
> Hence, we achieved the goal set for the reconnaissance. By reconnaissance in force we ascertained the real forward edge of the enemy defenses, and we learned from the statements of prisoners that he had the impression that our offensive had failed.[41]

By virtue of the reconnaissance in force, 5th Tank Army learned that the enemy had withdrawn his troops from the forward edge to a depth of two to three kilometers. This made it possible to alter the artillery fire plan and engineer plan in good time and adjust the missions of first echelon forces.

Troop *razvedka*, routinely conducted prior to the offensive, and planned reconnaissance in force materially contributed to a more accurate intelligence picture of enemy tactical defenses. At the same time, systematic establishment of an observation post network and personal reconnaissance (*rekognostsirovka*) by commanders at all levels across the entire front supplemented troop *razvedka* and the reconnaissance in force. To complete the intelligence picture of enemy tactical defenses, prior to the offensive the Soviets conducted extensive artillery and engineer *razvedka*.

Artillery Razvedka

One of the most important aspects of *razvedka* prior to the conduct of a penetration operation was the necessity for identifying correctly enemy fire systems, command and control posts, and other targets whose destruction would facilitate successful penetration. Determining the enemy fire and defense system was the task of artillery *razvedka*.

By late 1942 regulations had established specific tasks for artillery *razvedka* and procedures for the accomplishment of those tasks. Artillery *razvedka* was to be "conducted in any weather, in the day time and night time, both when forces are on the defensive and when they are on the offensive."[42] Regulations stipulated that the principal basis of artillery *razvedka* was troop artillery *razvedka* which was conducted "from all observation points of battery, battalion, regimental, and division commanders." In essence, this involved "a thousand eyes" equipped with optical equipment such as binoculars, battery commander scopes, and stereoscopes. Extensive observation networks were designed to reveal all features of enemy defenses which could be seen by the human eye. To penetrate areas covered by forests, buildings, and the terrain itself, the Soviets employed artillery instrumental *razvedka* (AIR) and corrective-reconnaissance aviation.

Ground observation was the task of separate reconnaissance artillery battalions (ORAD) which consisted of sound, optical, photographic, and topographical reconnaissance subunits. "Sound ranging units played a decisive role in reconnaissance of enemy firing systems by determining their location from the sound of the shot. By means of frequentive intersection of shots, the accuracy of determining the coordinates of the largest was rather high."[43]

Supplementing the ground reconnaissance artillery battalions were separate corrective-reconnaissance aviation squadrons (OKAE) and regiments (OKAP) which used visual and photographic means to identify and catalogue targets in the enemy defenses and subsequently adjusted artillery fire on distant targets. While these artillery *razvedka* means tackled the formidable challenge of identifying targets, they also had to be alert to enemy deception and extensive use of camouflage to conceal key targets. "The difficulty of *razvedka* rested in the fact that the enemy changed units, the combat formation of artillery and observation posts. Often, information about targets obtained today is already inaccurate tomorrow."[44] In order to complete the artillery *razvedka* mosaic, Soviet combined arms commanders employed reconnaissance groups or detachments to penetrate into the enemy rear area. Artillerymen routinely participated in these missions.

The artillery staff of forces at all levels planned and conducted artillery *razvedka* and processed the information received. The force chief of staff was ultimately responsible for the completeness, credibility, and timeliness of the data. Staff intelligence departments or sections then integrated artillery reconnaissance data with other intelligence information. Harsh climatic and combat conditions during the period preceding the Stalingrad offensive made artillery *razvedka* very difficult. Weather was generally bad, the German-occupied right bank of the Don River dominated the left bank and inhibited observation of German positions, and German air superiority ruled out extensive air reconnaissance by artillery aviation units. These negative conditions prevented identification of almost 70 percent of hostile firing points during the preparatory period.[45]

The three *fronts* involved in planning the operations allocated all available resources to artillery *razvedka*. The Don Front artillery staff intelligence section instructed subordinate headquarters to prepare uniform reconnaissance documents in a single copy. It then formulated reconnaissance missions for the artillery staffs of penetration armies and established tasks for reconnaissance battalions within those armies to fulfill. Intelligence officers and artillery staffs visited subordinate units to provide personal assistance and supervise the detailed reconnaissance work. They were particularly interested in the work of observation battalions to detect the nature of enemy defenses and topographical work done to create a topographical base for artillery fire. Reconnaissance staffs and battalions of the 27th Guards, 204th and 264th Rifle Divisions of 65th Army and the right flank divisions of 24th Army dispatched forces to verify the data obtained by observation. When defects in observation were noted, artillery intelligence officers corrected procedures on the spot.[46]

Prior to the preparatory period for the offensive, the Southwestern and Don Fronts had no means of artillery instrumental reconnaissance. After regrouping and during the preparatory period, all *fronts* received AIR assets which were distributed as follows:

Front	Army	Observation Unit(s)
Don	65th	709th Separate Reconnaissance Artillery Battalion
Southwestern	21st	816th Separate Reconnaissance Artillery Battalion 45th Separate Corrective-Reconnaissance Aviation Squadron
Stalingrad	57th	838th Separate Reconnaissance Artillery Battalion 31st Separate Corrective-Reconnaissance Aviation Squadron

Front	Army	Observation Unit(s)
	51st	32d Separate Corrective-Reconnaissance Aviation Squadron
	62d	8th Guards Separate Reconnaissance Artillery Battalion

(plus four separate reconnaissance artillery battalions assigned immediately prior to the offensive)[47]

Most of the reconnaissance artillery battalions lacked their full complement of observation equipment. The corrective-reconnaissance aviation squadron in the Southwestern Front had neither radios nor an operating base, nor fighter escorts. Consequently, they were seldom able to operate. The two observation squadrons assigned to the Stalingrad Front were better equipped but, for the same basic reasons, were able to fly only 13 sorties during the preparatory period.[48]

The 57th Army's actions typified the way these *razvedka* assets were employed. The army had ten to 13 days for its artillery units to organize and conduct *razvedka*. In addition to using ground observation, the army employed both artillery instrument reconnaissance and aerial spotting. These means, in combination with ground reconnaissance, provided precise data concerning the strength and deployment of enemy artillery:

> The precision of work of these forms of *razvedka* was subsequently confirmed by the large number of enemy guns knocked out and gun crews destroyed. Of the 30 batteries located by [sound] intersection, the accuracy of location was confirmed in 25. The coordinates of the combat formation of the artillery battalion of 20th Rumanian Infantry Division, determined on the basis of a captured firing chart, fully coincided with the coordinates determined by our reconnaissance.[49]

On the other hand, 51st Army, which lacked AIR and spotter assets, had to rely solely on ground reconnaissance.

Three days before the offensive began, the Stalingrad Front provided army artillery staffs with aerial photographs of separate sectors of the enemy defense. Throughout the *front* sector, *razvedka* of all types had ascertained the outline of the main line of resistance, areas where observation was still underway, firing positions and

135

points, and enemy defensive installations. Later critiques identified some intelligence shortfalls, stating:

> However, we should note that it was not possible to determine the exact location of the enemy fire system in the depths of his defenses, in view of the fact that the enemy did not reveal his system of fire; and deep reconnaissance was conducted only to a limited extent.[50]

Throughout the planning period and while artillery was being regrouped to support the offensive, *front* intelligence personnel assisted subordinate intelligence organs, particularly in establishing observation procedures. Regular, round-the-clock observation was required of commanders at all levels; and artillery staff officers personally reconnoitered all new artillery observation posts.

Targeting procedures also improved through the use of observation equipment, sound and flash ranging, and ground reconnaissance patrols to supplement simple visual observation. Artillery scouts accompanied reconnaissance groups to determine the precise locations of potential targets. Data provided by reconnaissance units was then verified by interrogation of prisoners of war captured by troop reconnaissance units. In addition, artillery units established advanced observation posts well forward in rifle unit positions. All this work produced daily updates of reconnaissance maps.

The most active aspect of artillery instrumental *razvedka* was sound ranging conducted by sound ranging batteries. The platoons of these batteries occupied positions five kilometers from the front and sent warning personnel down to front line units. Sound ranging earned high praise in after-action reports.

> Sound ranging batteries disclosed fairly accurately the grouping of enemy artillery across the entire front (especially on the eve of the operation). At the beginning of the operation, the 709th Separate Reconnaissance Artillery Battalion, by means of sound ranging batteries, had in the course of two weeks, located 17 batteries; the 816th Separate Reconnaissance Artillery Battalion during the same period had located 64 batteries (6 mortar; 4 75mm; 46 105mm; 6 150mm; and 2 210mm batteries).
>
> On the front of 57th Army, the 838th Separate Reconnaissance Artillery Battalion, in a short period of time (10–12 days) revealed 30 artillery and mortar batteries, developed a topo-

graphic network in an area of 50 square kilometers, and tied in six artillery regiments.[51]

By the time the offensive began, sound ranging had accurately determined the positions of many hostile batteries. In time, after prolonged practice, these subunits established a uniform system of cooperation with firing units.

Topographic subunits also made an enviable beginning to their work. The 709th Separate Reconnaissance Artillery Battalion's topographic battery surveyed a 389 square kilometer area in 20 days, frequently while under fire. Its work located 260 enemy strongpoints and established a topographic (survey) base for all army artillery positions.[52] Although artillery–air *razvedka* played an insignificant role in observation, some work was carried out. The 31st Separate Corrective-Reconnaissance Aviation Squadron of 57th Army photographed the enemy main line of resistance, separate centers of resistance, and enemy artillery positions. Deciphered aerial mosaics prepared by this unit were used as one of the bases for the artillery offensive in 57th Army's sector. The squadron also photographed the entire inner line of German defenses around Stalingrad.

Soviet contemporary assessments concluded that, despite the problems encountered, "As a result of proper distribution of means of artillery instrumental reconnaissance and of sufficient time for preparations (up to 10 days), full success was achieved in uncovering the enemy's artillery grouping and his defensive systems on the main directions."[53] On the basis of the extensive intelligence data gathered by artillery *razvedka*, by 18 November the Soviets had completed planning for the artillery offensive.

Engineer Razvedka

While artillery staffs were conducting *razvedka* to determine the nature of enemy firing systems, engineer forces sought to obtain intelligence on engineer aspects of enemy defenses. Engineer *razvedka* provided a basis for successful creation and implementation of the engineer plan at every level. Plans for the Stalingrad operation required engineer forces "to carry out careful engineer *razvedka* of the 'forward edge' and depths of the enemy defense in the areas of penetrations."[54] Specifically, engineer *razvedka* was to determine the nature of the defense; enemy engineer preparations; and the number and disposition of engineer obstacles, in particular,

137

minefields. The principal means of conducting the *razvedka* were engineer observation posts (INP), reconnaissance and search groups, and engineers assigned to combat units carrying out reconnaissance in force.[55]

The experiences of the Stalingrad Front typified engineer efforts. Once the *front* had been notified of its penetration sectors, the engineer staff established 75 observation posts and observation points across the penetration sector. The density of these posts and points was one to three per kilometer of front, depending on the importance of the sector. In sectors where reconnaissance in force was underway, the network of observation points was doubled or tripled. Most observation posts and points were located along the forward edge of the *front*'s defenses. Each consisted of heated dugouts and covered rifle pits with accommodation made for observation. Twenty-three of the posts were equipped with optical devices, field glasses, and telescopes borrowed from artillery and mortar crews. The posts were manned by three to four engineers supervised by a junior officer or highly trained enlisted men whose duty was to supervise group activities and maintain observation records. Observation went on around the clock and the resultant data was plotted on a map and passed daily to the unit engineer officer who in turn summarized it, recorded it on a more general map, and transmitted the information daily to his unit's chief of engineers.

Between 1 October and 18 November, Stalingrad Front engineers organized and conducted 27 engineer *razvedka* raids deep into the enemy rear along main attack axes. These raids sought to disclose the antitank and antipersonnel mine and obstacle systems and determine the location of rear defense lines. In 51st Army's sector, where terrain was open and enemy defenses weakest, tankers and cavalrymen participated in the raids. North of Stalingrad, in 62d Army's sector, *front* organized seven engineer *razvedka* groups, which, at night, penetrated five kilometers into the enemy defenses, camouflaged themselves "in haystacks, straw, or deep shell holes" and, during daytime, observed enemy engineer and other activities. One group of three men remained in the enemy rear for three days and, during that time, moved 11 kilometers and developed detailed field sketches of enemy defenses throughout the sector.[56]

Post-offensive engineer surveys in 57th Army's sector indicated that pre-offensive assessments of existing minefields and barbed-wire entanglements over a considerable portion of the penetration sector were accurate. Further south, in 28th Army's sector, engineers discovered 37 trenches, 32 firing positions, and ten mortar positions. This comprised 79 of a total of 102 enemy defensive positions discovered before the offensive, including three of seven existing minefields. In the *front* main attack sector of 57th Army, where engineer *razvedka* assets were concentrated, engineer reconnaissance identified 35 firing positions for machine guns, five earth and timber pillboxes, 12 mortar positions, and 28 artillery positions, of which five were concealed. Engineers correctly identified 70 of 95 existing defensive positions. In addition, deeper engineer reconnaissance parties "correctly identified the defenses of the enemy second echelon." The critique concluded by stating, "Hence, in the main, engineer *razvedka* discovered the system of German-Rumanian defenses in the direction of the main attack, thus facilitating to a considerable extent the success of the breakthrough of the enemy defenses."[57]

The Southwestern and Don Fronts employed techniques similar to those used by the Stalingrad Front with similar results. By the time the Stalingrad operation began, artillery and engineer *razvedka*, used in close coordination with other types of ground *razvedka* and refined by the extensive use of reconnaissance in force, had painted a fairly accurate picture of German and Rumanian tactical defenses, including the boundaries between defending enemy units. This was particularly the case in main attack sectors of *front* shock groups. These *razvedka* measures paved the way for successful conduct of the penetration operations. It remained to be seen whether operational *razvedka* had provided adequate data at greater depths, essential for successful conduct of the exploitation operation.

Intelligence and Deception

Throughout the planning and preparatory period there was a direct and important relationship between Soviet deception (*maskirovka*) plans and *razvedka*. Although deceptive measures could have a salutary effect in themselves, they would be most effective if means existed to validate how well German forces had "taken the bait." Soviet deception planning had strategic, operational, and tactical aspects. Strategically, the High Command postured to convince the Germans a Soviet counteroffensive would occur on the Moscow–Smolensk axis. In mid-October, *STAVKA* ordered *fronts* in southern Russia to engage in defensive operations only. Simultaneously, in the Moscow region, the Kalinin and Western Fronts prepared for active offensive operations against German Army Group Center. The *STAVKA* hoped the Germans would perceive these actions to be Soviet intent to renew the offensive toward Smolensk, which had been suspended in April 1942. German intelligence organs picked up the activity and assessed that Soviet attacks were likely west of Moscow.

More important, Soviet intelligence collection in the Moscow sector detected (and even over-assessed) German force concentrations in that region. This led Soviet intelligence to conclude that no major transfers of German forces to the south were occurring. The Soviets were equally concerned over possible German force redeployments from deep within the Caucasus or from the west. The former was clearly unlikely in the light of German activity in the region. The latter could occur, but probably only after German intelligence had detected the presence of a major threat in the Stalingrad region. To confirm these judgements, throughout October and November the Soviets employed their few long-range *razvedka* assets (principally air) to reconnoiter main rail and highway lines running into southern Russia. They detected no major troop movements.

Operationally and tactically, Soviet deception sought to mask the major force build-up northwest and south of Stalingrad and conceal the secret movement of new shock forces (principally 5th Tank Army) into the Stalingrad region. Most of these deception measures were passive in nature, although most Soviet forces deliberately demonstrated a defensive posture except those in the area immediately northwest of Stalingrad where Soviet counterattacks had occurred in the recent past. To verify the effect of operational and tactical deception, Soviet intelligence had to insure that the Germans had not detected Soviet plans and shifted large forces into the threatened sectors. Short-range air and long-range ground *razvedka* could only marginally detect movements of major enemy forces at operational depths. This problem was eased by the fact that the Germans and their allies had few operational reserves. It was even more difficult for the Soviets to detect last minute, short distance moves by those few German divisions available as tactical reserves, such as the 14th and 22d Panzer Divisions. The course of the offensive vividly underscored this Soviet weakness.

Soviet *razvedka* was best able to validate the results of tactical deception. The variety of ground and air reconnaissance means available to the Soviets made it difficult for the Germans or their allies to reinforce significantly tactical defenses without detection —

certainly to a depth of up to 20 kilometers. The supreme test for Soviet intelligence would occur after the operations had commenced; but, by that time, the deception would have already succeeded or failed.

Conclusions

Soviet assessments regarding the effectiveness of intelligence operations prior to the Stalingrad offensive range from overly optimistic to starkly realistic, depending on who wrote them, in what circumstances, and when they were written. Post-war open source studies, memoirs, and articles vary in their degree of candor but generally reflect Soviet satisfaction regarding how well *razvedka* operated. Soviet contemporary classified critiques emphasized general success as well; but, in the spirit of self-criticism and a desire to improve procedures, they also catalogued failures which required remedying in the future.

The memoir literature speaks virtually with one voice. *STAVKA* representative Zhukov wrote:

> We had learned from POW interrogations that the overall combat standard of Rumanian forces was not high. In these sectors we would enjoy considerable numerical superiority provided the Nazi Command did not regroup reserves by our offensive zero hour. Thus far, our intelligence had not discovered any signs of regrouping. Paulus' 6th Army and part of 4th Panzer Army were tied up at Stalingrad by troops of the Stalingrad and Don Fronts.
>
> Our forces were massing in the designated areas according to plan. As far as we could judge, the enemy was ignorant of our regrouping. We had taken steps to envelop all movement of troops and material with the utmost secrecy.[58]

Vasilevsky reached the same conclusion:

> In brief, our conclusions consisted of the following: The German troop grouping would basically remain as before; the main forces of the 6th and 4th Panzer Armies would continue to be involved in protracted fighting in the area of the city. The Rumanian units would remain on the flanks of these forces (that is, in the areas of our major attacks). We had not observed any more or less substantial reserves being brought up to the Stalingrad area from the interior. And we had not noted any essential regroupings taking place in the enemy

troops operating there. On the whole, the strength of both sides at Stalingrad, as far as we could judge, was roughly equal at the beginning of the offensive. We would manage to assemble powerful shock groups at the points of the impending attacks of our *fronts* by calling in the GHQ reserves and taking off troops from secondary battle sectors; this gave us a superiority in men and equipment that would enable us to count on invariable success.[59]

STAVKA representative and artillery commander Voronov asked himself the rhetorical question, "Did the Hitlerite Command know anything about the preparations for our offensive?" He then answered his own question, stating:

According to all information of our ground and air *razvedka*, the enemy suspected nothing. We followed the enemy with all our eyes. Observation went on around the clock. Sound *razvedka*, which detected enemy artillery and mortar batteries, worked uninterruptedly. From the skies, we systematically photographed enemy positions, especially those regions where we intended to penetrate his defenses. Generals and artillerymen wore out the seats of their pants behind stereoscopes at observation points for hours.[60]

Army commanders echoed these conclusions. General I. M. Chistiakov, 21st Army commander, wrote:

Our *razvedka* worked very actively. It established that, in the army offensive sector, units of 4th and 5th Rumanian Corps defended. The enemy defense had two belts to a depth of 15–20 kilometers. Both in the forward area and in the depth, it consisted of a system of strong points and centers of resistance, located on dominant heights. Everywhere the enemy had erected barbed-wire entanglements and established mine fields.

Running ahead, I will tell of such an episode. At Golovski Farm we crushed a Rumanian division. The captured commander of this division was brought to me. During the interrogation I showed him our intelligence map. The Rumanian division commander gazed at it for a long time and finally, with amazement, said, "The Soviet map reflects the positions of our forces more exactly than the operational map of my staff."[61]

General P. I. Batov, 65th Army commander, when describing his intelligence efforts, noted some last-minute changes in German dispositions. Reconnaissance in force by his 304th and 24th Rifle Divisions on 10 and 12 November netted 31 prisoners from the Rumanian 1st Cavalry Division and 30 German prisoners. Batov suspected that German units were moving. Subsequent reconnaissances from 14–16 November confirmed that elements of 14th Panzer Division were, in fact, redeploying into his sector.[62]

Soviet operational studies and unit histories also insist that Soviet *razvedka* provided sufficient intelligence information for sound planning and successful conduct of the operation. Although, in general, events bore this out, the fact was that this was the first major offensive in which the Soviets employed a coordinated intelligence collection effort. Many of the individual component parts of that system were incomplete, and personnel involved in operating each part were still inexperienced in preparing for large-scale offensive operations.

Classified Soviet critiques of all aspects of *razvedka*, compiled shortly after the operation, provided an accurate appreciation of how well the intelligence system functioned. In general, while they supported the favorable postwar views of the participants, the critiques highlighted problems which had to be solved in the future. Analysis of operational *razvedka* emphasized the growing importance and potential of long-range air, agent, reconnaissance-diversionary, partisan, and radio *razvedka* which, in some sectors, "attained the depth of 450 kilometers" during the period of the Stalingrad operation.[63] To illustrate the point, one study provided details of *razvedka* activities in an unnamed area of the front using fictitious place names and unit nomenclatures. The general situation and configuration of the *front* indicated the analysis pertained to the Western Front sector.

While praising the thoroughness of *razvedka* planning and the integrated use of intelligence obtained from many sources, the study highlighted weaknesses applicable to the entire Eastern Front. The first was a Soviet tendency to treat every piece of intelligence with equal credibility. Despite the fact that *razvedka* noted virtually all actual enemy troop transfers:

> On several occasions, the intelligence section at headquarters, though not in possession of sufficiently substantiating information, reported the presence of a number of formations and units which, in actual fact, never opposed our *front* ... sometimes on the flimsiest evidence.[64]

This was so because:

> Generally speaking, the intelligence section at our *front* head-quarters was extremely eager to record new formations, using the argument that, if no confirmation should be forthcoming for any of them, they could be very easily deleted. On particularly frequent occasions, the intelligence section was easily deceived by the appearance in the enemy area opposite our *front* of light motor vehicles bearing emblems of various divisions.[65]

In the case of the Western Front, aerial *razvedka* of enemy airdromes and engineer *razvedka* was quite effective, an observation which applied as well to *razvedka* in southern Russia. The study noted, however, that, even in the fall of 1942, *front* intelligence was still affected by the earlier preconceived notion that the Germans would undertake new offensive action in the Moscow sector. This perception tainted intelligence, which, in turn, focused undue attention on detecting a build-up preparatory for that offensive.

Drawing on the experiences of the Western and other *Fronts*, the study drew some conclusions regarding operational *razvedka*, beginning with the claim that "*front* headquarters have gained a great deal of experience regarding organization of operational *razvedka* which enables them to solve successfully any problem pertinent to the situation." While noting that "in actual practice all intelligence sources and means (radio, agents, air, partisans) are fully able to execute the tasks assigned to them," positive results are best attained if all elements work as a team.[66] This required that close attention be paid to staff cooperation.

Despite the praise, intelligence collection produced a profusion of reports and information which strained analytical capabilities. Hence, more attention had to be paid to verification of reports and careful sorting and analysis of collected data. This could be solved by implementation of a more rational system for verification and sifting of intelligence information. Another deficiency which compounded the collection and analysis problem was the lack of tactical expertise, "often the simplest military literacy," on the part of agents and air reconnaissance crews.[67] Because they lacked training, these sources reported virtually everything they saw, whether or not the information was worthwhile or valid. The study recommended more substantive training for their personnel and more thorough briefings before they undertook their missions.

Radio *razvedka* proved its worth during the fall and produced numerous reports. Here also, the inexperience of radio operators conditioned them to deception by the enemy. Better training was also the remedy for this problem. Critiques noted the immense value of captured prisoners and documents and urged all commands to expand the scope and duration of scouting and reconnaissance missions. Likewise, critiques of engineer *razvedka* cited the "profitable experience gained by the forces of the Don Front and Stalingrad Front" noting, "Their engineer reconnaissance teams, despite the greater operational and tactical density of enemy groupings there, penetrated deep into his rear areas, took their time in reconnoitering them, and collected extremely valuable information."[68]

Whereas during the Stalingrad operation intelligence sections at *front* and army compiled separate plans monthly or bi-weekly for each type of intelligence collection means, the study recommended creation, in the future, of a common *razvedka* plan for 15-day increments, supplemented by a single detailed list of intelligence data to be obtained by air, radio, or ground reconnaissance. The study urged commanders and staffs to integrate their general intelligence needs into operational planning so as to avoid irrational or untimely requests for special or operational intelligence or situations where staffs simply avoided requests for intelligence out of fear of compromising planning secrecy. This comment reflected heightened concern for planning security as well as the existence of separate types of intelligence, including "special" from national and NKVD sources and "operational" from military sources.

Finally, the study enjoined all *fronts* to resist in the future the tendency to overestimate enemy forces and to consider the situation in each sector within the context of the entire front. It then called for more efficient staff work (staff culture), stating, "The execution of this task must be given the highest priority in the work of *razvedka*, which represents the most important element of the command of forces."[69]

Several major Soviet war experience studies analyzed both the defensive and offensive phases of the Stalingrad operation. These addressed virtually every aspect of combat including *razvedka*, although primarily in a tactical sense; and they concluded that marked improvements had occurred during the fall of 1942. In analyzing Soviet counterattacks conducted northwest of Stalingrad in September and early October, one critique painted a bleak picture of pre-offensive reconnaissance:

The troops went into battle without knowing the enemy defense system. *Razvedka* was conducted in a superficial manner. Often there was no observation of the battlefield. As a result of insufficient study of the enemy defenses, his line of combat security was often taken for the forward edge of the main defense zone. During the period of artillery preparation, shells were fired into vacant areas; and, when the infantry advanced to the attack, it had to go a great distance to reach a system of enemy defenses which had not yet been neutralized.[70]

This contrasted sharply with subsequent descriptions of *razvedka* techniques used in the November offensive and their results:

Carefully planned and continuous conduct of *razvedka* made possible the timely discovery of the enemy defense system, the grouping of his forces and weaponry, his system of engineer installations and entanglements, and also the character of the terrain. In the study of the enemy, a great part was played by local military actions of the *front* and the verification by reconnaissance in force of enemy groupings for several days prior to the attack.[71]

The study attributed improvements to the existence of new detailed regulations and instructions, a higher level of command interest and involvement in planning, the improved efficiency of staffs, and the higher state of unit training.

Despite wholesale improvements in *razvedka* during the Stalingrad operation, deficiencies still existed. At the highest level, although sufficient intelligence was available, the Soviet commands underestimated the size, strength, and resilience of German forces in the Stalingrad region. Consequently, the encircled German group was over twice as large as expected; and a major operation had to be mounted to reduce the group. "This explains the drawing-out of the operations, which, instead of lasting seven days as planned, lasted 23 days."[72]

The Stalingrad Front also underestimated German capabilities to mount a counterattack from the southwest into the Stalingrad area. Based on this estimate, it assigned only light screening forces of 51st Army to cover approaches along the Aksai River. When the unexpected German threat materialized, major troop regroupings were necessary to forestall German relief of the encircled Stalingrad force. However,

For a number of reasons, first of all the careful preparation of the operation as a whole by the *STAVKA* and by its representatives on the spot (Marshals of the Soviet Union Comrades Zhukov, Vasilevsky, and Voronov), the afore-mentioned mistakes and a number of less essential weaknesses did not have any serious consequences.[73]

The study then cited a document captured from German VII Army Corps which assessed Soviet performance before the attack and during the period 19–24 November. Among other points, the Germans praised the apparent efficiency of Soviet *razvedka*:

> ... an extremely careful feeling-out of all the front by the method of ordinary actions of shock detachments (strength up to a regiment) separated by long intervals of time for the purpose of determining precisely the weak places on the front. This reconnaissance in force was particularly intense two or three days before the beginning of the offensive.[74]

Another specific study, which focused on 5th Tank Army operations, detailed its *razvedka* accomplishment. It concluded that, in the critical penetration sector, reconnaissance forces had determined the true forward edge of defenses, the location of engineer obstacles and the most important weapons systems, and the location and strength of the second line of defense. *Razvedka*, however, had not provided a completely accurate picture of German tactical reserves. The 5th Tank Army's pre-offensive *razvedka* indicated the presence on its front of two infantry divisions occupying weak positions in the enemy tactical rear "on the line Pronin, Peschany (Ust–Medveditski), Perelazovski."[75] As the operation commenced and 5th Tank Army's two tank corps advanced into the penetration, they encountered stronger forces than anticipated. The study stated, "Actually, however, in the course of the operations, the Army in this sector fought the 7th Cavalry Division (in dismounted formation), units of 1st Motorized Rumanian Division, and the German 22d Tank Division."[76] This unexpected encounter produced only temporary problems for one of the advancing Soviet tank corps.

Soviet critiques noted problems associated with air *razvedka* but attributed most to German air superiority and lack of crews and requisite modern equipment. Principles governing the conduct of air *razvedka* were sound; and, in several important instances, reconnaissance units were able to contribute positively to the overall intelligence effort, particularly by observing major rail and road networks. There was every reason to expect greater contributions in the future when Soviet air power gained ascendancy and when more modern equipment (radios) and aircraft were available.

Thorough Soviet analysis of artillery *razvedka* lauded overall accomplishments but also recommended areas for improvement. Special praise was reserved for artillery commanders at every level who conducted joint reconnaissance with appropriate ground commanders. Reports also praised the work of operations sections within *fronts* and armies, stating, "It becomes clear that, in this team, the working-out of all questions relating to coordination and planning of the operations worked very well."[77] Such was not the case, however, regarding coordination between intelligence sections where "there was no clearly organized exchange of reconnaissance data. The various intelligence sections did not establish proper relations among each other and, most important, at each of them there was no sense of responsibility for complete and timely collection of *razvedka* data, and also for correct conclusions regarding the enemy."[78] Often orders received by commanders were not passed on to respective artillery commanders.

On the other hand, the critiques spoke highly of the work of artillery reconnaissance agencies, stating that their activities "in connection with the rout of Hitler's army in the Stalingrad area ensured great effectiveness of the artillery offensive. It was only because of the great operational importance of the reconnaissance and the reliability of the target data that the large masses of artillery were able, in a short space of time, to pulverize the elite German-Fascist army."[79] This occurred in spite of the fact that artillery staffs and commanders did not provide their intelligence sections with sufficiently accurate missions. Consequently, they learned about the impending operation from "secondary personages."

The extensive pre-offensive regrouping severely overburdened artillery intelligence officers since the *razvedka* sectors constantly changed. This required considerable complex coordination between army reconnaissance, artillery observation battalions, and troop units. Intelligence officers' lack of familiarity with instrumental and artillery air reconnaissance subunits they were to manage, combined with the lack of requisite observation and communication equipment, compounded the regrouping difficulties. Frequent assistance from assistant intelligence officers of *front* artillery helped solve these problems. Although shortages in observation equipment (particularly battery commanders' scopes) inhibited formation of combined observation in all battalions, nonetheless, "there was not a single division artillery regiment or GHQ reserve unit in which battalion combined observation was not operative."[80]

Among the other problems cited in critiques were: limited exchange of reconnaissance data between relieved and relieving units; inadequate training of some scouting and ground reconnaissance personnel; the lack of a specific officer on division artillery staff who could devote his entire attention to artillery *razvedka*; weak battalion artillery reconnaissance due to observation equipment shortages; and terrain difficulties which inhibited observation and reduced the number of targets disclosed by flash ranging. Finally, artillery air *razvedka* "played no essential role in view of the almost complete absence of artillery observation aviation." Despite this problem, considerable aerial photography "facilitated study of the depth of the enemy defense."[81] This critique and critiques of subsequent phases of the Stalingrad operation as well as those of associated operations provided a sound basis for recommended improvements to the artillery *razvedka* structure.

Engineer *razvedka* was clearly the most effective of all the types of *razvedka* conducted during the preparatory period. Yet even in this realm Soviet critiques specified two areas where improvements could be made. More extensive double-checking and analysis of data received from ground reconnaissance patrols could have improved the process of detecting minefields. In addition, more thorough use of photography and, in certain cases, interrogation of POWs could have supplied a further check on data provided by units performing engineer *razvedka*. As was the case in virtually all areas of reconnaissance, critiques recommended creation of more engineer *razvedka* assets and more extensive use of those already in being, specifically more extensive fielding of engineer observation posts and the addition of engineers to virtually all troop reconnaissance efforts.

One of the most important *razvedka* innovations employed in the Stalingrad operation was the general use of reconnaissance in force (*razvedka boem*) prior to the operation to verify data received from other intelligence sources. Although the technique proved beneficial, analysis indicated some problem areas and some aspects of reconnaissance in force which could be exploited to a greater extent in the future. Conduct of the reconnaissance over an extended period of eight days failed to provide the most up-to-date data on enemy force dispositions. Likewise, since the reconnaissance occurred in different sectors and at different times, the Germans could have shifted forces between sectors without Soviet intelligence noting the shifts.

The limited size of many of the reconnaissance detachments hindered their operations, as German and Rumanian forces often blocked them and prevented their determining deep enemy dispositions. More important, large-scale conduct of reconnaissance in force could become a potential offensive indicator in its own right. If conducted well before a planned offensive, enemy forces could use the indicator as justification for reinforcing defenses in regions where the reconnaissance in force had occurred. Fortunately for the Soviets, this did not occur during the first phase of the Stalingrad operation. It would, however, occur in the second phase when Soviet forces attacked along the middle reaches of the Don River.

In general, despite the problems they encountered, Soviet intelligence organs made more than a modest contribution to Soviet success in the initial phases of the Stalingrad operation. It remained to be seen whether intelligence could maintain its record of success during the flow of combat which followed the initial Soviet attack.

RAZVEDKA DURING THE OFFENSIVE

General

On the morning of 19 November 1942, Soviet Southwestern Front forces burst from their bridgeheads along the south bank of the Don River and struck defensive positions of Third Rumanian and Sixth German Armies (see Maps 4 and 5). By mid-day Soviet infantry had penetrated Rumanian defenses; and the 1st and 26th Tank Corps of 5th Tank Army went into action, smashing the remnants of the Rumanian defenses. The next day, forces of the Stalingrad Front attacked Rumanian forces south of Stalingrad and committed 4th Mechanized Corps in an exploitation. By 23 November the mobile forces of the two Soviet *fronts* had linked up near Kalach west of Stalingrad, entrapping most of German Sixth and part of Fourth Panzer Army in the Stalingrad pocket.

Once the encirclement was complete, Soviet forces immediately attempted to reduce the encircled German force and simultaneously extend the offensive westward with attacks against Italian and Rumanian forces defending along the middle sector of the Don River. Meanwhile, 51st Army of the Stalingrad Front erected a screen along the Aksai River, southwest of Stalingrad, to defend against German efforts to relieve the Stalingrad garrison. While the

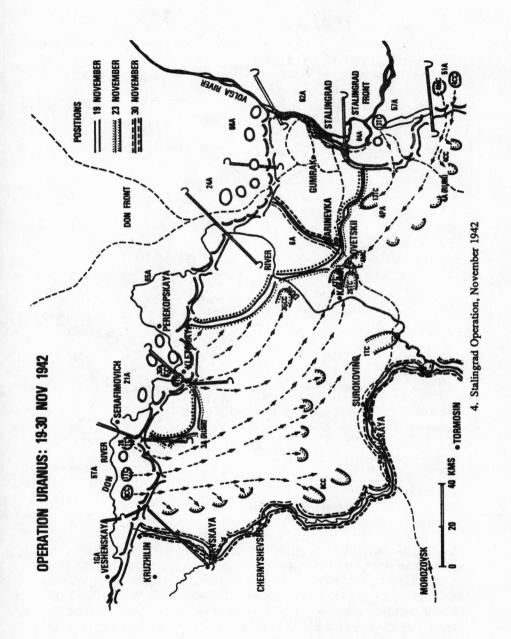

4. Stalingrad Operation, November 1942

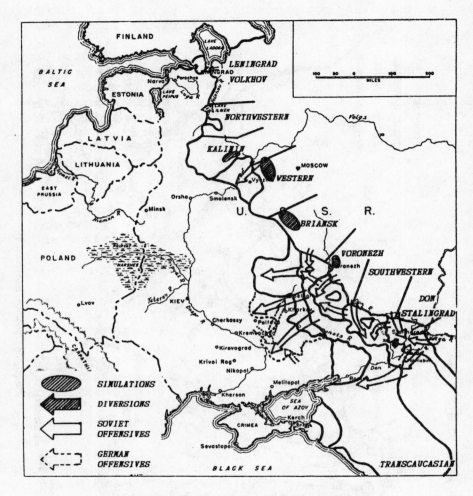

5. The Winter Campaign, November 1942–March 1943

Don Front and major portions of the Stalingrad Front fought to reduce the Stalingrad pocket, the Southwestern Front, reinforced by the Voronezh Front's 6th Army and 2d Guards Army from *STAVKA* reserves, planned so-called Operation Saturn against Eighth Italian Army and Rumanian and German forces defending along the Don and Chir Rivers. Originally, this operation was designed to thwart German relief attempts toward Stalingrad from the west and, ultimately, penetrate to Rostov to create an even larger encirclement of all German forces in the Tormosin and Caucasus regions.

By 4 December, after repeated futile attempts to crush the Stalingrad pocket, the Soviets realized they had woefully underestimated the size of the encircled force. Consequently, the *STAVKA* stripped 2d Guards Army from Southwestern Front control for use at Stalingrad and delayed the commencement of Operation Saturn from 10 to 14 December. The deep objectives of Operation Saturn remained unaltered. No sooner had planning begun in earnest for Operations Saturn and Kol'tso (Ring – the reduction of the Stalingrad encirclement) than, on 12 December, the Germans commenced a relief effort by LVI Panzer Corps across the Aksai River toward Stalingrad from the southwest. The *STAVKA* reacted quickly to this new threat. On 13 December it halted planning for Operation Kol'tso and ordered 2d Guards Army southward to block and ultimately defeat the German relief columns. Simultaneously, it truncated Operation Saturn into Operation Little Saturn. The new operation, scheduled to begin on 16 December, had shorter objectives (essentially the defeat of Eighth Italian Army and Army Detachment Hollidt).

This frenetic planning resulted in the conduct of two operations: one along the middle Don River and the second southwest of Stalingrad. The first, Operation Little Saturn, was conducted by the Southwestern Front and part of the Voronezh Front between 16 and 27 December 1942. It resulted in the defeat and destruction of Eighth Italian Army and Rumanian and German forces defending along the upper Chir River. By 28 December the Germans had abandoned their relief attempt into Stalingrad from the Tormosin region and were hastily attempting to erect new defenses further to the west. The second operation, the Kotel'nikovo operation, lasted from 12 to 30 December 1942. Initially, from 12–23 December, German forces drove to within 50 kilometers of encircled Sixth Army. Thereafter, the Stalingrad Front, reinforced with 2d Guards Army, drove German forces westward, frustrating the German relief attempt. By 30 December all German hopes of rescuing the beleaguered German garrison had faded. After a long siege, on 2 February 1943, German forces in Stalingrad finally surrendered.

During the course of these operations, Soviet intelligence organs were severely tested. It was one thing to prepare for an offensive over an extended period while the front was relatively static. It was an altogether different matter to conduct intelligence work while the situation was in a state of flux. Between 19 November and 30 December, Soviet intelligence simultaneously had to support the conduct of the Stalingrad operation, prepare for the Middle Don and Kotel'nikovo operations and then support the conduct of each of these operations.

Throughout the duration of the Stalingrad, Middle Don, and Kotel'nikovo operations, Soviet intelligence organizations employed the same basic techniques they had used in preparing for the Stalingrad operation. Whenever possible, they altered their procedures to correct deficiencies apparent in earlier phases, but these corrections were limited by the paucity of available time and the rapidly changing situation. Within time constraints, the South-western and Stalingrad Fronts planned for the Middle Don and Kotel'nikovo operations in much the same fashion as they had planned the Stalingrad operation. For the latter this was very difficult, as responsibility for reducing the Stalingrad pocket had just passed to Don Front control.

Fronts employed their longer range air and radio collection assets to conduct operational *razvedka* by monitoring movement of German operational and tactical reserves. They were assisted in this effort by the general Soviet presumption that the Germans would attempt relief missions and by geography, which dictated the regions from which those attempts would have to emanate. The adjacent Voronezh and North Caucasus Fronts assisted this effort using their long range aviation assets. Soviet *fronts* employed shorter range troop, artillery, engineer, and combat *razvedka* assets to prepare for and conduct operations in their respective sectors. Soviet commanders and staffs also confronted the new challenge of conducting *razvedka* on the march, particularly in support of deep operating mobile forces. Here again, the primary Soviet concern was the location and movement of German reserve units, in particular panzer corps and divisions which could disrupt Soviet offensive efforts.

The Stalingrad Operation 19 November–12 December

The Stalingrad operation developed so swiftly that Soviet intelligence had no time to alter its initial assessments of German strength and dispositions around Stalingrad. Soviet forces simply had to cope with the pre-offensive intelligence data until the encirclement had formed. Thereafter, intelligence worked to determine just what size force they had encircled and how it was disposed. Initially, Soviet armored and mechanized forces advanced rapidly and formed the encirclement just as planned in spite of errors in the intelligence picture and in the conduct of *razvedka*. Those errors, however, did pose minor problems during the penetration and exploitation phase of the operation.

As they advanced into the penetration, the tank corps and rifle units tended to become involved in prolonged battles to overcome small enemy groups or strong points which should have been detected by reconnaissance and bypassed. Soviet critiques noted, "If the commander of a mobile group or the commanders of large units get timely information from their reconnaissance concerning such centers of resistance, the loss of time in executing detour maneuvers may be reduced to a minimum."[82] The failure of *razvedka* to detect the presence of 22d Panzer Division prior to the offensive had a temporarily adverse effect on the operation. "The 1st Tank and 8th Cavalry Corps had an unexpected encounter with units of 22d German Panzer Division in the area of Peschani ... in doing so we lost more than a day."[83] As a consequence of this case and experiences of other mobile corps, the Soviets recommended that, in the future, these groups conduct reconnaissance independently, using their own ground reconnaissance in concert with dedicated air reconnaissance both during the penetration and exploitation phases of the operation. In addition, they recommended creation of movement detachments to clear obstacles, mark advance routes, and share in the reconnaissance function. These proposals were the first of many which would contribute to more effective operations of the fledgling mobile force in the future.

A more critical intelligence error had serious consequences for the subsequent Soviet operation to reduce the encirclement. Vasilevsky explained the failure:

> Unfortunately the offensive [against the Stalingrad pocket] did not bring the expected results. In our initial calculations, on which we had based the decision to destroy the surrounded enemy grouping by a single drive, we had made a serious mistake. According to intelligence information from the *fronts* participating in the counteroffensive and from General Staff intelligence agencies, the total number of men in the surrounded grouping ... was put at 85,000–90,000. In fact, as we learned later, it had over 300,000 men. Our notions of enemy equipment, especially artillery and tanks, and the arms available to the surrounded Germans also fell far short of

actuality. We had not taken into consideration the reinforcements which joined formations of the 6th Field and 4th Tank German Armies in the process of their offensive and defence, and the huge number of units and subunits of all types of special and auxiliary troops that had become involved in what was known as the "cauldron" or pocket. What is more, the personnel of these troops were mostly used subsequently for reinforcing the combat units. Thus, we had completely left out of consideration the anti-aircraft defence division, more than ten detached sapper battalions, medical organizations and units, numerous construction battalions and the engineering detachments of the former Todt organization ... units of the field gendarmerie, the secret military police, and so on.[84]

In short, Soviet intelligence made the age-old mistake of an inexperienced, green intelligence organ. It simply counted division, corps, and army flags without considering the size of the total force. By 4 December the Soviets were aware of their mistake. Consequently, Vasilevsky received 2d Guards Army to help carry out the reduction operation.

Ominously, at about this time, Vasilevsky noted intelligence reports to the effect that Field Marshal Erich von Manstein had taken command of the newly-formed German Army Group Don and was preparing plans to form two shock groups – at Tormosin and Kotel'nikovo – to mount relief operations to Stalingrad.[85] Although this threat prompted some Soviet regrouping of forces, Vasilevsky continued his plans to reduce Stalingrad. Soon, however, intelligence reports from the Southwestern and Stalingrad Fronts indicated "that large enemy forces were building up in the Kotel'nikovo and other areas. German air activity also heightened against our 51st Army."[86] Ground operations soon confirmed the reports that panzer units were concentrating at Kotel'nikovo. This brought operations against the Stalingrad cauldron to a temporary halt as 2d Guards Army was readied to move to the Kotel'nikovo area.

During the short-lived Soviet attempt to reduce the Stalingrad pocket, *razvedka* was poor, in part because of over-confidence caused by Soviet under-estimation of the size of the German force. Since the pocket shrank quickly after the initial assault because the Germans withdrew to more defensible positions, "the artillery *razvedka* agencies ... lost contact with the enemy and, at the moment of the approach of our units to his new defense line, they did not possess sufficiently complete and reliable data concerning the character of the enemy defense." By 28 December, after the smaller pocket had evolved, "the number of targets disclosed by artillery *razvedka* was very small."[87] Engineer *razvedka* suffered from the same problems. Air surveillance over the encircled German force was inhibited by generally inclement weather and by the fact that most 8th Air Army *razvedka* aircraft were conducting *razvedka* missions in support of 51st Army operating along the Aksai River to the southwest. These problems would be addressed and overcome when Soviet forces resumed reduction of the Stalingrad pocket in early January. Meanwhile, Soviet attention shifted to action along the Don and Aksai Rivers northwest and southwest of Stalingrad.

The Middle Don Operation, 16–28 December

Preliminary planning for the Middle Don operation began on 3 December after the *STAVKA* had approved Vasilevsky's initial plan and continued after the operation was scaled down in scope on 12 December. Thereafter planning was under Voronov's supervision. The concept of the operation called for an assault by two armies of the Southwestern Front southward across the Don River and westward across the Chir River (see Map 6). The 1st Guards Army and the Voronezh Front's 6th Army were to attack from bridgeheads across the Don River near Verkhnyi Mamon, penetrate Eighth Italian Army defenses and then commit four tank corps which would fan out and advance to the south and southwest to the Millerovo and Morozovsk area deep in the Italian rear area. Simultaneously, 3d Guards Army was to attack westward across the Chir River from the Bokovskaia region. The 1st Guards Mechanized Corps would exploit westward and southward in concert with 1st Guards Army's mobile forces. By joint action, the two armies were to encircle and destroy Italian, Rumanian, and German forces between the Don and Chir Rivers and then advance to seize key airfields at Tatsinskaia and Morozovsk, which the Germans used to resupply Sixth Army at Stalingrad.

Razvedka for the attack began soon after 2 December and culminated in an extensive reconnaissance in force conducted between 11 and 13 December. The Southwestern Front's 17th Air Army and Voronezh Front's 2d Air Army conducted air *razvedka* during the preparatory period of the operation. Twenty-three of the army's 632 aircraft were dedicated solely to reconnaissance, while a total of 106 PO-2 and R-5 aircraft conducted reconnaissance,

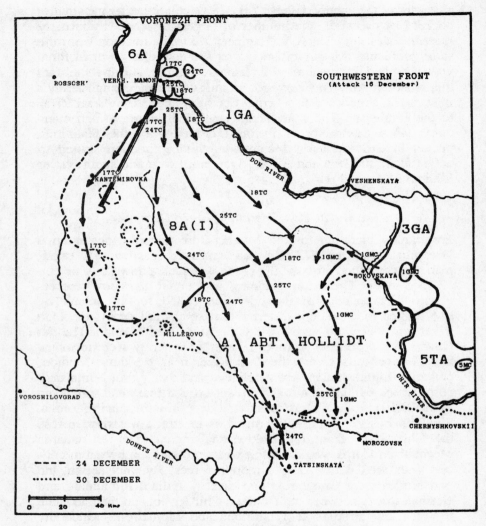

6. Middle Don Operation, December 1942

liaison, and night bombing.[88] Throughout the operation, Soviet air forces had only a slight numerical advantage over their opponents.

During the preparatory period, the two air armies received the mission "to conduct *razvedka* in the interest of the forthcoming operation, photograph the enemy defensive sector on the right bank of the Don, and uncover the beginning and direction of transport of his operational reserves to the front."[89] Poor weather inhibited the performance of this and other missions. "In fact, aviation was most fully able to fulfill only the *razvedka* missions and cover the concentration of our own forces," in part because German aircraft were inactive prior to the offensive in 1st Guards' and 6th Army's sectors and only marginally active in 3d Guards Army's sector.[90]

Bad weather restricted all air *razvedka* prior to 8 December. From 8 to 15 December, the two air armies conducted 1,263 sorties, of which 212 were dedicated to reconnaissance of enemy positions along the front and in the depths. These reconnaissance flights "fully uncovered the enemy's defense system and photographed the main defensive belt on the right bank of the Don and Chir Rivers in the sector from Rossosh' to Nizhne–Chirskaia; the dimensions of the photographed region reached a depth of 12–15 kilometers. Besides this, aerial photographs were taken of enemy concentration areas and aerodromes in Kantemirovka, Chertkovo, Millerovo, Tatsinskaia, and Morozovsk."[91]

Air *razvedka* also confirmed the absence of large enemy reserves opposite Soviet main attack axes and established that the enemy had not occupied any of the prepared defenses in the operational depth of their rear area. Assessments noted, "One must mention that the quality of air *razvedka* was very good, and ground commanders disposed of exhaustive data upon which to base their decisions in penetrating the enemy defensive sector."[92] Well-organized *razvedka* of enemy air bases provided information which prompted heavy Soviet air strikes on German air force units at Millerovo, Tatsinskaia, and Chernyshkovsky. Soviet aircraft destroyed 120 German aircraft in these strikes, thus assisting Soviet air forces in achieving air superiority in the initial phase of the operation.[93]

The Soviets employed reconnaissance-diversionary teams and agents in the operation under control of the special and intelligence sections of *front*. Radio units continued intercept activities as well, but few details exist regarding either reconnaissance/agent activity or radio intercepts except Soviet general references to the fact that they occurred. Soviet orders of battle noted a destroyer (commando) brigade assigned to the Voronezh Front's 6th Army, and accounts noted the use of "specially selected teams ... whose task was to penetrate ... into the rear of enemy positions ... for disorganization of command and control."[94] Although the Soviets had a sound general idea about the nature of the enemy defense (since they had observed these positions continuously since August), more precise data was required to plan the artillery offensive. The task of gathering this information fell to the artillery intelligence staffs of *front* and armies. Artillery *razvedka* employed observation, use of artillery instrumental *razvedka* (AIR), and participation of artillerymen in ground reconnaissance operations.

The 6th Army's conduct of artillery *razvedka* was typical of the *front*'s efforts. By 5 December, the army had created 123 observation posts across the front from Novaia Kalitva to Krasno–Orekhovoe. In addition, four sound-ranging platoons, two flash-spotter platoons, two photographic platoons, and three sections of geodetic survey troops identified targets and enemy positions using basic triangulation procedures.[95] Staff officers from the army artillery intelligence section supervised the work and made frequent visits to subordinate *razvedka* units and observation posts. By 18 November, within a 30-kilometer sector of the front, *razvedka* had spotted about 100 targets and determined accurate coordinates for 28 of them. By the end of the operation, in the same sector 277 of 350 spotted targets had their coordinates determined. Most of this work was accomplished by the 399th Separate Army Artillery Observation Battery which identified the coordinates of 148 of these targets.[96] The Soviets used aerial photographs and ground *razvedka* to confirm many of the targets.

In some instances, artillery *razvedka* had difficulty determining specific targets or identified erronous positions. This applied particularly to enemy positions in the depth of the defense where the lack of aerial spotter support and poor weather limited the effectiveness of *razvedka*. Aerial photography did not extend beyond the depth of 12 kilometers. Despite faults in the organization and conduct of artillery *razvedka*, the Soviets judged in the end that it was possible "to gain fairly adequate information on the disposition of enemy artillery ... including the location of enemy firing points, his fire system, and the outline of the forward defense line."[97] The Southwestern Front also conducted standard engineer *razvedka* using a network of OPs and engineers assigned to reconnaissance detachments and patrols. Although engineer work identified most Italian field positions in the tactical depths, it had less success in locating minefields in the region.

To verify the work done by other *razvedka* organs, between 11 and 13 December Soviet armies conducted reconnaissance in force in company or battalion strength across the entire offensive sector.[98] During this period these companies and battalions secured new bridgeheads across the Don and Chir Rivers or expanded existing bridgeheads and sought to determine the strength and dispositions of enemy forces. Specific reconnaissance forces in 1st Guards and 6th Armies' sectors were as follows:

Date	Army	Rifle Division	Reconnaissance Force
11 December	1st Guards	195th	Reinforced Battalion
	1st Guards	44th Guards	Reinforced Battalion
	1st Guards	1st	Reinforced Battalion
	1st Guards	38th Guards	Reinforced Battalion
12 December	6th Army	127th	Three Reinforced Battalions
	6th Army	127th	Reinforced Company
13 December	6th Army	127th	Reinforced Battalion
	6th Army	127th	Reinforced Battalion
	6th Army	350th	Reinforced Battalion

The reconnaissance in force improved Soviet jumping-off positions for the main attack and prompted Italian forces to conduct counterattacks and reveal their artillery positions. In several sectors the Soviets capitalized on the success of the reconnaissance by reinforcing their forward positions in the bridgeheads. However, the reconnaissance also had an adverse effect by alerting Eighth Italian Army to the imminence of an attack. Consequently, between 13 and 15 December, elements of the German 385th and 27th Panzer Divisions deployed forward and occupied some of the Italians' forward defensive positions.[99] Despite this unpleasant reality, when Soviet forces attacked on the morning of 16 December, they had a more-than-adequate picture of Italian and German defenses.

The *razvedka* situation, however, abruptly changed after the Soviets commenced the offensive. In the Soviets' own words:

> If during the preparatory period of the operation, our *razvedka* – air, ground, and agent – was able almost fully to determine the enemy's defense, weapons, and strength, during the course of battle, and the decisive development of the operation, *razvedka* did not always provide the command with full and timely required information about the enemy.[100]

These problems ranged across the entire spectrum of intelligence collection means. Air *razvedka* suffered seriously from bad weather. During the entire operational period of 16 days and nights, 17th Air Army was able to operate only nine days and seven nights and 2d Air Army only six days and eight nights.[101] Virtually no aircraft operated during the first four days of the operation.

After 15 December air *razvedka* finally began reporting on enemy troop movements in the region. For example, on 20 December reconnaissance aircraft of the 282d Fighter Aviation Division detected a concentration of 80 tanks, 30 vehicles, and infantry around Nizhne Solonovsky north of Tormosin which were subsequently attacked by air units. Although not identified by the Soviets, this turned out to be elements of XXXXVIII Panzer Corps' 11th Panzer Division. A day before and for several days thereafter, air *razvedka* also detected heavy German rail traffic into Rossosh' and Mitrofanovka, to the northwest, Kantemirovka and Kamensk in the west, and Chernyshkovsky in the south.[102] Although Soviet air units did not engage these targets, it was apparent German reinforcements were arriving in the region.

In his 28 December situation report to the Supreme Command, Vatutin, Commander of the Southwestern Front, described the progress of the offensive:

All forces facing our Front (around 17 divisions) have been wiped out and their stocks captured. We have taken more than 60,000 prisoners, about the same number have been killed. The few remaining forces are hardly offering any resistance, except on rare occasions.

Ahead of us, the enemy continues stubborn resistance along the Oblivskaya and Verkhne–Chirskaya line. Today in the vicinity of Morozovsk we took prisoners from the 11th Panzer Division and the 8th Air Field Division which had previously faced Romanenko's army. The greatest resistance to Lelyushenko's army and to our mobile forces is coming from the enemy formations which moved from the Kotel'nikovo sector across the Don and to the line extending from Chernyshkovsky, through Morozovsk, and Skosyrskaya to Tatsinskaya. These troops are trying to dig in to obstruct the further advance of our mobile units and thus give their own forces a chance to retreat. Given favourable circumstances, the enemy may attempt to hold the entire salient with the aim of further rescuing his encircled grouping. He will get nowhere though. Every effort will be made to cut off that salient.

Every day air reconnaissance spot detraining of enemy troops near Rossosh, Starobelsk, Voroshilovgrad, Chebotovka, Kamensk, Likhaya and Zverevo. Though it is hard to tell what the enemy plans to do, evidently he is establishing his main line of defence along the Seversky Donets. The enemy is compelled primarily to fill in the 350-kilometre-wide breach our troops have made. It would be a good idea to continue to strike at the enemy without affording any respite. However, that calls for reinforcements as the forces available here are busy finishing up the Small Saturn Operation. Additional forces are required to initiate Big Saturn.[103]

The report reveals that a combination of *razvedka* sources and ground combat reports formed a fairly accurate picture of the situation by 28 December, but only after considerable damage had been done to the Southwestern Front's mobile forces. Throughout the operation, communications difficulties inhibited rapid reporting of air *razvedka* data and disrupted coordination of *razvedka* with ground units. Consequently, "daily combat work began with reconnaissance of the position of the [our own] ground forces."[104] Throughout the exploitation and pursuit phase of the operation, out of 1,252 sorties flown by the two air armies, 409 were devoted to *razvedka*.

During the penetration and exploitation phases of the operation, Soviet ground units, in particular the mobile groups, experienced difficulties produced, in part, by poor *razvedka*. When committed to combat late on 17 December, lead elements of Soviet 17th, 18th, and 25th Tank Corps suffered heavy tank losses from unreconnoitered minefields. Voronov later wrote, "When our tanks were penetrating the forward edge of the enemy defense, they were suddenly blown up by mines. It turned out that, in a series of places, mines were laid in three layers: the first had been laid by the Italians in summer conditions; the second, in autumn; and the third, at the beginning of the winter period."[105] Soviet critiques faulted the engineers, who had failed to ensure unobstructed movement of the tank forces through the enemy defense zone. They recommended that, in the future, engineer forces be assigned to tank and mechanized corps to perform that function.

Critiques recommended preparations for similar operations in the future should incorporate measures for thorough reconnaissance of the sector of mobile corps commitment. It was essential to gather information about the enemy defense system throughout the tactical depth of the penetration sector, the location of his reserves, and the capabilities and times of arrival of these forces within the corps' area of action in the enemy operational depths. Within the tank and mechanized corps themselves, critiques recommended use of organic reconnaissance elements "whose task it is to observe the action of the infantry, to reconnoiter the routes of march and to keep the corps headquarters informed on the situation. ... Officers from corps headquarters will accompany the reconnaissance elements."[106]

Once in the operational depths, because of a lack of reconnaissance means, mobile forces usually operated in isolation, blind to what was going on around them. As a Soviet critique stated:

> The matter of reconnaissance during their action in the depth of enemy operational defenses is another matter of vital importance to tank (mechanized) corps. Experience shows that, in a number of cases, tank (mechanized) corps had no clear idea about the disposition of enemy operational reserves or the probable time of their arrival in the area of forthcoming action. Because of that, the corps' action was diffident and their advance slowed down.[107]

Experience bore this out. Although 17th Tank Corps operated successfully along the western flank of the operation, the other three tank corps (18th, 24th, 25th) and lst Mechanized Corps ended up, after ten days of operations, isolated from one another 100–120 kilometers deep in the enemy rear. By this time, 18th and 25th Tank Corps had lost over 80 percent of their tank strength and were unable to seize their ultimate objectives. The stronger of the three corps (24th), with 59 tanks, took the German base at Tatsinskaia but was subsequently encircled by German 11th and 6th Panzer Divisions. After three days of siege, during which the neighboring tank corps could provide no assistance, the corps escaped from encirclement after losing most of its equipment.

Analysis of these cases led the Soviets to conclude that a mobile corps commander, operating in the depth of enemy defenses, often fighting in encirclement, must know beforehand about the approach of enemy reserves and about their movements. "Hence, a corps must have its own reconnaissance aircraft with the aid of which it could conduct reconnaissance within a radius of not less than 100 kilometers."[108] The crews of these aircraft required special training in cooperating with tanks and ground reconnaissance forces. Organic mobile corps tactical reconnaissance elements had to be accorded "greater initiative in the selection of ways and means for the performance of their assigned tasks." These elements would have to operate with the "greatest mobility, daring, and impetuosity."[109]

The critique noted that strong ground *razvedka* must always be closely coordinated with air *razvedka*, and ground elements must be supplied with powerful mobile radios to ensure that cooperation. At times, these reconnaissance elements would perform tactical combat missions similar to those performed by forward detachments such as the seizure and retention of key positions pending the arrival of the main force. Lack of intelligence could not only cause material damage to the mobile corps. It could also "be used to some extent as an excuse for cautious and even hesitant action of some of our corps in the depth of the enemy defense zone."[110] Adoption of these recommended measures could, in the future, remedy the problems experienced by the mobile corps late in the operation.

Thus, there was a striking difference between the efficiency of Soviet *razvedka* during the planning phase of the operation and the performance of *razvedka* units once the operation was under way. While effective *razvedka* paved the way for a successful penetration operation, the reverse was true once the operation had begun. "Forces often unexpectedly pushed into large and small enemy groups and engaged them in combat, not knowing the extent of enemy defenses or their strength. As a result, forces conducted protracted battles with enemy rearguards, while large enemy groups were slipping away from encirclement and withdrawing to favorable natural positions."[111]

The Kotel' nikovo Operation

The Kotel'nikovo operation southwest of Stalingrad developed in two phases (see Map 7). During the first phase (12–23 December), the Stalingrad Front's 51st Army conducted a mobile defense against German LVII Panzer Corps from the Kotel'nikovo area northeast to the Myshkova River line. In the second phase (24–30 December) 2d Guards and 51st Armies attacked German forces and drove them back to the Sal River. The first phase of the operation was particularly delicate for the Soviets since German forces advanced to within 50 kilometers of encircled Sixth Army's perimeter.

Razvedka played an important role prior to 23 December, for accurate intelligence information was absolutely vital if Soviet forces adequate to halt the German advance were to be sent to the threatened region. Initially, on 27 November, Soviet 51st Army attempted to capture Kotel'nikovo but encountered strong counterattacks and was forced to withdraw. While ground combat indicated the presence of a substantial German force, reports from air *razvedka* were even more ominous. The 17th Air Army reconnaissance aircraft soon reported:

On 30 November a mixed column of vehicles is moving from Kotel'nikovo to Verkhne–Kumskii. At Kotel'nikovo the station is jammed with rail cars and seven trains with locomotives. Movement of mixed columns from Kotel'nikovo to Verkhne–Kumskii and the concentration of tanks and vehicles in the Tormosin, Suvorovskii region merits attention.[112]

Over the next few days further reports from ground and air *razvedka* "discovered the approach and concentration of enemy tanks and motorized columns a long time before the beginning of the enemy offensive. This made it possible to undertake timely countermeasures which subsequently led to the defeat of the enemy Kotel'nikovo group."[113] General K. A. Vershinin of 4th Air Army confirmed these reports, stating:

Great help was provided to our forces by air reconnaissance crews. Completing four to five flights per day, they observed all important objectives in the enemy defense. ... In determining the intentions of the enemy, the intelligence section of Lt. Col. G. A. Drozdov played a large role. Having analyzed various data received in the course of several days, he reached the correct conclusion: the Hitlerites are withdrawing two tank divisions from the Prokhladnyi, Mozdok region and are transferring them to the Stalingrad area.

Further observation of the pilots of Major Bardeev's regiment confirmed Drozdov's conclusions. Having passed through Armavir and Tikhopetsk, enemy trains returned to Sal'sk. As it later became clear, two tank divisions – 23d and SS "Viking" – were being transferred to Manstein's group, which was being created to relieve Sixth Army of Paulus, encircled in Stalingrad.[114]

Vasilevsky reacted promptly to the 12 December German attack by alerting 2d Guards Army on 13 December to prepare to move to the region southwest of Stalingrad and reinforce 51st Army's defense. After receiving Stalin's consent, 2d Guards Army moved southwest early on 15 December. Heavy fighting raged from 13 to 23 December as German forces drove northward and crossed to the northern bank of the Myshkova River where 51st Army, reinforced by lead elements of 2d Guards Army, finally halted the German advance.

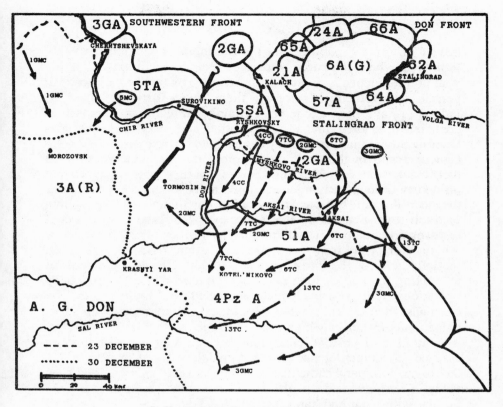

7. Kotel'nikovo Operation, December 1942

The remainder of the Kotel'nikovo operation developed almost in the fashion of a meeting engagement. The Soviet counterstroke began immediately after the German advance had ceased. The absence of prepared German defenses made formal planning for a penetration operation fruitless and, with it, planned *razvedka*. Thereafter, Soviet intelligence kept track of the operation's progress by means of air *razvedka*, radio intercepts, and, most important, ground combat reports. By 30 December, with German relief attempts thwarted, the Stalingrad operation was almost at an end. Subsequently, on 2 February after an extended reduction operation, German Sixth Army surrendered.

CONCLUSIONS

Soviet *razvedka* capabilities in the Stalingrad operation markedly improved when compared with their earlier performance. If the goal of intelligence is to provide an accurate picture of the enemy to permit achievement of victory, then Soviet *razvedka* must be judged to have been adequate. Certainly the Germans themselves contributed to their precarious situation and eased the task confronting Soviet intelligence. By choosing to operate both in the deep Caucasus and in the Stalingrad region, the Germans so strained their manpower and material resources that they were forced to rely on poorly trained and under-equipped allied forces to defend their extended flanks. This was an invitation for Soviet attack. By virtue of their over-extension, the Germans also lacked operational reserves and could create them only by further thinning out some other sector of the front, with all the incurrent risks. This situation partially solved the most serious Soviet *razvedka* problem of attempting to conduct long range surveillance of the German deep operational rear with inadequate air, agent, and radio assets. The Germans themselves created propitious circumstances for their defeat, circumstances which also eased the task of Soviet *razvedka*.

A number of positive conditions besides poor German strategy assisted Soviet intelligence efforts in the fall. After 18 months of war the Soviet command cadre had developed a keen appreciation of the value of *razvedka* and the effects of intelligence failures. All were familar with what had happened at Khar'kov in May 1942; and all realized this could not be permitted to happen again, for they could no longer trade away another 1,000 kilometers in order to restore a stable front. At Stalingrad, Soviet commanders and staffs understood what had to be done and, to an increasing extent, how to do it. Equipped with new and thorough regulations based on analysis of vast war experience, they had only to implement the regulation's provisions. Events proved that this was no mean task. At Stalingrad, the Red Army contained the nucleus of an articulated force structure necessary to carry out required *razvedka* tasks. The course of operations demonstrated that additional personnel training at all levels and more equipment was required to achieve full combat expectations. That, quite naturally, would also take time.

Equally important was the fact that the *STAVKA*, General Staff, and *fronts* had the time necessary to plan the operation thoroughly, a luxury they had not enjoyed a year before at Moscow. The one-month preparatory period permitted a studied Soviet approach to the problem of mounting a strategic offensive, and Soviet performance vividly demonstrated the value of that planning time. The planning process itself was the subject of study and analysis after the operation, a process which, in time, produced even greater dividends as the Soviets overcame problems evident in the Stalingrad operation. It was no coincidence that the Soviet system for analyzing war experiences emerged in the context of the Stalingrad operation.

Soviet *razvedka* performance was uneven in its effectiveness, but was markedly better than in the previous year. Strategic *razvedka* was still weak, due in part to the fragility of strategic collection systems and in part to lingering misperceptions on the part of the General Staff and *STAVKA* which tinged strategic estimates. The High Command, *fronts*, and armies had a crude air *razvedka* system and force structure, but a combination of factors including German air superiority, equipment shortages, and communications problems inhibited the system's performance. Air *razvedka* took place but was only partially effective. It detected many important German troop movements and concentrations in the deep German rear before and throughout the operation, but it could neither determine unit identification with any certainty nor could it precisely detect the direction of movement or ultimate destination of these units. Fortunately for the Soviets, there were few German reserves to detect.

A Soviet agent and reconnaissance-diversionary structure functioned during the Stalingrad operation but seems to have had only marginal effect on the operation's outcome. Moreover, no substantial partisan organization existed in southern Russia to emulate contributions of the partisans during the winter campaign of 1941–42 or to anticipate the extensive partisan warfare which would rage throughout central and northern Russia in 1943 and 1944. A few specialized radio *razvedka* units attempted radio intercepts in late 1942; and these, as well as regular communications units in the force structure, were able to log the identity of enemy units. However, their range was limited to the tactical and shallow operational depths.

At operational depths, Soviet intelligence relied on a combination of air, agent, reconnaissance-diversionary, radio, and long-range troop *razvedka*. While each means was subject to severe limitations, used in combination they were able to "sense," and sometimes clearly detect, changes in German dispositions and major troop movements. This was evident in all three operations. However, *razvedka* information was not exact enough to tell *precisely* where these units were heading. Consequently, the Stalingrad Front located German 22d Panzer Division by engaging it; and, later, the Southwestern Front, having detected reserves moving to Rossosh' and Kantemirovka, met and identified those reserves (German 385th Infantry and 27th Panzer Divsions) in combat south of the Don. Later in the same operation, 24th Tank Corps fell victim to German reserves (11th and 6th Panzer Divisions) at Tatsinskaya after Soviet air intelligence reports had earlier detected general German troop movements west of Tormosin. In short, collection systems were incomplete and thus imprecise. At Stalingrad this impeded but did not halt or abort operations. More refined systems were essential in the future lest the reverse be the case.

Soviet tactical *razvedka* made striking progress at Stalingrad in comparison with its earlier performance. This was so because it was absolutely necessary to solve the problem of penetrating enemy defenses; in part because the General Staff and higher commands paid tremendous attention to the problem; and, finally, in part because Soviet commanders now had the ability and the will to effect positive changes. Consequently, despite equipment problems, artillery *razvedka* worked particularly well in the 19–20 November attack. The 30 percent of total targets identified is impressive when one realizes most of these were in penetration sectors. Difficulties encountered along the middle Don resulted not from lack of proper procedure or target identification but rather from fog and bad weather which curtailed planned observed fire. Engineer *razvedka* was effective and also proved its worth, particularly in the November operation.

The tactical-scale reconnaissance in force preceding offensive operations also proved effective. They upset the stability of German and Axis defenses, clarified enemy firing and defensive systems, and improved jumping-off positions for main attacks. On several occasions they also induced complacency on the part of enemy units which felt they had successfully repelled an offensive and gained a respite from further combat. In time, however, the Soviets realized reconnaissance in force could become an attack indicator in its own right. They also learned that reconnaissance in force conducted unevenly across the front too many days prior to an offensive could defeat its own purpose if the enemy shuffled his forces prior to the attack. This was part and parcel of a learning process which prompted Soviet improvements of these techniques in the future.

Soviet *razvedka* was most effective during preparatory periods prior to major offensives. It was markedly less effective once operations had begun and during fluid combat. The Soviets also had difficulty in organizing *razvedka* while planning operations on the march. This recurring problem would have deadly consequences later in the winter during operations around Khar'kov and in the Donbas. In short, Soviet employment of *razvedka* at Stalingrad was a modest, if successful, beginning. Experiences at Stalingrad, both positive and negative, provided Soviet commanders and staffs with a blueprint for future improvements. The challenge to the Soviets was to act on that blueprint so that they could continue to achieve success in the future.

CHAPTER SIX

THE KURSK OPERATION

BACKGROUND: THE WINTER CAMPAIGN

After frustrating German attempts to relieve encircled Sixth Army, the *STAVKA* ordered its *fronts* in southern Russia to undertake a series of operations simultaneously with the destruction of the encircled force (see Map 8). The *STAVKA* applied maximum pressure on the Germans and their allies by conducting a series of successive *front* operations to collapse German defenses on the entire southern wing of the Eastern Front. Initially, these operations were well-planned, but as time passed, each successive operation became more hasty in nature. The last operations, begun in early February, were literally planned and conducted from the march. Initial operations incorporated detailed *razvedka* and *maskirovka* plans. Later operations were characterized by adequate intelligence collection but poor interpretation of data and lax implementation of *maskirovka* as increasingly overtaxed and exhausted Soviet units sought to deliver that last blow required to produce German collapse.

In January the Soviets initiated their offensives. As had been the case in November and December 1942, the Soviets sought first to smash the forces of Germany's allies. Simultaneously, the Soviets conducted operation *Kol'tso* (Ring) from 10 January to 2 February to reduce the Stalingrad pocket. German Sixth Army contributed to German efforts in the south by tying down seven Soviet armies of General K.K. Rokossovsky's Don Front, which could have had a telling effect if used to reinforce operations in other sectors of the front.

While operations to reduce Stalingrad proceeded, new Soviet offensives rippled along the front. On 13 January, General F. I. Golikov's Voronezh Front struck at the Hungarian Second Army and the remnants of Italian Eighth Army along the upper Don River. In the ensuing Ostrogozhsk–Rossosh' operation, which lasted until 27 January, the Soviets destroyed the Hungarian Second

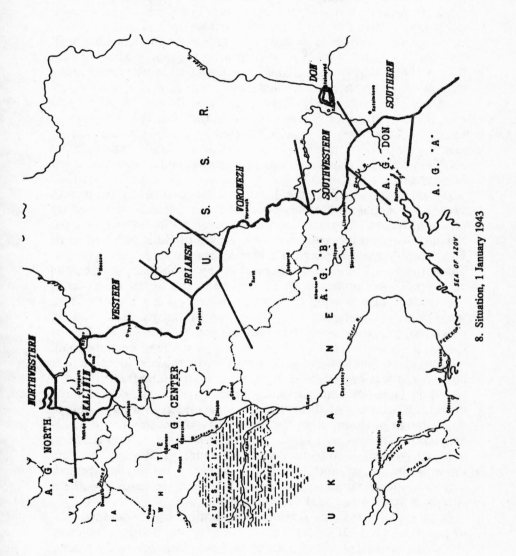

8. Situation, 1 January 1943

Army and Italian Alpine Corps and created a major gap south of German Second Army defending in the Voronezh sector. Simultaneously, General N. F. Vatutin's Southwestern Front resumed a slow, grinding advance westward. Further south, General A. I. Eremenko's (later Malinovsky's) Southern Front pushed toward Rostov, while Soviet forces in the northern Caucasus pressured the by now almost isolated German Army Group A. First Panzer Army of Army Group A barely escaped through Rostov to join Army Group Don before the Soviets slammed the door shut on German forces in the northern Caucasus by seizing the city. German Seventeenth Army (of Army Group A) withdrew slowly into fortified positions on the Kuban and Taman peninsulas and around the city of Novorossiisk.

By mid-January, with the Hungarian Second Army destroyed, the *STAVKA* planned a new operation to encircle and destroy German Second Army in the Voronezh area. On 24 January, the Briansk Front's 13th Army and three armies of Golikov's Voronezh Front began the Voronezh–Kastornoe operation against German Second Army. Within days, Second Army, with many of its units encircled, was forced to withdraw westward. It appeared as if the entire southern wing of German forces on the Eastern Front was about to collapse. In a burst of optimism, the *STAVKA* pondered plans to accelerate the offensive and force German forces back to the Dnepr River line and perhaps even beyond. Although the Soviets had displayed considerable skill at tactical and operational *razvedka* during and after the Stalingrad offensive and had standardized *razvedka* procedures to a considerable extent, the efficacy of those measures depended to a large degree on thorough planning. Thoroughness was a direct product of available time. Thus, where planning time was short or non-existent, although *razvedka* collection was adequate, processing the data tended to be sloppy, and the information was often mis-interpreted. This became apparent in the frantic Soviet drive across southern Russia in late January and February 1943.

Before the Voronezh–Kastornoe operation had concluded, the *STAVKA* ordered all its operating *fronts* in the south to conduct simultaneous offensive operations to force German Army Group Don to collapse (see Map 9). A collapse would result in destruction of that army group and Army Group A, which still occupied extended though hard-pressed positions in the Caucasus. While the Soviet Southern Front drove German forces westward toward

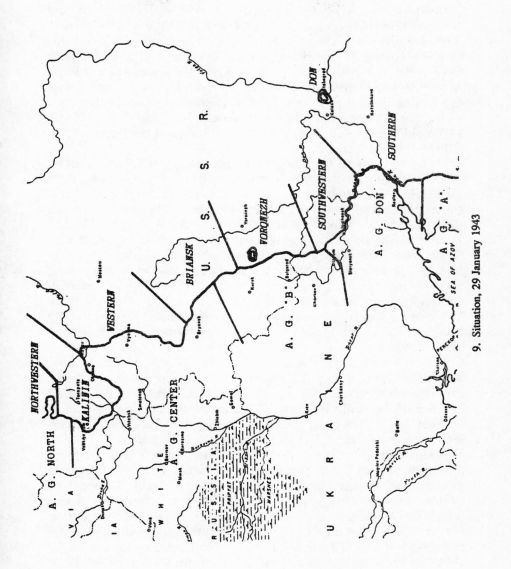

9. Situation, 29 January 1943

Rostov, the *STAVKA* ordered the Voronezh and Southwestern Fronts to strike the junction of Army Groups B and Don southeast of Khar'kov. The grand design of the *STAVKA* echoed Soviet offensive abandon evident in early 1942. The Voronezh Front was to seize Kursk, Belgorod, and Khar'kov and, if possible, push toward the Dnepr River southeast of Kiev. The Southwestern Front was to advance westward toward Izium and then swing south across the Northern Donets River, occupy Zaporozh'e and bridgeheads across the Dnepr, and ultimately reach the Sea of Azov near Melitopol', entrapping Army Group Don and isolating Army Group A in the Kuban area.

This grand design for a new and larger Stalingrad was fueled by *STAVKA* optimism that the Germans were nearing collapse, by a misreading of intelligence and German intentions, and by a woeful overestimation of their own force capabilities. The new offensives (later named the Khar'kov and Donbas operations) began in late January, from the march and without extensive planning. Although Soviet units individually conducted *razvedka*, it is doubtful if Soviet *front* and armies planned *razvedka* operations on the scale of those used at Stalingrad. The principal sources of intelligence in both operations were air and agent means, which apparently kept track of German troop movements in the operational depths, while troops in contact and ground *razvedka* determined German tactical dispositions.

Soviet forces swept westward through Kursk and Khar'kov, across the Northern Donets, and toward the Dnepr River in the rear of Army Group Don. While they advanced, unit strengths eroded because of the skillful German defense and the debilitating effects of time and distance on forces operating at the end of long and tenuous supply lines. The Germans reacted by holding firmly to positions along the shoulders of the penetration at Krasnograd and Slaviansk and by rapidly shifting large forces from the Caucasus through the Rostov "gate" into the Donets Basin (Donbas) to counter the exploiting Soviet forces. In one of the last major Soviet intelligence failures and the clearest cases of self-deception on the Eastern Front, the Soviets permitted optimism and over-confidence to cloud judgement. Soviet intelligence detected large-scale German redeployment of armored forces westward from Rostov toward the Dnepr but steadfastly interpreted those movements as a German withdrawal to new defensive positions along the Dnepr River. Consistently, the *STAVKA* and the *front* commands clung to their optimistic view as they spurred their advancing forces on, even as Soviet lower level commanders began to suspect and fear the worst.

By mid-February the Germans had contained the Soviet advance west of Kursk and short of Poltava, but Soviet forces were nearing the Dnepr River on a broad front north and south of Dnepropetrovsk. By this time Field Marshal von Manstein of Army Group Don had nearly completed orchestrating a regroupment which was about to bring to bear the force of three panzer corps against the flanks of advancing Soviet forces. Soviet army commanders' warnings went unheeded as message after message from the *STAVKA* and Southwestern Front headquarters urged their forces on. Soviet intelligence continued to misinterpret the clear evidence of major German troop concentrations south of Khar'kov and in the Donbas. A *STAVKA* directive dated 11 February reiterated the Southwestern Front's mission to block a German withdrawal to Dnepropetrovsk and Zaporozh'e and demanded the *front* undertake all measures to press the German Donets group into the Crimea, to close the passages into the Crimea through Perekop and Sivesh, and then to isolate these German forces from remaining German forces in the Ukraine.[1] This directive, and others, underscored the *STAVKA*'s belief that German forces were preparing to withdraw westward across the Dnepr River and that heavy German resistance at Slaviansk was designed to cover that withdrawal.

The advance of the Southwestern Front's armored spearhead (Mobile Group Popov) into the German rear area at Krasnoarmeiskoe reflected mistaken Soviet impressions. Even after Popov's force had been contained, on 19 February his lead 4th Guards Tank Corps received orders reflecting Soviet misperceptions. The corps commander, General P. P. Poluboiarov, received an order from the Front Military Council which read, "I order the encirclement and destruction of the enemy at Krasnoarmeiskoe. Fully restore the situation. Do not, in any case, permit an enemy withdrawal."[2] The order typified the air of unreality permeating the *STAVKA* and *front* headquarters. Within days, counterattacking German forces had decimated Popov's mobile force.

The mood of optimism within the *STAVKA* and General Staff persisted from the beginning of the operation and was based upon hard intelligence and the collective impression on the part of the Soviets of the immense damage done to German and their allied forces since 19 November. Three major armies: German Sixth, Italian Eighth, and Hungarian Second, had been erased from the German order of battle in the East. Fourth Panzer Army and

177

Second Army had been badly chewed up, and the remainder of German forces had suffered grievous losses. Surely, the Soviets reasoned, the trickle of reinforcements from the west could not compensate for these losses.

In a sense, Soviet High Command attitudes and actions in the winter of 1942–43 were a repeat, on a grander scale, of similar *STAVKA* behavior prevalent during the winter of 1941–42, when the *STAVKA* misread intelligence indicators and assigned unrealistic missions to overextended armies. That rashness and inability even to consider the necessity for restraint surfaced again in February 1943. As Soviet forces advanced, the *STAVKA* reverted to traditional offensive form and continually ignored the warnings of commanders who sensed impending disaster. *STAVKA* optimism also colored Soviet assessments of intelligence, which was collected in adequate quantities, but which was misassessed, since the High Command and the *fronts* placed their own rosy interpretation on German intentions. Information received from Western sources, although sketchy, tended to reinforce Soviet impressions.

Both the Southwestern and Voronezh Front commanders believed they were facing a panorama of German forces withdrawing towards the Dnepr River and safety. The Southwestern Front staff in particular erroneously assessed the large German regrouping as being the beginning of a German withdrawal. *Front* headquarters used that assessment to continue to rationalize the pursuit. Lt. General S. P. Ivanov, *front* Chief-of-Staff, and Maj. General A. S. Rogov, *front* Chief of Reconnaissance, signed an intelligence estimate which noted the concentration of large German armored units in the Krasnograd and Krasnoarmeiskoe region after 17 February but judged that these concentrations were designed "to strike a blow to liquidate a penetration of Soviet forces and to free communications for a withdrawal of forces in the Donbas territories across the Dnepr."[3] No partisan or agent reports contradicted this impression. The estimate concluded that "all information affirms that the enemy will leave the territory of the Don basin and withdraw his forces beyond the Dnepr." Vatutin underscored that judgement by stating, "Without a doubt the enemy is hurrying to withdraw his forces from the Donbas across the Dnepr."[4] He was so convinced of this German intent that he ignored repeated warnings from his army commanders that troop fatigue, equipment shortages, and growing enemy strength made it impossible to conduct simultaneous offensives in all sectors of the front. Instead he insisted on pressing to fulfill his mission of encircling and destroying the entire German Donbas group before the beginning of the spring thaw.

On the eve of the German counteroffensive (the afternoon and evening of 19 February and the morning of 20 February), Soviet air reconnaissance observed large German tank concentrations near Krasnograd, noted the forward movement of equipment from Dnepropetrovsk, and detected the regrouping of tank forces from the east between Pokrovskoe and Stalino toward Krasno-armeiskoe.[5] Nevertheless, in an estimate dated 1600 20 February, Lt. General S. P. Ivanov, Chief of Staff of Southwestern Front, assessed the movements of German XXXXVIII Panzer Corps as a withdrawal movement from the Donbas to Zaporozh'e. Based on that conclusion, Vatutin ordered his forces to continue their advance and demanded that the *front* mobile groups "fulfill their assigned mission at any cost."[6] According to 17th Air Army's official history, "Air *razvedka* carried out continuous observation of the withdrawal and regrouping of enemy forces and foresaw in timely fashion the approach and concentration of fresh enemy tank forces and infantry."[7] However, the higher commands consistently continued to misassess German intentions regarding these regrouped forces.

Southwestern Front optimism affected the attitude and actions of the Voronezh Front as well. A steady stream of information sent from the Southwestern Front to the Voronezh Front confirmed German intentions to withdraw and encouraged the Voronezh Front to speed up its offensive. German SS Panzer Corps' abandonment of Khar'kov on 16 February and its movement to Krasnograd simply reinforced that view. Golikov, the Voronezh Front commander, later admitted his error, stating, "It is necessary to recognize that at this stage I had an incorrect evaluation of the intent and capabilities of the enemy."[8]

As it had done earlier in the war, the *STAVKA* and General Staff reinforced the *front* commanders' optimism and compounded their mistakes. On 21 February, Lt. General A. N. Bogoliubov, Deputy Chief of the Operations Section of the General Staff, said, "We have exact data that the enemy in the evening is withdrawing in dense columns from the Donbas," when, in fact, those dense columns were about to participate in a violent counterattack.[9] These *STAVKA* and *front* misassessments persisted well after the Germans commenced their counteroffensive, and hindered Soviet ability to deal with the attacks. Only on 23 February, days after the devastating German counterstroke had begun, did the air of unreality enveloping the *STAVKA* and Southwestern Front head-quarters evaporate. By then it was too late, for Soviet forces were reeling back to the Northern Donets River after suffering heavy losses. Subsequently, in early March, von Manstein mauled the Voronezh Front and seized Khar'kov and Belgorod before Soviet reinforcements and the spring thaw brought operations to a halt.

The events of February and March had a sobering effect on the Soviet High Command. Once and for all it ended the Soviet tendency to launch offensives designed to succeed at all costs. Henceforth the Soviets would interpret intelligence data more cautiously and resist the natural impulse to let preconceptions rule over objective data. They also took a more jaundiced and prudent view of information provided by Western or "special" sources. A period of sober reflection on the part of the Soviets began, which endured to July 1943. That period was probably the most productive in the entire war for the Soviets in terms of force reorganization and analysis and incorporation of war experience into Red Army combat theory and practice. In the late spring and early summer of 1943 the Soviets created the basic force structure which would endure until war's end and drafted the directives and regulations which incorporated lessons learned at Stalingrad and during the winter. Subsequent Soviet combat performance at Kursk and there-after attested to the effectiveness of that Soviet study and analysis. In the realm of *razvedka* and *maskirovka* as well, the legacy of that analysis soon became clear.

GERMAN PLANNING FOR THE SUMMER OPERATION

After three months of almost constant combat activity had ended in the Soviet setbacks of February and March 1943, an operational lull set in on the Eastern Front (see Map 10). During the lull German planners pondered ways to regain the strategic initiative in the East by capitalizing on their March victories. Although the Germans considered several offensive plans, all in the south, their attention and that of Hitler was inexorably drawn to the Kursk bulge, which seemed to be a ripe target for envelopment. If the Soviets chose to defend it, it offered the opportunity to bleed the Red Army white in a relatively small sector without subjecting German forces to arduous operations over long distances, which had been the Germans' Achilles' heel in the past.

Ultimately, Hitler settled the issue. In Operational Orders No. 5 and No. 6 of 13 March and 15 April the High Command and Hitler

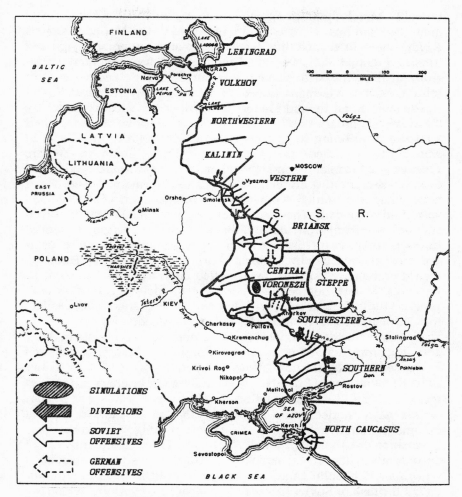

10. Situation, 4 July 1943: Soviet diversions, simulations, and counterstrokes, 12 July–16 August 1943

outlined German plans for projected operations against the Kursk Bulge, codenamed Zitadelle.[10] Operational Order No. 5 presumed Soviet forces would resume the offensive after the spring muddy season had ended. To forestall Russian action the order required Army Groups Center and South to prepare shock groups in the Orel and Khar'kov areas for a concerted attack converging on the Kursk bulge in mid-April. Thereafter Army Group North would strike again at Leningrad.

181

By 23 March the fluid situation around Kursk and Khar'kov had stabilized and Soviet forces had withdrawn to the Northern Donets River line. Hitler and the High Command temporarily ignored plans for "Zitadelle" and turned their attention to potential operations against the still shaken Russian forces defending east of Khar'kov. The Germans hoped to eliminate any renewed Soviet threat of a thrust toward Dnepropetrovsk (as in January and May 1942 and February 1943) and, at the same time, improve their strategic positioning for the conduct of "Zitadelle." On 22 and 24 March Hitler issued orders to Army Group South to prepare Operations "Habicht" and "Panther."[11] The former envisioned German seizure of a bridgehead across the Northern Donets River from Chuguev through Kupiansk to Izium as soon as the swollen river had subsided. The latter was larger in scale and involved seizure of territory on the east bank of the river from Belgorod through Sviatovo. This operation would definitely require postponement of "Zitadelle." On 2 April Hitler decided "Habicht" would commence on four days' notice any day after 13 April. If, however, it had not begun by 17 April, then "Panther" would proceed by 1 May. In the event that neither operation was feasible, the Germans would focus on "Zitadelle" instead.

Since the Northern Donets River did not recede until late in April and the commander of Army Group South, von Manstein, declared his forces unready for new offensive operations, on 15 April Hitler issued Operational Order No. 6 cancelling preliminary offensives and ordering full implementation of "Zitadelle," which was to start on six days' notice some time after 28 April. "Panther" would commence shortly thereafter to take advantage of Soviet preoccupation with the "Zitadelle" attack. Throughout subsequent periods up to the actual attack date, troop movements associated with both "Zitadelle" and "Panther" occurred in tandem, complicating the task of Soviet *razvedka* as it strove to determine where the German main effort would occur.

No sooner had Hitler established 3 May as the attack date than new problems arose, forcing delay after delay. First, slow deployment of Ninth Army into the Orel region forced postponement of the operation, and then heavy rains in the region prompted additional delays. Finally, on 30 April the High Command postponed the operation indefinitely until Hitler could confer with his commanders on a new attack date. At a subsequent 3 May conference with his staff and senior field commanders, Hitler debated the pros and cons of the operation, often heatedly, and raised the issue of delaying the operation until new critical weapons systems had been fielded in requisite quantities to affect the operation's outcome. Ultimately, the conference ended with yet another postponement, but with Hitler still committed to the concept of "Zitadelle." Three days later the High Command announced that "Zitadelle" would begin on 12 June, but that date was postponed as well. Despite considerable opposition from the OKW and field commands, on 20 June Hitler announced his final decision to go ahead with the offensive. Five days later he established 5 July as the date of the attack.[12]

Diminished German strength on the Eastern Front relative to 1941 and 1942 made it difficult for the German High Command to mask their attack intentions and the general location of the offensive. It was clear German strength permitted but one strategic blow along only a limited strategic axis. The very existence of the Kursk bulge made it the most obvious target. Despite these realities, there were compelling reasons to prompt Soviet uncertainty regarding when and where the attack would occur. As was the case in spring 1942, the Germans attempted some deception:

> In order to disguise the fact that this time Germany could only mount a limited offensive and as a hedge against the possibility that even this could miscarry, Jodl instructed Wehrmacht Propaganda to depict "Zitadelle" as a counteroffensive, thereby creating the impression of a strong defensive capability and establishing an alibi in advance in case "Zitadelle" failed.[13]

German indecision regarding attack timing certainly generated Soviet confusion, for the Soviets expected, and prepared for, German attacks on at least three occasions in the period from 1 May to 5 July. Each incorrect prediction tended to cast doubt on subsequent predictions. Moreover, the existence of several German plans ("Zitadelle," "Habicht" and "Panther"), and troop movements associated with each, made it difficult to ascertain exactly where the main blow would occur and how extensive the attack sector was to be. This confusion persisted, in fact, right up to 5 July, despite mounting positive attack indicators north and south of Kursk.

The German operational plan for the Kursk operation involved nearly simultaneous strikes by two large panzer forces against narrow sectors of the Soviet front north and south of Kursk.[14] The forces designated to deliver the dual blows would slash through Soviet defenses, unite near Kursk, and fan out to obliterate Soviet troops and weapons in the bulge. In the north, Ninth Army's XXXXVII Panzer Corps (2d, 6th, 9th Panzer Divisions, 20th Panzer Grenadier Division, 6th Infantry Division) would spearhead the attack by advancing south along the rail and highway line to Kursk in order to link up with Fourth Panzer Army forces advancing from the south. XXXXVI Panzer Corps (7th, 31st, 102d, 258th Infantry Divisions, von Manteufel Group) would cover XXXXVII Panzer Corps' right flank, and XXXXI Army Corps (86th, 292d Infantry Divisions, 18th Panzer Division) would cover the assault force's left flank. The 4th and 12th Panzer Divisions and the 10th Panzer Grenadier Division would be available to reinforce the attack. A total of over 1,200 tanks and self-propelled guns would strike the Soviet positions on a front of less than thirty kilometers with about 900 tanks and assault guns in units immediately available for combat.

In the south, Fourth Panzer Army and Army Detachment Kempf would strike north and northeast from positions west and south of Belgorod to smash Soviet defenses and link up with Ninth Army forces near Kursk. Fourth Panzer Army would deliver its main attack with XXXXVIII Panzer Corps (3d, 11th Panzer Divisions, "Gross Deutschland" Panzer Grenadier Division, 167th and 332d Infantry Divisions, Panther Brigade Decker) and II SS Panzer Corps (SS Panzer Divisions "Das Reich," "Totenkopf," and "Leibstandarte Adolf Hitler" advancing abreast north and northeast from positions west of Belgorod. On Fourth Panzer Army's right flank, Army Detachment Kempf would penetrate Soviet defenses west of Belgorod and push III Panzer Corps (168th Infantry Division, 6th, 7th, 19th Panzer Divisions) either northeast in cooperation with II SS Panzer Corps or eastward toward Korocha. The combined force of Fourth Panzer Army and Army Detachment Kempf's 1,500 tanks and assault guns would complete destruction of Soviet forces south of Kursk. Thus, the Germans amassed the most impressive armored armada yet assembled for a single attack. Considering the fact that up to July 1943 no German strategic offensive had ever failed to achieve immediate tactical and operational success, the Soviet High Command had genuine cause for concern.

SOVIET PLANNING FOR THE SUMMER CAMPAIGN

STAVKA planners had debated military strategy since German planners had begun their work in April. Stalin argued for a resumption of the offensive in the summer to pre-empt German actions, while Zhukov, Vasilevsky, and the General Staff urged caution and initial adoption of a defensive posture until the Germans had expended their offensive strength. Then, they argued, Soviet forces could launch a strategic offensive with a reasonable chance of success. On 8 April Zhukov dispatched to Stalin an extensive strategic appreciation concerning prospective German operations and the advisable Soviet response:

> To Comrade Vasilyev [Stalin's codename]
> 5:30 a.m., April 8, 1943
> I hereby state my opinion on the possible movements of the enemy in the spring and summer of 1943 and our plans for defensive actions in the coming months.
> 1. Having suffered serious losses in the winter campaign of 1942–43, the enemy would not appear to be able to build up big reserves by the spring to resume the offensive on the Caucasus and to push forward to the Volga to make a wide enveloping movement around Moscow.
> Owing to the inadequacy of large reserves, in the spring and first half of the summer of 1943 the enemy will be forced to launch offensive operations on a smaller front and resolve the task facing him strictly in stages, his main aim being the taking of Moscow.
> Proceeding from the fact that, at the given moment, there are groupings deployed against our Central, Voronezh and South-Western Fronts, I believe that the enemy's main offensives will be spearheaded at these fronts, in order to rout our forces on this sector and to gain freedom for his maneuvers to outflank Moscow and get as close to it as possible.
> 2. At the first stage, having gathered as many of his forces as possible, including at least 13 to 15 tank divisions and large air support, the enemy will evidently deal the blow with his Orel–Kromy grouping in the enveloping movement around Kursk from the north-east and likewise with the Belgorod–Kharkov grouping from the south-east.
> An additional attack on Kursk from the south-west aimed at

dividing our front must be expected from the west, from the area around Vorozhba between the rivers Seim and Psyel. The enemy will attempt by means of this operation to defeat and surround our 13th, 70th, 65th, 38th, 40th, and 21st Armies, his ultimate purpose at this stage being to reach the River Korocha–Korocha–Tim–River Tim–Droskovo line.

3. At the second stage, the enemy will attempt to come out on the flank and in the rear of the South-Western Front, his general direction being through Valuiki–Urazovo.

To counter this offensive, the enemy may deal a blow at the Lisichansk area on a northern, Svatovo–Urazovo sector.

In the remaining sectors the enemy will strive to reach the Livny–Kastornoye–Stary and Novy Oskol line.

4. At the third stage, after the corresponding regrouping, the enemy will possibly try to reach the Liski–Voronezh–Yelets front and, taking cover in a south-eastern direction, may launch an offensive as part of the wide enveloping movement around Moscow from the south-east via Ranenburg–Ryazhsk–Ryazan.

5. In his offensive operations this year the enemy may be expected to count chiefly on his tank divisions and air force since his infantry is at present considerably less well prepared for offensive action than it was last year.

At the present time, the enemy has as many as 12 tank divisions lined up along the Central and Voronezh Fronts and, by taking in three or four tank divisions from other sectors, he could pitch as many as 15 or 16 tank divisions with some 2,500 tanks against our Kursk grouping.

6. If the enemy is to be crushed by our defensive formations, besides measures to build up the anti-tank defences on the Central and Voronezh Fronts, we must get together 30 anti-tank artillery regiments from the passive sectors as rapidly as possible and redeploy them as part of the Supreme Command's reserves in the areas threatened; all the regiments of the self-propelled artillery must be concentrated in the Livny–Kastornoye–Stary Oskol sector. Even now it would be desirable for some of the regiments to be placed under Rokossovsky and Vatutin as reinforcements and for as many aircraft as possible to be transferred to the Supreme Command's reserves to smash the shock groupings with massed attacks from the air coordinated with action by tank and rifle formations and to frustrate the plan for the enemy's offensive.

I am not familiar with the final location of our operational reserves; therefore I believe it expedient to propose their deployments in the Yefremov–Livny–Kastornoye–Novy Oskol–Valuiki–Rossosh–Liski–Voronezh–Yelets area. The deeper reserve echelon should be deployed around Ryazhsk, Ranenburg, Michurinsk, and Tambov.

There must be one reserve army in the Tula–Stalinogorsk area.

I do not believe it is necessary for our forces to mount a preventive offensive in the next few days. It will be better if we wear the enemy out in defensive actions, destroy his tanks, and then, taking in fresh reserves, by going over to an all-out offensive we will finish off the enemy's main grouping.

"Konstantinov" [Zhukov's codename][15]

In his appreciation, Zhukov highlighted the most critical attack indicator – the movement and concentration of German armored forces.

Zhukov's assessment was reinforced by those of *front* commanders and chiefs of staff who forwarded their appreciations for *STAVKA* consideration. A 10 April report by the Central Front Chief of Staff, Lieutenant-General M. S. Malinin, echoed Zhukov's view:

From the Central Front, April 10, 1943
To the Operations Chief, General Staff of the Red Army
Colonel-General Antonov
4. The objective and most probable directions of the enemy offensive in the spring and summer period of 1943:
a) Taking into account the forces and means and, what is most important, the outcome of the offensives in 1941 and 1942, in the spring and summer period of 1943 an enemy offensive is to be expected solely in the Kursk and Voronezh operational direction.

There is hardly likely to be an enemy offensive on other sectors.

The general strategical situation being as it is at this stage in the war, it would be to the Germans' benefit to ensure a firm hold on the Crimea, the Donbas and the Ukraine and, for that purpose, to advance the front to the Shterovka–Starobelsk–Rovenki–Liski–Voronezh–Livny–Novosil line. To achieve this, the enemy will require no less than 60 infantry divisions with the corresponding air, tank and artillery support.

The enemy cannot concentrate such forces and means on the given sector.

This is why the Kursk–Voronezh operational direction is acquiring paramount importance.

b) Proceeding from these operational suppositions, the enemy is expected to direct his main efforts simultaneously along inner and outer radii of action:

along the inner radius – from the Orel area via Kromy to Kursk and from the Belgorod area to Kursk via Oboyan;

along the outer radius – from the Orel area via Livny to Kastornoye and from the Belgorod area to Kastornoye via Stary Oskol.

c) If we do not take measures to counter the intended enemy offensive, his successful operations on these sectors could lead to the rout of the forces of the Central and Voronezh Fronts, to the capture by the enemy of the vital Orel–Kursk–Kharkov railway line and to the attainment by his forces of an advantageous line to his firm hold on the Crimea, the Donbas, and the Ukraine.

d) The enemy cannot set about regrouping and concentrating his forces in the probable directions of his offensive and also building up the necessary reserves until the end of spring when the roads have improved and the floods ended.

Consequently, the enemy may be expected to go over to a decisive offensive in the second half of May 1943.

5. In the circumstances obtained in the given operational situation the following measures are deemed expedient:

a) To destroy the enemy Orel grouping by the joint efforts of the forces of the Western, Bryansk, and Central Fronts, thereby depriving him of the opportunity of dealing a blow at Kastornoye from the Orel area via Livny, of seizing the Mtsensk–Orel–Kursk railway, which is vital to us, and preventing the enemy from using the Bryansk network of railways and dirtroads.

b) To foil the enemy offensive operations, the forces on the Central and Voronezh Fronts must be reinforced with aircraft, mainly fighters, and anti-tank artillery, not less than 10 regiments being sent to each front.

c) For this purpose, it is desirable to have strong Supreme Command reserves in the Livny-Kastornoye-Liski-Voronezh-Yelets area.

Lieutenant-General Malinin
Chief of Staff, Central Front.[16]

Likewise, Vatutin and his staff provided a Voronezh Front assessment, which read:

To the Chief of General Staff of the Red Army, April 12, 1943

At the present time, it has been established that the Voronezh Front is confronted by:

1. Nine infantry divisions in the first line (26th, 68th, 323rd, 75th, 255th, 57th, 332d, 167th, and one unidentified). These divisions are positioned along the Krasno Oktyabrskoye–Bolshaya Chernetchina–Krasnopolye–Kazatskoye front. According to the information furnished by prisoners, the unidentified division is advancing toward the Soldatskoye area and is to replace the 332d Infantry Division.

These data are being checked. Information is available but has not been checked that there are six infantry divisions in the second echelon. Their position has not yet been established, and these data are also being verified.

According to radio intelligence, the headquarters of a Hungarian division has been located in the Kharkov area, which may be moved forward in a secondary direction.

2. At present, there are only six tank divisions (Gross Deutschland, Adolf Hitler, Totenkopf, Das Reich, the 6th and the 11th). Of these three are in the front line and the other three (Gross Deutschland, the 6th and the 11th) in the second line. According to radio intelligence, the headquarters of the 17th Panzer Division has moved from Alekseyevsky to Tashchagovka, which indicates that this division is moving northwards. With his present forces, the enemy can bring as many as three more tank divisions into the Belgorod area from the South-Western Front sector.

3. Thus, the enemy is likely to set up a shock group of up to ten tank divisions and not less than six infantry divisions, all in all as many as 1,500 tanks to counter the Voronezh Front; this concentration of forces may be expected in the Borisovka–Belgorod–Murom–Kazachya Lopan area. This shock group may have air support with an effective strength of approximately 500 bombers and no less than 300 fighters.

It is the enemy's intention to strike blows concentrically from the Belgorod area to the north-east and from the Orel area to the south-east in order to surround our forces deployed to the west of the Belgorod–Kursk line. Subsequently an enemy offensive is to be expected on the south-eastern sector at the flank and rear of the South-western Front with the objective of eventually pushing northwards.

It is not out of the question, however, that the enemy will decide not to launch an offensive to the south-east this year and will put another plan into effect, namely, after the attacks made concentrically from the Belgorod and Orel areas, he will pursue an offensive to the northeast for the purpose of a wide enveloping movement around Moscow.

This possibility must be taken into account and the reserves prepared accordingly.

Thus, opposite the Voronezh Front, the enemy will probably spearhead his main offensive from the Borisovka–Belgorod area on the Stary Oskol sector, with part of his forces moving toward Oboyan and Kursk. Additional attacks are to be expected on the Volchansk–Novy Oskol and Sudzha–Oboyan–Kursk sectors.

The enemy is not yet ready to launch a big offensive. The offensive is not expected to begin earlier than April 20, but most likely in early May.

However, individual attacks may be expected at any time. Therefore, we demand that our forces be in a constant state of full combat readiness.

Fedorov, Nikitin, Fedotov[17]

On 12 April, at a meeting in Moscow, Zhukov, Vasilevsky, and Chief of the General Staff's operations department, Lieutenant General A. I. Antonov argued their case with Stalin. Armed with messages of support from *front* commanders, the three convinced Stalin of the necessity for an initial defensive phase of the summer strategic offensive. General S. M. Shtemenko, First Deputy of the Operations Department, wrote:

> Ultimately it was decided to concentrate our main forces in the Kursk area, to bleed the enemy forces here in a defensive operation, and then switch to the offensive and achieve their complete destruction. To provide against eventualities, it was considered necessary to build deep and secure defenses along the whole strategic front, making them particularly powerful in the Kursk sector.[18]

Consequently, in late April the Central and Voronezh Fronts began constructing defenses in the Kursk area in accordance with *STAVKA* instructions signaling preliminary intentions to undertake at first a deliberate defense preparatory to launching a general strategic counteroffensive. At this stage it was fairly clear that the Voronezh, Central, Southwestern, and Briansk Fronts were to be the focal point of temporary defensive efforts. Of equal importance was the question of deploying strategic reserves to cover any eventuality. Zhukov described the rationale for distributing those reserves:

> At the same time it was decided in which sectors the Supreme Command's main reserves should be concentrated. It was intended to deploy them in the Livny–Stary Oskol–Korocha area where defences were to be organized should the enemy break through in the Kursk Bulge area. Other reserves were to be stationed behind the right flank of the Bryansk Front in the Kaluga–Tula–Yefremov area. The 5th Guards Tank Army and a number of other formations of the Supreme Command's reserves were to prepare for action beyond the junction of the Voronezh and Southwestern Fronts, in the Liski area.[19]

Shtemenko, on the General Staff, attested to Stalin's caution, writing:

> No one had any doubts that the Central and Voronezh Fronts would play the main role in the defensive actions. It was not impossible that the Briansk and Southwestern Fronts would also participate in this. Zhukov and Malinovsky were convinced that the Southwestern Front would be attacked. Since its own reserves were not strong enough, they insisted that an army or, at least, a tank corps, from the GHQ reserves should be stationed behind its junction with the Voronezh Front.[20]

Since Stalin would not rule out the possibility of German diversionary attacks in other sectors of the front, on 21 April he signed a directive reinforcing defenses elsewhere. Nevertheless, his principal strategic reserve force remained the Steppe Military District. This force, created in mid-March, by late April numbered six armies, one tank army, and several separate corps. On 23 April the *STAVKA* issued the Steppe Military District new instructions, which read:

> If the enemy assumes the offensive before the District's forces are ready, care must be taken to cover the following sectors securely: (1) Livny, Yelets, Ranenburg; (2) Shchigry, Kastornoye, Voronezh; (3) Valuiki, Alekseyevka, Liski; (4) Rovenki, Rossosh', Pavlovsk; (5) Starobelsk, Kantemirovka, Boguchar, and the Chertkovo, Millerovo area. ...[21]

SOVIET MILITARY INTELLIGENCE IN WAR

This placed Steppe Military District armies in position to counter German action across a broad front, from Orel in the north to Voroshilograd in the south. These dispositions covered virtually all potential German axes of advance, and, not coincidentally, dealt with all three German operational plans ("Zitadelle," "Habicht," and "Panther").

On 2 May, as defensive preparations proceeded apace, intelligence indicators produced the first of several *STAVKA* warnings that an attack might materialize in the near future. Zhukov noted:

> The Supreme Command had carried out thorough intelligence and aerial reconnaissance which had gained reliable information on the enemy flows of troops and ammunition towards the Orel, Kromy, Bryansk, Kharkov, Krasnograd and Poltava sectors. This confirmed the correctness of our forecasts in April. The Stavka and General Staff became increasingly of the opinion that the German forces might mount an offensive in the next few days.[22]

Although the attack did not materialize, the *STAVKA* heightened force readiness and on 5 May issued a directive which provided evidence for increased vigilance and mandated conduct of a preemptive air offensive. It read:

> Recently considerable movement of enemy forces and transport has been noted into the Orel, Belgorod, and Khar'kov regions as well as movement of forces to the front lines. This forces us to expect active enemy operations in the near future.
>
> The *STAVKA* of the High Command draws your attention to the necessity of
> 1. Full implementation of the plan to employ frontal aviation to destroy enemy aviation and disrupt the work of rail lines and highways.
> 2. Maximum attention to *razvedka* of all kinds, in order to reveal the enemy grouping and intentions. In these days without fail we must have prisoners daily, especially in important front sectors. ...
>
> A. Vasilevsky, Antonov[23]

Consequently, on 8 May the *STAVKA* sent the following directive to the Briansk, Central, Voronezh, and Southwestern Fronts:

> According to certain information, the enemy may begin an offensive between 10 and 12 May in the Oryol–Kursk or the

Belgorod–Oboyan direction, or in both directions at once. The GHQ instructs you to have all troops of both the first line of defence and the reserves in full combat readiness by the morning of 10 May on order to meet the possible enemy attack. Pay particular attention to aviation readiness so that you can not only repel the enemy air attacks in the event of the enemy launching an offensive, but you can gain air superiority from the very first moment of his active operations.

J. Stalin, A. Vasilevsky[24]

The *STAVKA* dispatched a similar message to the Steppe Front

> to speed up as much as possible the manning of the military district troops and, by the morning of 10th May, have all your available troops in full combat readiness both for defence and for active operation on GHQ instructions. Pay particular attention to the readiness of the air force meeting possible attacks by enemy aircraft on our airfields and troops.[25]

Characteristically, Stalin still harbored thoughts of conducting some sort of pre-emptive action. After extensive deliberations with his advisors and commanders, however, Stalin finally agreed to a strategic defense, but only after deciding to incorporate into those plans extensive pre-emptive air activity and planned counter-offensives, which would begin after the German assaults had been halted. Although the German offensive had not materialized, by mid-May Stalin and the *STAVKA* pressed on with their mixed defensive-offensive efforts. The first of those pre-emptive actions occurred between 6–13 May, when Soviet air units struck at German airfields. Once again in late May the *STAVKA* sensed an impending attack. This prediction was based, in part, on reports by Zhukov of the situation confronting the Voronezh and Central Fronts. Regarding the latter, on 22 May Zhukov reported:

> To Comrade Ivanov [Stalin's codename]
> The situation on the Central Front on May 21, 1943 was as follows:
> 1. By May 21 reconnaissance of all kinds has established that before the Central Front the enemy has 15 infantry divisions in the first line and 13 divisions, including three panzer divisions, in the second line.
> There is, moreover, information about the concentration of the 2nd Panzer Division and the 36th Motorised Infantry

Division south of Orel. The information about these two divisions requires verification.

The enemy's 4th Panzer Division, formerly deployed west of Sevsk, has been moved somewhere. Besides, there are three divisions, two of them panzer, in the Bryansk and Karachev area.

Consequently, as of May 21 the enemy can operate with 33 divisions, six of them panzer divisions, against the Central Front.

The Front's instrumental and visual reconnaissance has detected 800 artillery pieces, mainly 105 mm and 150 mm guns.

The enemy keeps the bulk of his artillery opposite the 13th Army, the left flank of the 48th Army and the right flank of the 70th Army, i.e., in the Trosno—Pervoye—Pozdeyevo sector. Behind this main artillery grouping there are 600–700 tanks on the Zmeyevka–Krasnaya Roshcha line. The bulk is concentrated east of the River Oka.

In the area of Orel, Briansk and Smolensk the enemy has concentrated 600–650 warplanes. The main enemy air grouping is in the Orel area.

Both on the ground and in the air the enemy has been passive in the last few days, confining himself to small-scale air reconnaissance and occasional minor artillery attacks.

In his forward line and his tactical depth, the enemy is digging trenches and intensively fortifying his positions in front of the 13th Army, in the Krasnaya Slobodka—Senkovo sector, where he already has a second defence line beyond the River Neruch. Observation reveals that the enemy is building a third defence line in this sector, 3–4 kilometres north of the Neruch.

Prisoners say the German Command knows about our grouping south of Orel and our planned offensive, and that German units have been warned. Captured airmen claim that the German Command is itself preparing for an offensive and concentrating aviation for this purpose.

I personally visited the forward lines of the 13th Army, observed the enemy defences from various points, watched his activity, and talked with divisional commanders of the 70th and 13th Armies, with commanders Galanin, Pukhov and Romanenko, and came to the conclusion that in the forward line the enemy was not making direct preparations for an offensive.

I may be mistaken. It may be that the enemy is camouflaging

his preparations for an offensive very skilfully. But an analysis of the deployment of his armor, the inadequate density of infantry formations, absence of heavy artillery groupings as well as the dispersion of reserves lead me to believe that the enemy will not be ready to launch an offensive before the end of May.[26]

According to Vasilevsky, Stalin again had fleeting thoughts of pre-emptive action:

On 20 May the General Staff, on the basis of freshly received information on enemy movements, warned the fronts with Stalin's permission that the Nazi offensive was expected no later than 26 May. After the first warning, when it had not been confirmed, the military council of the Voronezh Front regarded this as being due to a certain wavering on the part of the foe, perhaps even a rejection of the whole idea of an offensive; it therefore asked Stalin to decide on the question of whether to launch the initial blow at the enemy. Stalin took a serious interest in this proposition and it took all that we – Zhukov, myself and Antonov – could do to dissuade him from it.[27]

This scare, however, also passed; and by the end of the month the entire *STAVKA* resolved itself to the conduct of an initial strategic defensive.

As reported by Zhukov:

The final decision concerning the deliberate defense was accepted by the *STAVKA* at the end of May and beginning of June 1943 when it became known, in fact in all its details, about the German intention to strike the Voronezh and Central Fronts a strong blow by the use of large tank groups and new "Tiger" tanks and "Ferdinand" assault guns.[28]

The resulting strategic plan required the Voronezh and Central Fronts to defend the Kursk Bulge, flanked on the north by the Briansk Front and on the south by the Southwestern Front. In the rear the *STAVKA* created a large strategic reserve, the Steppe Military District, which would ultimately become the Steppe Front. Since, throughout April, Soviet planners were uncertain of the direction of the main German thrust, which they assumed would be against Kursk or south of Khar'kov, the *STAVKA* ordered all five *fronts* to erect strong defenses. Initially, the Steppe Military District's reserve armies, formed around the nucleus of 5th Guards

Tank Army, assembled in the Liski area east of Khar'kov in positions from which they could deploy to meet either German thrust. For the first time in the war the *STAVKA* formulated a general strategic plan incorporating broad *razvedka* and *maskirovka* measures which assisted in the defensive phase and concealed preparations for subsequent offensive operations.

The *STAVKA* assigned initial defensive missions to all *fronts* but, at the same time, ordered them to prepare two major counterstrokes, the first to begin during the German offensive and the second to follow shortly after the German offensive had ended. The *STAVKA* also ordered extensive *razvedka* measures to determine German intentions and dispositions and strict deception measures to conceal the assembly and redeployment of the strategic reserve – the Steppe Military District. During the defensive phase of the operation, based on intelligence information, the Soviets ordered *fronts* in other sectors to undertake diversionary offensives of their own, timed to draw German operational reserves away from the point where the Soviet counterstrokes would occur. The Soviets also planned to deliver against the concentrated German forces, once that concentration had been detected, major pre-emptive air and artillery counterpreparations to disrupt the final stage of German deployment.

Specific missions assigned to Soviet *fronts* reflected these extensive plans. The Voronezh and Central Fronts erected substantial defenses within the Kursk Bulge and, while concealing as much of their forces and preparations as possible, prepared to meet and defeat potential German assaults on Kursk from the north and south. Other *fronts* on the flanks defended along other critical axes and prepared counterstrokes as well. The Steppe Military District deployed at sufficient depth to cover all strategic axes; and, if the attack materialized around Kursk, it prepared to displace secretly northward to occupy assembly areas east of Kursk, back up the two forward *fronts*, repulse German penetrations, and launch a major counterstroke on the Belgorod–Khar'kov axis after the defensive phase at Kursk had ended. If Kursk was the German target, the Briansk Front and left wing of the Western Front postured to support the Central Front's defense and to prepare a major counterstroke against German forces at Orel as soon as the Central Front had halted the German advance. The Southwestern and Southern Fronts prepared diversionary attacks in the Donbas and along the Mius River, whose purpose Zhukov described, "In order to tie down enemy forces and forestall maneuver of his reserves, individual offensive operations were envisioned in a number of directions in the south of the country, and also in the northwestern direction."[29]

Thus, Soviet strategic planning called for one initial deliberate defense, followed by a massive counteroffensive, extensive use of *razvedka*, and implementation of a comprehensive strategic deception plan.[30] While initial defensive operations unfolded, large troop concentrations would secretly assemble and launch a massive counterstroke against German forces at Orel to support the Kursk defenders. Within days of the Kursk defenders halting the German advance, a second, secret, force regroupment would take place followed by a second massive counterstroke toward Belgorod and Khar'kov. During the interval between the first and second counterstrokes, the Southern and Southwestern Fronts would conduct diversionary offensives across the Northern Donets and Mius rivers into the Donbas. Preparations for these diversions would occur during the German offensive phase, and it was intended that the Germans detect those offensive preparations (which they did). The strategic plan also included pre-emptive artillery and air strikes and extensive defense preparations within the Kursk bulge, concealed as much as possible. Success in all aspects of the strategic plan depended, in part, on the accuracy of Soviet intelligence.

Zhukov and Vasilevsky supervised preparation and conduct of the Kursk strategic operation. *Front* and army commanders in the Kursk bulge exerted tremendous efforts to create deeply echeloned and firepower-intensive defenses while ensuring the secrecy of the preparations. *Razvedka* and deception measures were extensive. Building upon the experiences of earlier operations, the Central, Voronezh, and Steppe Front staffs prepared detailed *razvedka* and deception plans which exploited all intelligence collection assets and included concealment of preparations, creation of false troop concentrations, simulation of false radio nets and communications centers, construction of false air facilities and mock-up aircraft, and dissemination of false rumors along the front and in the enemy rear area.[31] These plans also included collation of information from all intelligence sources, secret movement of reserves, hidden preparations for counterattacks and counterstrokes, and concealed locations of command posts and communications sites.

As defensive planning progressed, tension built within the *STAVKA*. Vasilevsky later reflected:

As a result of constant and very careful military observation of the enemy on both the Voronezh and the Central Fronts, as well as the information being received from all forms of intelligence, we knew precisely that the Nazis were fully prepared for the offensive. And yet for some reason or other the offensive did not come. It was this "for some reason or other" that gave us some anxiety and knocked some people out of their stride.[32]

Anxiety produced renewed calls for offensive action by some commanders (Vatutin); but, regardless, the *STAVKA* held firm to its plans.

After 20 June most *STAVKA* members were convinced the attack would come in the near future. Vasilevsky and Zhukov thought it would occur during the week after 22 June, but, again, the time passed without incident, although intelligence indicators mounted. Zhukov described the impact of those indicators:

> The situation finally became clear in the last few days of June, and we realized that the enemy would mount an offensive in the coming days precisely here in the Kursk area and nowhere else.
>
> Stalin telephoned me on June 30. He ordered me to remain on the Orel sector to coordinate the operations of the Central, Briansk, and Western Fronts.
>
> "Vasilevsky is in command on the Voronezh Front," said the Supreme Commander.[33]

Zhukov added that on 2 July "the *STAVKA* warned the commanders of the Fronts that the enemy's offensive was anticipated between July 3 and July 6."[34]

Vasilevsky provided a more complete description of the measures he immediately undertook:

> On the night of 2 July the information received at General Staff from our intelligence section told us that in the next few days, at any rate no later than 6 July, the enemy's offensive on the Kursk Front was bound to begin. I instantly reported this to Stalin and asked permission to warn the Fronts at once. I then read to him the prepared draft GHQ directive: "From existing information, the Germans may launch an offensive on our front between 3 and 6 July. The GHQ orders you as follows: 1. To strengthen intelligence and observation of the enemy for the purpose of exposing his intentions in time. 2. To see

that the troops and air force are ready to repel a possible enemy attack. 3. To report on the instructions issued."

Stalin approved the text of the directive during the night of 2 July and it was dispatched to the commanders of the Western, Briansk, Central, Voronezh, Southwestern and Southern Fronts. I set off on the same day for the Voronezh Front. By evening I was at Nikolayev's [code name for Vatutin] command post.[35]

The event of 3–4 July, described by Vasilevsky, confirmed the information of 2 July:

All was quiet on the Voronezh and the Central Fronts on 3 July, as it had been on all preceding days. But at 1600 on 4 July the enemy carried out his reconnaissance in force on a wide sector of the Voronezh Front with approximately four battalions supported by 20 tanks, artillery and aircraft (some 150 sorties). All attempts by the enemy to drive a wedge into our forward line were repulsed. A prisoner captured during the battle, a German from the 168th Infantry Division, let us know that the soldiers had been issued with battle rations and a portion of schnapps, and that they were to launch an offensive on 5 July. From a telephone conversation with Zhukov I found out that this was confirmed by enemy deserters who had come over to us on the the Central Front on July 4.[36]

As a result of this intelligence, the Soviets responded with a pre-emptive artillery counterpreparation early on 5 July which preceded the German offensive by only a matter of hours. By nightfall on 5 July, the front was aflame. The long-awaited German Kursk offensive had begun.

RAZVEDKA PLANNING

During the operational lull which brought silence to the Eastern Front from March through June, Soviet intelligence organs used every means at their disposal to track the disposition of German forces and determine their intentions. The Steppe Military District commander described the immensity of the effort:

In the course of preparations for the battle in the Kursk area Soviet intelligence made an invaluable contribution to the defeat of the enemy. Starting in April, all the intelligence services worked to discover the plans of the Nazi Command.

Their attention was chiefly concentrated in the zone of the Central, Voronezh and Southwestern *fronts*. On instructions from Marshal Vasilevsky, Chief of the General Staff, the Intelligence Department of the General Staff and the Central Headquarters of the Partisan Movement were assigned the mission of ascertaining the presence and disposition of reserves in the enemy's tactical rear and the areas where troops from the West were being concentrated. Every *front* systematically conducted air and combat reconnaissance in its zone of operations ... Active reconnaissance was carried out in the enemy's deep rear.[37]

While routine intelligence collection continued, *razvedka* planning for the Kursk operations was coordinated by the *STAVKA* and implemented by detailed operational and tactical planning at every command level. The *STAVKA* and General Staff prepared general appreciations of German strategic intentions based on reports from *razvedka* sources and then tasked *fronts* to plan further intelligence collection. Formal *front* and army *razvedka* plans focused all intelligence activities by specifying who would conduct it, where, by what means, and to what end. *Front* and army *razvedka* plans included tasks for all air, agent, signal, special, and ground intelligence collection means available to respective commanders. At the same time, the High Command passed down to *front* all intelligence data received from its specialized collection means.

Soviet intelligence organs worked within the guidance of the 1942 *Staff Field Manual* and the new 1943 *Field Service Regulations*, both of which specified procedures and eliminated confusion and duplication of work within staffs. The 1942 Manual, issued late in the year, had incorporated lessons learned from analysis of war experience and provided a structural approach to the conduct of *razvedka*. By spring 1943, the Soviets had implemented most provisions of the 1942 regulation and had identified residual problems and their solutions in the 1943 regulation. Force chiefs of staff supervised *razvedka* planning in a well-ordered sequence of, by now, combat tested procedures. Functional staffs and forces designated to carry out the plan were better trained than had been the case earlier in the war.

To an increasing extent, the Soviets employed air and radio *razvedka* and, as the quality of intelligence data obtained rose, Soviet confidence in those collection means also increased. While expanding the scope of collection efforts, the Soviets worked assiduously to improve tactical collection techniques which had proved so critical in past operations. The 1943 regulations in particular drew upon the winter experiences to refine further staff procedures required to analyze effectively collected data and, more important, to pass that material in timely fashion to commanders and operations sections and departments. *Razvedka* planning by 1943 embraced definitive periods of the operations and were fully integrated into operational phases envisaged by the commander. This synchronization of planning aims and functions provided for smoother planning and closer cooperation between staff sections.

Armies relied for their own intelligence collection on reconnaissance units of subordinate headquarters (division reconnaissance companies and regimental reconnaissance platoons). By early 1943 combat subunits routinely assisted by conducting reconnaissance in force in support of the *razvedka* effort. Since armies and subordinate corps still had no organic intelligence-gathering personnel or facilities, they continued to rely on *front* for specialized support from air, agent, and reconnaissance-diversionary organs. Links with partisan units provided armies with their deepest intelligence-gathering asset. Otherwise, army collection efforts generally ranged to a depth of up to 15 kilometers and relied primarily on observation, night and day raids, ambushes, radio and telephone eavesdropping, and reconnaissance in force. To an increasing extent, armies employed long-range intelligence-reconnaissance detachments, often parachuted into the operational depths of the enemy rear.

By April 1943 refined principles of intelligence collection, processing, and analysis had emerged, and the Soviets had fashioned a logical system for the conduct of *razvedka*. Success, however, depended in large part on the efficiency of each collection means, on the creation of reliable communications means, and on efficient staff operations required to convert raw data into meaningful estimates which could be acted upon. While in the first two years of war, collection problems associated with each means had often frustrated these ends, by the spring and summer of 1943 centralized control of *razvedka*, tighter procedures, and extensive experience had solved many of the more nagging problems.

Intelligence departments (*razvedyvatel'nyi otdel* − RO) at *front* organized all *razvedka* activity, closely supervised by the Main Intelligence Directorate (*Glavnoe razvedyvatel'noe upravienie* − GRU) of the General Staff which provided *fronts* with strategic intelligence data. *Front* ROs worked out projects required by the plan, *razvedka* orders for subordinate armies and staffs of subordinate branches and types of forces, and directives for subordinate partisan detachments. Thereafter, ROs supervised collection of intelligence data, processed materials, prepared necessary reports and estimates, and kept commanders and operations departments informed of the intelligence situation. As the time of the offensive neared, ROs worked closely with operations departments and operational sections of the armies and lower level commands to plan effective troop reconnaissance of enemy tactical and operational dispositions.

A German study of Soviet intelligence organs and functions prepared by *Fremde Heere Ost* in October 1943 vividly highlighted Soviet capabilities. It captured the ubiquitousness of the system by portraying the linkages between military and political organs and the great scope and depth of intelligence operations (see Figure 6). The study's analysis of the GRU structure showed the interrelationship of agent and reconnaissance-diversionary activity and the linkages between *STAVKA* and General Staff level activities and those of the individual *fronts*. Most significant was the Soviet *razvedka* training effort and the growth of analysis organs within the GRU's information section. The study also noted the increased Soviet communications effort within the radio division and the presence of a cipher department to decode German transmissions (see Figure 7). The study detailed similar improvements in the entire intelligence structure from *front* down to regiment (see Figures 8–10).[38]

The Germans also recognized fundamental changes in the way the Soviets integrated *razvedka* and counter-*razvedka*. Prior to April 1943, *razvedka* and counter-*razvedka* (*kontrrazvedka* – counterintelligence) functions had been collocated in *front* and army headquarters and had been carried out by the *osobyi otdel'* (OO) (special department) and *razvedyvatel'nyi otdel'* (RO) (*razvedka* department) respectively. To increase the prestige and power of counterintelligence agencies, on 19 April 1943 the Defense Commissariat reorganized the OOs into *otdel kontrrazvedka* (OKR) which were shifted in subordination from the NKVD to the Commissariat of Defense (NKO) (see Figure 11).[39] Henceforth, they were directly responsible to one of the Assistant Commissars of Defense. These counter-*razvedka* organs came to be known by the acronym, SMERSH (*smert' shpionam* – death to spies). The extensive activity of these organs both to deal with enemy agents in the Soviet rear area and to assist intelligence and deception efforts

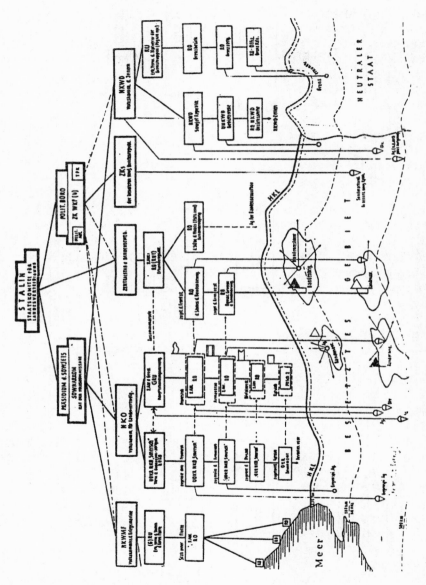

Fig. 6. Soviet reconnaissance-diversionary structure

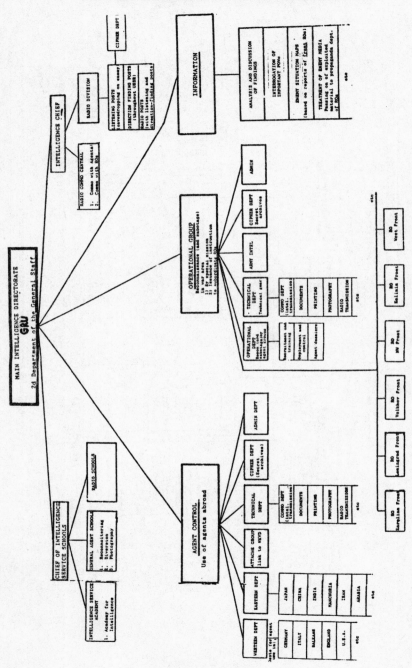

Fig. 7. Structure of the Main Intelligence Directors (GRU) of the Red Army

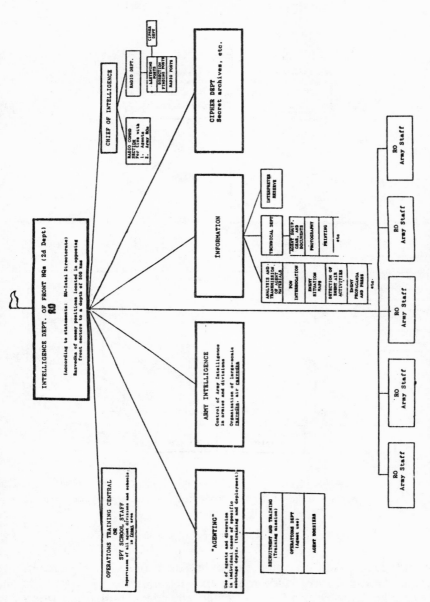

Fig. 8. Structure of the intelligence department (RO) of a *front* staff

205

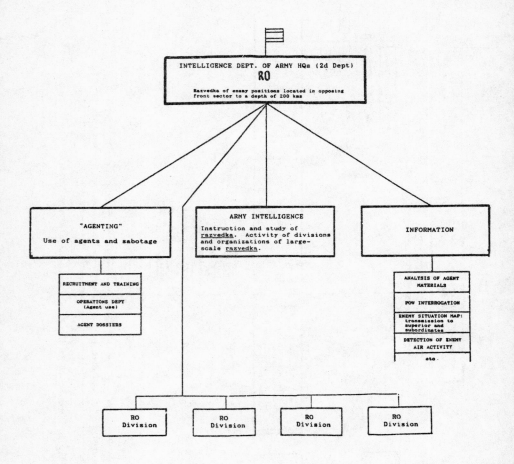

Fig. 9. Structure of the intelligence department (RO) of an army staff

by engaging in disinformation are beyond the scope of this book but, nevertheless, probably made major contributions.

Front intelligence staffs coordinated air, agent, radio, and troop *razvedka* activities, using specialized intelligence subunits under their control and assets of subordinated commands. *Fronts* also employed partisan detachments to conduct operational *razvedka* at

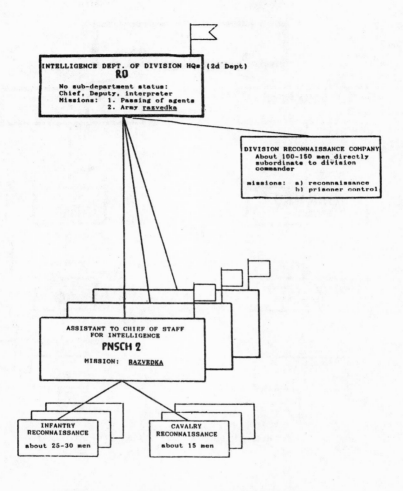

Fig. 10. Intelligence organs of divisions and regiments

greater depths in the enemy rear. Long-range air reconnaissance units assigned to *front* air armies gathered intelligence at strategic and operational depths by employing visual and photographic techniques, and army air *razvedka* units relied primarily on visual observation at tactical and shallow operational depths. Long-range air *razvedka* observed rail and highway networks deeper in the

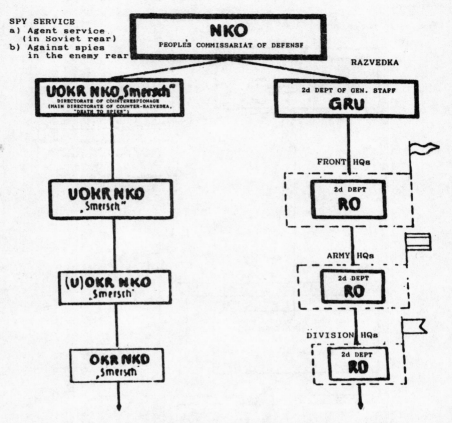

Fig. 11. Soviet military intelligence service after April–May 1943

enemy rear to determine the scale and direction of troop movements. All air reconnaissance units searched for potential tactical and operational assembly areas, and other deep objectives, but focused particular attention on identifying principal enemy defense lines, artillery firing positions, headquarters, supply installations, and reserve positions which could affect the development of the German offensive. Air *razvedka* data was passed to the staff which controlled the air assets and, if combat was under way, to all lower headquarters through regiment by clear text radio transmission.

Front staff departments controlled agent *razvedka*, special *razvedka* by reconnaissance-diversionary teams deployed from OMSBON and commando brigades, and partisan *razvedka*. They processed the intelligence information and, when appropriate, passed it to army headquarters. Specialized radio units at *front* level intercepted enemy radio transmissions, conducted radio location, and occasionally jammed enemy radio transmissions. Communications units at army and lower levels organized eavesdropping and tapped into enemy wire communications. Radio *razvedka* attempted to determine enemy strength and dispositions, the location of major enemy force groupings, and the time and location of his artillery and air strikes.

Armies, corps, divisions, and regiments organized ground *razvedka* through observation, troop *razvedka*, and reconnaissance in force to identify and determine the strength of enemy forces and the location of specific enemy defensive lines, weapons positions, and troop assembly areas. Soviet concern for ground *razvedka* reflected their belief that careful study of tactical positions could produce an intelligence mosaic which would assist in accurate assessments of enemy attack intentions and preparations. Consequently, the Soviets paid special attention to refining their ground *razvedka* techniques, which could supplement and verify information obtained in increasing amounts by more refined technical collection means. The most basic means of ground *razvedka* continued to be planned observation of enemy defenses. Commanders and staffs at every level organized extensive observation post networks manned by personnel specially trained in observation techniques and equipped with a variety of observation devices. The most important segment of this network was within army first echelon divisions and regiments.

Armies, divisions, and regiments also extensively employed small combat groups dispatched into enemy defensive positions to conduct sweeps, ambushes, and raids to obtain intelligence data. By summer 1943 these measures were facilitated by the close proximity of opposing force positions and by the vast experience in conducting such operations gained in the first two years of war. Small groups of five to eight men conducted sweeps and ambushes to seize prisoners, documents, and enemy weapons. Smaller groups of three to five men conducted diversionary and reconnaissance missions deeper in the enemy rear to perform like missions and also to locate, reconnoiter, and sometimes destroy enemy command posts, communications facilities, and logistics installations. Larger reconnaissance detachments from army and *front* conducted deeper operations against stronger objectives in the operational depths and cooperated with partisan detachments. Normally, these larger forces were controlled by the ROs of armies and *fronts*.[40] In addition, artillery and engineer staffs planned and conducted extensive artillery and engineer *razvedka*, fully integrated with other *razvedka* measures.

RAZVEDKA PRIOR TO THE OPERATION

Air

Soviet post-Stalingrad analysis of *razvedka* experiences concluded that air *razvedka* was often the only means of obtaining information about the enemy during fluid situations prior to or during operations. Since in the summer of 1943 radio intercept was relatively unsophisticated, and information obtained by agent networks and partisans was not always timely, air *razvedka* was especially crucial. By April 1943 the Soviet High Command had established procedures for existing air units to provide intelligence and had created specialized air units to serve intelligence staffs at *front* and High Command level. All combat aviation units in *front* air armies had the auxiliary mission of conducting reconnaissance. Smaller army aviation detachments performed similar missions for army commanders. Within *front* air armies and long-range aviation forces subordinate to the High Command, the Soviets created air reconnaissance regiments of four squadrons each to perform air *razvedka*. The former worked under *front* supervision, and the latter performed specialized missions and deep reconnoitering of the rail and highway network in the German rear. For example, in May 1943 the 2d Aviation Division of Special Designation, a long-range transport unit, formed for this purpose the 105th Separate Guards Aviation Squadron of Long-Range Night Reconnaissance, equipped with three to five C–47 aircraft.[41]

In theory, strategic air *razvedka* still extended to depths of up to 500 kilometers; but in actuality few aircraft penetrated to that depth. *Front* air *razvedka* units operated at shallower depths of up to 250 kilometers but normally concentrated their efforts on the tactical depths (up to 60 kilometers) and shallow operational depths of the enemy defenses.[42] Soviet air assets available to support ground forces in the Kursk operation consisted of the 16th Air Army (Central Front), 2d Air Army (Voronezh Front), 5th Air Army (Steppe Military District), 17th Air Army (Southwestern Front), and a portion of Soviet long-range aviation forces and forces of PVO Strany (national air defense). The High Command tasked these forces to fight for air superiority, disrupt movement of enemy reserves, cover Soviet ground forces from enemy air attack, and conduct *razvedka* of enemy positions and troop concentrations. The interdiction and *razvedka* missions were most important during the long period preceding the operation.

Twice during the preparatory period Soviet air forces struck at German airfields to weaken German air strength and fulfill other missions.[43] From 6 to 13 May six Soviet air armies (1st, 15th, 16th, 2d, 17th, and 8th) conducted 1,400 sorties across a *front* of 1,200 kilometers. Again, between 8–10 June, three air armies (1st, 15th, 2d) and long-range aviation units engaged 28 German airfields. While the first operation achieved considerable surprise, the second failed to achieve surprise and was less successful. Beginning in late March, Soviet long-range aviation and *front* air armies commenced a major operation against German rail lines and road networks to disrupt the flow of forces to the *front*. The extensive operation, which intensified right up to the time of the German attack, reached to depths of up to 600 kilometers and also produced considerable reconnaissance data on German movements.

Meanwhile, air army *razvedka* assets implemented *front* air *razvedka* plans to identify enemy troop assembly and concentration areas, air bases, air defense systems, defensive positions, strongpoints, firing points, and reserve areas. It was particularly important to identify the location and movement of panzer and panzer grenadier (motorized) divisions necessary to mount any sustained offensive. By mid-May, air *razvedka* had identified armored concentrations near Orel and Kromy numbering more than 900 tanks and pinpointed 16 airfields in the same regions.[44]

By Soviet admission, air operations during the preparatory period were not intensive. Each air army aircraft flew an average of .1–.2 sorties per day, for the Soviet command attempted to reserve maximum air assets for the offensive phase.[45] A Red Air Force directive of 16 June 1943 read, "During the period of quiet on the *front*, cease aimless combat flight other than *razvedka* and repulse of enemy aviation flights over our territory. ... Air armies are to preserve their strength, conduct intense staff training and support flying qualification of crews."[46] Nor were extensive assets dedicated solely to *razvedka*. Out of 2,900 aircraft in the committed air armies, only about 20 were reconnaissance type aircraft. These were supplemented by *razvedka* aircraft from long-range aviation units.

Within these constraints, *front* air armies cooperated closely with the *front* intelligence department and other intelligence collecting agencies. Separate aviation reconnaissance regiments and their subordinate squadrons carried out specific tasks required by the plan in timed sequence and were assisted by reconnaissance sub-units within other bomber, assault, and fighter aviation formations of the air armies. After-action critiques indicated that specialized reconnaissance unit aircraft flew fewer than 20 percent of recon-naissance sorties, while reconnaissance aircraft of line aviation units flew the remaining 80 percent. During the preparatory phase at Kursk, 16th Air Army flew 3,814 *razvedka* sorties (24.1 percent) and the 2d Air Army 1,925 sorties (16.1 percent).[47]

During the preparatory period for the operation, reconnaissance units attempted to reconnoiter the entire sector of their respective parent *front*. Seventy to 80 percent of the flights, however, occurred in the depths along only the principal approaches into the defense. Night flights concentrated on rail lines and major highways along which the Germans moved their forces, whereas day flights spanned the entire sector. Of the total number of reconnaissance flights, about 70 percent flew tactical missions; and the remainder focused on operational targets. This was because most aircraft had limited operating ranges, and the densest array of targets to be reconnoitered tended to be concentrated up to 30–40 kilometers in the enemy rear.[48] The *front razvedka* plan designated specific belts for tactical and operational *razvedka*. To improve the quality of *razvedka*, *front* commanders assigned specific belts and sectors to designated air army air reconnaissance regiments and reconnaissance subunits of other air formations. This division of responsibilities permitted air crews to become more familiar with the peculiar natural and manmade features of their sectors and to recognize changes more easily.

The General Staff and Red Army Air Force (VVS) employed special long-range reconnaissance regiments and separate crews assigned to Soviet Long-Range Aviation (ADD) to conduct strategic *razvedka* to a depth of up to 450 kilometers.[49] These units concen-trated on detecting and monitoring movements of enemy strategic reserves. Before the Kursk operation, this meant enemy formations moving into the region from the west or from adjacent army group sectors. Analogous activity went on within adjacent *fronts* to detect German troop movements out of sector and to verify the efficiency of deception plans (in particular in the Western, Kalinin, Briansk, Southwestern, and Southern Front sectors). Information from strategic reconnaissance aviation first went to the *STAVKA* and then to appropriate *fronts* and air armies so that their *razvedka* assets could verify the accuracy of the reports and detect further movement and forward deployment of those strategic reserves. During preparation for the Kursk operation, most reconnaissance aircraft still relied heavily on visual observation, while about 40 percent of the flights were capable of employing photography.[50] Good weather conditions further improved the utility of photography.

Air *razvedka* made significant contributions to Soviet intelligence-gathering before the Kursk operation commenced. One Soviet critique noted:

> In defensive operations of the Central and Voronezh *Fronts* at Kursk ... air *razvedka* long before the beginning of the defensive battle helped reveal the concentration areas of the enemy Orel and Belgorod–Khar'kov groups and determined the most probable directions of their main blows.[51]

On 14 May Marshal of Aviation A. A. Novikov dispatched the following intelligence report to the *STAVKA*:

> Report of Commander of Red Army Air Forces of 14 May 1943 to HQ Supreme High Command on Enemy Troop Build-Up for the Offensive Discovered by Air Reconnaissance in the Region of Orel, Kromy
>
> To Comrade Stalin
> To Comrade Vasilevsky
>
> My report is:
>
> Aerial photographic reconnaissance by the 4th Reconnaissance Air Regiment by the end of 14 May 1943 in the region of Orel, Kromy established over 900 enemy tanks and up to 1,500 motor vehicles.
>
> The tanks are located 5–10km behind the *front* line at the following points. 150 tanks and vehicles 2km to the west of Kurakino Station (50km to the southeast of Orel); 200 tanks and 100 vehicles to the south of Krasnaia Ivanovka (8km to the west of Kurakino Station); 200 tanks and motor vehicles in the forest to the north of Sobakino (23 km to the southwest of Kurakino Station); 220 tanks and vehicles in a grove to the south of Staroe Gorokhovo; 90 tanks and 30 vehicles near Rogovka (50km to the south of Orel).

In the villages adjacent to Zmievka Station (35km to the southeast of Orel), a significant number of motor vehicles and 50–60 tanks were noted. At Zmievka Station, 12 trains have unloaded with motor vehicles and freight; the station is covered by the fire of three antiaircraft artillery batteries.

The tanks located outside of population points and woods have been partially dug in and camouflaged. Moreover, systematic air observation over the last three days at the 16 airfields in the Orel region has noted more than 580 enemy aircraft. I conclude that the enemy with the tank and motorized units has taken up a jump-off position and has created an air grouping in the Orel sector for assisting the ground forces.

Commander of the Red Army Air Forces, Mar Avn Novikov 14 May 1943.[52]

Air Marshal S. I. Rudenko, commander of 16th Air Army, related another interesting and revealing incident in late June:

One day in June, Colonel G. K. Prussakov, intelligence chief of the 16th Air Army, came in to report and, along with the map, brought photographs of two small groves south of Orel. They concealed a large number of German tanks. Judging by the track traces and other evidence, the enemy was hiding about two panzer divisions in those groves.

Tank concentrations are always a tempting target for the air force. And so I immediately decided to bomb these two small groves and knock out two large panzer units.

Without losing a moment, I took up my suggestion to the Front commander. General Rokossovsky listened attentively and then said:

"Well, say we shake up these two divisions, and so tell the enemy we know much about him. He'll restore their combat power and hide them so that our recce will never find them.

"What we want now," he continued his argument, "is to make believe we know nothing and at the same time to find out his strength and his plans. And so we shouldn't alarm the Germans. Let them attack and then, if you want to, take a smack at those groves. Only it's hardly likely that you'll find any tanks there. You have to watch their movement and then shower them with bombs."

There was nothing for me to do but agree. We continued to send out recce planes every day to photograph all more or less suspicious spots. We estimated that the enemy had concentrated more than 1,000 tanks and assault guns against the Central Front at the end of June. The latest intelligence showed that the enemy had on the whole concentrated his troops for attack.[53]

Throughout the preparatory period daily reconnaissance flights photographed the roads, forests, and fields, as well as population centers, air fields, and enemy defenses. Photo-interpreters at *front* headquarters analyzed the photos to determine changes in terrain configuration and enemy dispositions. According to one assessment, "In May and June, in sectors chosen for the penetrations (during the counteroffensive), aviation photographed the enemy defense sector. The enemy defense system was transferred from aerial photographs to a map and helped support attacking forces."[54] Visual reconnaissance also detected what it could of German movements.

Despite notable successes, there were some limitations to air *razvedka*. Since the aircraft relied on visual and photographic observation, most flights took place during the day when German aircraft could contest the flights and when German units attempted to keep movements to a minimum. In addition, where visual observation or photography detected force concentrations, they often could not determine specific unit designations. This could only result from collation of air data with other intelligence information.

Agent-Diversionary (Special)

By late 1942 an articulated structure of reconnaissance-diversionary forces existed throughout the higher commands of the Red Army. Controlled by the General Staff's GRU and by the NKVD's special departments (*osobyi otdel*) at *front* and army level, these forces consisted of agents under GRU control; a Separate Motorized Rifle Brigade of Special Designation (OMSBON), which served NKVD Central and deployed teams and detachments across the entire *front*; and special detachments and groups subordinate to ROs and special departments of *fronts* and armies. These forces parachuted or infiltrated into the enemy rear to perform specific *razvedka* and diversionary missions as required by the *front razvedka* plan. Soviet agents and reconnaissance and diversionary detachments and groups cooperated with NKVD agents already in place and with partisan units to form an extensive network in the German rear area.

After 19 April 1943 the special departments (*osobyi otdel*) were reorganized into departments of counter-*razvedka* (*otdel kontrrazvedki* – OKR) subordinate to the People's Commissariat of Defense (NKO). The new departments focused on defeat of German intelligence units (*Abwehr*) in the Soviet rear area. The OMSBON remained subordinate to the NKVD and carried out operations in the deep German rear and liaison with partisan forces. As before, it operated with individuals, agents, detachments, and larger groups. During the period prior to Kursk, "Among its [missions] a special place was occupied by 'the railway war' of 1943 when on the eve of the Kursk battle almost all strategically important enemy railroads in Belorussia and the northern Ukraine were taken out of action. In several places German garrisons were destroyed as well."[55] While the NKVD conducted deep reconnaissance-diversionary activity with OMSBON, the GRU did likewise through its own agents and *front* ROs. According to one source:

> Energetic *razvedka* activity was conducted in the enemy rear. Thus the *razvedka* group of Senior Lieutenant S. P. Bukhtoiarovo conducted *razvedka* in the Khar'kov, Zolochev, and Belgorod region. For 54 days the '*razvedchkiki*' [scouts] traveled in the enemy rear more than 500 kilometers and captured 31 prisoners. The *razvedka* group destroyed seven airdromes and many warehouses. The group sent to the command more than 70 radiograms with information about enemy forces. The *razvedka* provided important information about the capability of the enemy to undertake an offensive in early July and reported about the presence of new types of tanks and assault guns.[56]

To supplement the operating forces of the NKVD and GRU, in October 1942 the Soviet High Command created separate guards battalions of miners (*miner*) (OGBM), special engineer forces tailored to operate against enemy lines of communications. One such battalion was assigned to each *front*. Each battalion formed special teams which operated in the enemy rear under supervision of the *front* chief of engineers in accordance with a specific plan. Often these groups coordinated closely with partisan forces in the region.[57] The principal missions of OGBM detachments were to conduct *razvedka* and carry out diversionary activity. Specifically:

> Miners operated in the enemy rear, as a rule in small groups

which allowed them to strike blows against enemy communications over a broad region. The maximum effect was realized when they were used simultaneously in several sectors of the *front*. Having received their mission, the miners passed through the *front* lines in small groups, usually at night, through intervals or gaps between enemy units or were dropped in the enemy rear by military transport aircraft. The drop occurred also at night, and the landing area was selected at a distance of about 15 kilometers from the operational objective.[58]

Often the OGBM cooperated closely with *front* engineer brigades of special designation which themselves carried out special missions at shallower depths in the enemy rear. Fragmentary Soviet order of battle data showed the 13th OGBM subordinate to the Voronezh Front in the summer of 1943.[59]

To support reconnaissance-diversionary forces and partisans as well, the Red Army Air Force created special air units within Long-Range Aviation to conduct air drops of personnel and supplies. By the end of 1942, the Soviets also created special aviation groups within each *front* to support partisans and deep *razvedka*-diversionary operations. In addition, Long-Range Aviation formed the 1st Aviation Transport Division to perform the same function. During the pre-Kursk period, the 1st Aviation Transport Division's 101st Long-Range Aviation Regiment flew numerous missions in support of partisan and *razvedka* forces in the Briansk region. In May 1943 the Red Army Air Force formed the 105th Separate Guards Aviation Squadron of Long-Range Night Reconnaissance within the 2d Aviation Division of Special Designation. This squadron of long-range aviation was also dedicated to transporting *razvedka* units into the German rear and supplying both those units and partisans.[60]

No comprehensive Soviet exposé of agent or *razvedka*-diversionary activities exists. However, numerous references appear in scattered Soviet sources. One general appreciation of the Kursk operation noted, "There were reports from partisans and organs of agent *razvedka*. From operational group *Pobediteli* (conquerors) operating near Rovno in the spring of 1943 information was received about the transfer of Hitlerite forces in the Kursk direction."[61] The official Soviet history of the war recognized the contributions of agents operating in the German rear as well as counter-*razvedka* organs:

While operating in the enemy rear, Soviet *chekists* penetrated their [German] *razvedka* and counter-*razvedka* organizations, uncovered plans for their underground activities against the USSR, and identified enemy agents, prepared for insertion in our rear. The operational groups of the Belorussian SSR NKVD alone, while located in the enemy rear, uncovered 22 *razvedka*-diversionary *Abwehr* schools, 36 residents and 1,142 agents of German-fascist *razvedka*.[62]

Sometimes this produced specific information:

In May [1943] an operational group of the security organ captured in the enemy rear an officer of the *razvedka* department of the Air Force Staff of Army Group Center who provided extremely valuable information about the preparation of the German command for a large-scale offensive in the region of the Kursk bulge.[63]

German assessments tend to confirm the vast scope of Soviet agent and *razvedka*-diversionary activities. A report of *Fremde Heere Ost* (Foreign Armies East) dated 30 December 1942 exemplified numerous subsequent reports and underscored the scope of the problem. It began by delineating the scope of Soviet agent recruitment: "The enemy calls upon all German-speaking Russians in the intelligence service to seek employment in work places which provide favorable conditions for their [agent] activities."[64] This included national minorities whom the Germans considered "more trustworthy" as well as former concentration camp inmates seeking redress from injustice. To supplement these sources, "the Russians place special detachments behind the German *front* for recruitment, training and organizing espionage groups. The Soviet intelligence service is trying to penetrate German intelligence activity."[65] This included recruitment of double agents and "dissatisfied members of the [German] armed forces" and exploitation of Russian dependents of German soldiers or civilians.

The Germans identified infiltration through *front* lines and paradrops, often amidst bombing raids, as the main means for deploying enemy agents into their rear area. Once in the German rear, agents sought "unwitting informants" and people working in German headquarters as major conduits of intelligence data. Once recruited, the informants were held in service by threats and blackmail. Every agent who was caught had a "skillfully produced 'history' with which he deceived German headquarters over and over, often with the help of suitable false papers."[66] According to the report, agents employed a variety of means to communicate with Soviet intelligence agencies, including "mailboxes," other persons (messengers), or radio transmissions. "Mailboxes" were specially designated message drop points, each of which was carefully camouflaged and equipped with a warning device such as pre-positioned stones or branches. Agents also used "books, news-papers, and bibles in which certain words have been specially marked" in order to pass messages.[67]

When discussing remedies to the growing agent problem, the report emphasized the need for more careful use and check of identity cards which, as during the summer of 1943, were "in many cases, very carelessly handled." It was especially important to interrogate captured agents to discover the means they used for collecting intelligence data and passing it to Soviet *razvedka* organs. The assessment ended with an admission and a warning:

> The German soldier is inclined, as is generally known, toward gullibility and, thereby, often causes great trouble. It is thus essential, time and time again, to draw the attention of the troops to, and warn them of, the activity of Soviet agents. This applies to fighting troops and more especially to the troops who are in the rear area.[68]

By the summer of 1944 German counterintelligence had identified 20,000 Soviet agents, and an estimated 10,000 fresh replacements were fielded every three months. Ominously, they estimated only one-third would ever be caught.[69] These agents or detach-ments were subordinate to the NKVD, GRU, or *front* and army commands, and they operated at varying depths in the German rear. Each group had specific missions to perform, the sum of which formed an imposing *razvedka* mosaic.

Some agents operated as deserters, responding to the German 1943 propaganda campaign *Silberstreif* in order to sow disaffection in German ranks and the ranks of German-Russian auxiliaries (*Hilfswilligen* – auxiliary volunteers). In II SS Panzer Corps alone, 186 Russian *Hilfswilligen* re-defected from April to June 1943, some carrying with them valuable intelligence information.[70] Other Soviet agents, deeper in the rear, infiltrated the German govern-mental, police, or railroad administrative apparatus. Thus, "The Abwehr monitored daily transmissions from one espionage net-work in Khar'kov that almost certainly related to Army Group South's preparations for Zitadelle."[71] The Germans noted the cooperation between agents and partisans. For example, German Ninth Army "attributed the bulk of Russian espionage in its sector during June and July 1943 to partisans infiltrating from the west rather than across the *front* lines."[72] This, in part, explains the major German effort prior to Kursk to clear partisan units from the Briansk region.

Another major study of Soviet intelligence activities compiled by German intelligence prior to October 1943 demonstrated both the size of the Soviet effort and German understanding of it.[73] The Germans recognized the organizational and functional aspects of GRU, NKVD, and OKR as well as their varied missions and subordinate organizations. Other similar reports outlined the operational methods of each organization. These reports evidenced growing German realization of the intelligence threat. It was, however, one thing to recognize the threat, but altogether another matter to deal effectively with it. Evidence indicates the Germans were unable to do so.

Outside the Soviet borders, the NKVD and GRU continued to be active through agents and various "spy rings" such as "Dora."[74] German radio intercepts of *Rote Drei* intelligence operations for the pre-Kursk period contain a number of predictions regarding attack dates, including the first week of May, 12 June, and 14 June.[75] The full message file probably contains other tentative dates. In any case, the time lag in transmission generally spanned several days. While the messages may have been of general assistance, actual Soviet decision-making was based on harder intelligence data, from sources more closely attuned to actual German actions. The same Soviet reaction pertained to assessments from Ultra passed directly by the British to the Soviets. The British continued passing Ultra-derived materials to the Soviets through the Military Mission in Moscow in early 1943. The usefulness of that material, however, depended directly on its source. The most valuable and regular of Ultra sources was German Air Force signal intelligence traffic and, from the spring of 1943, OKH non-morse teleprinter transmissions to Army Group South.[76]

While Ultra-derived SIGINT provided virtually no warning of the German 15 February 1943 counterattack, by March it presented a good view of German intentions. After 30 March intercepted traffic tracked German concentration of air assets in the Crimea and Kuban regions. The net effect of these and other intercepts was to focus attention on the Crimea and Kuban at the expense of other areas. The first references to future operations at Kursk appeared in the third week of March, when troop and air movements indicated a possible offensive at the end of April. On 13 April the codename "Zitadelle" first appeared. Thereafter, at the end of April, Ultra picked up a comprehensive assessment by Army Group South (see Appendix) of future German intentions at Kursk.[77] This was passed to the Soviets on 30 April along with a warning that the attack would take place in the near future. For the next two months, however, information collected and intelligence assessments were doubtful regarding future combat at Kursk:

> Except that AI [air intelligence] derived some indication of the imminence of "Zitadelle" from the cessation of the GAF's [German Air Force] preparatory bombing of industrial and communications centres in the Kursk sector which had begun during May, intelligence gave no advance notice of the opening of the much delayed German offensive. ...[78]

In fact, after fighting had commenced:

> On the progress of the fighting Whitehall's intelligence was limited to GAF Enigma and what was supplied by the Russians to the British Military Mission. The GAF Enigma was not very illuminating. Not until 10 July did it make it clear that the Germans were carrying out operation "Zitadelle."[79]

Agent reports and Ultra materials passed to the Soviets via official agencies were of some value to the Soviets. Strategic *razvedka* information from agents deep in the German rear or overseas provided illuminating information on German strategic intentions. However, its poor timeliness and often contradictory nature limited its operational use. In that regard, the Soviets found information from agents and *razvedka*-diversionary detachments and groups in the tactical and operational depths of the German defenses to be of greater import.

Partisan

By the end of 1942, the partisan movement was well-established in most German-occupied territory. The Central Staff of the Partisan Movement (TsShPD) provided unity to the effort, and the People's Commissariat of Defense Order of 5 September 1942 "concerning the Missions of the Partisan Movement" provided specific guidance for partisan operations. By March 1943 nagging communications problems were well on the way to solution, and more than 80 percent of the detachments had constant radio communications with staffs of the partisan movement. The various partisan staffs even established training courses for an estimated 23,000 specialists of which seven percent were trained in *razvedka*.[80]

The basic partisan military organization was the detachment (*otriad*) which was further subdivided into company, platoon, and special detachments operated independently or as a component of partisan brigades or divisions. The principal missions of the detachments were disruption of enemy communications, liberation of territory in the enemy rear, *razvedka*, and cooperation with *front* operating forces. By 1943 partisan missions, in particular those involving multiple detachments, were carefully coordinated with *front* headquarters. Partisan operational plans were, in fact, often integral components of Red Army offensive or defensive plans. Partisan detachments frequently cooperated with other *razvedka* organs, including agents and long- or short-range *razvedka*-diversionary forces of the NKVD, GRU, *fronts*, and armies. These included commando (*istrebitel'nyi*) detachments, battalions, and brigades operating under *front* control, formed either to combat German reconnaissance-diversionary forces or to replicate partisan action in cooperation with existing partisan detachments in the German rear.[81]

By 1943 Red Army Air Force units, in particular long-range aviation, cooperated closely with partisan forces. Dedicated air units flew in supplies and reinforcements, effected liaison, provided a means of communication, and, on rare occasions, contributed air support to partisan units when conducting major operations.

Operational guidance for the partisan movement became more specific in 1943. Building on the September 1942 order, on 19 April 1943 the *STAVKA* issued an order titled "Concerning the Improvement of *Razvedka* Work in Partisan Detachments." The order required partisans to broaden the range of their reconnaissance efforts into all occupied territories and focus *razvedka* efforts to serve Red Army units. In addition to establishing training programs, the order mandated use of trained Red Army officers and Chekists in key *razvedka* positions. Henceforth, partisan detachments were to cooperate closely with regular Red Army *razvedka* groups and "systematically transmit reconnaissance reports to the General Staff and *fronts* in timely fashion, each signed by the partisan commander and his assistant for *razvedka*."[82]

In the same month, Zhukov reported that in the middle of

April the *STAVKA* tasked the partisan movement with specific intelligence-gathering responsibilities:

> Vasilevsky gave the intelligence division and the Central Headquarters of the partisan movement the assignment of discovering the extent and distribution of the enemy's reserves in depth, the regrouping and concentration of troops moved in from France, Germany, and other countries.[83]

Party organs and partisan staffs cooperated more closely and, by July 1943, the Central Partisan Staff conducted conferences with the chiefs of intelligence of republic and regional staffs. The number of *razvedka* specialists grew significantly after issuance of the April order. From April to June 1943 the Ukrainian staff counted 20 assistant commanders for intelligence and 17 *razvedka* specialists in its subordinate units. Between February and July the number of assistant commanders for intelligence in detachments and brigades expanded from 70 to over 300.[84]

The *razvedka* sections of partisan movement staffs organized *razvedka* work in subordinate units and cooperated closely with respective *front* ROs. Throughout 1943 radio communications between partisan and *front* staff improved considerably:

> The increase in the quantity of radio means in partisan formations and the clear system of organized communications with them provided the capability, as noted by the chief of the communications section of the Central Partisan Staff, Major General I. N. Artem'ev, to secure for the army command exact information about the situation in the enemy rear (see Figure 12).[85]

For example, the Ukrainian partisan detachments had seven communications centers and 78 radio stations by July 1943. This permitted a 30 percent increase in transmissions between March and July.[86]

A German appreciation of partisan operations, prepared in the summer and fall of 1943, confirmed Soviet descriptions of partisan organization as well as the *razvedka* chain in the partisan structure (see Figure 13). This, combined with extensive German analysis of partisan order of battle, documented a considerable intelligence threat in the German rear.[87] Extensive German operations to clear the rear area, although often fruitless, further demonstrated growing German fears and frustrations over the festering sore in the rear area.

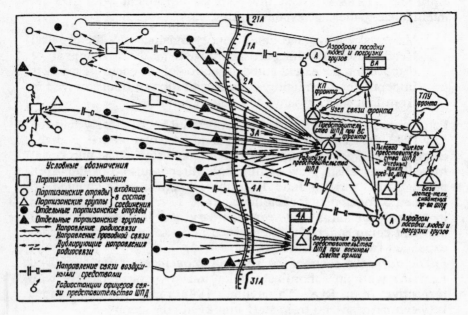

Fig. 12. Partisan communications with a *front* staff

Partisan forces, in the spring and summer of 1943, located in the Belorussian and Ukrainian republics and various provinces (*oblast'*) of the Russian republic, were directly or tangentially involved in the Kursk operation. Of primary concern were partisan formations in the Orel, Briansk, and Khar'kov provinces which were included in Soviet planning for the Kursk operation:

> In accordance with the *STAVKA* concept for the Kursk operation the Central Staff of the Partisan Movement received the mission to organize massive diversions and attacks on enemy communications in the enemy rear in the territory of the Orel, Briansk, and Khar'kov provinces.[88]

Included in the mission was the specific priority task of reporting on enemy movements and dispositions.

To insure close coordination of Soviet ground forces and partisans, in March 1943 the staff of the partisan movement, with the Military Council of the Briansk Front, worked out a plan of cooperative action which was approved by the *front* commander. The plan designated missions for partisan brigades in joint operations

THE KURSK OPERATION

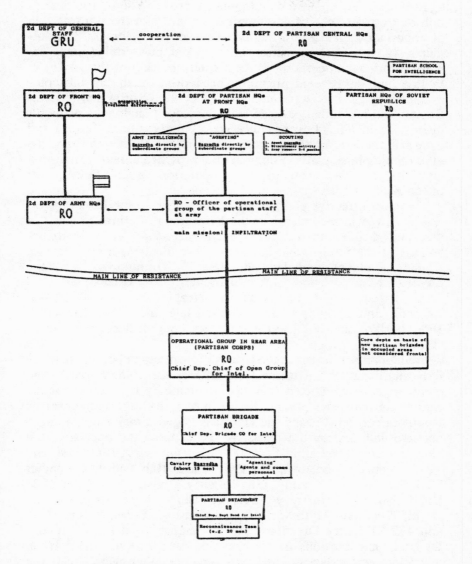

Fig. 13. Intelligence department of the partisan headquarters

against Briansk, against withdrawing German troops, for disruption of German lines of communication, and "for the transmission of important *razvedka* information to Soviet Army forces."[89] Simultaneously, the Orel province staff worked out similar plans for partisan brigades operating in the western portion of the province. In late June subsequent planning focused on disrupting rail communications in the operational sectors of the Central and Briansk Fronts. The Ukrainian partisan staff developed analogous plans for operations in Khar'kov province (particularly around Sumy) and deeper in the rear area in coordination with the Voronezh Front. To effect these plans, partisan units in Orel province united with the 1st and 2d Kursk Partisan Brigades for operations around Sevsk, west of the Kursk bulge.

The most effective partisan operations prior to the Kursk operation occurred in the sectors of the Briansk and Central Fronts. "In this period the partisans conducted *razvedka* and diversionary actions in the Orel, Briansk, Trubchevsk, Pochen, Mglin, Kletin, Karachev, Navel, and Unecha areas."[90] Throughout April the Suvorov, Kravtsov, and Shchors Brigades in the Briansk and Orel areas, together with forces in the Nezhin, Poltava, Akhtyrka, Liubotin, and Konotop regions, cut rail lines into Orel, Bukhmach and Khar'kov and collected intelligence data on the movement of German forces.

Soviet partisan forces in the Briansk forest region posed a particularly significant threat to the German rear area. There, more than eight brigades conducted *razvedka*-diversionary operations against critical German lines of communications to Orel. To rid themselves of this threat, on 22 May the Germans began a major operation to encircle and destroy the partisans. To conduct the operation, the Germans employed almost 50,000 men from the 707th, 221st, and 213th Security Divisions; 4th Panzer and 10th Panzer Grenadier Division; 7th, 292d, and 113th Infantry Divisions; and the 102d Hungarian Light Infantry Division (German records show the 707th, 710th, and 727th Security Divisions; the 318th, 404th, 407th, and 492d Infantry Divisions; the Hungarian 102d Light Infantry Division; and portions of 4th and 5th Panzer Divisions).[91] In an operation which lasted until late June, the Germans forced the partisans to disperse deeper into the forests and seized most population centers and communications routes in the region. Despite considerable losses, partisan activity continued around Briansk, although on a lesser scale, up to the beginning of the Kursk offensive.

While the German anti-partisan operation was in progress throughout June, it was unlikely the Germans would be able to mount large-scale operations elsewhere. The termination of the operation, in fact, became an indicator of German readiness to undertake the Kursk operation, particularly regarding the redeployment of panzer and panzer grenadier units necessary to participate in, or back up, the Kursk assault. Vasilevsky noted the contribution of partisan *razvedka* in a message he dispatched on 21 May from the Briansk Front to the *STAVKA*. The message also demonstrated continued Soviet concern for axes other than Kursk. Vasilevsky later paraphrased the message:

> According to information from air, military, and partisan intelligence, the enemy was continuing to bring up infantry and particularly tanks to the first two directions [Spas–Demensky and Zhizdra]. The partisans had seen one tank division arriving from the west in the Spas–Demensky sector. Although the presence of shock groupings enabled us to cover both the Kaluga and Tula directions more or less reliably, all the same I thought it worthwhile shifting the 19th Rifle Corps from the Gzhatsk area to Yukhnov and leaving it as part of 10th Guards Army.[92]

K. K. Rokossovsky, the Central Front commander, also attested to the value of partisan *razvedka*:

> We kept in close contact with their [partisan] headquarters, from which we received information on enemy troop movements. Our air reconnaissance observations were double-checked and augmented by the partisans, and our aircraft bombed targets which they located.[93]

Meanwhile, south of Kursk in the Sumy–Khar'kov region, several partisan groups operated in support of frontal efforts. The Kudinov Detachment operating in the Akhtyrka, Poltava, and Liubotin area cut the Khar'kov–Poltava rail line and, with other agents, reported on German troop movements. The Pribura and Shervorok Detachments did likewise around Romny and east of Kiev.[94] The Uncle Kolia (*Diadia Kolia*) Partisan Brigade, commanded by P. G. Lopatin, made an important contribution to the intelligence effort when it seized a German staff officer from Army Group Center and returned him to the "Big land" (*Bol'shaia zemlia*). The officer "reported valuable information about the preparations of the Hitlerite Command for the Kursk offensive in the summer of 1943."[95] Soon after, a partisan detachment under D. N. Medvedev achieved a real coup when "it succeeded in obtaining information about the location of Hitler's command post in Vinnitsa, the offensive plans of the enemy at Kursk in the summer of 1943, and preparations by Hitlerites for terrorist acts relating to the heads of those united powers at the Teheran Conference."[96]

These and other partisan actions in the spring and summer of 1943 formed a growing mosaic of reconnaissance and diversionary activities in the enemy rear. Considered singly, few acts warranted major attention. Together, however, partisan warfare began to have a major impact. *Razvedka* data, together with agent, air, and radio information, provided a far clearer indication of enemy intentions and dispositions than in the past, just as partisan operations, like those around Briansk and the "railroad war," began to have more than minimal operational impact. These developments, plus the numerous references in Soviet orders and messages to agent reports, are indicative of the contribution both partisan and agent *razvedka* made to Soviet development of a sound intelligence picture before Kursk.

Radio-Electronic

By late 1942 Soviet radio *razvedka* had begun making significant contributions to Soviet intelligence efforts. For the first time, the Soviets created specialized radio intercept and jamming units within *fronts* that could focus their attention on German communications. Moreover, regulations and instructions provided necessary structure for these activities and facilitated their interpretation and collation with other intelligence data.

Earlier in the war, Soviet communications units at every level routinely monitored German radio transmissions. This activity was best organized at *front* and army level where specific communications units conducted systematic "listening" for respective staff intelligence departments. In addition, the Soviets began experimenting with radio location although these early efforts failed to provide accurate enough information for targeting. During the Stalingrad operation the Soviets had also attempted radio-suppression (*radio podavlenie*). After encirclement of German forces, the Stalingrad Front created a radio suppression group equipped with several high-powered radio stations subordinate to the 394th Separate Radio Battalion. The *front* also created a series of special radio stations to feed German Sixth Army disinformation.

A major step forward in radio *razvedka* occurred on 17 December 1942 when the High Command created their first special purpose radio battalions (*radiodivizion spetsial'nogo naznacheniia*) tasked with conducting radio-*razvedka* and jamming. Initially, the *STAVKA* formed the 131st and 132d Special Purpose Radio Battalions and, later in the winter, formed three more (129th, 130th, 228th), each battalion subordinate to a *front*.[97] These new units had contributed to the success of Soviet radio *razvedka* late in the Stalingrad operation and continued to do so throughout the winter.

During preparations for defensive and offensive operations, *fronts* employed existing radio assets within their headquarters and those of subordinate armies to identify the enemy, in particular, newly arriving enemy mobile forces. Soviet classified critiques of operations during the fall of 1942 and winter of 1943 indicated a growing capability to intercept German radio traffic and determine the presence and location of forces in both the tactical and operational depths. Although seldom capable of identifying units in its own right, it provided an essential adjunct to information obtained by agent and air collection.

Soviet sources are extremely reticent about exposing details of radio-*razvedka* prior to and during the Kursk operation. While they mention jamming operations, they ignore the important corollary of interception. However, the equipment provided to special purpose radio battalions clearly indicated the ability of these battalions to intercept as well as jam enemy communications. From Soviet and other sources, it is obvious the Soviets employed three types of signal intelligence collection: interception of German clear text messages, interception and decoding of enciphered German transmissions, and location of German units by radio direction finding and recognition of call signs.

During earlier operations the Soviets had demonstrated a talent for capitalizing on lapses in German communications discipline through *podslushivanie* (listening-in). This continued at Kursk. According to one source:

> Once the offensive began, Fourth Panzer Army signals officers noted violations by the "Grossdeutschland" and especially SS "Das Reich" Panzer Grenadier Divisions in the use of clear text messages during operations. But the real shock came shortly thereafter, when a captured intelligence report of the Soviet 1st Tank Army dated 5 July 1943 revealed that radio intelligence had identified the positions of the headquarters

and units of II SS Panzer Corps, 6th Panzer and 11th Panzer Divisions before the offensive began. Other captured documents disclosed that 7th Panzer Division, XIII Corps and Second Army headquarters had been similarly "fixed" by Soviet radio intelligence.[98]

The Soviets employed two specialized radio units at Kursk to jam German radio transmissions and probably to intercept messages as well. The 130th and 132d Special Designation (Purpose) Radio Battalions "paid special attention to disturbing radio communications of the staffs of divisions and corps, attacking from the north and south toward Kursk and other communications officers of aviation force, supporting the ground force."[99] The 132d Radio Battalion supported the Voronezh Front from positions near Sidorovka, southeast of Belgorod, where it collected information on German dispositions prior to the assault and, after 5 July, tried to interrupt Fourth Panzer Army communications as it advanced to Prokhorovka. The 130th Radio Battalion supported the Central Front from positions southeast of Mtsensk, focusing primarily on transmissions of German Second Panzer and Ninth Army.[100]

Ultra intercepts and German intelligence data cast some light on Soviet decoding capabilities. By June 1943 British intelligence had determined the Russians had captured the German code used by the Air Force for air-ground signaling and a naval Enigma machine as well.[101] Moreover, German records note that German Second Army lost to the Soviets several Enigma machines and some cipher parts and documentation in December 1941. A warning went out from the signal officer of XXX Corps of Army Group North on 18 September 1942 that "well-organized Russian radio intelligence" had the capability of reading "every one of our messages."[102] Later, in January 1943, OKH Signals Division evidenced "certainty" that the Russians had deciphered some Enigma messages. Consequently, the OKH instituted changes in equipment and procedures to improve communications security. It is also reasonable to assume German loss of additional Enigma machines during and after the Stalingrad operation when it lost all of Sixth Army and part of Second Army.

As we shall see, the clear correlation between German troop movements associated with offensive preparations and the time the Soviets issued alerts to their forces sharply indicates that radio intelligence, in concert with air, agent, and partisan *razvedka*, was capable, to a considerable extent, of monitoring troop movements in the German operational rear. This deep collection capability, combined with refined Soviet tactical *razvedka* techniques, provided ample warning of the impending attack.

Troop

While the Soviets relied on air, agent-diversionary, partisan, and radio *razvedka* as principal sources of strategic and operational intelligence, they generated tactical intelligence by conducting thoroughly planned and extensive troop, artillery, and engineer *razvedka*. Only the performance of thousands of mundane and often hazardous tasks associated with these collection methods could reveal the nature of enemy tactical defense sufficiently to permit successful detection by Soviet forces. From April to July 1943, Soviet forces, participating in erecting defensive positions along the Eastern Front, undertook constant reconnaissance across their *fronts*.

Front and army *razvedka* plans assigned specific intelligence collection missions to all subordinate units. In addition, subordinate units conducted routine troop reconnaissance in accustomed patterns to conceal the focus of Soviet defensive efforts. Combat patrols, sweeps, ambushes, and raids occurred regularly across the *front* to determine changes in German tactical dispositions and to capture prisoners and documents. To an increasing extent, these measures produced significant results. The Soviets referred to troops engaged in these activities as *iazykoved* (linguists), engaging in *iazykovanie* (linguistics), or more properly, a search for "tongues" (*iazyka*).

The Soviets improved procedures associated with all troop *razvedka* techniques. For example, the size of forces conducting sweeps (*poisk*) was significantly reduced; and sweeps were conducted in daytime rather than just at night. Daytime sweeps, used extensively throughout all fronts, occurred either one or two hours after first light or in bad weather. Similar improvements took place regarding other techniques as well. Although few troop *razvedka* missions produced significant information, collectively they provided thousands of bits of data necessary to portray accurately enemy dispositions and future intentions.

To verify the data collected by troop *razvedka*, the *STAVKA* required Soviet forces to conduct systematic reconnaissance in force across the entire *front*. Zhukov, as *STAVKA* representative for the Stalingrad offensive, had issued orders to that effect in early

November. Reconnaissance in force was designed to determine the actual forward area of enemy defenses, the grouping of enemy forces in the immediate tactical depths, the enemy system of fires, and the nature of engineer preparations of the defense.[103] To carry out the reconnaissance, first echelon rifle divisions operating on main attack axes formed reconnaissance detachments, normally consisting of reinforced companies or battalions from first echelon regiments, supported by regimental artillery. Sometimes divisions dispatched several detachments in company strength. The army commander specified the time of the reconnaissance in accordance with the army *razvedka* plan and local conditions.

In the spring of 1943 the Soviets improved their capability for processing and analyzing intelligence information obtained by troop *razvedka*. This included further rationalization of the staff system which collected and processed information and similar beefing-up of analysis, particularly at corps and division level. In addition, the Soviets added an interpreter to division intelligence staffs to supplement the existing interpreter at corps level. This permitted earlier and more thorough interrogation of POWs and more rapid interpretation of documents and exploitation of their contents. In addition, in July 1943 division intelligence officers received an assistant, and the program of intelligence training for officers and NCOs continued to improve.

The cumulative scale of troop *razvedka* in the months before Kursk was impressive. According to one source:

> From April through June 1943, in the forward area of the Central and Voronezh Front, in addition to troop commander and artillery observation points, more than 2,700 *razvedka* observation points were erected. *Front* forces conducted 105 reconnaissances in force, more than 2600 night sweeps and 1500 ambushes, as a result of which 187 Hitlerite soldiers and officers were seized. During the interrogation of prisoners the dispositions of enemy forces in the main defense belt were defined more precisely as well as the location of command posts and airdromes.[104]

Information from troop *razvedka* certainly contributed to the intelligence picture upon which the Soviets issued alerts in May, although the Soviets have divulged little of this information. As the real date of the German offensive neared, troop *razvedka* provided significant information, much of which the Soviets have revealed.

In early spring, active Soviet troop *razvedka* picked up signs of German offensive preparations. General K. S. Moskalenko, commander of the Voronezh Front's 40th Army, reported that, on 10 April, his chief of staff noted the concentration of 15 infantry and three panzer divisions in the Voronezh Front sector with evidence that new formations were continuing to arrive. Two days later the Voronezh Front military council reported to the General Staff that the enemy opposing the front "can create a shock group of a strength of up to 10 tank divisions, the concentration of which is expected in the Borisovka, Belgorod, Murom, Kazach'ia Lopan' areas."[105] Moskalenko responded to these warnings by intensifying his troop *razvedka*:

> In the 40th Army sector, already in the first ten days of May we observed animated movement of enemy forces. On our right flank enemy reconnaissance in force and sweeps quickened. Prisoners [taken by Soviet *razvedka*] reported that conversations about an offensive went on among officers.[106]

At this stage Moskalenko admitted that, although the Soviets knew an attack would occur somewhere in the Kursk region, "It was not known to us, when, or in what sector of the front the offensive would begin."[107]

Razvedka in 40th Army's sector continued to clarify the situation despite the fact that warning signals issued in May proved erroneous. On 15 June a German deserter from the 3d Battalion, 164th Infantry Regiment, 57th Infantry Division reported to 40th Army intelligence that his unit, facing the right flank of Moskalenko's army, had the mission of holding firmly to its defense lines since the offensive would occur "in a more critical sector of the front." The deserter reported that, from the beginning of June, German forces were concentrating in the Khar'kov and Belgorod regions, east of 40th Army's sector.[108]

On 19 June another captured German prisoner from the 2d Battalion, 676th Infantry Regiment, 332d Infantry Division reported that for two or three weeks a rumor had circulated in his unit to the effect that his division would soon move eastward to a new concentration area near Golovchino, out of 40th Army's sector. Moskalenko noted, "Soon this information was confirmed: prisoners taken from that division at the end of June stated the division would move from its former defense positions in order to concentrate on 2 July against [Soviet] 6th Guards Army."[109] Moskalenko, in the light of previous German actions, was concerned about strengthened German defenses on his army's front. He later wrote:

We were not completely sure about the time or direction of the enemy strikes. In the data which we had at our disposal, doubt was aroused by the fact that the fascist command, which was always looking for weak spots in our defense, namely where it had attempted to achieve success, was now operating differently: it was concentrating its primary forces against a strongly fortified sector of the defense where, as the enemy undoubtedly knew, a tank and a combined arms army were deployed, as were *front* reserves, in the second echelon of the Voronezh Front. Was this not guile? And was this not done in order to distract the attention of the Soviet command from the actual direction of the strike they prepared? Therefore, we still did not discount the possibility of an enemy offensive in other directions, among which was the 40th Army sector.[110]

On the northwestern face of the Kursk bulge, General P. I. Batov, commanding 65th Army in the secondary defense sector of the Central Front, harbored similar misgivings. Every night during the last ten days of June German reconnaissance groups operated in 65th Army's sector. Batov noted his concern:

> The activity of German reconnaissance was a sign that the enemy was completing his preparations for an offensive. But why did his activity grow only on 65th Army's front? Was his main attack aimed at us? Rokossovsky answered me confidently regarding that question, "The Germans are cunning. The main grouping, as before, sits against the right flank of our front. However, be alert!"[111]

Experiences varied widely across the front throughout June; but, as July approached, troop reconnaissance activity intensified and produced significant results. A *razvedka* group of 6th Guards Army's 32d Guards Rifle Division in the Belgorod sector, over the course of several days, captured prisoners and documents "providing information about the location, grouping, combat capability, and offensive method of SS Panzer Division 'Totenkopf.' Besides this, scouts simultaneously forewarned our command about the approach of enemy reserves to the front."[112] A classified Soviet analysis of intelligence data, upon which the Soviet counterpreparation was based, confirmed the advance warning, stating:

> On the Voronezh Front (6th Guards Army) from 28 June we noticed accelerated movements of enemy forces on the Belgorod–Tomarovka road and, simultaneously with this,

enemy forces moved up closer to our forward positions. As a result of all types of *razvedka* we established there were four tank and three infantry divisions on the front of 6th Guards Army which had arrived from other sectors.[113]

On 2 July the Voronezh Front further confirmed this report when two prisoners taken that day reported that trains with a large quantity of tanks, artillery, infantry, ammunition, and foodstuffs were unloading at Belgorod.

The Central Front was equally attentive. From 29 June through 3 July *front* ground and air reconnaissance "noticed movements of German armor, artillery, and infantry units (subunits) and their arrival in the forward area in 13th and 48th Armies' sectors."[114] A formerly classified report noted that from 2 July "we noticed activity in enemy positions" and tallied up the number of newly arrived units as four infantry and three tank divisions.[115] By 5 July the Central Front had detected on 13th Army's front alone 90 artillery batteries, 22 mortar batteries and a large number of observation posts. Intensified troop *razvedka* further clarified this picture. On the night of 1–2 July, a German deserter of 68th Infantry Division near Sumy reported that an offensive would occur within three days.[116] Forty-eight hours later, on the night of 4 July

> a deserter from the 2d Squadron, 248th Reconnaissance Detachment of the 168th Infantry Division ... reported that on the night of 4–5 July the Germans intended to go on the offensive from the region north and northwest of Belgorod and that in preparing for the offensive, sappers of SS "Totenkopf" Tank Division had begun mineclearing on the night of 4 July.[117]

On the north side of the Kursk Bulge, in the State Farm Tarino sector of the Central Front's 13th Army, at 2230 4 July, a *razvedka* detachment from the 77th Separate Reconnaissance Company, 15th Rifle Division, captured a German from 6th Infantry Division who reported the German attack would begin at 0300 5 July.[118] Another German sapper, captured in 48th Army's sector, provided essentially the same information. On the basis of this latest troop *razvedka* information, the *STAVKA* ordered the Central and Voronezh Fronts to commence their artillery counterpreparation only hours before the planned German assault.

Artillery

One of the most important aspects of *razvedka* prior to the conduct of defensive or offensive operations was the necessity for correctly identifying enemy fire systems, troop concentrations, command and control posts, and other targets whose destruction would disrupt enemy plans. Determining the enemy fire and defense system was the task of artillery *razvedka*.

The 1942 regulations had established the tasks of artillery *razvedka* and procedures for the accomplishment of those tasks. Artillery *razvedka* was to be conducted in all weather, around the clock, and in all defensive and offensive situations. The principal means of artillery *razvedka* was troop artillery *razvedka*, based on thorough battlefield observation. Extensive observation networks, equipped with optical devices, were designed to reveal all features of enemy defenses which could be seen by the human eye. The Soviets employed artillery instrumental *razvedka* (AIR) and corrective-reconnaissance aviation to penetrate areas not visible from ground observation.

Separate reconnaissance artillery battalions (ORAD) conducted ground observation with sound, optical, photographic, and topographical reconnaissance subunits. Sound ranging proved particularly effective in determining potential targets. Separate corrective-reconnaissance aviation squadrons (OKAE) and regiments (OKAP) used visual and photographic means to supplement the work of ground reconnaissance artillery battalions and to identify targets in the enemy defenses and subsequently adjusted artillery fire on distant targets. To complete the artillery *razvedka* mosaic, Soviet combined arms commanders employed reconnaissance groups or detachments to penetrate into the enemy rear area. Artillerymen routinely participated in these missions. The artillery staff of forces at all levels planned and conducted artillery *razvedka* and processed the information received. The force chief of staff ultimately was responsible for the completeness, credibility, and timeliness of the data. Staff intelligence departments or sections then integrated artillery reconnaissance data with other intelligence information. Favorable weather during the period preceding the Kursk operation facilitated artillery *razvedka*.

The two *fronts* directly involved in planning the initial Kursk defense allocated all available resources to the artillery *razvedka* task. Beginning in April, both *fronts* conducted continuous *raz-*

vedka from an extensive network of artillery unit and formation observation posts. Observation identified appropriate targets to a depth of five kilometers into German forward defenses. The Central Front's 13th Army exemplified the high density of the observation network. By early July the army had created 1,300 artillery observation posts representing a density of about 40 OPs per kilometer of front. All posts observed in accordance with the artillery plan created and centrally controlled by the army artillery staff.[119]

For deeper observation and identification of specific enemy targets in the forward area and depths of the defense (primarily artillery), both *fronts* possessed reinforced means of artillery instrumental *razvedka* (AIR) and corrective-reconnaissance aviation. AIR was performed by separate reconnaissance artillery battalions organic to artillery divisions, each of which consisted of two sound *razvedka* batteries, an optical *razvedka* battery, a topographical *razvedka* battery, and photogrammatric and meteorological platoons. The Central Front included four such artillery battalions, two in 13th Army and one each in 48th and 70th Armies. The Voronezh Front fielded seven separate reconnaissance artillery battalions with two assigned to 6th Guards Army and one each to 7th Guards, 38th, and 40th Armies.[120] In addition, both *fronts* included separate corrective-reconnaissance aviation squadrons which, in the spring, were shifted from artillery division control to *front* control.[121] By virtue of the shift, each *front* possessed one corrective-reconnaissance aviation regiment (OKAP), each with four subordinate squadrons, as well as a separate squadron (by 1944 fighter aircraft elements were also added to the regiments to provide protection).[122] The adjacent Briansk, Western, and Southwestern Fronts also contained air assets, but did not have full corrective-reconnaissance aviation regiments.

Sound *razvedka* remained the most important function of the reconnaissance artillery battalions. During April Central Front battalions deployed their sound *razvedka* batteries in five separate posts two to three kilometers from the forward edge. A central sound recording station, situated in the rear, performed all calculations and provided data for answering fire.[123] Sound ranging activities were closely integrated with visual optical observation and ground patrol *razvedka* activity. Meanwhile, topographic units worked to tie together Soviet artillery units and to plot the locations of enemy positions received from ground and air reconnaissance.

The role of artillery air *razvedka* grew in the period prior to the

Kursk operation, but its effectiveness was still dependent upon the availability of fighter aircraft cover. Where the skies were safe, results were impressive. For example:

> During the course of the Orel offensive operation in July 1943 the 50th Separate Corrective-Reconnaissance Aviation Squadron on the main axis of the Briansk Front completed 44 sorties to photograph defensive sectors, to conduct visual *razvedka* of batteries and to correct fire on them. As a result we succeeded in detecting up to 1,200 individual targets and destroying eight enemy batteries.[124]

The Soviets, however, encountered difficulties as well, exemplified by the experience of the Briansk Front's 61st Army operating on the Bolkhov axis in July. Although 61st Army possessed separate reconnaissance artillery battalions and separate corrective-reconnaissance aviation squadrons, "weak command and control of them by the army artillery staff led to their ineffective use."[125] This, in turn, led to ineffective artillery fire.

Conversely, many Soviet units experienced marked success. In the Central Front sector, the 98th Separate Corrective-Reconnaissance Aviation Regiment worked effectively. As a result:

> In the preparatory period this regiment accomplished a great deal from its multiple, repetitive, large scale photographing of the entire depth of the enemy defense. By the beginning of the defensive battle all artillery staffs of armies on the main attack axis were equipped with maps with detailed decoded information about the enemy.[126]

By mid-April Central Front *razvedka* "had a full representation of the enemy. The 258th, 7th, and 72d Infantry Divisions defended in *front* of 70th Army."[127]

Late during the preparatory period, artillery observation posts detected an attempt by the Germans to deceive the Soviets regarding their intended attack sector. The lst Guards Artillery Division observers after 1 July reported:

> Once a group of officers in SS panzer force uniforms openly, without any attempt at concealment, conducted personal reconnaissance in *front* of the positions of the 280th Rifle Division. From the OP of Col G. V. Godin it was apparent how the fascists checked their maps of the terrain and pointed among themselves in the direction of Moloticha. The SS were

located in the same sector where we had prepared an artillery concentration, but the commands did not open fire on them; it was more important to establish enemy intentions. Later we detected still other reconnaissance groups. As a result we reached a rather clear impression of enemy intentions to attack in the direction of the left flank sector of 70th Army's 28th Rifle Corps. True, the suspicion quite fully arose that the demonstration was an attempt to deceive Soviet forces.[128]

Despite the fact that artillery instrumental *razvedka* was still not fully sufficient:

On the Central Front alone, from March to July reconnaissance artillery battalions detected 364 artillery and mortar batteries, 416 separate guns and mortars, 124 strongpoints and covered firing positions and 51 machine guns. On the Voronezh Front instrumental *razvedka* means discovered 80 percent of enemy artillery, up to 50 percent of the mortars, and more than 50 percent of engineer structures in the forward area and in the immediate depths of the enemy defense.

As a result of the work of all artillery *razvedka* organs of the Central Front, by the opening of battle a total of 3,722 targets, among which were 329 artillery and 129 mortar batteries, 2,095 firing points and pillboxes, 521 covered firing positions, and 238 observation posts, were inventoried.

On the Voronezh Front 6th Guards Army *razvedka* discovered 1,076 targets including 94 artillery and mortar batteries, 179 pillboxes and bunkers, 37 observation points, 597 machine guns, various engineer structures, warehouses, and regions of concentration of enemy forces.[129]

The overall Soviet artillery *razvedka* plan built upon the successes of the Stalingrad period to complete a fairly comprehensive picture of German tactical defenses. This picture was sufficiently detailed to permit detection of major changes in German dispositions days prior to the beginning of the offensive.

Engineer

While artillery staffs were conducting *razvedka* to determine the nature of enemy firing systems, engineer forces sought intelligence on German engineer preparations for the offensive and on physical aspects of the area of operations. Engineer *razvedka* provided a basis for successful creation and implementation of the engineer plan at every level. Plans for the Kursk operation required engineer forces to carry out careful engineer *razvedka* of the "forward edge" and depths of the enemy defense adjacent to all threatened areas. Specifically, engineer *razvedka* was to determine the nature of the defense; enemy engineer preparations; and the number and disposition of engineer obstacles, in particular, minefields. The principal means for conducting *razvedka* were engineer observation posts (INP), reconnaissance and search groups, and engineers assigned to combat units carrying out reconnaissance in force.[130]

The engineer force staff of armies organized *razvedka* through corps and division engineers and through army staffs to attached engineer-sapper units and formations. The *front* chief of engineers organized the entire engineer *razvedka* effort for the *front*. Engineer staffs and forces planned and carried out engineer *razvedka*. Plans included specific missions, sectors of action, composition of forces, method and means of conduct, period of fulfillment by stages, organization of communications, and reporting sequences and procedures. A series of standard orders and reports provided means for compiling *razvedka* data and transmitting it to appropriate operational organs. ROs at *front* and army level maintained all data on a map and passed necessary information to artillery staffs, air armies, engineer forces, and *front* topographic departments.

Soviet analysis of engineer *razvedka* procedures during operations in early 1943 provided a rationale for this tightened system. In part, the Soviets concluded:

> Engineer *razvedka* produces positive results only when it is conducted within a unified system of cooperation of all types of land and air *razvedka*. In order to decipher aerial photographs, use information of ground *razvedka*, and form a collective scheme, it is very beneficial to organize a special group of officers in the *razvedka* department (RO) of the staff. It is obligatory that engineer officers be members of this group.[131]

The critique went on to emphasize the value of aerial and ground engineer photography in offensive and defensive preparations.

Engineer *razvedka* focused simultaneously on determining enemy offensive preparations and detecting specific firing and defensive positions in the depths of the enemy defense to facilitate counteroffensive action. All the while engineers studied the terrain on both sides of the *front*. After late 1942 engineer obstacle battalions of special designation engineer brigades (engineer brigades of special designation/IBrSH) formed engineer *razvedka* subunits. Later, army engineer battalions employed platoon size forces for engineer *razvedka*, and engineer-sapper brigades used engineer-*razvedka* companies. Assault engineer-sapper brigades of *fronts* and army motorized engineer brigades used motorized engineer reconnaissance companies. These units were equipped, insofar as possible, with vehicles, radios, and optical observation equipment. The assistant chief of staff for engineer *razvedka* of engineer formations and *fronts* and armies supervised their activities. Within the sapper battalion of rifle divisions, the first platoon of the first company was specially trained for and assigned the task of conducting *razvedka*. The same applied to the first squad in the sapper platoon of rifle regiments.[132]

Although engineer *razvedka* was either conducted independently or as a part of another *razvedka* force, more often it was combined with other means. Thus, engineers participated in observation, sweeps, deep reconnaissance, photography, and interrogation of civilians, prisoners, and deserters. They also employed engineer-observation posts, photographic posts, engineer-sweep groups, engineer groups for long-range *razvedka*, and engineer-reconnaissance patrols.

Engineer observation posts (INP) deployed in the first line of trenches. These conducted round-the-clock observation and, during the night, dispatched patrols and established listening posts near or within German defenses. These posts were particularly dense in the first echelon rifle division defensive positions on suspected enemy attack axes. For example, during April and May 1943 the Central Front's 65th Army deployed 39 INPs as follows:

Force	Engineer Observation Posts
149th Rifle Division	3
69th Rifle Division	8
194th Rifle Division	4
37th Guards Rifle Division	7
60th Rifle Division	4
246th Rifle Division	5
115th Rifle Brigade	4
321st Army Engineer Battalion	2
Attached Front Engineers	2[133]

An even denser array of engineer observation posts existed on 13th and 70th Armies' *fronts*.

These posts assisted materially in the detection of German offensive preparations:

> Engineer *razvedka* at the end of June and beginning of July discovered lanes made by the enemy through his obstacles. On the night of 5 July observation from an engineer observation post fixed the cutting of lanes by the enemy through the obstacles in front of our forward edge. This helped determine the direction of the enemy main attack and affirmed the correctness of information from other types of *razvedka* about the time his offensive would begin.[134]

Photographic observation was carried out from photographic posts equipped with a periscopic long-focusing photo apparatus (PDF), which prepared photographic panoramas of the enemy defenses. *Front* photo interpreters then analyzed these photographs to determine minute changes in enemy dispositions.

The most mobile means of engineer *razvedka* were the engineer *razvedka* groups (IRG) which had the task of conducting ground *razvedka* to verify observation data and of carrying out diversionary activity as well. These forces, formed from division, army, and *front* engineer units, operated at night on foot or were delivered into the enemy rear by parachute.[135] By the time of Kursk, the Soviets also employed mobile engineer observation posts, detailed from regimental sapper platoons, division sapper battalions, army and *front* engineer units, and especially, from mobile obstacle detachments of division and corps. These mobile observation posts operated principally after enemy offensive operations had commenced.

In addition to seeking information on enemy dispositions, engineer *razvedka* thoroughly surveyed terrain conditions on both sides of the *front*. Engineers took part in personal reconnaissance (*rekognostsirovka*) conducted by command groups at each level and employed numerous engineer patrols as well. For example:

> From 28 March to 5 July 1943 engineer units of the Voronezh Front conducted engineer *razvedka* of the Psel', Northern Donets, Vorskla, Seim and Oskol Rivers, their tributaries, streams, and lakes in the *front* sector. Detailed descriptions of them provided the capability of precisely determining conditions for crossing them, the capability of constructing here and there types of crossings, and the necessary degree of

strengthening water barriers so that they could be used as obstacles.[136]

Engineer *razvedka* measures, integrated into a thorough system of troop *razvedka* and artillery *razvedka*, provided sound ground intelligence information. Army and *front*-level intelligence staffs had the task of integrating this data with information obtained from higher level, more sophisticated collection systems.

Summary

The cumulative data obtained from troop *razvedka*, combined with information from operational and strategic means and technical data from artillery and engineer *razvedka*, alerted the Soviets. On 29 June, a Central Front intelligence summary concluded that the Germans had occupied jumping-off positions for the offensive. Daily summaries for 30 June, 1, 2, and 3 July repeated the warning. Suddenly, on 4 July, the Soviets noted all activity had sharply halted:

> On the enemy side, where we expected the offensive, suddenly all was quiet. Nothing could be observed in front of Central Front forces. The field of battle was lifeless. Enemy firing activity fell off. On the Voronezh Front to the left it was the same. Moreover, operational *razvedka* [agent, air, radio] determined that tanks, vehicles, and tractors stretched along roads running east and west in the Donbas, 150–200 kilometers south of Khar'kov. It seemed as if from the Kursk bulge all were rushing back and heading for the Donbas. However, these and other measures conducted by the enemy not only did not deceive our *razvedka* but also alerted them even more. All forces and means of *razvedka* of units, formations and large formations intently followed the enemy actions.
>
> Hour after hour passed and in the enemy camp as before quiet ruled. What did it mean? Why did the enemy act so unusually? That question also extremely interested officer-*razvedchiks* and commanders at all levels.
>
> There were of course hypotheses and proposals in search of the truth.
>
> Finally we decided. You see, it was all in order. In the course of the last five days the enemy had moved his forces and equipment to the forward edge and regrouped in preparation for the offensive.

243

On the night of 4 July the enemy had occupied jumping-off positions for the attack. Therefore on 4 July no regrouping or movement of forces from the depths could be detected. You see, the enemy needed at least one day to rest, inspect, and prepare the personnel of his subunits and units for the attack.

Such a conclusion was written in the intelligence summary of the Central Front for 4 July. In particular it said that the enemy had finished his force concentration and was preparing to go over to the offensive, which was expected to occur in one–two days.[137]

Despite this assessment, the Soviets still did not know the precise time of the offensive or the precise main attack axes. Based on this summary and a like summary prepared by the Voronezh Front, all forces were directed "to strengthen all types of *razvedka* to establish the exact time of the enemy offensive."[138] This order reinforced similar orders issued by the *STAVKA* on 2 July which mandated intensification of air *razvedka* and seizure of prisoners. In response to these orders the Soviets intensified aerial *razvedka* and sweeps, searches, and ambushes organized by first echelon rifle divisions. One of the many groups was one consisting of a sergeant and 14 men from the 15th Rifle Division, which at about 2200 hours seized a prisoner from the German 6th Infantry Division. Interrogation of the prisoner revealed that the attack would occur at 0200, 5 July. Acting on the basis of that, plus other information from the Voronezh Front, the *STAVKA* authorized the two *fronts* to commence their counterpreparation. One Soviet assessment focused on this single, seemingly inconsequential episode to generalize about the importance of low-level troop *razvedka*:

It is not difficult to note, that the prisoner sapper of the 6th German Infantry Division, his testimony in the interrogation, and conclusions reached by our commands had not only tactical or operational, but also strategic importance.[139]

ANALYSIS OF *RAZVEDKA*

By analyzing the course of combat, existing Soviet orders and assessments, accounts of Soviet *razvedka* activities, actual Soviet force dispositions, and documented German orders and troop movements associated with preparations for the summer offensive, one can reconstruct by fact, circumstance, or inference, the basis for Soviet judgements and actions.

The heavy combat which raged throughout February and March, during which the Germans drove Soviet forces back to the line of the Northern Donets River and threatened Kursk, left as a legacy the Kursk salient jutting westward from what was otherwise an almost linear front. When action subsided in late March, the bulk of German operational reserves, the panzer corps, were concentrated along the flanks of the Kursk bulge or opposite Soviet defenses in the Izium sector of the Northern Donets River line. These dispositions, the focus of German thrusts in March, and the configuration of the front served as a basis for initial Soviet assessments of German intentions.

In late March and early April, the *STAVKA* and General Staff exchanged opinions on the matter and sought advice from *STAVKA* representatives and *front* commanders as well. Underlying their concern was a paucity of hard intelligence information resulting from the onset of the *razputitsa* (thaw) and the absence of combat action. A General Staff Directive of 3 April underscored the problem:

> Because of the spring thaw and cessation of large combat on the front for most armies receipt of information from troop *razvedka* has diminished. As a result enemy regroupings in many cases remain undetected.[140]

As a result, the *STAVKA* collected assessments from subordinates. Shtemenko summed up the resulting General Staff view on German intentions:

> The question as to "where" was not then too difficult. There could be only one answer – in the Kursk Salient. This was where the enemy had their main strike forces, which represented two possible dangers for us; a deep outflanking thrust round Moscow or a turn southwards. On the other hand, it was here, against the enemy's main concentration, that we ourselves could use our manpower and weapons to the greatest effect, particularly our big tank formations. No other sector, even if we were very successful there, promised so much as the Kursk salient. This was the conclusion eventually reached by GHQ, the General Staff and the *front* commanders.[141]

Zhukov and the Central and Voronezh Front staffs echoed Shtemenko's opinion in their appreciations of early April 1943. Zhukov believed German strategic weakness and the configuration of the front would make Kursk a likely target, with Moscow the ultimate objective. The Central Front assessment detailed German troop movements in its sector and highlighted shifts of forces from the Kalinin and Western Front sectors into that of the Central Front. It estimated it was opposed by German Second and Second Panzer Armies which had 18 divisions forward and 19 in reserve and second echelon. The bulk of these forces (15 divisions) faced 65th Army's sector covering the approaches to Novgorod–Severskii and Sevsk. While Rokossovsky was concerned about future German action in the Ponyri–Kursk sector and beyond to Voronezh, he assessed no action would occur until after the thaw had ended.[142]

Vatutin and his Voronezh Front staff counted nine infantry and six panzer divisions confronting his defenses with a capability for further reinforcement by three more panzer divisions from the Southwestern Front sector. Vatutin noted that radio intercepts had already detected the movement of 17th Panzer Division from Aleksievskii northward to Tashchagovka along the Northern Donets River. Thus, Vatutin estimated the Germans could assemble a shock group of up to ten panzer and more than six infantry divisions in the Borisovka–Kazach'ia Lopan area for an advance northward toward Stary Oskol and additionally toward Oboian, Sudzha, and Novy Oskol. Like Rokossovsky, Vatutin thought terrain conditions would forestall a major attack until after 20 April and, more likely, early May.[143]

A subsequent 12 April STAVKA meeting agreed that Kursk was the most likely German target. Meanwhile, on 23 April, the STAVKA ordered the Steppe Military District to erect a safety net of reserve armies deep in the rear from Elets through Voronezh to Millerovo south of the Don River. Simultaneously, the STAVKA ordered all fronts to be vigilant against the German practice of mounting diversionary attacks elsewhere across the front.[144] On 20 April, Rado ("Dora") in Switzerland relayed intelligence that set 14 June as the date of the offensive but observed, "Only modest operations were planned." Subsequent messages over the next nine days from "Dora" indicated postponement of the offensive from early May to 12 June.[145]

The first concrete Soviet warning of an impending attack occurred on 2 May when the STAVKA radioed front commanders that an attack was expected at any moment. Zhukov reported, "The Supreme Command had carried out thorough intelligence and aerial reconnaissance which had gained reliable information on the enemy flow of troops and ammunition toward the Orel, Kromy, Briansk, Khar'kov, Krasnograd, and Poltava sectors."[146] A 5 May

STAVKA directive requiring *fronts* to intensify *razvedka* echoed Zhukov's view, stating, "In recent days considerable movement of enemy troops and transport has been detected in the Orel, Belgorod, Khar'kov region, as well as an approach of forces to the front lines. This forces us to expect active operations by the enemy in the shortest time."[147] The 2 May warning order coincided closely with Soviet receipt from the British of the 25 April Ultra intercept, which summarized an Army Group South assessment of Soviet dispositions and anticipated actions. On 30 April the British passed this assessment to the Soviets, along with a warning of an impending German attack on Kursk.[148] Soon, however, available Ultra material decreased in quality and quantity.

Soviet assessments made in late April and early May, however, also coincided closely with the most apparent indicator of impending offensive action, German troop movements, in particular movements of panzer and panzer grenadier divisions. In late April German panzer forces adjacent to the Kursk bulge were controlled by eight panzer corps (see Map 11). North of Kursk the XXXXVI, XXXXVII, and XXXXI Panzer Corps concentrated their divisions in the depths of the Orel salient. South of Kursk the XXXXVIII, II SS Panzer, and XXIV Panzer Corps deployed forward and in the depths of the Belgorod–Khar'kov salient. LVII and XXXX Panzer Corps elements stretched along the rail line south of the Northern Donets River from Balaklaia to east of Slaviansk.[149]

In late April, specifically on the 29th and 30th, a significant number of these divisions shifted sectors or moved closer to the front (see Map 12). In the Orel area, 12th and 20th Panzer Divisions shifted south toward the front from positions southwest of Orel, while, in the Belgorod–Khar'kov region, SS Panzer Divisions "Totenkopf" and "Das Reich" rotated forces between front and rear positions and SS "Das Reich" moved its assembly areas from south of Khar'kov to positions north of the city. At the same time, 7th Panzer Division moved into assembly areas south of Khar'kov and 106th Infantry Division shifted from positions east of Khar'kov into new positions near Belgorod. Simultaneously, Panzer Grenadier Division "Grossdeutschland" moved subordinate units from the Poltava region northward to new positions southwest of Belgorod in the rear of German front line positions.[150] Although the bulk of this movement was at night, daytime traffic intensified as well. It is reasonable to assume the rail net, particularly south of Khar'kov, was under observation by agent, *razvedka*-diversionary forces, or partisan reconnaissance patrols, for later in the period, the same

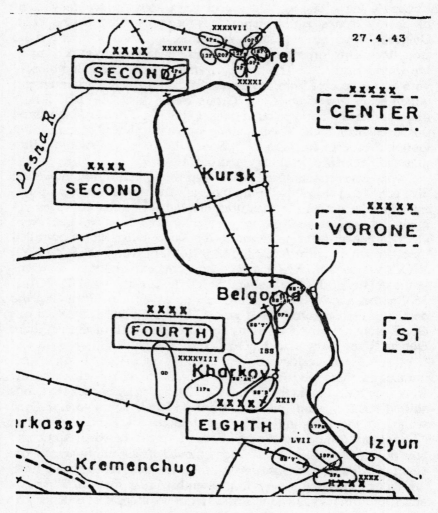

11. Position of German operational reserves, 27 April 1943

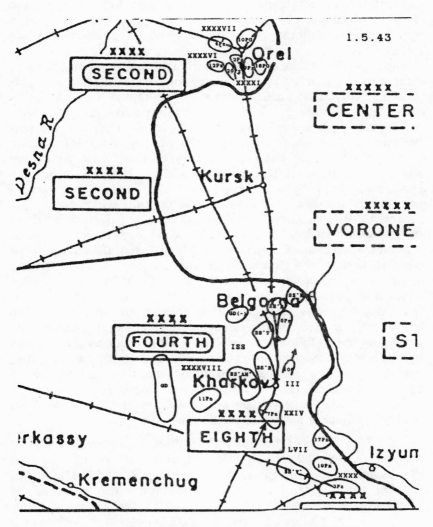

12. Position of German operational reserves, 1 May 1943

segments of rail line came under diversionary attacks. Detection of this movement by agent, air, or radio reconnaissance, or a combination of all three, probably prompted Soviet issuance of the 2 May alert.

Although the expected attack did not materialize, German forces maintained their advanced positions for several days. This, plus additional Soviet *razvedka* information, prompted the *STAVKA* to issue a second warning on 8 May, which postulated a new attack time of 10–12 May. Shtemenko failed to specify the nature of the new intelligence data, simply stating, "On May 8, 1943 information reached the General Staff by various channels that an enemy offensive on the Orel–Kursk Sector and the Belgorod–Khar'kov Sector might begin between May 10 and 12."[151] In part, this warning reflected the continued movement of those units which had begun changing positions in late April (despite Hitler's decision to defer the attack until 10 June at the earliest – within days he set 12 June as the date). Lieutenant General K. S. Moskalenko affirmed that the principal indicator of German intentions on both occasions in May was troop movements, writing, "Unusual troop movements were detected on the enemy side twice in May."[152] In addition, intensified troop *razvedka* produced a new batch of prisoners which undoubtedly echoed rumors circulating in the German camp concerning an impending offensive. Heavy air activity associated with the 6–13 May Soviet air offensive produced new air *razvedka* data confirming heavier German troop movements forward. Despite the warnings, however, the offensive did not materialize.

After mid-May a new spate of *razvedka* information forced the *STAVKA* to issue a further alert. Shtemenko reported:

> On May 19, 1943, the General Staff received fresh and what to us then seemed reliable information that the enemy intended launching their offensive between May 19 and 26. The text of the second warning to the same Fronts was prepared by Antonov and, after being reported to the Supreme Commander by phone, was sent out at 0330 hours on May 20 to the addressees. As before, they were instructed not to relax their vigilance and battle readiness, including that of the air forces, and, by reconnaissance patrols and taking prisoners, to uncover the strength of the enemy's forces and actual intentions.[153]

The *STAVKA* Directive of 20 May, which contained the warning, specified the source of its data, stating, "According to information received from agent *razvedka*, the Germans intend to begin the offensive on our front during the period 19–26 May."[154] The same day Vasilevsky claimed the General Staff "received [fresh] information on enemy movements" which prompted the alert.[155] This probably referred to actual German troop movements involving a shift of 7th Panzer Division to positions north of Khar'kov, the forward deployment of elements of 11th Panzer Division to Borisovka and "Grossdeutschland" Panzer Grenadier Division to Akhtyrka, and a wholesale shifting of forces within LVII and XXIV Panzer Corps south and west of Izium (see Map 13).[156]

The following day the Central Front reported similar movements were occurring on its front, particularly involving 2d Panzer and 36th Panzer Grenadier Divisions and other forces south of Orel. The same Central Front report, however, ended by discounting the likelihood of an offensive before the end of May. This judgement was made on the basis of troop, artillery, and engineer *razvedka* of the German forward area which reported, "The enemy was not making direct preparations for the offensive."[157] In essence, a warning based on operational and strategic *razvedka* of deep German movements was discounted when it failed to match the assessments based on shallower tactical *razvedka*. Meanwhile, on 23 May, after Soviet determination that an offensive was not in the immediate offing, "Werther" in Switzerland reported Army Groups South and Center had completed preparations for a 1 June attack.[158] Despite this report, as May gave way to June, Soviet anxiety over an impending attack lessened. Although "the General Staff was receiving reports [primarily agent and partisan] of huge transfers of tanks from west to east – apart from information about troop concentrations, there was no other evidence that an offensive would be launched."[159]

In early June, to confirm that an attack was not imminent, the General Staff's operations section again ordered *fronts* to focus *razvedka* assets on German force dispositions, particularly panzer units. This order may have been prompted in part by a 6 June "Werther" report that forward movements of Second and Fourth Panzer Armies' motorized units had been cancelled on 28 May.[160] An air of distrust surrounded the Soviet reaction. The 6 June order produced a reassuring assessment, "Five days were allowed and when they had elapsed, reassuring reports came back that there had been no change at the front and the enemy's tank concentration was still the same."[161] In fact, actual German dispositions reflected the accuracy of this assessment. German panzer forces remained in

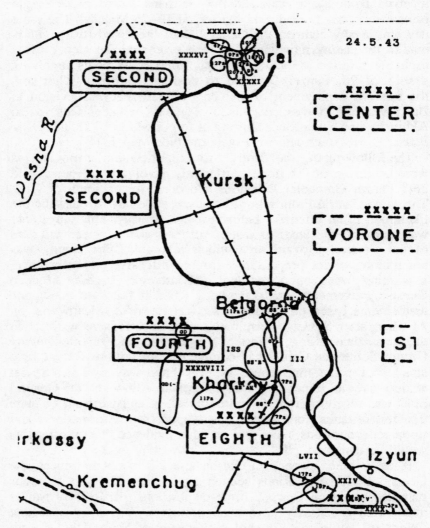

13. Position of German operational reserves, 24 May 1943

assembly areas, the bulk of which were in the Khar'kov area (see map 14).[162]

By mid-June Vasilevsky, Zhukov, and others in the General Staff were convinced an offensive was in the offing. Vasilevsky later wrote:

> As a result of constant and very careful military observation of the enemy on both the Voronezh and the Central Fronts, as well as the information being received from all forms of intelligence, we knew precisely that the Nazis were fully prepared for the offensive. ... We were both convinced that the enemy would be the first to launch an attack during the following week [after 22 June].[163]

This judgement reflected new actual German troop movements which began on 16 June and continued to about the 20th (see Map 15). During that period 3d Panzer Division moved from the Slaviansk region northwest to new positions southeast of Khar'kov. Simultaneously, 17th Panzer Division consolidated in assembly areas near Barvenkovo and began movement to Slaviansk.[164] These movements affected German offensive posture in both the Belgorod–Khar'kov and Izium sectors, where German planners had prepared distinct plans for "Zitadelle," "Panther," and "Habicht." This warning, however, also turned out to be premature as confirmed on 23 June when "Lucy" (Rudolph Rossler) reported from Lucerne, "The very latest news from Fuehrer headquarters ... the German attack against Kursk, contemplated since the end of May is no longer planned."[165] Hard on the heels of "Lucy's" news, "Werther" also sent a message (23 June) which read:

> OKW does not wish to provoke a large-scale Russian offensive in the central sector under any circumstances. Therefore one considers the German preventive attack planned for May–early June in the southern sector no longer serves a purpose. ... Soviet build-up in the Kursk area since early June is now so great that German superiority there no longer exists.[166]

In essence, "Werther" stated the offensive would not occur. Within ten days, however, German offensive indicators mounted to such an extent that a new warning was warranted.

On 29 June German forces began forward deployment of forces for the 5 July offensive. Movements associated with these final preparations were substantial and literally dwarfed movements which had prompted previous Soviet alert orders. From 29 June

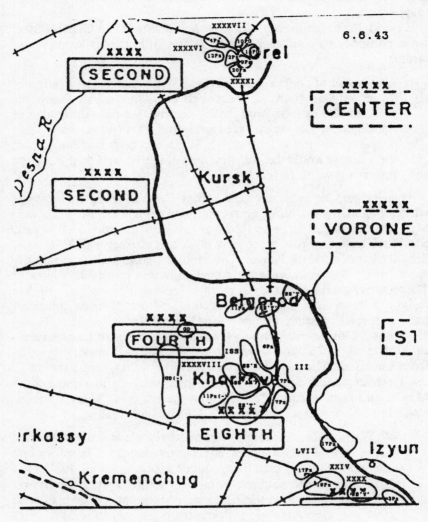

14. Position of German operational reserves, 6 June 1943

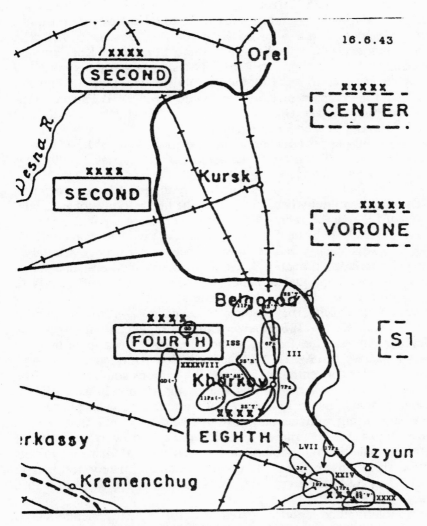

15. Position of German operational reserves, 16 June 1943

through 1 July, II SS Panzer Corps' SS Panzer Division "Totenkopf" moved north from assembly areas south of Khar'kov into positions in the tactical depth west of Belgorod (see Maps 16–18). The remaining divisions of the corps assembled north of Khar'kov. III Panzer Corps deployed 7th Panzer Division to positions northeast of Khar'kov and moved 19th Panzer Division from the Barvenkovo area into positions near Khar'kov while XXXXVIII Panzer Corps moved both Panzer Grenadier Division "Grossdeutschland" and 11th Panzer Division into assembly areas 60 kilometers from the front and 3d Panzer Division to new positions west of Khar'kov. In addition, the 328th Infantry Division moved into assembly areas south of Khar'kov.[167]

These extensive troop movements prompted Zhukov to write, "The situation finally became clear in the last few days of June, and we realized that the enemy would mount an offensive in the coming days precisely here in the Kursk area and nowhere else ... [June 30]."[168] This clearly indicated what was already understandable. Soviet *razvedka*, probably agent and air, but perhaps also radio, detected the scope and direction of redeployments sufficiently to determine once and for all the general sectors where the blows would fall. During the ensuing three days (2–4 July), German XXXXVIII, III, and II SS Panzer Corps completed their large-scale deployment into the tactical dispositions of forces mounting the attack (see Maps 19–22).[169] At the same time, German panzer corps finished their concentration into attack positions south of Orel. The scale of these movements was staggering, involving as it did the movement and assembly of over 1,500 armored vehicles plus countless supporting vehicles into positions west and south of Belgorod and almost 1,200 armored vehicles on a narrow front south of Orel. It was at this juncture that Soviet tactical *razvedka* organs began receiving a flood of reports which ultimately resulted in the 2 July *STAVKA* alert order for an attack expected from 3 to 6 July.

An intelligence report prepared on 3 July by Moskalenko's 40th Army indicates the degree of detail concerning German concentration available to Soviet commanders defending south of Kursk:

> Information about the Enemy in the 40th Army Sector on 3.7.43
> 1. Three German infantry divisions defend in the first line in the army sector.
>   a) 57 ID – division commander Lt. Gen. Pikko. It defends

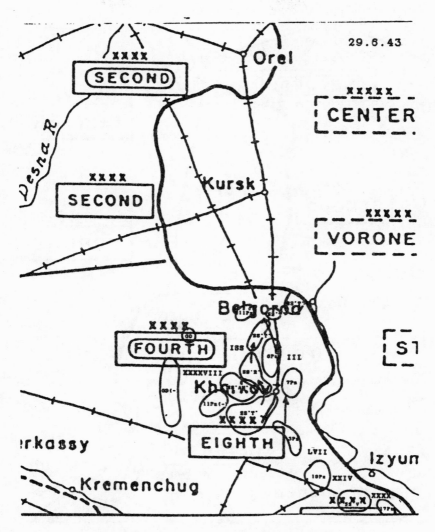

16. Position of German operational reserves, 29 June 1943

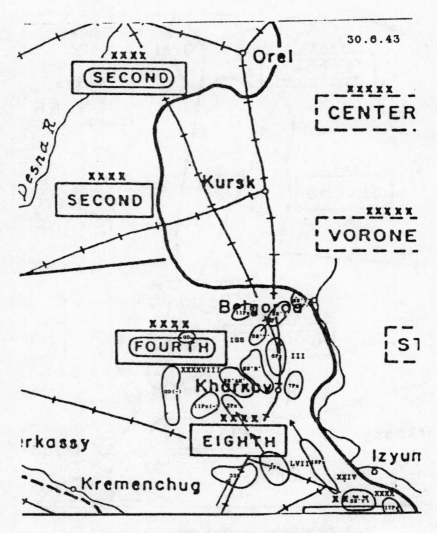

17. Position of German operational reserves, 30 June 1943

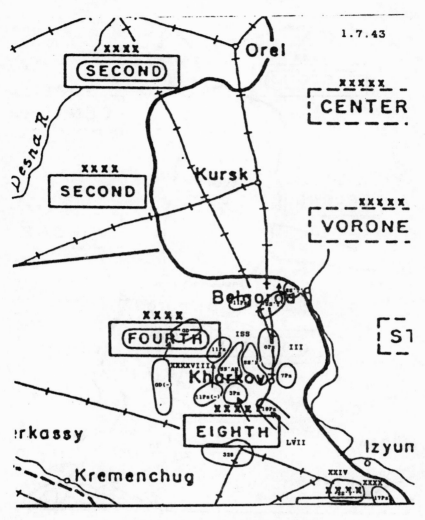

18. Position of German operational reserves, 1 July 1943

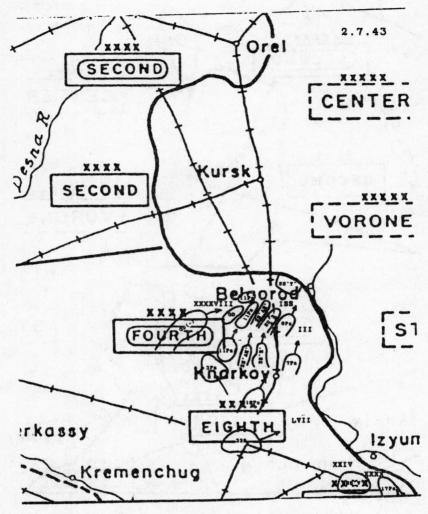

19. Position of German operational reserves, 2 July 1943

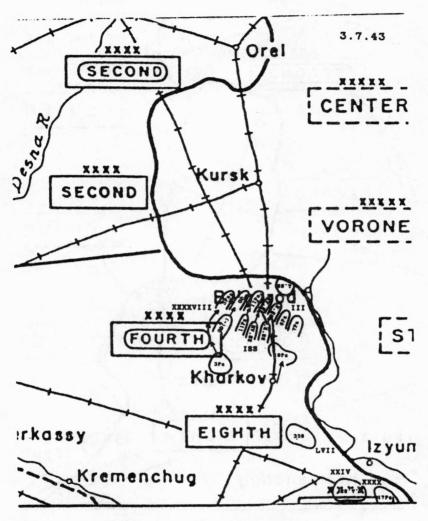

20. Position of German operational reserves, 3 July 1943

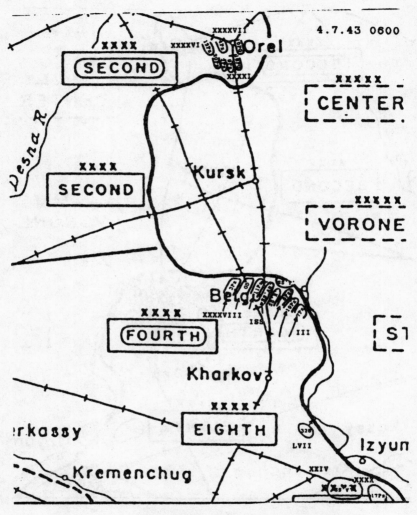

21. Position of German operational reserves, 0600 4 July 1943

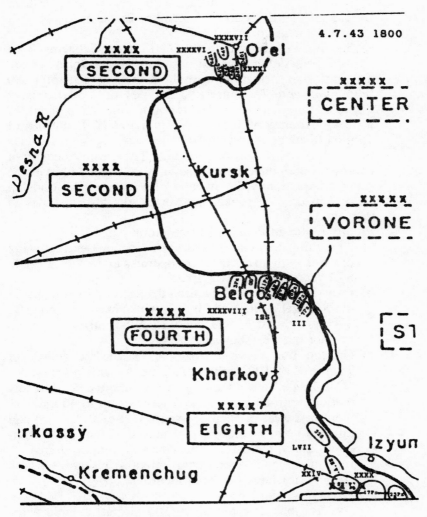

22. Position of German operational reserves, 1800 4 July 1943

a sector of 18km, with three regiments in the first line.

b) 255 ID -- division commander Lt. Gen. Poppe. It defends a sector of 17km.

c) 332 ID – division commander Lt. Gen. Schaefer. Two regiments defend against our army in a sector of 18km. The indicated formations include in their composition 120 field guns and 77 mortars. All types of *razvedka* have disclosed the existence of 8 batteries of 150mm (29 guns), 25 artillery batteries of 105mm (83 guns) and 20 batteries of 75mm (78 guns). A total of 54 batteries – 190 guns. Besides these, there are 27 separate mortars. The greatest density of enemy artillery is in the Pochaevo, Kasilovo, and Nikitskoe regions. Apparently the artillery of a reserve tank division located in the Borisovka, Graiveron area also operates in this region.

2. Enemy motor-mechanized force grouping:

a) According to aviation [*razvekda*] an unidentified tank division with up to 200 tanks operates in the Sumy, Nizh. Syrovatka, Bol. Bobrik area.

b) From 20.6 to 26.6.43 aviation detected up to 20 tanks in the Starosel'e area and up to 15 tanks at Slavgorod (10–20km southeast of Krasnopel'e). Whom they belong to has not been established.

c) On the line Novo–Berozovka, Kazatskoe (north of Tomarovka) 100 tanks belonging to tank division SS "Das Reich" are operating in the infantry combat formation, with an immediate reserve of up to 40 tanks in the forest west of Blizhnii (southwest of Belgorod) and up to 60 tanks belonging to tank division SS "Totenkopf" are in the Streletskii, Krasnoe, Belgorod area.

3. Immediate and operational infantry reserves in the army sector have not been identified.

5. Enemy aviation:

Aviation has detected up to 100 aircraft at field aerodromes at Belopol'e, Lebedin, Graivoron, Borisovka, and Mikoianovka, presumably from the Khar'kov aerodrome center, which conducts *razvedka* of our combat formation.[170]

This report generally conformed to actual German dispositions and, with similar reports, provided adequate data upon which to base the 2 July alert order. As indicated, air *razvedka*, plus troop *razvedka*, played a major role. Radio intercept probably contributed to precise identification of German units.

Even as late as early July, after concentration of the German armored armada had been completed, and after the Germans had conducted their 4 July pre-offensive reconnaissance west of Belgorod, the Soviet command, having determined the general timing of the attack and the general attack sectors, still lacked refined data concerning what unit would attack where and where the precise main attack axis was located. The Chief of the Voronezh Front Operational Department, Major General V. A. Svetlichnyi, later wrote:

> The staff of the Voronezh Front, having known about the beginning of the enemy offensive, did not undertake necessary measures to strengthen the defense of 6th Guards Army [on the Oboian axis], since it considered that he [the enemy] would deliver the main attack on Stary Oskol and part of his force in Oboian.[171]

Lieutenant General M. E. Katukov, 1st Tank Army commander, echoed the uncertainty, commenting that he anticipated the attack could materialize from Suzhda, Rakitnoe, Belgorod, or Korocha toward Oboian.[172] This inability to detect precisely the direction of the main German attack explained why the Germans made their greatest offensive progress in the Voronezh Front sector.

It is clear that ample information was available to the Soviets regarding German intentions to launch a summer offensive. Precedent alone indicated the Germans would do so. Moreover, by late April 1943, a variety of indicators pointed to the likelihood of an attack in the vicinity of Kursk, including geography, the disposition of German operational reserves as determined by air and agent *razvedka*, and information provided by Ultra. All played a part in shaping Soviet decisions to conduct a strategic defense prior to launching a strategic counteroffensive.

Between early May and late June, *razvedka* data permitted the Soviets to refine their estimate and reach the conclusion that the most likely direction of German attack would be along the Orel and Belgorod axes toward the base of the Kursk bulge. Throughout the period, however, the Soviets remembered past experiences and remained cautious in their assessments. In fact, Soviet dispositions as late as 5 July reflected an intent to defend every major axis along which German forces might advance.

There were good reasons for this caution, among which were

a healthy Soviet appreciation of German deception capabilities, respect for the ability of the Germans to move forces quickly between sectors, and skepticism born of experience regarding the veracity of intelligence sources, information, and assessments. On several occasions, but most notably in the spring of 1942, the Soviets had been deceived by the Germans regarding where the strategic blow would occur, with tragic consequences. More recently, in February 1943, the Soviets badly misread accurate intelligence indicators which led to their subsequent defeat in the Donbas. From these and other unfavorable but enlightening experiences, the Soviets were determined to cover all eventualities while exploiting intelligence whenever possible.

Knowledge of prior Soviet experience, as well as an examination of German archival sources, indicates Soviet skepticism was prudent. Originally the Germans had planned for operations in sectors adjacent to that of Kursk proper. As the date of the offensive neared, the Germans resurrected these plans ("Habicht" and "Panther") either for deceptive purposes (as diversions) or as adjuncts to the actual Kursk offensive. An order to First Panzer Army on 29 June required deceptive measures by that Army in the Izium region (see Figure 14).[173] As late as 7 July, two days after the German assault at Kursk, new orders to First Panzer Army postulated delivery of a supporting attack in that region (see Maps 23–24).[174] Consequently Soviet strategic planners prepared for every eventuality and concentrated their forces in a wide band from Moscow in the north to Voroshilovgrad in the south.

The Soviets were also skeptical of some of the intelligence data they received. Information from the Swiss agent network, in particular "Werther's" transmissions, ostensibly based on OKW information, was contradictory and often unreliable. The Soviets tended to note it but accorded it little value. "Dora," "Lucy," and "Werther" provided valuable material regarding overall enemy intentions, as did Ultra, but only during early spring. Thereafter the information either dried up entirely or contained little detail upon which to base operational or tactical assessments. In the end, by their own resolve and by habit, the Soviets relied upon what they themselves had developed – an intricate network of *razvedka* sources which covered the entire combat spectrum and which they understood and, hence, tended to trust. Ultimately, this was the most important source of intelligence data upon which the Soviets based their assessments in May and June and, finally, their judgements prior to the German attack in July.

Message entitled: to KR. G.KDOS, CHEFSACHE HZOX/Z C253 + KR--
HZOXZ C253/55 29.6.43 1130--AN PZ-A.O.K. 1, from HEERESGRUPPE SUD, ROEM
EINS A NR. 0594/43 GEH. KDOS. NAM T-313/60. The message read:
To Pz. A.O.K.1'

1st Panzer Army from day x-3 to day x is simulating
[feigning] the continuation of deployment from the
outskirts of Lozovaya, Krasnopavlovka, and
Mechebilovka toward the Donetz Front. At the
same time, the impression of an upcoming change
of course is to be aroused in the enemy by
exhibiting bridging materials.

Fig. 14. Order to First Panzer Army, 29 June 1943

While undertaking a massive and systematic *razvedka* effort
to refine their defensive capability and prepare for subsequent
offensive action, the Soviets also erected an immense safety net to
avoid repetition of the disasters of 1941 and 1942. They prepared a
strategic defense which could adequately check a German thrust
along every potential German axis of advance. This is not apparent
in most general Soviet sources, nor have Western accounts realized
the unique configuration of Soviet strategic deployments.

Actual Soviet dispositions in the summer of 1943 were not recognized by German intelligence at that time. Nor did German commanders writing long after the war understand the realities of July.
Most general Soviet studies of the Kursk operation reinforce that
false picture. Maps of the Kursk operation show an immense
concentration of forces at Kursk, including those initially in the area
on 5 July and those which joined combat in the region over the
course of the operation (see Map 25). These maps show the defending armies of the Central and Voronezh Fronts, reinforcing armies
of the Steppe Front, and arriving strategic reserves. The narratives
which accompany the maps point out that the Central and Voronezh
Fronts included 26 percent of the personnel, 33.5 percent of the
aircraft, 46 percent of the tanks, and over 25 percent of the artillery
and mortars deployed on the Eastern Front.[175] The presence
of strategic reserves and reinforcements increased the numbers
significantly.

What was striking about actual Soviet strategic force deployments on 1 July 1943 was the breadth of their defensive orientation

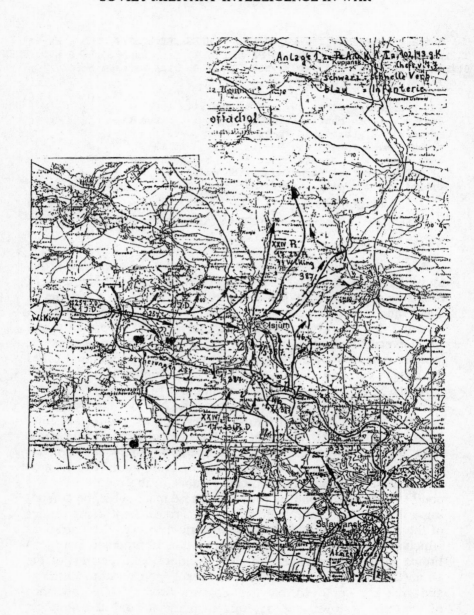

23. First Panzer Army planning map, 7 July 1943. Inclosure 1

24. First Panzer Army planning map,
    7 July 1943. Inclosure 2

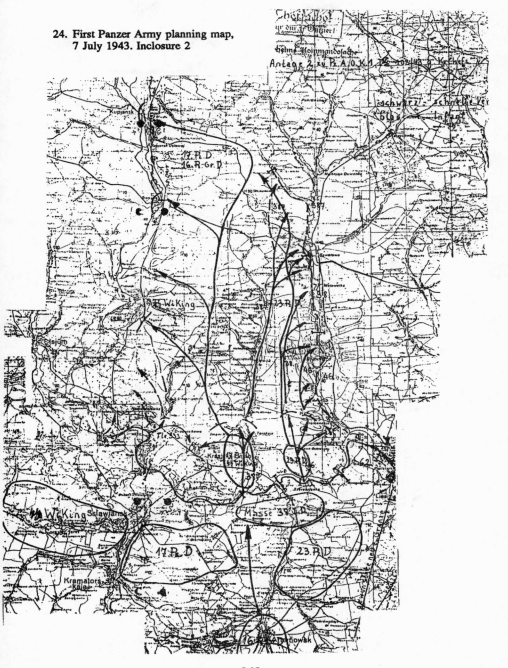

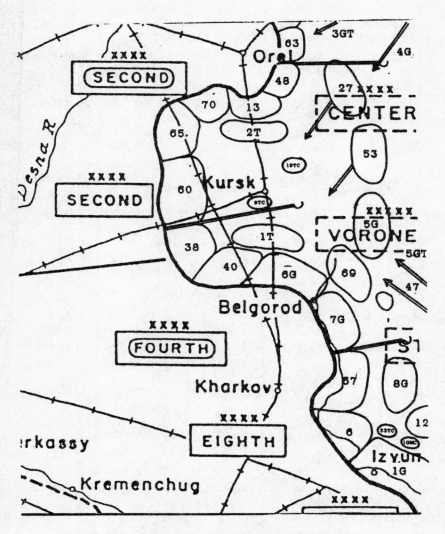

25. Concentration of Soviet forces at Kursk, 4–21 July 1943

(see Maps 26–28). Fully 57 percent of the Red Army (3.8 million men) was deployed in the sector from Viaz'ma to Voroshilovgrad covering the Rosslavl'–Moscow, Orel–Moscow, Belgorod–Voronezh, and Izium–Voronezh axes. The strongest Soviet *fronts*, each exceeding 600,000 men, defended the Viaz'ma, Kursk salient, and Izium sectors. These defenses more than covered all German offensive plans for 1943. Large combined arms reserves backed up these forces on the Moscow, Kursk, and Voronezh axes; and the five Soviet tank armies were distributed evenly across the most critical sectors, each closely coordinating with combined arms armies (10th Guards and 4th Tank Armies southwest and west of Moscow, 4th Guards and 3d Guards Tank Armies south of Moscow, 1st and 2d Tank Armies with armies in the Kursk bulge, and 5th Guards Tank Army with 5th Guards and 47th Armies south and west of Voronezh). Along each strategic axis, German forces confronted at least two echelons of combined arms armies backed up by a tank army.[176]

A more detailed view shows the diversity and configuration of forces on all three major axes (see Map 29). Two echelons of combined armies with two tank armies in between created a veritable bastion out of the Kursk bulge. On the Moscow approaches were deployed two echelons of combined arms armies, two tank armies, and two additional armies, 10th Guards and 4th Guards, further to the rear. Further south, around Izium, the Southwestern Front formed two echelons of combined arms armies backed up by 47th Army and 5th Guards Tank Army of the Steppe Military District. This concentration defended against a German thrust across the Northern Donets River called for in operations "Habicht" and "Panther."

Contemporary German intelligence assessments failed to note the concentrations, and 20 years later Field Marshal von Manstein's appreciation scarcely reflected the realities of 5 July (see Map 30).[177] In fact, German intelligence data and postwar works continued to reinforce the popular view that the bulk of the Red Army was initially at Kursk, ready to meet the 5 July assault. Instead, the larger concentrations would ultimately form at Kursk, but only well after the Germans had initiated their action and only when it became crystal clear that Kursk was the target.

A composite view of actual Soviet dispositions and the armies German intelligence identified and failed to identify provides a clear indication of German intelligence failures and evidence that Soviet dispositions were not unduly affected by advance warning

26. Distribution of Soviet strength along strategic directions, 4 July 1943

27. Strength of Soviet *fronts*, 4 July 1943

28. Soviet second echelon and reserve armies, western and southwestern directions, 4 July 1943

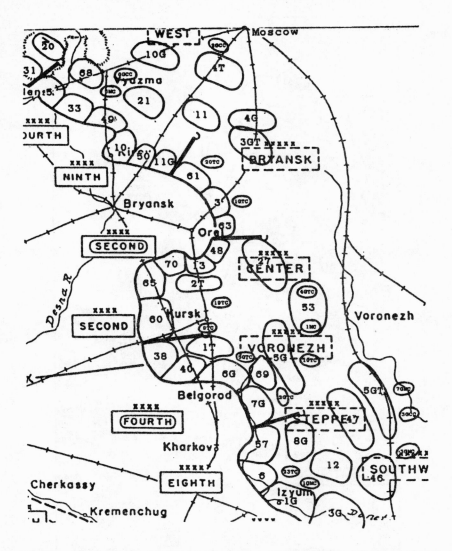

29. Disposition of Soviet armies along the western and southwestern directions, 4 July 1943

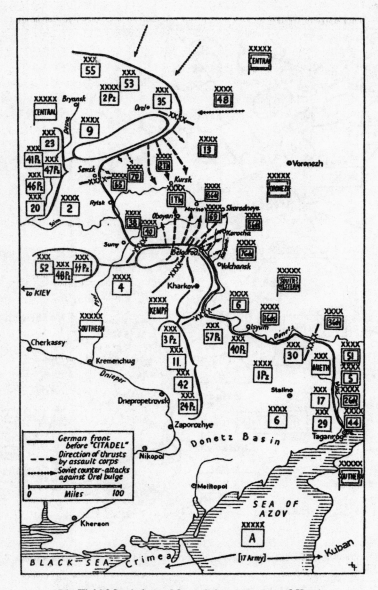

30. Field Marshal von Manstein's assessment of Kursk

of a German attack at Kursk (see Map 31). German intelligence failed to detect ten armies, two of which were tank. It held six of these armies to be located in the Northwestern and North Caucasus Front regions. It only tentatively identified 3d Guards Tank Army south of Moscow. Thus it missed the majority of the Soviet second echelon armies on the Moscow and Izium–Voronezh axes and much of the Soviet strategic reserves deployed on the southwestern direction. These were the armies which not only halted the German thrust at Kursk but also initiated the strategic counteroffensive across the breadth of the front. This was indicative of similar, though greater German failures to detect Soviet reserves in later operations, particularly in the summer campaign of 1944 and the winter campaign of 1944–45.

As the German offensive unfolded after 5 July, the *STAVKA* patiently waited until German offensive intentions were vividly clear. Then, and only then did it dispatch orders to its reserve armies to concentrate at the decisive point and halt the German drive, which by then had suffered greatly hacking its way through deep Soviet tactical defenses. On 6 July Commander of the Steppe Military District, Colonel General I. S. Konev, arrived at 5th Guards Tank Army's headquarters and ordered Lieutenant General P. A. Rotmistrov to move his tank army forward to Stary Oskol where it would become subordinate to the Voronezh Front. At 0130 on 7 July the army began a two-day forced march which covered 230–250 kilometers. At 0100 on 9 July it received new orders which propelled it to its fateful meeting with II SS Panzer Corps at Prokhorovka.[178]

That night, at 2400 hours, Konev received an order redesignating the Steppe Military District forces as the Steppe Front. The order read:

2. Include in the Steppe Front 27th Army with 4th Guards Tank Corps, 53d Army with 1st Mechanized Corps, 47th Army with 3d Guards Mechanized Corps, 4th Guards Army with 3d Guards Tank Corps, 52d Army with 3d, 5th, and 7th Guards Cavalry Corps, 5th Air Army and all reinforcing units, rear service units and institutions of the Steppe Military District.
3. Armies of the front will deploy in accordance with verbal orders given by the General Staff.
4. Movement of forces will be carried out only at night.

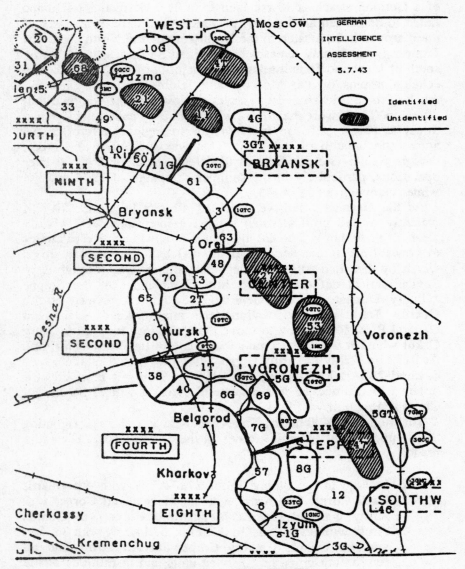

ASSESSED LOCATIONS (FRONTS)

68A – Northwestern	4GA – Central	46A – North Caucasus
11A – Northwestern	53A – Northwestern	47A – North Caucasus
21A – Unidentified	27A – Northwestern	12A – Unidentified

31. German intelligence assessment, 5 July 1943

5. Command post of the Steppe Front from 12 July will be in the Gorianovo region.

STAVKA of the High Command

J. Stalin

Antonov[179]

Within a week other reserve armies (3d Guards Tank, 4th Tank, 11th) received similar orders which collapsed the structure of strategic reserves toward the Orel–Kursk sector. Soon, simultaneously, multiple Soviet armies struck the exhausted German spearhead while others initiated counteroffensive action at Orel.

Soviet strategic dispositions mirrored the maturity of Soviet planning in the summer of 1943 and reflected realistic Soviet interpretation of intelligence indicators. Those dispositions prudently defended every critical strategic axis and disposed of reserves flexibly so that they could regroup to meet any eventuality. The Soviets did not repeat the mistakes of May and June 1942 and February 1943 when they had placed too much faith in agent intelligence and their intuition and deployed accordingly, only to be surprised and defeated. Moreover, they positioned their reserves to resume the offensive whenever the energy of the German offensive had expired. Strategic warning produced by *razvedka* was helpful, but not critical. Operational warning produced by *razvedka* was even more important, but even it was not decisive. The greatest contribution was made by efficient tactical *razvedka*, for, in the final analysis, it contributed to Soviet success in blunting the German thrust before it had penetrated into the operational depths. In the end, tactical warning plus skillful Soviet tactical, operational, and strategic deployments spelled doom for the German offensive.

INTELLIGENCE AND DECEPTION

By 12 July the German offensive against the north flank of the Kursk bulge had expired, worn down to exhaustion in the Soviet defenses. Shortly thereafter, forces from Konev's Steppe Front met and defeated German forces which had penetrated Soviet tactical defenses in the south. After 12 July the defensive phase of Kursk ended as Soviet forces near Orel went over to the offensive.

The Soviet Kursk counter-offensive unfolded in sequence according to plan. The first counterstroke began on 12 July against German Army Group Center northwest of Orel and expanded on 13 July as the Soviet Central Front went into action south of Orel. On 17 July the Southern and Southwestern Fronts opened major diversionary assaults across the Mius and Northern Donets Rivers against Army Group South. Finally, on 3 August, the Voronezh and Steppe Fronts, after a major regrouping, assaulted Army Group South's defenses around Belgorod. Both major counterstrokes required extensive regrouping of forces, elaborate *maskirovka* plans, and extensive *razvedka* support to ensure the *maskirovka* plans achieved their intended effects. The two diversionary operations were also carefully prepared, although from the *STAVKA* perspective it was not so critical to mask their preparations. In fact, German detection of Soviet attack preparations in those sectors played a major role in the success of the more critical counterstrokes at Orel and Belgorod.

No sooner had the German offensive begun at Kursk than Soviet forces elsewhere along the Eastern Front began to play their role in the strategic game of cat and mouse. The *STAVKA* plan had stipulated "as soon as the Kursk battle unfolded several neighboring *fronts* would go on the offensive in order that Hitler's High Command would not be able to strengthen its forces on the Kursk direction."[180] Accordingly, the Southwestern Front was to begin a diversionary attack across the Northern Donets River on Barvenkovo, and the Southern Front was to conduct a smaller attack across the Mius River toward Stalino. The two offensives were designed to draw German operational reserves from the Belgorod region and hold them elsewhere until after the 3 August planned Soviet offensive at Belgorod had achieved its initial aims. Soviet *razvedka* was tasked with determining whether those reserves had moved south and tracking their progress during the diversionary operations. Once those operations were complete, *razvedka* would monitor subsequent movement of the German reserves.

General R. Ia. Malinovsky's Southwestern Front attacked across the Northern Donets River in the Izium sector on 15 July. Although the attack had clearly failed by 17 July, the *STAVKA* insisted it continue. Meanwhile Soviet air and ground *razvedka* tracked the arrival, deployment, and commitment to combat of German reserves. Already, *razvedka* had determined the presence of 17th Panzer Division and SS Panzer Grenadier Division "Viking." The 8th Guards Army commander Lieutenant General V. I. Chuikov reported, "At first light [on 19 July] reports began arriving in the army staff from aviation *razvedka* about the movement of German forces into our sector of the front. German tanks, artillery and self-propelled guns moved along the roads." By matching this information against prisoner-of-war interrogations:

> We established that the commander of Army Group South, Eric von Manstein, had shifted 24th Tank Corps from Khar'kov and introduced 17th Panzer Division into combat against our army. On the heels of 24th Tank Corps the 3d Tank Division of 2d SS Tank Corps with reinforcements were shifted from Belgorod and Khar'kov in close order into the Donbas.[181]

Despite the deteriorating situation, Malinovsky continued his fruitless attacks until 27 July. By that time it was clear German forces would be unable to return to Belgorod in time to thwart the Soviet 3 August offensive. In fact, that proved true as the second Soviet diversionary offensive further distracted German operational reserves after 27 July.

On 17 July Colonel General F. I. Tolbukhin's Southern Front struck across the Mius River against the defenses of German Army Group South's Sixth Army. In a situation analogous to that at Izium, Soviet forces crossed the river, established a bridgehead, and committed two mechanized corps; but then the advance abruptly ground to a halt against well-prepared German defenses. Subsequently, German reinforcements shifted from the north; first 23d Panzer Division and ultimately II SS Panzer Corps and XXIV Panzer Corps contained and smashed the Soviet bridgehead by 3 August and drove Soviet forces eastward across the Mius. That same day, to the north, the Soviets launched the second great Kursk counterstroke against German forces near Belgorod, forces now deprived of most of their operational reserves.

Again, along the Mius River, the Soviets stubbornly clung to their minute gains despite the fact it was obvious the Germans would ultimately prevail. Throughout the operation, first Soviet air *razvedka* and then ground *razvedka* tracked German troop movements to assure the attacks achieved their desired effect of attracting German operational reserves from the Belgorod–Khar'kov region. After it was clear they had, the *STAVKA* discontinued the attack. Quite naturally, after 3 August these same operational reserves streamed back northward to stem what, by then, had turned into a major successful Soviet penetration of German defenses near Belgorod. Soviet *razvedka*, principally air and troop, then had the task of monitoring German troop movements back into the Khar'kov region as the Soviet offensive developed.

While Soviet air *ravzedka* detected the general flow of German forces back toward Khar'kov, it was ground reconnaissance groups and patrols of Soviet 1st Tank Army that established German presence by ground contact. On 6 August 1st Tank Army's 6th Tank Corps' reconnaissance group crossed the Sukhoi Merchik River west of Khar'kov and met advanced elements of II SS Panzer Corps' "Totenkopf" Panzer Division. The day before, reconnaissance units of 3d Mechanized Corps had encountered SS Panzer Division "Das Reich" north of Liubotin. In light of these reports, Vatutin ordered his two tank armies to sweep west of Khar'kov to complete the encirclement of the city before German reinforcements consolidated their positions.[182] This initiated a vicious ten-day struggle for the city fought by mobile groups ranging west of the city.

Ultimately, on 23 August Khar'kov fell and, within weeks, the Germans began a harrowing withdrawal to the Dnepr River line. The Kursk operation, by Soviet definition, ended with the fall of Khar'kov. During the counteroffensive phase of the Kursk strategic operation, Soviet *razvedka* fulfilled the task of monitoring German troop units sufficiently for Soviet forces to complete the investiture and capture of Khar'kov. In concert with, and in the service of, successful *maskirovka* (deception), German Army Group South was forced to abandon its positions east of the Dnepr River line.

CONCLUSION

Razvedka, in close concert with deception, played a significant role in the Soviet strategic defense at Kursk and during the strategic counteroffensive which followed. By late April, Soviet intelligence assessments, assisted by data from the British, were accurate enough for the *STAVKA* to decide to plan strategic offensive operations incorporating a defensive phase, a significant counteroffensive, and a complex strategic deception plan. Despite the accurate strategic *razvedka* assessments, the Soviets avoided earlier mistakes by treating the assessments skeptically and by creating powerful defenses on every major potential strategic axis the Germans could employ. Thus, throughout the planning phase they took into account potential German deception like that which had been so effective in the spring and summer of 1942.

Having created a strategic "safety net," the Soviets focused on operational and tactical *razvedka* to refine their appreciation of German intentions. These measures, focused primarily on detecting German troop movements, produced the warnings of May and June and, ultimately, of the actual German attack in July. Careful and patient control over strategic reserve units enabled the Soviets to redeploy those forces and commit them to combat at the most critical times and in the most important sectors. *Razvedka* thereby detected and helped thwart the German offensive. Subsequently, *razvedka* provided requisite information for successful implementation of the strategic deception plan and paved the way for the successful counteroffensives. To a far greater degree than before, the Soviets were able to monitor German troop units in the operational and strategic depths. This increased sophistication in *razvedka* was absolutely vital for such an equally sophisticated deception plan to succeed. Succeed it did, in large part due to improved Soviet intelligence!

At Kursk the Soviets successfully detected German strategic, operational, and tactical intent, while masking to a considerable degree their own counteroffensive intent. This combination of factors spelled doom for German offensive plans in the summer of 1943 and, more important, ultimately sealed the fate of German fortunes on the Eastern Front as a whole.

CHAPTER SEVEN

THE VISTULA–ODER OPERATION

INTO THE THIRD PERIOD OF WAR

After the Kursk operation, the Soviet High Command commenced a general offensive across the breadth of the Eastern Front from west of Moscow to the Black Sea. By September the concerted drive had slowly forced German forces westward to the line of the Dnepr River. In November the Soviets skillfully employed operational *maskirovka* to concentrate secretly sufficient forces for a breakout across the river north of Kiev. The Kiev operation created a strategic *platsdarm* (bridgehead) west of the river from which Soviet forces launched renewed offensives deeper into the Ukraine in December 1943. Throughout the drive to the Dnepr in the fall of 1943, Soviet *razvedka* effectively monitored the movement of German operational reserves and facilitated both successful Soviet *maskirovka* and the accomplishment of Soviet objectives. As the second period of war ended, Soviet forces commenced operations which, by late spring, would clear the Ukraine of German forces.

Unlike 1943, in 1944 strategic initiative was continuously in Soviet hands. Beginning in January 1944, with a major strategic offensive in the Ukraine, throughout the year the Soviets orchestrated a series of successive strategic offensives, each more successful than its predecessor. In the winter and spring the Soviets conducted a series of *front* operations – at first successive and then simultaneous – which, by April, cleared German forces from virtually the entire Ukraine. When German forces concentrated to repulse an expected Soviet assault through southern Poland or Rumania in the summer, the Soviets instead struck at German Army Group Center in Belorussia. Within weeks the Soviets had destroyed three German armies and advanced westward toward the Nieman and Narev rivers. As German forces shifted northward to stem the Soviet tide in Belorussia, Soviet forces drove westward toward L'vov, Lublin, and Warsaw on the line of the Vistula River. By August German Army Group North Ukraine had been badly shaken and strained to contain Soviet forces along the Vistula. In August Soviet forces struck the by-now depleted German Army Group South Ukraine defending in Rumania. Within two weeks that force had been decimated, and Soviet forces drove deep into the Balkans, conquering Rumania and Bulgaria and threatening the German southern flank in Hungary.

The series of Soviet strategic offensives were prepared and launched within the context of an effective strategic deception plan which played on German misperceptions and used both active and passive *maskirovka* measures to take advantage of German force dispositions and to conceal similar Soviet dispositions. As a result, virtually all Soviet offensives achieved a significant degree of surprise and greater than anticipated success.[1]

Razvedka played a critical role in the achievement of these successes by closely monitoring German force movements and by checking the effectiveness of Soviet *maskirovka* measures. Throughout 1944 all types of *razvedka* capitalized and improved on 1943 experiences. These improvements, most apparent in the Belorussian offensive of June 1944 and in subsequent operations in southern Poland and Rumania, pertained both to the effective operations of each type of *razvedka* and to the integrated use of all means of intelligence collection.

REFINEMENTS IN *RAZVEDKA*

Throughout 1944 coordination of *razvedka* became even more sophisticated, and that sophistication was reflected in the 1944 *Red Army Field Regulation*.[2] The regulation reiterated the importance of *razvedka* but underscored Soviet insistence that raw intelligence information be treated skeptically, stating, "The operations of reconnaissance units or subunits must be bold and active. The enemy can be forced to show his strength only by combat."[3] In the main, the regulation repeated the contents of the 1942 and 1943 regulations, but it did place even greater emphasis on certain types of *razvedka*. It recognized the importance of aerial *razvedka*, noting, "Aerial photo *razvedka*, which permits studying reconnoitered objectives with great reliability and completeness, is of greatest value."[4] The indices of aerial *razvedka* depth increased to 100 kilometers for army and 500 kilometers for *front* (strategic) reconnaissance aviation. Communications had improved to such an extent that aircraft were expected to "pass observation data by radio in the clear, encoding only the designation of points."[5] Aerial *razvedka* reports were "received from the aircraft simultaneously by the radios of combined-arms and air staffs which had sent the aircraft on reconnaissance."[6]

The regulation went on to subdivide *razvedka* into three categories: operational, tactical, and special. Operational *razvedka* by *fronts* and armies relied primarily on aircraft, mobile forces, and radio intercept supplemented by tactical *razvedka* data and information from partisans. Tactical *razvedka* by corps, divisions, and regiments relied on aircraft and ground force actions, while special *razvedka* was the task of the chiefs of combat arms and services (artillery and engineers).

By 1944 a wide array of ground *razvedka* forces had evolved, including reconnaissance detachments (*otriad*), separate reconnaissance groups (*gruppa*), separate reconnaissance or mounted patrols (*dozor*), and dismounted reconnaissance subunits, each with unique composition and specific methods and sectors of operations.[7] These forces reflected the more sophisticated Soviet force structure, in particular its mobile elements. In general, *razvedka* units ranged to depths of from 1–30 kilometers in advance of a main force.

The 1944 regulation also emphasized the importance of signals intelligence, stating, it "provides an opportunity for determining the location of headquarters and probable enemy groupings; intercepting radio messages; and monitoring individual conversations, instructions, and reports being passed over wire facilities."[8] Finally, it specified in detail the required contents of *razvedka* plans but, for security's sake, enjoined divisions and corps to assign *razvedka* missions to subunits "only verbally" and only to the extent necessary for performing the *razvedka* mission. In addition, it "categorically prohibited" reconnaissance units from carrying combat documents or maps with notes about friendly force dispositions along on reconnaissance.[9]

Organizationally, the 1944 regulation created new officer positions at *front* and army headquarters to facilitate smooth processing of information. "Agent" officers were required to know "constantly, and in detail, the situation and state of large units assigned to them, to report on their large units to the commander and chief of staff, immediately on demand, and to acquaint the large units with the combat missions assigned by the commander and oversee their execution." Their use reduced the number of stages in information gathering and eliminated "parallelism."[10] Designated information officers manned information control points within armies to centralize control over all data from senior or subordinate headquarters. These officers worked closely with agent officers "to considerably improve the gathering and study of information on the combat situation at all control levels."[11] While information gathering was streamlined, the Soviets refined reporting procedures, created reporting schedules, and established new report formats. Of particular importance was a new summary of information covering 24 hours of combat activity.[12] In the summer of 1944, while new regulations were being published and circulated, a Soviet staff reorganization upgraded the *razvedka* department (*otdel'*) of each *front* into a *razvedka* directorate (*upravlenie*) with its own expanded subordinate functional departments. The efficiency of these new systems became apparent in the Vistula–Oder operation.

Soviet intelligence collection and analysis improved in tandem with increased Soviet operational and strategic success. This applied in particular to longer range and more complex collection means across the entire spectrum. The number of Soviet aircraft specifically engaged in air *razvedka* steadily increased throughout 1944. For example, from 1 January 1944 to 1 July 1944, 1st Ukrainian Front's *razvedka* aircraft strength rose from 30 to 52. By 1 January 1945, 93 reconnaissance aircraft were available.[13] These figures, however, comprised less than five percent of total aircraft strength and paralleled overall aircraft strength increases. By 1944 reconnaissance missions averaged between 25 and 30 percent of aircraft sorties but, on some occasions (the Bobriusk operation), reached as high as 47 percent of the total flights.[14] Of this increased number of sorties, photographic flights rose to 50.3 percent by the summer of 1944.[15] This translated into more effective photographic coverage of enemy tactical defenses and more rapid detection and identification of enemy forces moving in the operational and strategic depths.

Agent and reconnaissance-diversionary *razvedka* increased in importance as operators and operational groups and parties increased in number and quality of work and as communications means matured. German intelligence assessments continued to attest to the effectiveness of these forces and their adverse impact on German defensive posture. *Fremde Heere Ost* records are replete with detailed assessments of which group was operating where and what each group was equipped with (see Map 32).[16]

Partisan *razvedka* became an important source of Soviet intelligence data in 1944, if not the most important, and materially contributed to Soviet success in the Ukraine and, in particular, in Belorussia. Soviet and German critiques alike agree on the pivotal

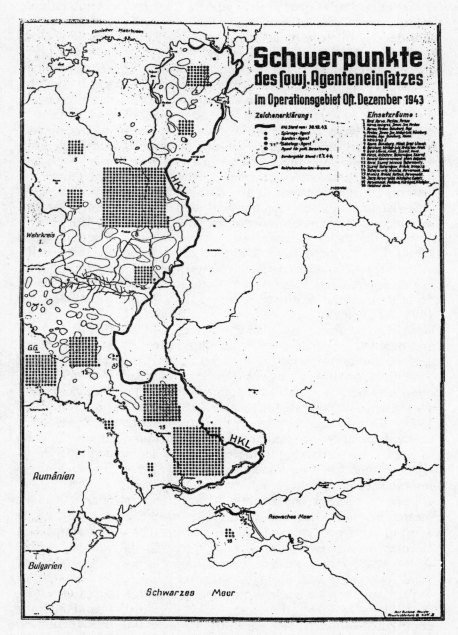

32. German assessment of Soviet reconnaissance-diversionary activity, December 1943

role played by partisans. A comprehensive postwar German assessment of partisan *razvedka* noted that while "the contribution of the bands to the overall Soviet intelligence effort tends to be somewhat obscured ... by 1943, the Soviets relied almost exclusively on the partisan intelligence service in some areas."[17] As Soviet armies plunged into Poland and Rumania in late 1944, the value of partisan *razvedka* diminished, since many underground groups were as hostile to Russians as to Germans. The Soviets did make a conscious attempt to establish contacts with some underground elements, in particular in Poland and Slovakia. These contacts would pay considerable dividends in early 1945.

The scope and impact of radio *razvedka* grew in 1944 as radio interception and decoding means spread from *front* level down into armies and as new units were created at *STAVKA* and *front* level. Typical of this expanded radio *razvedka* capability was the case of 4th Guards Army of the 2d Ukrainian Front in the Uman'– Botoshany operation of March 1944. During the short period of preparation for that operation (eight days), among other collection means the army employed a telephonic and radio interception platoon. Within a tightly organized plan, the platoon, in concert with other collectors, aided in the formation of a fairly clear picture of enemy dispositions.[18]

During the Belorussian operation in June and July 1944, the 130th and 131st Special Designation Radio Battalions jammed and intercepted German radio transmissions. By this time the Soviets had developed a similar capability within the GRU and also within army headquarters. During the Belorussian operation, 61st Army formed a communications equipment close reconnaissance team (GBRSS) to monitor enemy radio and telephone transmissions. It contained two radio monitoring squads of four men each to monitor VHF and HF bands and two line communications monitoring squads of ten men each, all from the 106th Separate Signal Regiment. In addition, it contained a radio technician, six military translators, and two vehicle drivers.[19] According to Soviet critiques:

> The intelligence personnel of the GBRSS obtained valuable intelligence on the composition and strength of enemy forces, numerical strength of subunits and units, and the time and place of delivery of hostile artillery attacks. This made it possible to determine enemy intentions in a timely manner.[20]

By late 1944 radio monitoring practices had been standardized at all Soviet levels of command from the High Command through army headquarters. Despite the proliferation of radio intercept equipment and forces and Soviet claims of significant results, German critiques downplayed the importance of Soviet signals intelligence, noting:

> It was interesting to note that Soviet signal reconnaissance attained only mediocre results, despite their plentiful and excellent equipment. Correct information was obtained through signal reconnaissance only when German units violated basic rules of signal discipline and transmitted their messages in clear text.[21]

Evidence from the Stalingrad, Kursk, and Belorussian operations, as well as other operations in 1945, indicate massive German underassessment of Soviet capabilities in this area.

The sophistication of troop *razvedka* grew as Soviet armies and corps employed ever larger specialized reconnaissance detachments and groups which operated at greater depths in the enemy rear (up to 50 kilometers) and often cooperated with partisans and air-dropped agents or teams. Throughout 1943 and 1944 the Soviets improved their techniques for conducting reconnaissance in force and adopted variations which prevented the Germans from using the reconnaissance as an attack indicator. At Kursk, reconnaissance in force occurred from one to three days before the Soviet offensive across a broad front to clarify enemy dispositions, provoke enemy reaction, and, at times, deceive the Germans regarding where the main Soviet thrust would occur. By this time armies employed for this purpose multiple reinforced battalions from first echelon rifle divisions. Often these battalions operated in close coordination with artillery firing the initial preparation. In Belorussia reconnaissance battalions in several army sectors actually began the offensive, which then developed without an artillery preparation in order to achieve surprise. In general, the role and importance of reconnaissance in force increased both as a reconnaissance and an offensive tool. By 1944 reconnaissance in force occurred one day before or on the day of the actual offensive. This virtually negated any possibility of the reconnaissance being used as an important attack indicator. The Soviets judged that by 1944 "reconnaissance in force became an operational factor and not [just] tactical."[22]

Both artillery and engineer *razvedka* continued to function on the basis of procedures developed earlier in the war, but increased quantity and quality of equipment, in particular within OKAPs and

ORADs, improved their capabilities. All these collective improvements in *razvedka* would become apparent in the Soviets' most successful large-scale offensive of the war, which would occur in Poland in 1945.

SOVIET PLANNING FOR THE VISTULA OPERATION

General planning for the 1944–45 winter strategic offensive began in late October 1944, while Soviet forces on the main strategic direction, along the Vistula and Narev Rivers, were fighting to extend the offensive deeper into Poland. The Soviets assessed the condition of their forces and concluded, at Zhukov's urgings, that Soviet forces needed a rest before resuming the offensive. Consequently, while operations continued on the flanks, after 3 November Soviet forces in the central sector of the front went over to the defensive.

In late October the *STAVKA* and general staff developed the general concept for a two-stage campaign, commencing in November, which would end the war. The concept's aims were:

(a) to rout the East Prussian grouping and occupy East Prussia;
(b) to defeat the enemy in Poland, Czechoslovakia, Hungary, and Austria;
(c) to advance to a line running through the Vistula mouth, Bromberg (Bydgoszcz), Poznan, Breslau (Wroclaw), Moravska Ostrava, and Vienna.

The Warsaw–Berlin line of advance – the zone of the lst Belorussian Front – was to be the direction of the main effort. Routing the Courland enemy grouping (the 16th and 18th Armies) was assigned to the 2d and 1st Baltic Fronts and the Baltic Fleet. They were also to prevent the enemy forces pressed to the Baltic Sea from being transferred to other fronts.[23]

Shtemenko later explained the rationale for a two-stage campaign:

It was assumed from the start that the last campaign of the war against Hitlerite Germany would be carried out in two stages. In the first stage, operations were to continue mainly on what might be described as the old line of advance – the southern flank of the Soviet–German front in the Budapest area. It was calculated that a breakthrough could be achieved here by inserting the main forces of the Third Ukrainian Front between the River Tisza and the Danube, south of Kecskemet.

From there they would be able to assist the Second Ukrainian Front with thrusts to the north-west and west. ... We had no doubt that the grave threat to their southern flank would force the German command to transfer some of their forces from the Berlin sector, and this in its turn would create favourable conditions for the advance of our main forces – the Fronts deployed north of the Carpathians. The General Staff firmly believed that by the beginning of 1945 the Soviet Army on the lower Vistula would reach Bromberg, capture Poznan and take over the line running through Breslau, Pardubice, Jihlava and Vienna; in other words, advance a distance of between 120 and 350 kilometers. After that would come the second stage of the campaign, which was to culminate in Germany's surrender.[24]

During November and December, the Soviet assaults in the Baltic region and in Hungary confirmed the *STAVKA*'s judgement that the Germans would react to threats against their flanks by transferring reserves from their center. Meanwhile, the Soviets began detailed planning for the January strategic offensive, which included two large-scale operations, both focused on the western strategic direction (see Map 33). The first, conducted by the 3d and 2d Belorussian Fronts, would strike the heavily entrenched German East Prussia group and protect the northern flank of the main strategic drive across Poland.

The 1st Belorussian and 1st Ukrainian Fronts would jointly launch the main strategic thrust. As described by Zhukov:

> The immediate strategic objective for the 1st Belorussian Front was to break the crust of the enemy defense in two different areas simultaneously, and having knocked out the Warsaw–Radom enemy grouping, to move out to the Lodz meridian. The subsequent plan of action was to advance towards Poznan up to the line running through Bromberg (Bydgoszcz)–Poznan and further south until tactical contact with the troops of the 1st Ukrainian Front was made.
>
> The subsequent advance was not planned, as General Headquarters [*STAVKA*] could not know beforehand what the situation would be by the time our forces reached the Bromberg–Poznan line.[25]

The original Warsaw–Poznan operation became the Vistula–Oder operation only after the plan was exceeded, and Soviet forces

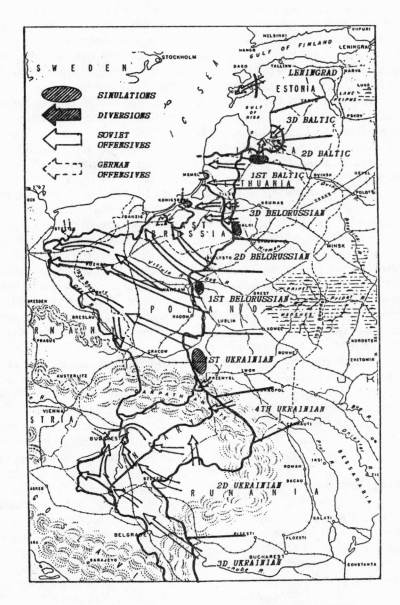

33. The Soviet Winter Campaign, January–February 1945

had reached the Oder River. The *STAVKA* and Stalin did not use a *STAVKA* representative to plan and coordinate the operations and instead coordinated directly through each *front* commander. On 15 November Zhukov took command of the 1st Belorussian Front, and Vasilevsky took charge of 1st and 2d Baltic Front operations to the north. In mid- and late December the *STAVKA* approved initial *front* plans, altered the concept slightly, and designated an attack date of 12 January, eight days earlier than planned, to assist the Allies then struggling in the Ardennes.[26]

From the standpoint of conducting strategic and operational *razvedka* and *maskirovka*, the Soviet High Command and *fronts* faced a different set of circumstances and problems in 1945 than they had faced earlier in the war. The Eastern Front's length had shrunk considerably, producing increased concentration of Soviet and German forces along the front. The Germans knew the Soviets were going to attack, probably in many sectors; and the geographical configuration of the front also posed definite problems. Soviet forces now faced heavy defenses on the East Prussian–Konigsberg direction and heavy German concentrations on the western outskirts of Budapest. Soviet forces were mired in mountain fighting across the width of the Carpathian Mountains; and on the western direction they occupied restrictive bridgeheads across the Narev and Vistula Rivers from which they would have to launch their new offensive. Thus, the Soviets would have difficulty masking their intent to attack and the attack's location, strategically and operationally. Continued operations in Hungary could distract the Germans, but only regarding the scale of offensives elsewhere.

To solve these problems, strategically the Soviets sought primarily to conceal the scale of their offensives rather than their location or timing. The plans included operational and tactical deception measures to blur German perceptions regarding attack timing and location. This required strenuous *STAVKA* efforts to conceal regrouping and concentration of forces on the critical western direction. All the while the Soviets continued operations in Hungary to fix German reserves in that region and postured forces in the western direction to distract German attention from the key Konigsberg approach and the Narev and Vistula bridgeheads. *Razvedka* plans fulfilled the important functions of validating the effectiveness of deception plans, monitoring the movement of German reserves, in particular from East Prussia and Hungary, and facilitating a rapid and complete penetration of German defenses along the Vistula River.

By early December 1944 the *STAVKA* had established the direction and zones of attack and the depth of immediate and subsequent objectives for each *front* and had assigned *front* commanders who would coordinate directly with the *STAVKA* while preparing and conducting the operation. On 16 November Zhukov took command of the 1st Belorussian Front. Konev retained command of the 1st Ukrainian Front. Although, by mid-November, the offensive plan was complete, with the attack date set for 20 January, to maintain secrecy the *STAVKA* did not issue detailed directives to the *fronts* until late December.[27]

The *STAVKA* concept required the 1st Belorussian Front to launch three attacks (see Map 34). It would launch its main attack from the Magnushev bridgehead, using three combined arms armies (61st, 5th Shock, and 8th Guards) to penetrate German defenses; and two tank armies (1st Guards and 2d Guards), and one cavalry corps (2d Guards) to conduct the exploitation toward Poznan. The 69th and 33d Armies, backed up by 9th and 11th Tank Corps and 7th Guards Cavalry Corps, would conduct a secondary attack from the Pulavy bridgehead toward Lodz; and the 47th Army, cooperating with the 1st Polish Army, would launch another secondary assault to envelop Warsaw. The 3d Shock Army was in *front* reserve.[28]

Konev's 1st Ukrainian Front was to conduct one powerful assault from the Sandomierz bridgehead. The 6th, 3d Guards, 5th Guards, 13th, 52d, and 60th Armies, supported by the 25th, 31st, and 4th Guards Tank Corps, would penetrate German defenses; and the 3d Guards and 4th Tank Armies would conduct the exploitation. The 21st and 59th Armies, in *front* second echelon, were to join the attack shortly after it had begun. Konev's *front* was to attack toward Radomsko and subsequently develop the offensive toward Breslau. The two *fronts* would attack in time-phased sequence with Konev's forces initiating their attack on 12 January from the Sandomierz bridgehead and, two days later, Zhukov commencing his assaults from Pulavy and Magnushev.[29]

The geographical disposition of the two Soviet *fronts* made deception extremely difficult. The Germans knew an attack was likely and had been predicting precise attack dates since late November. Repeated failure of the attack to materialize, however, dulled the credibility of these predictions. They also knew the attack would have to come from the bridgeheads across the Vistula or from the area south of the Vistula to the Carpathian Mountains. The primary indicator of an imminent attack would be the obligatory

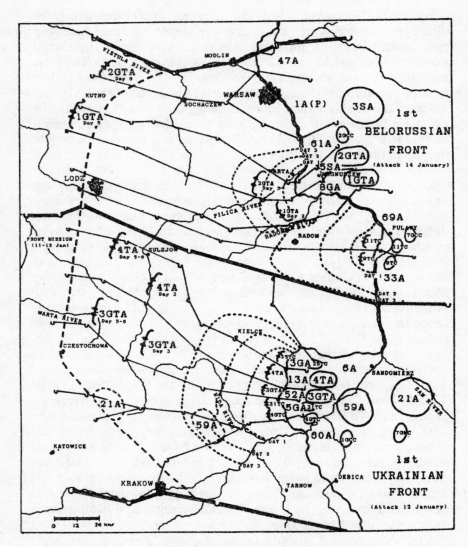

34. Soviet Vistula–Oder operational plan

build-up of Soviet forces along the front, in particular within the bridgeheads. Therefore, to confuse the Germans regarding the time of attack, the Soviets would have to keep secret the build-up of forces while attempting, in so far as possible, to deceive the Germans regarding attack location.

Both Zhukov's and Konev's *fronts* required large-scale reinforcement before they could mount decisive offensives, which they could then sustain through the depths of Poland. This meant increasing the strength of Soviet forces in central Poland by as much as 50 percent by the assignment and movement into the area of significant strategic reserves. Consequently, the *STAVKA* reinforced the 1st Belorussian Front with three combined arms armies (33d, 61st, and 3d Shock), one tank army (1st Guards), and numerous supporting units. The 1st Ukrainian Front received four combined arms armies (6th, 21st, 52d, 59th), one tank army (3d Guards), and one tank corps (7th Guards). Total reinforcements amounted to almost 60 rifle divisions, four tank corps, one mechanized corps, and over 120 artillery regiments.[30] Regrouping of these forces had to be accomplished secretly if the Soviets were to achieve any degree of surprise.

The deception plan required by the *STAVKA* and implemented by Zhukov and Konev sought to achieve two distinct aims. First, it sought to conceal the size of the regrouping effort and the timing and the scale of the offensive. Second, the Soviets sought to focus German attention on secondary sectors, in particular on the region south of the Vistula River. The Soviets had no misconceptions concerning the German belief that an attack would occur in the near future. Their overall intent was to weaken the German capability to resist the attack, principally by concealing its scale.

The elaborate deception planning and planning for the penetration operations from the Vistula bridgeheads placed a high premium on implementation of an effective and thorough *razvedka* plan exploiting all *razvedka* means. *Razvedka* had to reveal the nature and depth of German tactical defenses and the forces deployed in them. More important, *razvedka* had to monitor movements and dispositions of German operational reserves, in particular those which had earlier moved into East Prussia and Hungary. Although the Soviets were certain of penetrating German defenses, intervention of fresh German reserves could significantly limit the depth of the Soviet advance, given the existence of extensive pre-planned, but unmanned, German defense lines existing at varying depths across Poland. In addition, *razvedka* had the task of verifying the effects of Soviet deception. In fact, the Soviet *razvedka* plan itself incorporated measures designed to deceive the Germans regarding where the main attack would occur.

Within an atmosphere of strict secrecy, Zhukov and Konev prepared deception plans which incorporated active measures to disinform the Germans about the location of the attack and passive measures to conceal the arrival of reserves and concentration of attack forces in their respective bridgeheads.[31] Zhukov created a simulated force concentration on the extreme left flank of the 1st Belorussian Front near Joselow and on the army right flank north of Warsaw to attract German reconnaissance and reserves. Meanwhile, in the *fronts'* actual attack sectors, troops continued defensive work and maintained strict *maskirovka* discipline. All this activity was closely coordinated with the real regrouping and concentration of forces in the Magnushev and Pulavy bridgeheads, and conducted under a cloak of extreme secrecy.

Konev's *maskirovka* plan was far more elaborate that Zhukov's, in part because it had to be, given that Konev's attack would occur from only one bridgehead, and also because Konev could use the region south of the Vistula River as a part of his deception plan. Konev realized the difficulties he faced and later modestly wrote:

> I do not insist that our deceptive measures enabled us to achieve a complete tactical surprise in the direction of our main attack from the Sandomierz bridgehead, although I can vouch for the fact that they were helpful.[32]

These helpful measures included a major active simulation on the *front*'s left flank and Draconian measures to conceal the concentration of resources and the build-up in the Sandomierz bridgehead.[33]

Throughout the period of these intensive preparations, the Soviets supplemented their active and passive deception measures with intensive security activity conducted by the NKVD [*Smersh*] in the rear to uncover agents and counter German diversionary activity. Only one example is cited by the Soviets, who wrote:

> In the beginning of January Abwehrkommand 202 alone dispatched behind the front lines more than 100 diversionary reconnaissance groups. Their liquidation was the basic task of the NKVD, all of whose activity occurred in accordance with the orders of the *front* military councils. They maintained close ties with the local party and democratic organizations, which helped expose the enemy and his agents. The security organ of the staffs and rear services played an important role in the search for diversionary forces.[34]

The increased efficiency of Soviet rear security services, which were employed in ever greater numbers, partially explained the deterioration of German human intelligence sources in this as well as in previous operations.

RAZVEDKA PLANNING

Throughout late fall 1944, continuous conduct of *razvedka* enabled *STAVKA* planners to adjust their concept for the Vistula–Oder operation and formulate a thorough *razvedka* plan. Within the *STAVKA*, the GRU surveyed conditions along the front and provided the context within which operational planners at other levels could formulate operational *razvedka* concepts. In late October the *STAVKA* estimated that, given German strength in Poland, the 1st Belorussian and 1st Ukrainian Fronts would be able to penetrate to a depth of up to 140–150 kilometers. A subsequent, more thorough assessment in early November indicated German strength was still too formidable for a large-scale Soviet attack to succeed in the near future.[35] At that point the decision was made to mount a two-phase campaign with the Polish phase commencing in January. This would accord well with the planned final Allied drive into Germany expected early in 1945.

Throughout November and December, Soviet *razvedka* focused on German troop transfers to East Prussia and Hungary in response to the first phase of the Soviet offensive against German positions in East Prussia and Hungary. Shtemenko noted:

> Our expectations were confirmed. Soviet attacks in November–December 1944 caused the enemy, according to our calculations, to concentrate 26 divisions (including seven Panzer divisions) in East Prussia and 55 divisions (including nine Panzer divisions) near the capital of Hungary. ... The German command was once again compelled to obey our will and left only 49 divisions, including a mere five Panzer divisions, on what was for us the main sector of the front.[36]

If this was not enough information upon which to base a decision to attack, news received in late December and early January confirmed the Soviet decision. In early January Soviet intelligence detected the movement of German IV SS Panzer Corps, a critical operational reserve, from the Warsaw area to Hungary. Specifically:

> On 30 December 1944, our radio *razvedka* established that radio stations of the enemy's 3d and 5th Tank Divisions and 4th Tank Corps had ceased to operate. On 1 January 1945, *razvedka* agents reported that soldiers wearing the insignia of 5th Tank Division had been spotted in Czestochowa and on 3

January, radio *razvedka* detected movement of radio stations of the 3d and 5th Tank Divisions in the direction of Kryukov. Finally, the seizure of a prisoner from the 3d Tank Division in the area of Komarno definitely confirmed the transfer of the 4th Tank Corps to the new area.[37]

Fresh intelligence assessments made in late November of both enemy force dispositions and Polish terrain prompted *STAVKA* adjustments in the offensive scheme. Initially, the 1st Belorussian Front was to have attacked due west from the Pulavy and Magnushev bridgeheads while 1st Ukrainian Front did likewise from the Sandomierz bridgehead toward Kalisz on 1st Belorussian Front's left flank to avoid the heavily built-up Silesian industrial region. New data brought by Zhukov to a 27 November meeting in Moscow altered this plan.

> On November 27, Zhukov arrived in Moscow in answer to a summons from GHQ. On the basis of Front reconnaissance data he had reached the conclusion that it would be very difficult for the First Belorussian Front to attack due west because of the numerous well-manned defense lines in that area. He thought that success was more likely to be achieved by aiming the main forces at Lodz with a follow-up toward Poznan. The Supreme Commander agreed with the amendment and the operational aspects of the plan for the First Belorussian Front's initial operation were slightly modified.
> This altered the position of the Front's left-hand neighbor. There was no longer any point in the First Ukrainian Front's striking at Kalisz, so Marshal Konev was given Breslau as his main objective.[38]

While the *STAVKA* sifted through its data and modified its strategic plans, the two *fronts* developed *razvedka* plans to complement their offensive concepts. The *razvedka* plans were designed to fulfill two groups of concrete missions: *razvedka* of enemy defenses along the Vistula River and *razvedka* of enemy dispositions throughout the depths of Poland up to the Oder.[39] The first group involved

> determining the exact disposition of the enemy combat formation and of elements of the enemy defense down to company strong points and the location of artillery and mortar batteries to a preciseness of 100 meters; revealing the location of staffs and command and observation posts down to

battalion; and discovering the weakest places in the enemy defense along the Vistula.[40]

The second group of missions required determining the strength and composition of enemy defensive positions in the depths and detecting, identifying, and tracking operational reserves and potential reinforcements for German forces defending along the Vistula. Both *fronts* ordered *razvedka* missions to be fulfilled by 1 January – during a period of 45 days.

Unlike earlier operations, the *razvedka* plan encompassed the entire period of preparation and conduct of the offensive rather than only 15–20 days.[41] This provided greater unity of purpose for the effort. To provide total planning secrecy, both *fronts* often abandoned the practice of preparing written *razvedka* orders for subordinate headquarters and instead transmitted appropriate sections of the *front razvedka* plan verbally to those units which would fulfill them. Periodically, *front* headquarters held conferences with army RO chiefs and representatives of other involved staffs (artillery, engineers) to explain the plan and clarify missions assigned to each *razvedka* organ. The *front* commanders also organized staff war games attended by the chiefs of army ROs to refine missions and surface unanticipated *razvedka* problems.

Fronts took considerable care to plan for the use of each type of *razvedka* and to ensure all means were fully integrated with one another. This included *front* assets (reconnaissance aviation regiments, reconnaissance-corrective aviation regiments, separate special designation radio battalions (OSNAZ), and organs of agent *razvedka*) and reconnaissance subunits of 35 first echelon divisions and fortified regions of armies, as well as eleven artillery instrumental *razvedka* battalions (AIR).[42]

Unlike earlier operations, the Soviets were now operating on non-Soviet soil. As Zhukov explained, this posed new problems for intelligence:

> Preparations for the Vistula–Oder operation were largely different from those of similar scale on Soviet territory. Previously, we were fed with intelligence by guerrilla [partisan] detachments operating in the enemy rear. We did not have this advantage any more.
>
> Now we could only gather intelligence through secret service agents and by means of aerial and ground reconnaissance. ... Our supply routes along railroads and motor roads now lay in Poland where, besides true friends and the people loyal to the

Soviet Union, there were enemy intelligence agents. Special vigilance and secrecy of maneuvers were required in the new conditions.[43]

Once *fronts* had formulated initial *razvedka* plans, they then prepared oral orders for subordinate formations. One such order issued to 38th Army on 22 December 1944 read in part:

1. Study the enemy in the entire depth of his tactical defense (8–10km.), especially the forward area and defenses on the western bank of the River Vislok. Enemy firing positions must be revealed to commanders at all levels up to corps inclusive; they must be tied in with topography on the ground, logged in the observation journal and numbered. Special attention must be paid to the organization of generals' and officers' *razvedka*, which must be conducted continuously.[44]

Within the armies, subordinate corps, divisions, and regiments now implemented their planning to complete the *razvedka* continuum. The actions of the 5th Army were representative:

All commanders and staffs devoted great attention to the organization and conduct of continuous and active *razvedka* of the enemy. Constant observation of troop scouts, artillerymen, and sappers was organized over the enemy defense. Ambushes and radio interception were systematically organized, small groups were sent into the enemy rear, and reconnaissance in force was conducted, as a result of which, every three to five days we secured prisoners. We had sufficiently full information concerning all that occurred in the enemy rear from aviation *razvedka*. The enemy defense was systematically photographed. All of this provided a full and accurate picture of enemy dispositions, his defense and his intentions.[45]

Planning periods for army-level *razvedka* varied according to *front* missions, conditions, and policies. Most armies, however, organized *razvedka* within specific planning periods. For example, 60th Army of 1st Ukrainian Front planned for 15-day periods, its corps for periods of 5–10 days, and rifle divisions usually for 2–3-day periods.[46] The 60th Army relied principally on sweeps, ambushes, ground and aerial observation, and artillery and engineer *razvedka*.

The 5th Guards Army, which planned *razvedka* in similar time frames, also instituted special periodic meetings between army and corps commanders and staffs and *razvedka* officers from corps, divisions, and specialized forces. These sessions reviewed all *razvedka* data and determined subsequent *razvedka* missions. In addition, "special attention was paid by commanders and chiefs of staff to the organization of close cooperation of all types of *razvedka*."[47] In 5th Guards Army the RO formulated a detailed *razvedka* plan, based on chief of staff guidance, which specified tasks for subordinate *razvedka* organs and the period for their completion. In addition, to ensure continuity of *razvedka* up to the time of the attack, the army formulated an overall plan encompassing the entire preparatory period, which sought to determine "enemy dispositions and intentions; enemy defense systems and defensive structures; organization of firing systems and engineer obstacles; and enemy combat methods."[48] Other armies implemented similar procedures. It was then the task of various *razvedka* organs to implement the elaborate plans and pave the way for the offensive.

RAZVEDKA PRIOR TO THE OPERATION

Air

The Soviets conducted air *razvedka* with units subordinate to the High Command and to the two *fronts* involved in the operation. The High Command employed separate reconnaissance aviation regiments of Long-Range Aviation to conduct deep observation and photography while *front* air armies carried out *front* air *razvedka* plans employing all *front* aviation assets. Specialized *front* reconnaissance aviation regiments and squadrons conducted about 19 percent of the sorties, while TOE (establishment) assets conducted the remaining 81 percent. Between 70 and 80 percent of the sorties concentrated on the main axes of the *front*'s offensive with over 70 percent of these concentrated on targets in the tactical depths.[49]

General S. I. Rudenko's 16th Air Army supported Zhukov's 1st Belorussian Front. Rudenko's army consisted of six aviation corps and 14 separate aviation divisions and regiments totalling 2,396 aircraft. Of this force, the 16th, 47th, and 72d Reconnaissance Aviation Regiments and fighters of the 286th Fighter Aviation Division and 6th Fighter Aviation Corps performed dedicated reconnaissance missions. A total of 96 aircraft engaged solely in reconnaissance activity. General S. Krasovsky's 2d Air Army provided similar support for Konev's 1st Ukrainian Front. Krasovsky's army contained eight aviation corps, one separate aviation division, and three separate aviation regiments. As in Zhukov's *front*, the separate regiments provided reconnaissance capabilities. The 2d Air Army included 2,273 aircraft, of which 93 were dedicated to reconnaissance missions. In addition, air armies possessed over 150 PO-2 light night bombers, which were often used for reconnaissance.[50]

The 1st Belorussian Front's air *razvedka* plan, developed by air army chief of staff Lieutenant General P. I. Braiko, called for continuous deep reconnaissance and concentrated planned reconnaissance activity for six days prior to the offensive. Rudenko later noted that Zhukov

> demanded that we discover the nature and system of enemy defense throughout the entire tactical depth and also detect the presence, nature, and degree of preparation of intermediate and rear defensive positions (lines) from the Vistula to Poznan. We were charged with providing a clear picture showing the disposition of aerodromes, field and anti-aircraft artillery, especially in the bridgehead regions, the concentrations of enemy reserves, in particular tanks.[51]

A total of 5,025 aircraft sorties during this period covered force concentrations, protected airfields, and conducted air *razvedka*.[52] For 40 days prior to 12 January Braiko's plan required intensive air *razvedka* between the Vistula and Oder Rivers to a depth of 400–500 kilometers.

To foster more efficient use of air assets, the *razvedka* plan subdivided the enemy defense sector opposite 1st Belorussian Front into two zones — close and distant. Reconnaissance-corrective aviation regiments and close *razvedka* aviation squadrons reconnoitered the former, and long-range reconnaissance regiments and long-range night reconnaissance aircraft concentrated on the latter.[53] These flights produced aerial photographs and mosaics of virtually all German defenses in the depths. Later in the operation, shorter-range air *razvedka* missions prepared similar photos of enemy tactical defenses. Up to seven such efforts permitted *front* analysts to compare and detect changes in defensive positions and troop dispositions at frequent intervals. A total of 109,200 square kilometers of territory in 1st Belorussian Front's offensive sector were thoroughly photographed.[54] The three reconnaissance aviation regiments (16th, 47th, and 72d) accomplished most of this work using PO-2 aircraft for night observation and IL-4 aircraft to photograph enemy positions as far west as Poznan.

Weather conditions prior to the offensive were characteristically bad, and reconnaissance sorties were primarily limited to two days in November, six in December, and only one in early January. Despite the bad weather, a total of 1,759 sorties were flown in good and bad weather, an average of 25 per day. Heavy German flak and bad weather also made tactical photography difficult. Despite the difficulties, aircraft photographed German tactical defenses from a depth of 4 to 8 kilometers three times before the attack. In the immediate environs of the Magnushev and Pulavy bridgeheads, German trenches and strongpoints were photographed four times, and mosaics of German defenses in these main attack sectors stretched 25–40 kilometers to the west.[55] This permitted detection of an additional six antitank barriers extending 20–40 kilometers from north to south and a series of intermediate positions and defense lines. Close and careful aerial *razvedka* also facilitated detection of false enemy defenses and simulated artillery positions; for example, in the region north of Warka.[56] Other photographic flights con-centrated on communications lines, key road junctions, and German airfields. Rudenko noted:

> From the air we succeeded in discovering active army aerodromes and determined what units were located there. In the interests of our aviation all crossings over the Vistula from Modlin to Vlotslaveka, across the Pilitsa from Warka to Tomashuv and railroad centers and cities to the meridian of Kutno were photographed.[57]

This reconnaissance facilitated their future destruction.

Assault aircraft of the 6th Assault Aviation Corps detected movement of German artillery westward from the Warka region, and reconnaissance aircraft of the 2d and 11th Guards Assault Aviation Divisions discovered that German forces had abandoned the first line of trenches in the bridgehead regions (to avoid the effects of the artillery preparation). The Soviets subsequently adjusted their artillery preparation accordingly.

With Zhukov's approval, Rudenko also employed experimental motion picture filming of German forward defensive positions using assault aircraft. Rudenko noted, "The information from film and photographic *razvedka* helped specify and complete conditions marked on maps. New structures, antitank ditches, and roads were discovered."[58] As in earlier operations, air crews were assigned specific sectors in which to operate, thereby increasing their ability to detect even the slightest change in enemy disposition and terrain conditions.

Analogous activity took place on Konev's 1st Ukrainian Front, where Major General A. S. Pronin developed and implemented an air *razvedka* plan whose objectives were similar to those of the 1st Belorussian Front. Planned photographic missions of German tactical defenses by the 1st Ukrainian Front's air recce aircraft took place on 6, 16, 21, and 28 December and immediately prior to the offensive. This facilitated comparison of photo-images and notation of changes in the defense.[59] Marshal Konev noted, "Accurate *razvedka* data was collected, the entire enemy defense was photographed ahead of time, and changes occurring there subsequently were detected in timely fashion."[60] Long- and short-range *razvedka* by the three reconnaissance aviation squadrons photographed 193,587 square kilometers of territory, including intermediate defensive positions, road and rail junctions, towns, and, most important, tactical defenses around the Sandomierz bridgehead. Just before the offensive, while Soviet forces occupied jumping-off positions for the attack, four to five pairs of reconnaissance aircraft per day conducted continuous reconnaissance to detect enemy troop and tank concentrations, movement of enemy reserves, and antiaircraft artillery positions in key offensive sectors.[61]

In general, the growing number of Soviet aircraft available to perform *razvedka* missions and near-total dominance of Soviet aircraft in the skies made air *razvedka* a powerful Soviet offensive tool. Only poor weather inhibited Soviet air *razvedka* plans, but to a minimal extent.

AGENT-DIVERSIONARY-PARTISAN

For the first time in the war, in January 1945 the Soviets had to do without large-scale partisan *razvedka*, since combat operations would take place on Polish soil. Instead, the Soviets relied on agent and reconnaissance-diversionary forces to gather strategic and operational intelligence. Because the Polish population was understandably suspicious of Soviet intent, only greater Polish hatred of the Germans fostered limited support for Soviet operatives in the German rear. Further complicating the milieu in which Soviet intelligence forces operated was the split in the Polish underground between the London-based Polish Home Army and forces supported by the Soviet-sponsored Lublin Committee. To compensate for these difficulties, the Soviets relied on a small indigenous agent network and more numerous agent and diversionary-reconnaissance teams inserted into the German rear by air drop or ground infiltration. Characteristically, the Soviets say little about these activities, so one must rely on earlier patterns of Soviet agent use and information in German intelligence records.

In Poland the Soviets employed four types of human intelligence collectors in the German rear. The NKVD and GRU both employed operatives either already in Poland or inserted before the Vistula–Oder operation commenced. The former conducted extensive counter-*razvedka* work against the Abwehr, and the latter used a variety of agents and special teams of various sizes to collect intelligence data or engage in diversionary activity (often from the OMSBON). *Front* RUs and army ROs also fielded long-range reconnaissance groups or detachments from *front* commando brigades at shallower depths, and formations below army-level employed shorter-range *razvedka* detachments and patrols. All these activities were coordinated by the GRU and the RUs and ROs in the intelligence chain of command.

Somewhat more shadowy were links between Soviet intelligence and Polish anti-Nazi factions which German reports show to have existed. Although these did not replicate the full scale of earlier partisan organizations, they were undoubtedly controlled in the same centralized fashion. Soviet sources make numerous references to agent-diversionary operations but primarily at lower command levels. A 5th Guards Army history recognized "well organized" use of *razvedka* groups dispatched into the enemy rear.[62] General V. I. Chuikov, commander of 8th Guards Army, described in some detail deep *razvedka* in his sector:

> Before [the army] stood the mission – in the interests of other armies and the *front*, to conduct deep, careful *razvedka* of enemy forces with which we now anticipated close struggle. We well knew what units were located in the forward line of the enemy defense. But these were very little. We needed to know what forces were located in the second echelon and in the entire depth of the enemy defense. It was necessary for our *razvedchiki* [scouts] to slip into the enemy rear, secure prisoners there, interrogate them and, through personal observation, obtain exact additional information.[63]

Chief of 8th Guards Army's RO Colonel Gladky formulated a *razvedka* plan involving insertion of several *razvedka* groups up to

25–40 kilometers into the enemy rear to observe German movements and identify units. Those groups deployed forward on foot
by infiltration, and the army RO used radio and PO-2 aircraft
operating at night to communicate with them. The first *razvedka*
group, made up of a sergeant and a private, infiltrated into the
German rear in early October north of Czeczylovka and penetrated
the forests 12 kilometers southwest of Warka to survey German
defenses and note force dispositions. After three days, they found
no German units and were ordered to create a base for a larger
razvedka group which could continue to monitor German troop
movements toward the Magnushev bridgehead. The new group of
seven men, commanded by Lieutenant I. V. Kistaev, operated for
two months from the hidden base. Chuikov stated that the group

> secretly penetrated into the forest, camouflaged themselves
> there and successfully worked for more than two months,
> transmitting to the army staff very valuable information about
> the enemy obtained from observation and interrogation of
> prisoners. Enemy artillery, six barrel mortars, and tank unit
> positions were discovered. Special attention was paid to the
> daily life of enemy forces and their daily routine. We knew
> when the fascist soldiers went to the field kitchen and when
> they left and when changes in security were made. All of this
> had to be studied to deliver a surprise attack.[64]

Shtemenko, in his memoirs, alludes to agent activity in southern
Poland that helped track the transfer of IV SS Panzer Corps from
southern Poland to Hungary.

One reference to higher level, longer-range reconnaissance
activity probably accurately typifies the operations of GRU-level
razvedka forces. In January 1945 an OMSBON operational group
of fifteen experienced men, code-named "Groznyi" (Formidable),
parachuted into the Althorst region, 100 kilometers northeast of
Berlin. There they operated in the forests through the spring of 1945
when the front lines reached the area. The operational group
"radioed the command information about the dislocation of enemy
forces, the position of military objectives, and the construction of
defensive structures on the approaches to Berlin."[65] To emphasize
this was not an isolated incident, one Soviet critique added, "Other
large groups of OMSBON men greeted the 'Day of Victory' in the
Berlin area."[66]

While the Soviets are reticent to detail agent *razvedka* operations, German records reflect the extent of those operations and

provide hints as to their effectiveness. Among the many documents highlighting agent activity, four illustrate the scope of the problem and evidence German concern for it. A report prepared by German Army Group A logged enemy activity in the rear area from 1 November to 31 December 1944 and assessed the impact of that activity on lines of communications.[67] It identified 38 separate "Banden" (bands) operating throughout Poland in November. It further subdivided the "bands" into Soviet, Polish, and Slovak and recorded identified *Kundschaftergruppen* (Scouting groups) and the location of known Soviet parachute drops (see Map 35). At this point, the highest density of Soviet agent and reconnaissance-diversionary forces was in the region southeast of Lodz (Litzmann-stadt), due west of the Magnuslav and Pulavy bridgeheads, and along the projected main axis of advance of the two Soviet *fronts*.

A *Fremde Heere Ost* assessment of Soviet *Kundschaftergruppen* operating during November 1944 identified 26 such groups, under High Command (GRU) control, active across the front. The 1st Belorussian Front controlled an estimated 19 groups which operated primarily northwest and southwest of Warsaw, while the 1st Ukrainian Front controlled 19 groups operating from the Iaslo region south of Krakow northwestward to the region just southeast of Lodz (Litzmannstadt).[68] A third document, prepared by Army Group Center in January 1945, showed "Banden" activities in December 1944 using the same notation system as the earlier report.[69] It evidences the same general pattern as the Army Group A report but notes increased activity (in particular parachute drops) in the region south of Krakow.

A higher level report prepared by *Fremde Heere Ost* recorded the operations of Soviet "scouting detachments" from 1 December 1944 to 4 January 1945 (see Map 36).[70] It noted that Soviet teams under GRU (*STAVKA*) control operated primarily in the region north and south of Krakow; 1st Belorussian Front teams concentrated on the area west and southwest of Warsaw, and 1st Ukrainian Front reconnaissance-diversionary groups and detachments focused primarily on the region south of Krakow toward Iaslo. This report identified 23 groups (teams) under High Command control and 33 under control of the two *fronts*, probably only a fraction of those actually operating in the German rear. Subsequent reports in February identified up to 58 such groups by name or code number. In addition, reports counted more than 20 "regiment" size groups operating under the auspices of National Polish authorities (*Armia Krajova* – National Army) and another eight–ten brigades

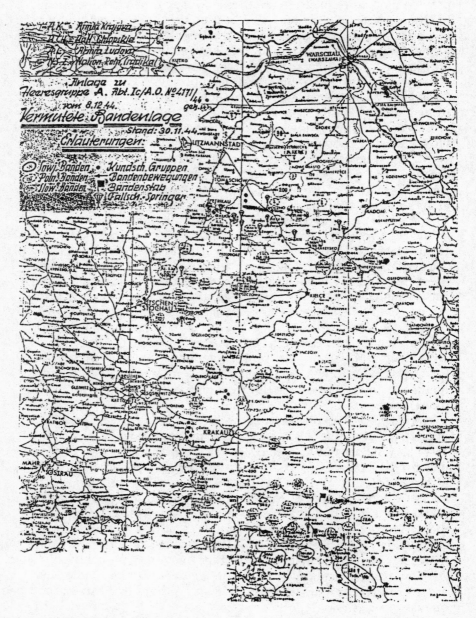

35. German Army Group A assessment of Soviet reconnaissance-diversionary activity, December 1944

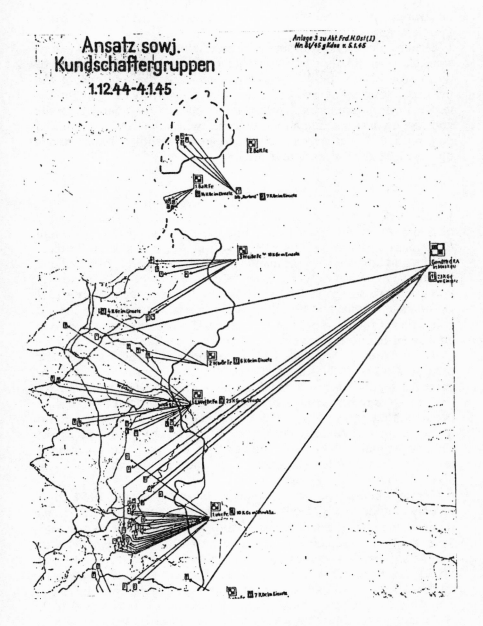

36. German *Fremde Heere Ost* assessment of Soviet reconnaissance-diversionary activity, 5 January 1945

or groups under communist Polish command (*Armia Ludova* — People's Army).

Sketchy Soviet descriptions of agent *razvedka* activity and extensive German documentation underscored the extensive scale of these activities. Clearly, by 1945 agent *razvedka* was one of the principal sources of Soviet strategic and deep operational intelligence information. Moreover, close cooperation of Soviet agents and reconnaissance-diversionary forces with some Polish bands in part replicated earlier extensive cooperation with partisan forces operating in the German rear area.

Radio

Radio-electronic *razvedka* was more extensive in 1945 than at any time earlier in the war. Radio intercept assets operated at High Command level under the GRU, within *fronts* under RU supervision, and under army command as well. Each Soviet *front* had one special designation radio battalion both to intercept and jam enemy communications. The 130th Radio Battalion supported the 1st Belorussian Front, and the 132d Radio Battalion supported the 1st Ukrainian Front.[71] The High Command probably assigned two additional battalions as reinforcements for each *front*.[72]

As was the practice in 1944 operations, armies created their own internal radio intelligence capability by forming special radio *razvedka* teams from the army signal regiment. For example, six such radio *razvedka* groups supported the armies of 1st Belorussian Front. Although the Soviets provide little detail concerning radio intercept operations, fragmentary reports attest to its effectiveness, such as the claim, "On 30 December 1944 our radio reconnaissance established that radio stations of the enemy's 3d and 5th Tank divisions had ceased to operate."[73]

German intelligence reports throughout 1943 and 1944, previously cited, recognized the seriousness of communications security problems and the likelihood that German transmissions were being intercepted and decoded. Additional judgements will remain speculation until Soviet archival materials cast light on real Soviet capabilities, but Soviet claims of success with radio *razvedka* track closely with subsequent Soviet operational performance. Certainly the success of the Soviet deception plan indicated high probability that the Soviets were able to verify German troop movements by other means, if not of radio.

Troop

During preparations for the Vistula–Oder operation the Soviets continued to display their mastery of troop *razvedka.* They employed the entire panoply of techniques, including sweeps, ambushes, and raids, associated with ground *razvedka*; observation and commanders' personal reconnaissance; and sophisticated techniques for conducting reconnaissance in force (*razvedka boem*). All these measures, carefully integrated into *front*, army, corps, and division *razvedka* plans, reached a new scale of intensity and variety. For example, during the preparatory period, 1st Belorussian Front forces conducted 509 sweeps and ambushes, including three of regimental scale, 14 daylight raids, 12 extractions from the enemy rear, and 22 series of reconnaissance in force. These measures produced 78 prisoners and 38 captured documents.[74]

Literally hundreds of examples of troop *razvedka* are detailed in Soviet works ranging through every combat level. In a typical example, on the night of 3 December 1944, a *razvedka* group of the 244th Guards Rifle Regiment, 82d Guards Rifle Division of 8th Guards Army conducted a sweep which carried it up to the forward German trench where it was halted by antipersonnel mines. Based upon prior experience, the 246th Guards Rifle Regiment dispatched a large *razvedka* group to the same region several nights later. Covered by special flank security groups, the new reconnaissance force burrowed under the minefield and reached the German trenches where they captured a German corporal. Documents on the prisoner identified him as a member of the 1st Battalion, 184th Infantry Regiment, 221st Infantry Division. The prisoner also provided information about neighboring units. To verify the data, on 16 December the regiment conducted a second sweep using the same methods to confirm the information obtained earlier.[75] Another 8th Guards Army division commander noted:

> *Razvedka* sweeps occurred every day. However, *razvedka* was conducted with all comprehensible means. By virtue of its results, we recreated the enemy defense system, his firing system, the presence of reserves and his dispositions. *Razvedchiki* tried as exactly as possible to determine the trace of trenches and the position of firing points. All of this was recorded on maps, and artillery fire and aviation strikes were directed against the revealed targets. ... In a word, we decided

many questions without which it would have been impossible to count on a successfully developing offensive.[76]

Similar extensive use of troop *razvedka* occurred on the 1st Ukrainian Front. In 5th Guards Army's sector, sweeps and ambushes were conducted by small groups consisting of a combined arms nucleus, one to two sappers to study engineer obstacles, and a similar number of artillerymen to determine the enemy firing system. Ambushes were generally employed where the enemy defenses were less dense and where enemy reconnaissance units were active, either in advance of or to the rear of the front. Where defenses were continuous, ambushes took place during sweeps. Groups conducting sweeps which were not detected by the enemy left detachments in the enemy rear to operate night ambushes.[77] Extensive ambush and sweep activity by both *fronts* provided a steady flow of German prisoners and facilitated almost daily updating of the assessed configuration of enemy tactical defenses. These active measures went hand-in-hand with more passive planned observation by front-line units.

By 1945 the Soviets had developed thorough procedures for visual and optical observation. Formal networks for observation, complete with optical equipment, existed from *front* down to battalion level. This network employed maps to record data and reported observation data to higher headquarters through a formal communications and data-collecting system. Observation points, distinct from those employed for artillery observation, formed a dense network at corps and division level and were tied in closely with main and rear command posts. In the forward area, commanders created observation posts as close as possible to the front lines or first echelon subunit positions, where the commander could personally observe the field of battle, especially on the main axis of advance.[78] Division commander observation posts were co-located with those of the division artillery group commander. "Often the location of the observation or command post was selected by the higher level commander."[79] Routinely, representatives of each branch (artillery, engineer, armor) manned OPs.

An even denser network of battalion and regimental OPs supplemented those of divisions and corps. OPs were placed in first and second trench lines and on any commanding terrain. Ideally, these posts conducted continuous observation to a depth of 2–3 kilometers into the enemy rear. Staff officers manning these posts were required to note all observed data in an "observation journal," which was subsequently forwarded to and "systematically studied by the staff."[80] Observation posts often acted as bases for both patrol activity and eavesdropping on enemy wire communications lines; thus, inevitably they were critical nodes in the *razvedka* system. By late 1944 first echelon battalions customarily employed one eavesdropping post, while regiments and divisions fielded from two to three posts each. High level observation posts were sited to increase the range of observation up to five kilometers, depending on terrain conditions. Typically, an army preparing for offensive operations created over 1,000 OPs of various types. In the Vistula–Oder operation, 69th Army employed up to 750 combined army observation posts and up to 520 artillery observation posts.[81]

The 1st Belorussian Front's 5th Shock Army formed army observation posts in the offensive sectors of each first echelon rifle division and also created one mobile observation post of three to five men to deploy forward once the offensive had begun.[82] The 129th Rifle Corps of 47th Army, by 4 January, had created one to two observation posts for each of its companies, battalions, regiments, and divisions of the first echelon. These posts were able to observe routinely up to 3 kilometers into the enemy defenses and, in some critical sectors, up to 4 kilometers. Artillery OPs operated either as part of this OP system or adjacent to individual OPs to facilitate more responsive and accurate artillery fires.[83] An officer of neighboring 61st Army described the scene at his observation post:

> Beside the stereoscopes lay maps and forms with the results of aerial photography, all speckled with conditionally designated pillboxes, machine gun positions, and artillery and mortar batteries. I carefully compared them with the observed panorama of the enemy defense.[84]

Careful, disciplined conduct of commanders' personal reconnaissances (*rekognostsirovka*) increased the effectiveness of the observation post system.[85] All pre-war and wartime regulations required such reconnaissance, and Soviet commanders attested to its value. Konev later wrote:

> In preparing for the breakthrough we also counted on a powerful artillery blow. To make this blow effective, the command of the Front, the commanders of armies, corps, and divisions, as well as the artillery commanders concerned, made the most careful reconnaissance of the entire penetration sector. We, the command of the Front, commanders of armies,

corps, divisions and regiments, together with the artillerymen and airmen, literally crawled all over the front line, mapping out the main objects of the attack.

Incidentally, it is my profound conviction that such a reconnaissance of the terrain, even to the point of crawling on all fours, is in no way at variance with the operational art. Some theoreticians are inclined to overestimate the operational art and hold that the rough work on the spot is, so to speak, the business of the lower commanders, not the operations planners. My opinion, however, is that thorough preparation on the spot and the subsequent practical realisation of the theoretical postulates go very well together. The operation I am describing is a good example.[86]

Soviet commanders conducted personal reconnaissance in sequence from higher level to lower level command over a number of days. Senior commanders normally accompanied their subordinates in groups of up to five or six individuals.

All work was conducted from operating observation posts. (It was forbidden to bring along maps with conditions noted on them.) Cooperation on the terrain was organized during the following periods: 6–9 January – by the corps commander with regimental commanders and attached force commanders with participation of the division commander; 9–11 January – by the commander of the division with battalion and attached subunit commanders with participation of the regimental commanders; 11 January – by the rifle regiment commanders with company commanders with participation of battalion commanders.[87]

Marshal Zhukov conducted his personal reconnaissance in the Magnushev bridgehead with individual corps and division commanders on the terrain across which they would operate. "On this *rekognostsirovka* the orientation, missions, and combat formation of units, the subordination of artillery, and the order of infantry support tank use was specified."[88] Division commanders of 5th Shock Army supervised their personal reconnaissance process after 10 January. Since the first German trenches were only 500–1,000 meters distant, company, battalion, and regimental commanders could often observe to four kilometers depth – that is, through the second German defensive position.[89]

Standardized personal reconnaissance procedures throughout

both *front* sectors often served two purposes. It certainly contributed to a clearer understanding of enemy defenses. When skillfully orchestrated, it also served as a means of disinformation regarding attack intentions and main attack location. While camouflaged parties of officers conducted real personal reconnaissance, bogus parties, dressed and posturing to draw enemy attention, often tricked enemy reconnaissance, since by 1945 it was clear that personal reconnaissance by Soviet officers was a major attack indicator. Often the Soviets included in these parties armor force officers with their characteristic garb and badges to indicate the likely commitment of a Soviet tank army in the sector.

One of the most critical means of last minute *razvedka* was the reconnaissance in force (*razvedka boem*), a technique which by 1945 had become far more sophisticated than it had been in earlier years. The purpose of reconnaissance in force had not changed. Its task was to verify intelligence data received from all *razvedka* means and note any last minute changes in enemy dispositions before the attack commenced. By 1945, however, the general purpose of reconnaissance in force had expanded. Often the reconnaissance, if successful, became an integral part of the overall offensive. For example, during the Belorussian operation, when 43d and 6th Guards Armies' reconnaissance forces succeeded in seizing the first German defensive positions, the *front* commander ordered the remainder of his forces into action to exploit the reconnaissance in force's success, without firing an artillery preparation.

To further confuse the Germans, by late 1944 reconnaissance in force often occurred immediately before the attack (up to one day) and in all sectors, so as not to reveal the main attack direction. Often reconnaissance in force also became a diversionary measure. Since they had become a clear attack indicator, Soviet commanders employed them in secondary sectors to draw German attention away from the main attack sector or conducted them well in advance of a planned attack to confuse the enemy regarding offensive intentions and timing. For example:

> Sometimes reconnaissance in force would be conducted at an earlier time in order to delude the enemy. On 5 January 1945, for example, that is, 10 days prior to the start of the Vistula–Oder offensive operation, the 1st Rifle Battalion of the 240th Guards Rifle Division, with an antitank battalion, a 76mm battery, and a combat engineer company, supported by two artillery regiments and a mortar battalion, conducted recon-

naissance in force with the objective of reconnoitering the forward edge of the enemy's main defensive position, to take prisoners for identification purposes, and to demolish anti-personnel obstacles in a sector 500 meters north of Grabow–Zalesny (south of Warsaw). The mission was accomplished. Raids, ambushes and dispatch of reconnaissance parties and detachments behind enemy lines were for the purpose of capturing prisoners, documents, specimens of weapons and combat equipment, and inflicting losses on the enemy. The raid and the ambush were the most effective and widely-used techniques. In January 1945 alone (during the period of defense) the army mounted 60 and 23 respectively. These actions killed 70 officers and men and took five prisoners. Reconnaissance party losses totaled four killed and 45 wounded.[90]

The latest guidance for conducting reconnaissance in force appeared in the 1944 *Instructions on Penetrating a Positional Defense* which, first and foremost, required the reconnaissance in force in up to battalion strength to verify existing defensive positions and ensure the Soviet artillery preparation did not strike unoccupied positions. The instructions required "advance battalions" conducting reconnaissance to pave the way for successive operations by the main force. Advance battalions were assigned deeper missions, often including "tactically important objectives in the enemy defense."[91] To accomplish these missions, the Soviets attached reinforcements to the advance battalions, including tanks, SP guns, sappers, etc. "Thus *razvedka* became an operational factor, and not [just] tactical."[92]

Advance battalions in the Vistula–Oder operation conducted reconnaissance immediately before the main force attack (see Figure 15).[93] The battalions were often reinforced by minesweeper tank platoons and assault companies, and an artillery preparation preceded their advance. Konev described the methods he used in the 1st Belorussian Front:

Reconnaissance in force was nothing new; it had been made before the beginning of the offensive in many other operations. We realised, however, that it had acquired a certain stereotype pattern to which the Germans had become accustomed and against which they had found an antidote. The stereotype part of it was that the reconnaissance in force was usually made the day before the offensive, then the data obtained was collected and analyzed, assault positions were taken up correspondingly and the offensive was begun the next day.

This time we decided to act differently, so as to prevent the enemy from reorganizing his defenses after our reconnaissance in force. To achieve this, we resolved to deliver a short but powerful artillery attack and immediately follow it up with reconnaissance in force by our forward battalions; if we then discovered that the enemy had not withdrawn his troops, we were to bring down the whole power of our artillery fire upon his positions. Such was our plan. If it had turned out, however, that the Nazis had withdrawn their troops, we would have immediately shifted our fire without wasting any shells, to where they had taken up their new positions.

Apart from my natural desire to see the beginning of the offensive with my own eyes I came to the Front observation post to be able to make the necessary decisions on the spot, if the operations of the forward battalions showed that the enemy had withdrawn.

The enemy might withdraw to any depth, including one that would require redeployment of some of the artillery and, consequently, a certain lull. In short, a situation might arise in which I, as the Front commander, would have to make urgent decisions which it would be desirable to check on the spot so that I could issue appropriate instructions.

The observation post in the immediate proximity of the battle formations, provided with all means of communication and control was the most suitable place. I arrived at the observation post together with Generals Krainyukov and Kalchenko, members of the Front Military Council, and General Sokolovsky, Chief of Staff of the Front.

At 0500 hrs, after a short but powerful artillery attack, the forward battalions launched an assault and soon captured the first trench of the enemy defences. The very first reports made it clear that the enemy had not withdrawn, but had remained in the zone of all the artillery attacks we had planned.

Despite its short duration the artillery attack was so powerful that the enemy thought it was the beginning of the general artillery preparation. Taking the action of the forward battalions for the general offensive of our troops the Nazis tried to stop it with all the fire weapons at their disposal.

This was just what we had counted on. After capturing the

Formation	Reconnaissance Force	Dedicated Support	Timing	Results
1st Belorussian Front				
69th RC, 61st A	Reinforced rifle bn per first echelon division	3–4 arty/ mortar bns; regiment and division arty	0855 14/1/45	Confirmed enemy dispositions
29th Gds RC, 8th Gds A	Assault bn per first echelon division	ditto	ditto	Confirmed enemy dispositions
26th RC, 5th SA	Reinforced rifle bn per first echelon division	ditto	ditto	Secured first defensive position to depth of 2–3 km
1st Ukrainian Front				
73d RC, 52d A	Reinforced tank- minesweeper and assault rifle company per first echelon division	ditto	1500 12/1/45	Confirmed first defensive positions unoccupied, secured prisoners

Abbreviations: SA – Shock Army, A – Army, RC – Rifle Corps, bn – battalion, arty – artillery

Fig. 15. Reconnaissance in Force Plan, Vistula–Oder Operation

first trench our forward battalions took cover between the first and second trenches. This was when our artillery preparation started. It lasted one hour and 47 minutes and was so powerful that, judging by a number of captured documents, it seemed to the enemy to have lasted not less than five hours.[94]

In essence, Konev's reconnaissance in force transformed itself into the first phase of the main attack. While doing so it simulated a main attack and forced the Germans to reveal all their troop and firing positions.

Zhukov devised a different plan for reconnaissance in force preceding the 1st Belorussian Front's assault. He planned a 25-minute heavy artillery preparation followed by a reconnaissance in force by advance battalions and companies. If the reconnaissance by the 22 reinforced battalions and 25 reinforced companies succeeded in seizing advanced German positions, the main attack would commence without further artillery preparation. If, however, the reconnaissance in force failed, an extended second artillery preparation would precede the main attack. This reconnaissance in force by advance battalions and companies (called a "special echelon" – *osobyi eshelon*) succeeded in overcoming the first two German defensive positions. Zhukov, in due course, ordered his main forces to continue the attack without the additional artillery preparation.[95]

An example from 47th Army illustrates another variation in the conduct of the reconnaissance in force:

> For conducting reconnaissance in force, during the night of 14 January, the two previously created and reinforced groups of 400 men each covertly moved up to the enemy barbed wire obstacles where they prepared to blast passages through them for the [subsequent] attack. In the morning, after a 10-minute intense shelling by all the corps artillery which caught the enemy by surprise, a detachment from the 143d Rifle Division, without a pause, captured two trenches; and a detachment from the 132d Rifle Division captured one along a front of 150–200m. The enemy, having considered the reconnaissance in force as an offensive by the main forces, committed a larger portion of its weapons to battle and began to bring up reserves to the penetration sectors. During the following 24 hours, the enemy's attempts to drive our reconnaissance forces from the captured trenches were unsuccessful. As a result of the reconnaissance in force, the personal observation of the commanders, and with the aid of artillery reconnaissance and observation, the enemy grouping and fire plan had been ascertained while the enemy was confused about the nature and aims of our troops.[96]

In essence then, the reconnaissance turned into the main attack which, within hours, had torn apart the entire first German defensive position.[97]

The reconnaissance in force, combined with systematic troop reconnaissance measures conducted earlier during the preparation phase, rendered German defenses virtually transparent and satisfied the principal task assigned troop *razvedka* by 1944 regulations – to verify enemy dispositions and facilitate conduct of a rapid penetration operation.

Artillery

Extensive artillery *razvedka* assets were available to both *fronts* during preparation for the Vistula–Oder operation. These included TOE subunits of troop artillery *razvedka*, separate reconnaissance aviation battalions, aeronautic battalions for aerostatic observation (VDAN), and separate corrective-reconnaissance aviation regiments. Eighty-five percent of these forces were concentrated on the army main attack sectors of both *fronts*. This provided an artillery instrumental *razvedka* (AIR) density of one reconnaissance battalion to every 4–5 kilometers of front.[98] All artillery *razvedka* assets were closely integrated with collection activities of other *razvedka* forces (for example, observation).

The most effective aspect of artillery instrumental *razvedka* was sound ranging, as indicated by this critique of 61st Army (1st Belorussian Front) artillery *razvedka*:

> Artillery reconnaissance was conducted by artillery reconnaissance and fire subunits with the aid of optical, sound ranging and other devices. Its mission was to spot promptly and to determine precisely the coordinates of important targets. The SChZM-36 sound ranging unit was the most sophisticated. From July 1943 through April 1945 sound ranging took part in the major operations of the Great Patriotic War in determining coordinates on the average of up to 90 percent of the total number of reconnoitered targets by all artillery weapons.[99]

All armies on main attack axes possessed dedicated artillery *razvedka* assets. For example, the 1st Belorussian Front assigned the following artillery *razvedka* assets to its subordinate armies:

Army	Reconnaissance Artillery Battalions	Corrective Aircraft	Aerostatic Observation
61st	45th ORAD	4 aircraft, 98th OKAP	3d Detachment, 6th VDAN
5th Shock	725th, 821st ORAD, Recon aviation battalion, 44th Guards Army Gun Artillery Brigade	6 aircraft, 98th OKAP, 3d Night OKAP	1st, 2d Detachments 4th VDAN
8th Guards	OKAP, 6th Artillery Penetration Corps	6 aircraft, 98th OKAP	3d Detachment, 4th VDAN
69th	810th ORAD, Recon aviation battalion, 62d Army Gun Artillery Brigade	8 aircraft, 93d OKAP, 3d Night OKAP	2d Detachment, 6th VDAN

The 13th Army's artillery group consisted, in part, of the 14th Guards Separate Reconnaissance Artillery Battalion and the 1st Aeronautic Detachment, whose mission was to detect enemy artillery and mortar positions and engage them with counterbattery fire during and after the artillery preparation.[100] The 5th Guards Army was supported by the 118th Separate Corrective-Reconnaissance Aviation Regiment consisting of four IL-2 and four IaK-9 aircraft plus ground artillery instrumental units similar to those supporting 13th Army.[101]

It was the task of division, corps, and army artillery staffs to integrate all artillery *razvedka* collection means. An account by an officer in 61st Army's 9th Guards Rifle Corps described how it was done:

> Special attention was paid to artillery *razvedka*. A large network of observation posts was deployed in corps artillery. From the army artillery staff we were sent a large scale map with aerial photographic data. Each battery of the corps artillery group and countermortar group was assigned specific targets. The German-fascist command employed various methods of disinformation and a system of false firing positions, in which they placed actual weapons served by truncated crews. This occurred during preparation for the operations in the Magnushev and Pulavy bridgeheads. *Razvedchiki* [scouts] of our army and of the *front* artillery staff sounded the alarm about the former. When the results of *razvedka* were generalized and analyzed on the basis of various sources, we discovered that the quantity of artillery exceeded the combat strength of defending enemy formations several times over ... the data of aerial photographs, visual observation, and corrective-reconnaissance aviation affirmed the [actual] presence of enemy artillery batteries.
>
> Careful observation by artillery *razvedka* in the forward area over the flashes and timing of enemy fire by various means confirmed the firing activity of batteries. From battery and battalion OPs we received intelligence information, and before sending the next *razvedka* report and map to corps artillery staff, I sat for a long time, thought over, and calculated how many and what kind of detected artillery and mortar batteries fired shells on our force dispositions.[102]

By careful analysis 61st Army was able to decipher most enemy artillery positions deployed across its front.

In total, the two *fronts* employed about 20 separate reconnaissance artillery battalions (one per artillery division), three to four aeronautical battalions of aerostatic observation, and four separate corrective-reconnaissance aviation regiments.[103] The openness of the terrain on the west bank of the Vistula River mitigated the negative effects of unfavorable weather to produce better than adequate artillery observation data.

Engineer

Engineer units assigned to *front* and army and the TOE sapper battalion organic to rifle divisions provided engineer *razvedka* support for the Vistula–Oder operation. *Front* assets included engineer-sapper brigades, some motorized, and usually one special designation engineer brigade to handle specialized tasks such as mineclearing and demolition in the enemy rear area. Armies had brigades or engineer battalions attached from *front* as well as organic engineer units. The rifle division sapper battalion, according to the new 1944 TOE, assigned to one combat engineer platoon the mission of combat reconnaissance and provided it with specialized training for that mission.[104]

Engineers established a dense network of engineer observation posts (INP) closely intertwined with their combined arms and artillery counterparts. Usually rifle divisions established two such posts, each manned by three men, but in main attack sectors the density of INPs reached three to four per kilometer of front. Each INP was equipped with optical devices (binoculars, stereoscopes), compasses, and watches; and troops manning them maintained observation journals and maps or sketches of the region. Often INPs photographed enemy defenses using periscopic cameras. All data collected by the INP was dispatched through engineer channels to the division, army, and ultimately *front* intelligence directorates for processing and collation.

To verify the information recorded by observation and photography, engineers either organized or participated in sweeps to study the defenses first-hand and take prisoners. These sweeps, usually conducted at night, were made by parties of four to five men armed with machine guns, grenades, mine detectors, and wire cutters. The sweep group was normally led by the engineer *razvedka* platoon or company commander.[105] The average depths of the sweeps were 1 to 2 kilometers; but, by January 1945, larger groups occasionally penetrated up to 40 kilometers.[106]

Engineer activity during the preparatory period was intense. The 1st Ukrainian Front Chief of Engineers, Lieutenant General I. P. Galitsky, established over 180 engineer observation posts and supervised the conduct of 1,300 sweeps, 118 of which penetrated into the operational depths (greater than 20 kilometers).[107] For the most part, these posts and sweeps were organized and conducted by division and corps sapper battalions and by army engineer *razvedka* companies (for example, the 460th Separate Reconnaissance Company of 5th Guards Army).[108] The 60th Army, operating on a broad front from the southern portion of the Sandomierz bridgehead south to the Tarnow region, organized INPs on the basis of one per first echelon rifle battalion, one per first echelon rifle regiment, and two to three per rifle division. Every ground *razvedka* group contained two to three sappers; and, in addition, special engineer parties conducted deeper engineer *razvedka*.[109]

Similar activity took place on the 1st Belorussian Front, where the density of INPs reached three to four posts per kilometer of penetration sector. The 8th Guards Army established 28 INPs along a 7-kilometer front in the Magnushev bridgehead, while 69th Army deployed 42 INPs on a 10.5-kilometer front in the Pulavy bridgehead. The 8th Guards Army conducted 50 sweeps and 69th Army 56 to a depth of up to 25 kilometers.[110] During the four days prior to the offensive, 47th Army conducted 45 sweeps in the area north of Warsaw.[111] According to one Soviet critique:

> The results of engineer *razvedka* permitted composition of a full picture of the state of enemy engineer structures and obstacles and helped determine the most expedient form of combat use of engineers and means of performing their engineer work.[112]

In addition, engineer forces actively participated in the reconnaissance in force which immediately preceded the offensive. In the 1st Belorussian Front:

> To fulfill the former mission [clear routes for reconnaissance advance battalions] a destruction group consisting of a sapper squad and automatic weapons squad was included in each company of first echelon assault battalions. In the 1st Belorussian Front the 166th and 92d Engineer Tank Minesweeper Regiments were also used to clear passages. They secured passages through minefields for two tank brigades and seven tank and SP artillery regiments during the penetration of the defense.[113]

Engineer forces operated analogously within the 1st Ukrainian Front.

EFFECTIVENESS OF *RAZVEDKA*

Comparison of German defensive dispositions and force transfers during the two months prior to the offensive with Soviet accounts of *razvedka*, and examination of the course of the operation indicates that Soviet *razvedka* organs did their job well. The Soviet *maskirovka* plan was successful, the Soviets were able to pinpoint the location of German reserves, and the penetration operation developed more rapidly than planned. The effectiveness of Soviet forces in the early phases of the operation did such damage to defending German forces that ultimately the offensive plunged westward well beyond the planned objective of Poznan to the Oder River, only 60 kilometers from Berlin. Certainly some of this success was attributable to the weakness of German defenses and the absence of large German operational reserves due to the large German transfer of forces southward from September to November 1944 in response to Soviet activity in the Carpathian Mountain region and in Hungary (see Map 37). Soviet intelligence was able to monitor movement of these reserves and was aware of their location in early January. The clearest example was Soviet tracking of the movements of IV SS Panzer Corps from the Warsaw region to Hungary in December and January.

Soviet strategic and operational *razvedka* collection organs, responsible for monitoring these movements, and for determining the nature of German defenses across the expanse of Poland, accomplished both tasks successfully. During the nine favorable flying days between mid-November and 12 January, Soviet 1st Belorussian Front air *razvedka* conducted 1,700 reconnaissance aircraft sorties, with these results:

> The total area of aerial photography comprised 109,000 square kilometers. Of this total enemy defensive positions to a depth of 8 kilometers were photographed three times over, and the enemy defense sectors in front of the Magnushev and Pulavy bridgeheads to a depth of 25–40 kilometers [were photographed] four times every 10–12 days. Perspective [oblique] photography of the forward edge and the entire tactical defense zone in front of the bridgehead occurred repeatedly. All of this provided the capability of discovering the nature and

Переброска войск противника в полосы действий 38-й и 1-й гвардейской армии (сентябрь—ноябрь 1944 г.)

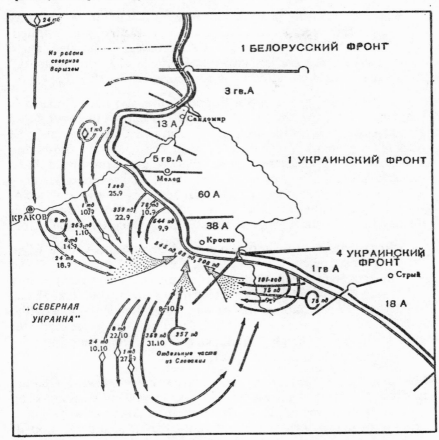

37. German force regroupings, September–November 1944

system of the defense and the grouping of enemy field and antiaircraft artillery throughout the entire tactical depth.

In the operational depth army rear positions and cut-off positions along the Pilitsa River were photographed twice and the Warta and Poznan defensive positions once. As a result of the survey a series of intermediate positions between the Vistula and rear belt were revealed, six antitank positions from 20 to 60 kilometers long were uncovered, as well as an entire aerodrome net with aviation forces based on them.[114]

The 16th Air Army commander, General S. I. Rudenko, commented:

> The air *razvedka* plan, drawn up by the staff of the air army under the supervision of General P. I. Braiko, was fulfilled. Our RO led by Colonel G. K. Prussekovy applied much creative effort and organizational skill in order to employ all types of aviation effectively and purposefully.[115]

Chuikov, commander of 8th Guards Army, seconded Rudenko's judgement, stating, "With satisfaction I mention that our army air *razvedka* coped with its missions. Information gathered by it received high marks from the *front* staff and staffs of neighboring armies."[116] The 1st Ukrainian Front achieved similar results as its air *razvedka* photographed over 103,000 square kilometers of territory and monitored movement of German reserves in the key sector south of the Vistula River.[117] Finally, a critique of the Soviet Air Force command and staff during the Vistula–Oder operation noted:

> Reconnaissance aviation uncovered beyond the Vistula River enemy prepared defensive belts, six antitank positions ... and determined concentration areas of enemy reserves and enemy artillery groupings. All crossings over the Vistula and Pilitsa Rivers were photographed, and airfield nets with aviation units were uncovered. The information from air *razvedka* permitted the High Command and *front* commands to plan correctly the offensive operations.[118]

Radio *razvedka* by *fronts* and armies helped reveal German tactical defensive dispositions and movement of reserves. The Soviets have revealed little about their achievements except a critique of 1st Belorussian Front radio *razvedka* and mention of radio *razvedka*'s role in tracking the southerly move of IV SS Panzer Corps. The critique of 1st Belorussian Front radio *razvedka* declared:

> Radio *razvedka* of the *front* ascertained the dispositions of 9th Army, and the staffs of all corps and five (of seven) enemy divisions, operating in the first line. It had undoubted merit in revealing the operational regrouping occurring in this period in the sector of this army. Thus radio *razvedka* was the first to notice the withdrawal by the German-Fascist command of 4th SS Tank Corps to Hungary where a counterattack was being prepared. According to its data, the *front* staff succeeded in

establishing the transfer of the left flank 56th Tank Corps from 4th Panzer Army to 9th Army, as well as the change in the defensive sector of 8th Army Corps.

The successful activity of radio *razvedka* organs was caused first of all by the presence in the *front* composition of radio equipment which was powerful for its times (four radio battalions OSNAZ and the forces themselves had six army groups for close communications *razvedka*).[119]

Soviet sources are less exact regarding the impact and effectiveness of agent and reconnaissance-diversionary *razvedka*. Scattered accounts of agent actions cited earlier obviously supplemented the intelligence picture. For example, "On 1 January, *razvedka* agents reported that soldiers wearing the insignia of 5th Tank Division [SS] had been spotted in Czestochowa."[120] One Soviet critique, referring to agent *razvedka* as "*spetsial'naia*" (special), stated:

> For example, in the Vistula—Oder operation special *razvedka* of the 1st Ukrainian Front revealed the basing of aviation and the capacity of the aerodrome net in the *front* sector, and also established the concentration regions of three divisions, the 17th and 4th Tank Army staffs, the 48th Tank and 42d Army Corps staffs, and added other information concerning the grouping of enemy forces, and his operations and intentions.[121]

Once again, German reports illustrated the extent of Soviet agent and reconnaissance-diversionary *razvedka*. German periodic intelligence studies assessed significant numbers of agents, bands, and reconnaissance units in the rear labeled under the categories of bands, agents, scouting groups, and detachments, etc. German documents also illustrated how the Soviets used these agents or groups for deceptive purposes. For example, a study of German intelligence procedures employed in the east contained a section on how intelligence dealt with enemy agents. In addition to cataloguing all agent activities, German intelligence concluded:

> The places at which the agents were detected or apprehended, as these entries increased in density in certain sectors of the front, were found through experience to indicate very closely where the Russians were planning to engage in large scale operations.[122]

A report on agent activity prepared on 5 January 1945 revealed agent activity to be concentrated west of Warsaw and south of

Krakow. In fact, these were the regions where Soviet deception plans were attempting to simulate attack preparations to distract German attention from the rear main attack sectors adjacent to the Vistula River bridgeheads. These and other German documents vividly attest to the effective Soviet use of agents and reconnaissance-diversionary teams in deception operations. At the same time, they tacitly underscore the growing role of these *razvedka* organs in the more common role of intelligence gathering.

As had been the case since late 1942, Soviet troop, artillery, and engineer *razvedka* were particularly effective and contributed to rapid Soviet success in the penetration operation. All sources indicate the Soviets gathered detailed information on enemy troop and artillery dispositions throughout the tactical depths of the German defense. It is apparent that Soviet intelligence knew German operational reserves opposite the Sandomierz bridgehead were deployed within the tactical depths. Hence, the Soviets were able to target these units during their artillery preparation and, as a result, destroy their command and control and inflict heavy losses. German 16th and 17th Panzer Divisions suffered severe damage during the preparation.

Extensive sweeps, ambushes, and raid activity produced a steady stream of prisoners and documents to confirm data obtained from ground and aerial observation:

> As a result, troop *razvedka* studied in detail all groupings of enemy forces within the limits of the main defensive belt. By the beginning of the operation, *front*, army, and division staffs had sufficiently complete information about the composition of the combat formation of fascist formations, defending in first echelon.
>
> In cooperation with engineer [*razvedka*], troop *razvedka* found out the true outline of the forward edge of the defense, the engineer obstacle system in the forward region and particularly in the depths of the defense, as well as the junction [boundary] of divisions, regiments and battalions; and on the Pulavy bridgehead even the junction between companies. Together with artillery [*razvedka*] it revealed the enemy firing system.[123]

Moskalenko, commander of 38th Army, reinforced this judgement, stating, "As a result, by the beginning of the operation the system of enemy trenches, fortifications, obstacles, and observation posts was uncovered and studied by all officers down to company and battery commanders, inclusive."[124] An account of 47th Army offensive preparations echoed Moskalenko's view:

> As a result, by the start of the offensive the configuration of the forward edge had been determined, the fire plan and weapons of the enemy defenses had been discovered down to the individual submachine gun, the coordinates had been determined for 18 artillery and mortar batteries, 12 assault guns, 17 machine guns, 11 covered trenches and 2 pillboxes. This comprised around 70 percent of the basic enemy weapons in the corps' sector of advance.[125]

Reconnaissance in force conducted during the preparatory period and just prior to the offensive deceived the Germans regarding attack timing and location and verified the results of earlier *razvedka*. In 47th Army's sector north of Warsaw, where the Soviets planned diversionary operations, the reconnaissance fulfilled both functions:

> The plan of operations foresaw the conduct in our sector of a reconnaissance in force which was timed to correspond with the beginning of the shock group's offensive from the Magnushev bridgehead. The mission – to disorient the enemy and at the same time feel out his force and secure prisoners. The *razvedka* was successful. The so-called Modlin junction, on which the Hitlerites placed great hopes, judging by all, was not as strong as it had been in October of the previous year. Our advance battalions succeeded in penetrating the depth of the enemy defense by almost a kilometer and seized several tens of prisoners.[126]

Elsewhere the reconnaissance in force succeeded, and in the 1st Ukrainian Front sector it served the purpose of both confusing the enemy and permitting refinements in artillery fire plans. "Information obtained by reconnaissance in force allowed the *front* commander to make several changes in the artillery support of the offensive. In particular, the artillery preparation was planned with a pause for platoons to conduct demonstrative attacks."[127] This demonstrative action forced the Germans to "show their hands" and the subsequent artillery preparation pulverized German defenses.

Thorough artillery *razvedka* simply added to the detailed picture composed by Soviet intelligence staffs. This was particularly true in main attack sectors where 90 percent of artillery intelligence-gathering assets were concentrated (for example, in 34 kilometers of 1st Belorussian Front's 230-kilometer sector).[128] Artillery instrumental *razvedka*, reconnaissance-corrective aviation, and the dense network of artillery observation posts within rifle and artillery units provided an accurate picture of enemy defenses:

> As a result of these measures, in the penetration sector [of 1st Belorussian Front] artillery *razvedka* uncovered and determined the coordinates of 468 artillery and mortar and 57 antiaircraft batteries, 1,480 open firing points, 245 firing points with covers (pillboxes), 406 blindages and 154 observation posts.[129]

In addition, artillery *razvedka* assisted in analysis of forward enemy defenses and the identification of antitank and antipersonnel obstacles and other defensive structures.

Engineer *razvedka* contributed to success in the preparatory period and during the reconnaissance in force as well. Joint artillery and engineer observation in 5th Guards Army's sector "illuminated" the enemy defensive system, located 36 105mm artillery batteries, 15 75mm batteries, 33 antiaircraft batteries, 12 81mm mortar batteries, and 17 119.8mm mortar batteries. In addition, *razvedka* revealed that German forces manned only the first and second positions of the main defensive belt. "All this permitted the army command to have complete information about the enemy and make correct decisions."[130] A 60th Army critique of engineer *razvedka* noted the work of engineer observation posts and engineer reconnaissance parties dispatched deep into the enemy rear and concluded:

> Such organized [engineer] *razvedka* permitted us to determine the overall grouping of enemy force operations on our army's sector and ascertain the nature of his defensive structures which, in turn, provided the possibility of more exactly determining the missions of army formations.[131]

Engineer *razvedka* forces also played an important role in the reconnaissance phase just prior to the main attack. According to a senior engineer:

> By the start of the Vistula–Oder Operation of the 1st Belorussian and 1st Ukrainian fronts (January 1945), it had been possible to remove all our own minefields in the jump-off areas and make passages in the enemy minefields in front of the

forward edge of its defenses. Here, just on the bridgeheads in front of the breakthrough of the defenses on the 1st Belorussian Front, the combat engineers removed 80,000 anti-personnel and about 42,000 antitank mines. As a total in this operation, in the zone of the 1st Belorussian Front, the engineer troops made 872 passages in the enemy minefields. Here 19,483 antitank and 14,201 anti-personnel mines were removed.[132]

Extensive Soviet *razvedka* prior to the offensive provided a basis for accurate Soviet assessments of German strength throughout the depth of Poland. By the end of December 1944, the General Staff assessed that there were 49 German divisions, including five panzer divisions, in the main sector of the front.[133] Assessments of German forces defending in individual Soviet army sectors were even more accurate, in part because of efficient *razvedka* and in part due to the smaller number of German formations.

A 1st Belorussian Front order issued in early December to 5th Shock Army revealed the intelligence picture at that time:

To the Commander of 5th Shock Army
Copy: to chief of the Red Army General Staff

1. Units of the enemy 251st and 6th Infantry Divisions, reinforced by six RGK [reserve of High Command] artillery battalions, two RGK antitank battalions, an RGK assault gun brigade, and one RGK mortar regiment, defend strongly fortified positions on the line: Varka, Grabuv, Zales'ny, Vyboruv, Grabuv Pilitsa, Bzhozuvka, Stzhizhina, Gelenuvek, Gelenuv, Lipa, Lezhenitse. The enemy has fortified these positions for more than four months and has developed them to a depth of from 10 to 15 kilometers. The most developed defense system and the densest enemy combat formation is in the sector Tsetsyliuvka–Lezhenitse.

The main artillery groupings are in the regions:
(a) Up to four battalions – Zbyshkuv (5 kilometers south of Varka), Budy Boskovol'ske, Boska Volia;
(b) Up to three battalions – Stanislavuv, Dutska, Volia, Male Bozhe.

Enemy reserves are in the regions: presumed 383d Infantry Division – M. Brone; tank division of an unknown number – Bialobzhegi, Charnotsin (22 kilometers west M. Edlinsk) (17 kilometers southwest of Varka); infantry division of unknown number — Nove Miasto, Tomashuv; presumed 25th Tank Division — Stanislavitse (4 kilometers southwest of Kozenitse), Pionki; grenadier division of unknown number and presumed 174th Reserve Division — Radom. ...

Commander of 1st Belorussian Front Forces Marshal of the Soviet Union G. Zhukov	Member of the Military Council Lieutenant-General Telegin

Chief of Staff of 1st Belorussian Front
Colonel-General Malinin[134]

This assessment accurately plotted the tactical defenses of German 251st and 6th Infantry Divisions and the strength of their fire support. It correctly assessed the location of 25th Panzer Division; and the second panzer division identified corresponded to 19th Panzer Division, which was also located in this sector. The grenadier division referred to was either 10th or 20th Panzer Grenadier Division, operating between the Magnushev and Sandomierz bridgeheads. The reserve division identified replicated the German security division operating to the rear of German tactical defenses.

In late December intense *razvedka* activity by 47th Army north of Warsaw accurately determined German tactical dispositions:

> On 29 and 30 December 1944, the Nazi Command regrouped its troops, having positioned two infantry regiments of the 73d Infantry Division in the first echelon and one regiment in the second. In the reserve were around 1.5 infantry battalions and up to 15 tanks. The basic portion of the enemy artillery was positioned in the forests to the west of Hotomow (around 16 batteries).[135]

Further south, in the Sandomierz bridgehead 5th Guards Army also formed an accurate picture of the dispositions and strength of defending German units:

> Before the army front, in the sector of the penetration defended units of the 168th, 304th, and 68th Infantry Divisions reinforced by tanks, artillery, and mortars. The strength of enemy divisions reached 6,000 men, and companies were 60–80 men strong, predominantly German but with small quantities of Austrians. The average density of artillery

reached 10–12, and in some sectors up to 20–25 guns per kilometer of front, and up to 10 machine guns, 3 tanks, and 150–170 rifles per kilometer. In the Buska–Zdrui areas, the corps tank reserve was located – the 501st Separate Tank Battalion with 50 machines. Enemy operational reserves were located in the depth of the defense. In the army offensive sector we expected two infantry and one tank division to appear.[136]

A critique of 1st Belorussian Front *razvedka* summarized its overall achievement regarding German order of battle:

> As a result of the complex and purposeful use of forces and means of all types of *razvedka*, missions assigned by commanders to *front razvedka* during the preparatory period were fully carried out: by the beginning of the offensive the 1st Belorussian Front staff possessed accurate information about the compositions, grouping, and the combat capabilities of formations and units of German-Fascist forces operating in the sector of the forthcoming offensive. The enemy tactical defense zone on the direction of the *front* main attack was especially revealed in detail.[137]

Once in possession of this data, the *front* ensured it was put to good use:

> The *front* staff made great efforts to provide generalized data to the forces. In particular, they were sent detailed characteristics of enemy divisions defending the Vistula defensive line, schemes of defensive positions throughout the entire depth of the defense, maps of aviation unit basing and his aerodrome network and reconnaissance sketches of the main defense belt on a scale of 1:25,000 and 1:50,000, which during the ten days before the offensive were passed down to company and battery commanders.[138]

Soviet *razvedka* deprived German defenders of what little chance they had to defend successfully along the Vistula. The devastating nature of the ensuing assaults ensured that Soviet forces would penetrate far beyond their ultimate objective of Poznan, in this case all the way to the Oder River.

RAZVEDKA DURING THE OPERATION

The conduct of *razvedka* during a prolonged static period prior to an offensive was a skill Soviet forces had learned well since the summer of 1943. It took considerably longer, however, for Soviet forces to develop a similar talent for *razvedka* on the march – during active operations. It is axiomatic to a marksman that it is far more difficult to detect, identify, and strike a moving target than a stationary one. Moreover, the noise and confusion of active fluid operations naturally pose challenges to intelligence collection of all sorts. By 1945 the Red Army relied primarily on air, radio, and mobile ground *razvedka* means during the course of an operation to determine enemy dispositions and intentions. Soviet performance during the Vistula–Oder operation vividly illustrated the strides Soviet commanders had made in this regard since the first tentative, partially successful Soviet attempts to keep up with German force movements during the Stalingrad period.

Once an operation had begun, a major portion of *razvedka* forces had to concentrate on carrying out pre-planned missions in support of the ongoing attacks. Since, however, the situation was constantly changing, these missions often had to be adjusted, while some *razvedka* forces received entirely new missions suited to the changing situation. In addition, the rapid tempo of development required that some of these new missions be operational in nature, as well as tactical.

The principal missions of *razvedka* during the offensive were:

> to determine the degree of suppression of the enemy defense;
> to specify the dispositions of firing means and obstacles hindering the forward movement of forces;
> to determine areas of concentration, combat composition, and the degree of combat readiness of close enemy reserves and monitor their movements;
> to establish the time and direction of enemy staff displacements;
> to detect the moment of enemy preparation for withdrawal.[139]

Fulfillment of these missions was principally the responsibility of ground *razvedka*, which included the actions of numerous separate reconnaissance patrols, detachments and groups; raids, sweeps, ambushes, observation, officers' reconnaissance patrols, as well as artillery, engineer, and air *razvedka*. Separate reconnaissance groups and patrols from divisions and regiments usually consisted of a reinforced reconnaissance platoon or a rifle squad, while battalions employed rifle squads.

Reconnaissance groups and patrols serving divisions and regiments during the tactical penetration received a direction or objective on which to orient their sweep, ambush, or raid activity, while battalion-size reconnaissance detachments, leading mobile corps and brigades in the exploitation and pursuit phase of the operation operated along a direction (axis) or in a distinct sector.[140] By 1945 most reconnaissance detachments were fully motorized and had their own armor and antitank support. An average motorized reconnaissance detachment consisted of one to two automatic weapons platoons mounted on vehicles, a tank platoon, an antitank gun platoon, and one to two platoons of machine gun motor-cycles.[141] Detachments routinely employed their own subordinate reconnaissance patrols.

Once the penetration phase had been completed, Soviet mobile forces (tank or mechanized) routinely led their advance with re-connaissance detachments and combat-oriented forward detach-ments (*peredovoi otriad*). The former served as the eyes of the latter and of the main force. Every tank battalion in first echelon tank brigades of tank or mechanized corps on the march dispatched a combat reconnaissance patrol (BRD) forward. It also formed special mobile observation posts which were arrayed in front of and on the flanks of the main brigade force. Tank brigades formed their own separate reconnaissance patrols (ORD), and tank (mechanized) corps and armies designated reconnaissance detach-ments to lead the pursuit.[142] Because of the large number of water obstacles to be crossed in the offensive, mobile forces often employed engineer reconnaissance groups or forward detachments reinforced with engineers to effect river crossings.[143] In few opera-tions was Soviet ground *razvedka* as effective as it was in the Vistula–Oder operation. In part, this explains how the Soviets were able to sustain operations to such extraordinary depths.

On the mornings of 12 and 14 January, respectively, the 1st Ukrainian and 1st Belorussian Fronts commenced combat opera-tions. Within hours each *front* had devastated German tactical defenses and begun an operational exploitation. Ground *razvedka* measures employed by 1st Belorussian Front typified actions across the entire front. Following a 25 minute artillery preparation, *front* forces commenced reconnaissance in force by one to two rifle battalions from each first echelon rifle division reinforced by tanks and self-propelled artillery and supported by artillery fire and air strikes. Unable to halt the advance battalions and thinking them to be the actual main attack, the Germans began withdrawing from the forward defensive positions to other prepared defenses in the rear. Soon the Soviets ordered a general advance; and, by day's end on 14

January, German defenses had been penetrated to a depth of from 15 to 20 kilometers. The following day, after Soviet forces developed the offensive to a depth of 20–50 kilometers, 1st Belorussian Front's two tank armies began their exploitation.

While Soviet forces conducted the penetration and approached the enemy army rear defense lines, they employed aerial and ground observation, reconnaissance groups and detachments, and other techniques to gather intelligence information. Mobile observation posts (PNP) mounted on armored vehicles and intermingled with attacking infantry conducted the most effective observation and reported back through intelligence channels at division. Each division operating on a main attack axis employed one to two such groups while corps fielded two to three and armies three to seven.[144] The PNPs also served the purpose of keeping the commander informed concerning the location of his own forces.

Reconnaissance groups (RG) of regiments, usually in squad strength, operated on the boundaries of adjacent regiments and sought to penetrate one to two kilometers deep into the enemy formation in order to observe, seize prisoners, and determine the enemy defensive posture. Larger divisional reconnaissance groups, of up to platoon size, operated in similar fashion but with expanded missions, often to determine the disposition of close operational reserves.[145] For example, a reconnaissance group of 8th Guards Army was tasked with determining the location and status of the German 19th and 25th Panzer Divisions, the principal operational reserves in the 1st Belorussian Front sector, last known to be located near Radom:

> The inability to conduct air *razvedka* because of bad weather created a threat of German secret movement of these units and their commitment into a battle with all the resulting implications. A reconnaissance group of 8th Guards Army's 82d Guards Rifle Division, sent late on 14 January into the enemy rear, by means of observation and comparison of information obtained from prisoners, ascertained movement of 19th Tank Division units to the penetration sector. This permitted the army commander to undertake necessary measures leading to piecemeal destruction of that division.[146]

Further north a major Soviet intelligence concern was the nature of German defensive positions on the north bank of the Pilitsa River between Warka and Belobzhegi, where the Soviets intended to commit 2d Guards Tank Army into the penetration. Troop *razvedka* also answered that question:

> On the night of 15 January a reconnaissance group of 5th Shock Army succeeded in penetrating into the enemy cut off position [along the Pilitsa River] and determined that the positions were occupied only by withdrawing German forces. This data assisted 5th Shock Army forces in forcing the Pilitsa and protecting the subsequent introduction of 2d Guards Tank Army into the penetration.[147]

Once through the tactical defenses, Soviet mobile forces commenced the exploitation led by forward detachments and reconnaissance detachments. Combined arms armies then formed their own reconnaissance detachments which operated well forward in the gaps between the exploiting mobile forces and less mobile main force infantry. These reconnaissance detachments of reinforced tank or rifle battalion size ranged 20–40 kilometers in advance of their parent forces, and cooperated closely with aviation units to reconnoiter enemy rear or intermediate defense lines and monitor German withdrawal or the arrival of reserves. For example:

> Reconnaissance detachments of 2d Guards Tank Army, arriving in the Sokhachev area (50 kilometers west of Warsaw), determined that part of the rear [defensive] positions were occupied by the 391st Security Division and that enemy 46th Tank Corps formations were withdrawing westward from Warsaw. By decisive action of 2d Guards Tank Army forces, the 391st Security Division was crushed, and with the arrival of 2d Guards Tank Army at Sokhachev, withdrawal routes of the Warsaw group westward were cut. As a result it [the Warsaw group] was forced to turn northwest where it crossed the Vistula under constant joint action of our aviation and ground forces and suffered great losses.[148]

Numerous examples exist of similar actions by reconnaissance groups and detachments late in the operation as Soviet mobile forces raced across central Poland. For example, on 19 January the reconnaissance detachment of 2d Guards Tank Army discovered that various specialized and reserve German units had established a fortified region in the Vrotslaveka region. The same day 5th Shock Army reconnaissance organs detected the presence of German Panzer Grenadier Division "Brandenburg" near Vlodavy, and 1st

Guards Tank Army reconnaissance detachments west of Lodz took prisoner elements of the German 412th Security Division. Armed with this information, on 19–20 January Soviet forces breached the Warta River line along its entire length. Several days later, from 20 to 24 January, the same occurred in the Poznan area when reconnaissance organs detected the presence of elements of the German 196th Reserve Division, the 130th Border Regiment, and more than ten other battalions, some of which were *Volksturm* (home guards). Early detection of these units prevented German establishment of a new defense line, and most of the units ended up encircled in Poznan.[149]

Further north Soviet *razvedka* organs detected the early stages of a German buildup in Pomerania:

> On 22 January in the Torun region, a prisoner was captured from the German 31st Infantry Division which had been located earlier in the Baltic. From *razvedka* organs, operating in the enemy rear, came information about the beginning of force transfers from Danzig to the southwest, that is to the front right flank. Simultaneously enemy opposition near Bromberg, Nakel and Schneidemuhl stiffened considerably.[150]

Subsequent identification by a reconnaissance detachment of 2d Guards Tank Army of the 15th SS Infantry Division near Nakel and knowledge that few German forces were south of Schneidemuhl raised concern for security on the right flank. As a consequence:

> That *razvedka* information predetermined the decision of the *front* commander to employ 3d Shock Army (the *front* second echelon) to cover the *front* right flank. Simultaneously, armies operating on the Kustrin and Frankfurt directions were ordered to increase the tempo of their offensive in order to rapidly overcome enemy fortifications and reach the Oder.[151]

Meanwhile to the south on 25 January, while 4th Tank Army was advancing toward the Oder River near Steinau, a reconnaissance detachment assisted in a preemptive river crossing. The 16th Guards Mechanized Brigade of 4th Tank Army's 6th Guards Mechanized Corps had the mission of seizing a crossing site for future use by the army. A reconnaissance group commanded by Lieutenant M. Ia. Radugin, consisting of a rifle company, a platoon of T-34 tanks, a heavy machine gun platoon, two SP guns, a radio squad, and three sappers, led the brigade. Its mission was "to determine the strength and composition of enemy reserves approaching the Oder, determine whether defenses along the river were manned, conduct terrain reconnaissance, and ascertain the trafficability of routes to the river."[152] Most important, it was to seize a bridge over the Oder near Steinau and hold it until the brigade's forward detachment arrived.

Traveling at a speed of 45 km/hour on the road to Steinau, the group met little resistance. At 1500 hours near Steinau they captured a prisoner who reported the bridge was defended by four 105mm artillery battalions, tanks, and *Panzerfausts* (hand-held antitank weapons). Having confirmed the prisoner's report, the group swept northward along the east bank of the Oder, occasionally exchanging fire with German units on the west bank of the river. That night near Liuben, 10 kilometers north of Steinau, the group found an undefended crossing site and conducted a night river crossing. They held the crossing until the arrival the next day of 16th Guards Mechanized Brigade, which consolidated the bridge-head. Combining stealth, rapid movement, and skillful analysis of intelligence data, the group played a significant role in obtaining a key bridgehead over the Oder.

In general, ground reconnaissance organs of combined arms and tank armies, operating flexibly well in advance of their parent forces, prevented German preparation of intermediate defense lines. They anticipated German movements and negated the impact on combat of newly arrived operational reserves. These actions were fully integrated with activities of higher level *razvedka* organs such as radio and air.

Radio *razvedka* organs at *front* and army level (the four special designation radio battalions and numerous radio *razvedka* groups within armies) during the penetration operation concentrated on detecting changes in German dispositions and the arrival of new German formations once the operation began:

> *Radiorazvedka* on the first day of the offensive revealed the dislocation of staffs of not only formations [corps and divisions], but also many units [regiments] of the enemy first echelon, and in the course of the operation constantly tracked their movements. They discovered, in timely fashion, the location of operational reserves and determined the direction of withdrawal of German-fascist forces.[153]

Soviet critiques reserved special praise for army close communication *razvedka* groups, which assisted the commanders of divisions and corps to recognize the immediate plans of the enemy to counter the advance of our forces and to undertake necessary measures. Thanks to these, in the 61st Army sector in the course of the first two weeks of the offensive we disrupted five counterattacks by companies and battalions and detected the withdrawal of the enemy to the third [defensive] position in front of our army's left flank corps.[154]

Once the penetration operation had ended and weather had improved, air *razvedka* began playing a key role in determining enemy intentions and dispositions. In fact, the deeper Soviet forces advanced, the more important was air *razvedka*. *Frontal* air forces began flying *razvedka* missions on 16 January after the weather improved, although earlier bomber and fighter flights had conducted minimal aerial observation. The priority missions of both 16th and 2d Air Armies were to monitor the movement of enemy reserves and continuously observe conditions on the field of battle. Soviet control of the skies facilitated accomplishment of both missions. Subsequently:

> Special attention was paid to the assault aircraft and ground forward detachment which cleared the path for all formations. Cooperation with this detachment in the operational depth meant that pilots had to conduct *razvedka* in its interest, discover enemy units, especially artillery and tank, and crush them from the air.[155]

Compared with earlier operations, the Soviets devoted a larger percentage of sorties to *razvedka*. For example, 2d Air Army supporting the 1st Ukrainian Front allocated 11 percent of its sorties to that function. This placed inordinate demands on communication and staff procedures, especially in the light of the rapidly changing conditions. Air *razvedchiki* (scouts) passed information about the enemy to the combined arms army staffs, which, in turn, provided the aircraft with new targeting information. To a greater extent than before, aviation commanders exercised considerable initiative required to deal with unexpectedly detected enemy reserves or withdrawing German units. Often they operated on the basis of information received from their own *razvedka* rather than orders from *front* or air army commanders.[156]

Improved air-ground radio communications procedures and equipment prompted smoother operation of the system. According to Rudenko:

If air and ground crews were to communicate with one another through their staffs, this required considerable time. Therefore we decided to employ such a communications system which included the following aspects. Our aviation commanders had to be collocated with commanders of tank subunits and direct assault aircraft strikes on those targets, which were of the highest priority to destroy.[157]

Whenever possible, air *razvedka* used the same direct ground line. On numerous occasions close air-ground cooperation facilitated more effective ground operations. For example, when 11th Tank Corps approached German defenses at Radom on 15 January, "Aviation conducted *razvedka* of enemy withdrawal routes, directed pursuing formations on their attack objectives, and supported forward detachment operations and operations of the main force."[158]

Almost immediately after the offensive had begun, *razvedka* data flowed in from fighter and assault aircraft. On the morning of 13 January, in 1st Ukrainian Front's sector, pilots of 2d Air Army reported movement and concentration of enemy forces on the flank of 4th Tank Army south of Kielce and north of Chmel'nik. Subsequent air strikes by 8th Bomber and 2d Assault Aviation Corps disorganized the planned German counterattack; and, by evening of 13 January, German forces began withdrawing to their third defense belt. "Air *razvedka* reported the movement of withdrawing enemy columns toward Czestochowa, Sosnovets and Krakow," and again air units struck at German columns.[159] This scattered air activity on the first few days of the offensive helped rout German forces defending at Sandomierz.

On 16 January after the weather had cleared, air *razvedka* expanded to encompass the entire front. Opposite the Magnushev and Pulavy bridgeheads reconnaissance aircraft "determined the direction of withdrawal of German forces and the location of friendly forward detachments and main force formations."[160] Subsequently, they directed bomber and fighter strikes on German columns along the Sokhachev–Lodz, Skernevitse–Tomachuv–Mazovetsky and Radom–Opochno roads and identified for destruction enemy concentrations and strong points at Rava–Mazovetsky, Strudzianka, Inovludz' and at river crossing sites near Skernevitse where German 25th Panzer Division forces defended.[161] During 17 January 16th Air Army aircraft flew 2,500 sorties. Photographic *razvedka* missions confirmed destruction of bridges at Seradz,

Vyshorrud, and Kutno and the destruction of eight railroad trains.[162]

Most important, on 17 January 16th Air Army detected the arrival in the sector of significant German reserves:

> Air *razvedka* determined that tanks were unloading in the Lodz region. This was tank corps "Grossdeutschland" transferred from Prussia. The commander of 16th Air Army assigned the 241st Bomber Division the mission of launching air strikes. Operating in eight groups, the crews in three passes destroyed the railroad railbed at the arrival and departure switches and almost fully knocked out the rail center. Bombing from various directions and various heights disorganized the German air defense. Tankers soon secured Lodz, seized 400 rail cars with military equipment and cargo and 28 repaired engines. Because of the blows of aviation and *front* mobile forces, tank corps "Grossdeutschland" suffered considerable losses and was forced to withdraw, having failed to advance into battle.[163]

Shortly thereafter, 16th Air Army *razvedka* detected German occupation of the "Warta defensive line with up to five infantry divisions."[164] These units subsequently also suffered heavily from air attacks.

Air *razvedka* also contributed to detection and identification of German forces concentrated in the Silesian industrial region on 1st Ukrainian Front's left flank. By 19–20 January resistance stiffened in the area, forcing Konev to shift the axis of 3d Guards Tank Army's advance from Breslau southward toward Oppeln and Ratibor. By 23 January air, radio, and combat *razvedka* had identified elements of the German force:

> In the evening of 23 January we worked out from our reconnaissance data the composition of the enemy group defending the Silesian industrial area. It consisted of nine infantry divisions, two panzer divisions, several so-called combat groups, two separate brigades, six separate regiments and 22 separate battalions, including several machine-gun training battalions and an officers' penal battalion. Judging by appearance we could have expected the arrival of 2–3 more infantry divisions and one panzer division in the near future.[165]

By 28 January, 3d Guards Tank Army and 21st, 59th, and 60th

Armies had isolated the German forces; and within days they withdrew to escape destruction.

Late in the operation, *razvedka* data convinced the Soviets to halt their forces along the Oder River and, instead of driving on Berlin, to mount operations to clear their flanks (in Pomerania and Lower Silesia). Earlier, Stalin had expressed doubts as to whether Soviet forces should attempt to breach German fortified positions along the old border west of Poznan (the Mezeritz line) in the light of reported German concentrations in Pomerania, the separation of 1st Belorussian Front from its neighboring *fronts*, and German resistance in encircled cities (Poznan, Breslau). At that time, Zhukov had been able to convince Stalin to continue to advance to the Oder. Zhukov recalled:

> On 26 January the reconnaissance party of the 1st Guards Tank Army reached the Miedzyrzecz fortified line and captured a large group of men and officers. From prisoners' statements it appeared that in many places the line was not yet manned, that units were just moving out to fill in the gaps. The *front* command decided to step up the advance of the main forces towards the Oder and to try to take bridgeheads on the western bank in their stride.[166]

Subsequently, between 30 January and 2 February, 1st Belorussian Front forces penetrated the heavily fortified region, reached the Oder River, and secured several small bridgeheads on its western bank. During this period Zhukov received ominous *razvedka* reports which reinforced Stalin's earlier impressions of a growing threat from Pomerania. His air army commander Rudenko recalled:

> At the time it became well known; the Germans were urgently forming 11th Army under the command of Himmler. ... For air *razvedka* over Pomerania we selected our best pilots and navigators. They were required to inspect in detail the vast region daily and not miss one column which could be moving east – the more so since the forested area and bad weather also assisted the hidden movements of the enemy.
>
> *Razvedchiki* flew in PE-2 aircraft and photographed the territory. By the pictures we could exactly determine where the forces were going and how they were organized.[167]

However, bad weather and German security measures prevented continuous observation and Soviet aircraft were unable to detect any significant movements. Rudenko's airmen persisted in their efforts:

> We continued intensively to conduct *razvedka* from the skies, reporting in timely fashion to the *front* staff about all that the enemy did in the so-called "tent" hanging over us from the north. Finally all types of *razvedka* succeeded in determining that by the beginning of February between the Oder and the Vistula two fascist armies had concentrated: the 2d and the 11th possessing over 20 divisions. Our air searches discovered that the flow of forces to Eastern Pomerania was continuing. Actually the quantity of enemy divisions there, as was later revealed, rose to 40.[168]

These reports, plus others received from ground *razvedka* units reporting the German build-up along the Oder River prompted the Soviets to terminate the Vistula–Oder operation in early February.

Air *razvedka* during the course of the operation proved effective and assisted the development of deep ground operations. It "discovered enemy reserves moving toward the field of battle, ascertained the location and movement of enemy columns withdrawing to rear defensive lines, detected the weakest defensive sectors" and assisted combat aircraft in fulfilling their missions.[169] Most important, it functioned in close cooperation with other equally mature means of *razvedka*, in particular radio and mobile ground reconnaissance. Together those *razvedka* organs played a significant role in the successful Soviet sustainment of continuous operations to depths of 500–700 kilometers.

RAZVEDKA AND DECEPTION

Throughout all phases of the Vistula–Oder operation, *razvedka* played a major role in the formulation and execution of Soviet deception plans by providing data upon which planning was based and by verifying how well the plan was working. Throughout September and October Soviet intelligence kept track of German troop movements to the south. Operations in the Carpathians and south of the Dukla Pass drew away from Poland German 1st, 8th, and 24th Panzer Divisions and the 78th and 253d Infantry Divisions. Subsequent Soviet operations in Hungary drew 1st, 8th, and 24th Panzer Divisions further south to the Debrecen region. Later, in December, IV SS Panzer Corps shifted from the Warsaw area to Budapest. These strategic movements set the stage for the elaborate

Soviet Vistula–Oder deception plan. By posturing for assaults north of Warsaw and between the Vistula River and the Carpathian Mountains, the Soviets capitalized on previous attack patterns and German expectations.

Thereafter, up to 12 January, German operational reserves in central Poland remained relatively static. Soviet assessments in early December located the German 251st and 6th Infantry Divisions adjacent to the Magnushev bridgehead, one unknown panzer division southwest of Warka, 25th Panzer Division southeast of Radom, and a panzer grenadier division and reserve division at Radom.[170] These dispositions varied little to the date of the attack when the same two German infantry divisions defended the bridgehead, and 25th Panzer, 19th Panzer, and elements of 10th Panzer Grenadier Division remained in the operational rear (see Map 38).[171] Shtemenko reported a Soviet assessment that only 49 divisions defended along the Vistula front, five of which were panzer. In reality, the Germans had four panzer and the equivalent of one panzer grenadier division in the area. The fact that the Germans never reinforced their forces along the Vistula confirmed Soviet judgements regarding the success of their deception plans, as did German movement of tactical infantry reinforcements south of the Vistula River just before the offensive (in particular, the 344th and 359th Infantry Divisions).[172]

In one of the clearest cases to date, the Soviets used their intelligence collection techniques to deceive the Germans. Fully understanding that German intelligence viewed Soviet agent and reconnaissance-diversionary operations as indicators as to where the main attack would occur, the Soviets concentrated those activities during December and January in the regions west of Warsaw and south of the Vistula River city of Krakow. There is strong evidence that *front* RUs employed planted line crossers and also deserters to provide German intelligence with false information.

The Soviet deception plan succeeded to a considerable extent, in part, because of efficient intelligence work. German intelligence documents clearly indicated they expected an attack in the central sector of the Eastern Front. In fact, they had expected the attack to occur since late October and had continuously revised their estimates when the offensive did not occur. A 5 January assessment by *Fremde Heere Ost* (Foreign Armies East) stated:

The large scale Soviet winter offensive, for which definite dates (26 Oct, 7 Nov, end of Nov, 10 Dec, 19 Dec, 1 Jan) were

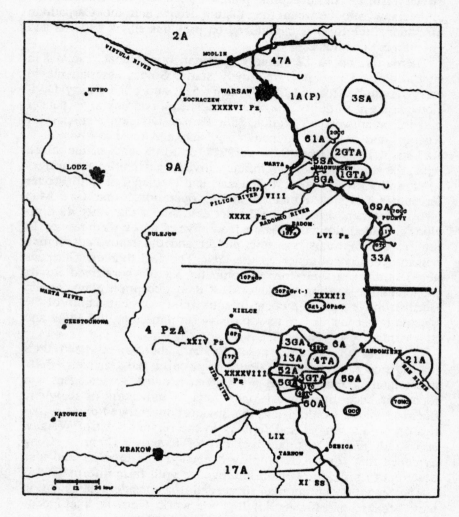

38. German force dispositions, 11 January 1945

determined during recent months on the basis of reliable reports, was again postponed because of unfavorable weather conditions and also, apparently, for political reasons. At present, the middle of January can be considered the next possible date of attack.[173]

The repeated postponements and frustrated expectations naturally cast doubt on the 5 January prediction. The 5 January estimate also claimed:

> The main effort of the entire operation is still obviously in the sector of Army Group A. The directions of the main effort, which from previous reports led by way of Crakow into the Czech region, had apparently been transferred to the northwest into the Silesian area, by way of the Upper Silesian industrial region.[174]

German uncertainty regarding precisely where the main attack would occur forced the Germans to recognize credible threats on every potential axis of Soviet advance. Annex 2 to the estimate assessed that Konev's 1st Ukrainian Front would make the main attack from the Baranov (Sandomierz) bridgehead toward the "Kattowitz–Tschenstochau region." Other strong forces would operate south of the Vistula toward Krakow.[175] This assessment was in direct response to Konev's deception plan. The estimate assessed 1st Belorussian would envelop Warsaw by advancing from the Warka (Magnushev) bridgehead to the southwest and then to the west and northwest.[176] This assessment recognized Zhukov's deception operation in 1st Belorussian Front's right flank sector north of Warsaw.

The Germans also recognized the adverse impact of earlier Soviet offensives in Hungary, which required the shifting of German reserves to the south:

> Since the enemy has been successful, through the development of the situation in Hungary, in forcing the withdrawal of strong German reserves from the main effort sector of Army Groups A and Center, it is necessary, from the standpoint of an estimate of the enemy, to point out the importance of corresponding German strategic reserves, which will make it possible to prevent great initial successes by the enemy, i.e., to defeat the enemy by not permitting him to retake the initiative.[177]

Soviet *razvedka* made this even more dangerous by successfully tracking German movements while the Germans failed to detect major Soviet regroupings.

German Army Group A assessed that it was opposed by two large Soviet groupings: four rifle armies and six mobile (tank and mechanized) corps of the 1st Ukrainian Front, with one additional army and three more mobile corps available for reinforcement; and three rifle armies, one Polish army, and three tanks corps of the 1st Belorussian Front, with two rifle armies and three mobile corps available as reinforcements (see Map 39).[178] At the time the 1st Ukrainian Front actually fielded nine rifle armies, six tank corps, and three mechanized corps; and the 1st Belorussian Front possessed eight rifle armies, five tank corps, and two mechanized corps (see Map 40).

The Germans missed the Soviet redeployment into Poland of 61st, 3d Shock, 33d, 52d, 21st, and 59th Armies from the *STAVKA* reserve. They assessed that these armies were either in their former sectors up to a thousand kilometers distant or were deep in the Soviet rear area. The Germans detected the possible presence of 6th Army headquarters, but the Soviets probably intended the army to be detected as a part of their deception plan on the right wing of the 1st Ukrainian Front. The Germans detected 5th Shock Army but believed it was assembled east of the Vistula, when actually it was concentrated in the Magnushev bridgehead. The Germans assessed that 2d Guards Tank Army was 100–150 kilometers east of the Magnushev bridgehead when it was actually concentrated on the east bank of the river. The 1st Guards Tank Army was located on German intelligence documents to the southwest of L'vov, when, in fact, it had also moved to concentration areas east of the Vistula River opposite the Magnushev bridgehead. The 3d Guards Tank Army was depicted as being southeast of the Vistula River east of Debica, thus positioned to attack either toward Krakow or from the Sandomierz bridgehead. German intelligence was more accurate regarding the location of 4th Tank Army. It assessed one corps as being in the Sandomierz bridgehead and the second corps as preparing to cross the Vistula. The Germans correctly located the Soviet army mobile groups, the 9th, 11th, 25th, and 31st Tank Corps. They assessed, however, that 4th Guards Tank Corps was located south of the Vistula River and north of Debica in the precise area of the simulated Soviet concentration area which 4th Guards Tank Corps was to animate.[179]

The net effect of this intelligence failure was staggering. In all three bridgeheads the Germans assessed they faced odds of about 3:1 or 3.5:1. Actually the Soviets created an operational superiority of between 5:1 and 7:1 in the bridgeheads. When Soviet concentration occurred, that translated into Soviet tactical superiority of between 8:1 and 16:1. The effect of such superiority was predictable. German defenses crumbled almost instantly on day one of the

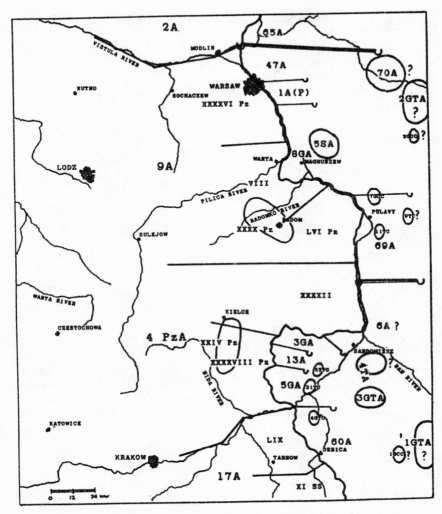

39. German intelligence assessment, Vistula Front, 11 January 1945

Soviet offensive. German reserve panzer divisions, although at more than full strength (17th Panzer Division, for example, had 210 tanks, half of them heavy tanks), were inundated and swept away in a Soviet advance that drove hundreds of kilometers into Poland. The German Vistula–Oder disaster was a Soviet deception success. Moreover, the deception success was conditioned in large measure by effective Soviet *razvedka* prior to the offensive.

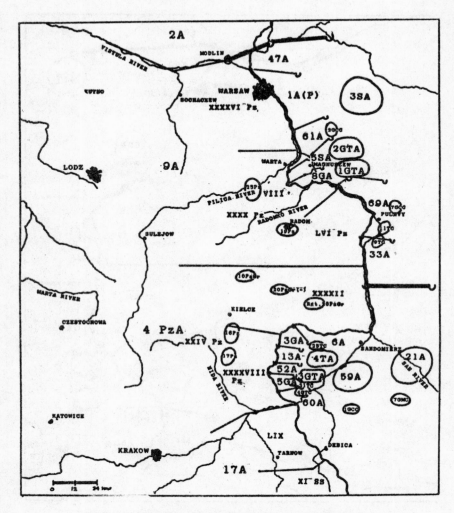

40. Soviet force dispositions, Vistula Front, 11 January 1945

CONCLUSION

Soviet *razvedka* proved to be one of the basic means of securing success in the Vistula–Oder operation. While Soviet numerical superiority remained the biggest factor in their achievement of victory, effective intelligence work contributed to the Soviet ability to generate that superiority without German knowledge. *Razvedka* contributed to the rapid development of the penetration operation by forming an initial accurate picture of German tactical dispositions. Once the operation had begun, sound intelligence ensured the initiative remained in Soviet hands until time and distance had taken their toll on advancing Soviet forces. This, in part, explained the extraordinary depth of the Soviet advance.

The Soviets drew upon more than three years' war experience to employ imaginative intelligence techniques within both the operational plan and the deception plan. In the words of one Soviet critique:

> In the organization and conduct of [*razvedka*] earlier obtained war experience was widely exploited and creativity, initiative, and flexibility were displayed in the implementation of all *razvedka* measures. This was expressed in a sufficiently thought out *razvedka* plan with the goal of continuously providing all staffs with full and trustworthy information, not only for making decisions on the operation, but also for refining them during combat operations.[180]

The Soviets effectively integrated all collection means, and when one means could not operate, others carried the load. Thus, "In bad weather reconnaissance detachments of armies operating a great distance away from their own combat formation secured for staffs information about enemy forces which should have been provided by aviation."[181] The depth of Soviet *razvedka* was also noteworthy for it enabled them to detect and counter, by ground or air action, every German attempt to restore stability by erecting new defensive positions east of the Oder River. Ultimately, long-range *razvedka* led to a discontinuance of the operation and the Soviet decision to clear their flanks before concentrating for a future drive toward Berlin.

Soviet critiques of the operation accorded special praise to radio *razvedka*, which, until 1945, had been one of the weaker links in the intelligence-gathering chain. While long-range radio intercepts, in concert with agents and aviation, had often detected movement of deep operational reserves earlier in the war, in the Vistula–Oder operation shorter-range radio eavesdropping, for the first time, proved extremely effective:

> Experience obtained in the use of close communications *razvedka* groups [within armies] deserves attention. In spite of the fact that radio-electronic *razvedka* was then only in its infancy

and a comparatively low-powered ultra-short-wave and short-wave radio apparatus was used, in many cases it assisted in disclosing the intentions of enemy subunits and units in his tactical depths.[182]

Although Soviet sources are reticent when describing agent and reconnaissance-diversionary operations, German records eloquently attest to the significance of this activity. Moreover, in addition to performing the accustomed tasks of reconnaissance and diversionary activity, by 1945 the Soviets had a mature enough appreciation of how German intelligence worked to employ *razvedka* measures as an integral part of Soviet deception planning. As attested to by the two air army commanders, Rudenko and Krasovsky, and by numerous other accounts and critiques, air *razvedka* continued to play a positive role in pre-offensive *razvedka*. More important, once the offensive had begun, air reconnaissance, in close cooperation with mobile ground reconnaissance units, effectively monitored movement of German reserves, thereby depriving the Germans of the opportunity to regain the initiative in virtually any sector. In large part, air and mobile ground *razvedka* conditioned successful Soviet deep operations.

While all this information taken together forms an impressive mosaic of intelligence capabilities, it probably does not adequately detail the full extent of Soviet *razvedka* efforts in 1945. The Soviets characteristically have left much unsaid. Without German archival materials, one would have to rate Soviet intelligence as good. When available German materials are taken into account, that evaluation rises even higher. It is likely full Soviet disclosure of their own archival materials will indicate an even greater Soviet capability. Until those materials are available, analysts will have to satisfy themselves with this assessment, which in itself should be a sobering reminder of what Soviet intelligence could achieve in the waning months of the Second World War.

CHAPTER EIGHT

THE LEGACY OF WAR: CONTEMPORARY *RAZVEDKA*

BACKGROUND

The Soviets emerged from the war with a healthy respect for all types of *razvedka*. While appreciating and employing more sophisticated means such as air, agent, and radio, they also emerged from war understanding that effective tactical *razvedka*, the sum of often petty and mundane acts, could produce profound results. On the basis of these judgements, the Soviets built their postwar *razvedka* system. That system has accentuated wartime trends. While keeping pace with technological advances in intelligence collection, the Soviets have not forgotten, and still stress, the more mundane low-level *razvedka* techniques.

Recent technological changes, as well as the changing nature of combat, have intensified Soviet concern for *razvedka*. The emergence of high-precision weaponry, the urbanization of terrain, and other factors have accentuated the importance of time in battle. The Soviets realize that rapid maneuver and effective command and control are keys to success in contemporary battle. So also is effective and timely collection and processing of intelligence data. For the Soviets, the latter has become a principal challenge of the 1980s and 1990s. Thus the Soviets are emphasizing new *razvedka* techniques such as employment of reconnaissance-artillery fire groups and are emulating the Western concept of the recce-strike complex. While doing so, they still emphasize what experience has convinced them is most effective – the simple, basic *razvedka* tasks which have proved so effective in the past.

TROOP *RAZVEDKA*

The most fundamental type of *razvedka* involving the tactical and, to some extent, the operational level is troop *razvedka*. Since the

Second World War, the Soviets have refined tested wartime concepts for troop *razvedka*. Although principles and basic procedures remain as before, fundamental changes in technology and the nature of ground forces have increased the requirements placed on forces conducting reconnaissance and the capabilities of those reconnaissance forces. The full mechanization and motorization of forces in the 1950s accelerated the pace of developing battle and increased the premium placed on effective and timely reconnaissance. Conversely, improved force mobility, while posing a dilemma, provided a solution to the dilemma as well. With the physical solution of increasing mobility at hand, it then became necessary to create a command and control system capable of complementing rapid operations. While the rapidity of operations increased throughout the 1960s, 1970s, and 1980s, the lethality of modern weaponry and their lethality range further increased the importance of *razvedka*. In the light of these trends and of former experience, the Soviets continued to emphasize the critical role of dynamic, flexible troop *razvedka* as the essential base of any comprehensive intelligence system.

Today troop *razvedka* may be conducted either before or during combat, while a force is moving forward into battle or when it is fully deployed for combat. When preparing to join battle or during the conduct of battle, Soviet forces are specifically arrayed to meet whatever situations arise. The Soviets term these arrays "march formation" (*pokhodnyi poriadok*) and "combat formation" (*boevoi poriadok*). The former is used on marches, during an approach to battle, during commitment into battle, and during exploitation and pursuit phases of an operation. The latter is used when forces prepare to engage and actually engage a defending enemy force. Each of these arrays (or formations) includes distinct force elements assigned to perform specific functions. Taken together, their actions form a logical and cohesive approach to resolution of combat situations, an approach designed to produce successful results. One of the most important military functions performed on the march or when deploying for combat is the reconnaissance function.

By Soviet definition, march formation is "the formation of subunits [battalions], units [regiments], formations [divisions], and groups of ships, with their reinforcing means, for the carrying out of a march. ..."[1] March formations facilitate rapid movement, quick deployment of forces into pre-combat or combat formation, and reliable and stable command and control. The myriad of specialized functional units which Soviet forces employ on the march and in combat is often confusing to all but the expert observer. Yet each of these functional units plays a critical role in the conduct of military operations. Although reconnaissance units represent but one of these functional categories, an understanding of the role of all these units is necessary to form an adequate context for identifying and understanding the role of the particular unit performing *razvedka*. Thus the extended passages which follow describe the interrelationships of all these functional units in order to focus better on the issue of where specific reconnaissance units fit into those well-ordered march and combat arrays.

The march formation of combined arms formations (divisions) and units (regiments) consists of several distinct elements including a forward detachment, march security forces, a main force, and rear service units and subunits. Each of these elements performs a distinct military function. The forward detachment (*peredovoi otriad*) is the lead combat element of the force; march security forces (*pokhodnoe okhranenie*) perform reconnaissance (*razvedka*) and provide protection (*obespechenie*) for the main body; the main body (*glavnaia sila*) represents the principal combat element of the force; and rear service elements (*tylovye chasti*) sustain all force operations.

A wide variety of functional units perform combat, reconnaissance, and protection missions in support of the main force (see functions listed below).

Function	*Force*
Combat	forward detachment (*peredovoi otriad* – PO) enveloping detachment (*obkhodiashchii otriad*)
Reconnaissance (*razvedka*)	reconnaissance detachment (*razvedyvatel'nyi otriad* – RO) reconnaissance group (*razvedyvatel'naia gruppa* – RG) separate reconnaissance patrol (*otdel'nyi razvedyvatel'nyi dozor* – ORD) reconnaissance patrol (*razvedyvatel'nyi dozor* – RD)
Protection	advance guard (*avangard*) advance party (lead march party) (*golovnaia pokhodnaia zastava* – GPZ) flank party (flank march party) (*bokovaia pokhodnaia zastava* – BPZ) rear party (rear march party) (*tylovaia pokhodnaia zastava* – TPZ)

(continued overleaf)

357

Function	Force
Others:	
Protection Against Weapons of Massive Destruction (*ZOMP*)	chemical reconnaissance patrol (*khimicheskii razvedyvatel'nyi otriad* – KhRO)
Engineer Protection	movement support detachment (*otriad obespecheniia dvizheniia* – OOD)
Sentry Security	outpost detachment (pickets) (*storozhevoi otriad*)

The forward detachment is a unique organization specifically designated to fulfill combat missions which, if successfully performed, contribute to the success of the force as a whole. It normally leads the march formation and will, in turn, field its own reconnaissance and advance, flank, and rear security elements.

The reconnaissance task of a force in march formation is fulfilled by one of several types of reconnaissance units, differentiated primarily by size. Combined arms formations or units employ a reconnaissance detachment (RO) to obtain information about the enemy and the terrain both on the march and in anticipation of a meeting engagement.[2] The reconnaissance detachment usually consists of a motorized rifle, tank, or reconnaissance company of a regiment or a motorized rifle, tank, or reconnaissance battalion of a division, reinforced by artillery, tanks, sappers, chemical reconnaissance forces, and other specialized units as required. It operates to a depth of from 35 to 50 kilometers and can cover a sector up to seven kilometers wide. A smaller version of the reconnaissance detachment is the reconnaissance group (RG) which is usually of reinforced company size.

Reconnaissance detachments can also form and employ reconnaissance patrols (RDs) in up to reinforced platoon strength operating at varying distances (normally 3 to 15 kilometers) from its parent reconnaissance unit. In addition, formations and units can employ separate reconnaissance patrols (ORD) in lieu of, or in addition to, regular reconnaissance detachments or groups. The separate reconnaissance patrols of up to reinforced platoon strength operate analogously to the other large reconnaissance units.[3] The mission of reconnaissance units is clearly distinct from that of the forward detachment. The function of the latter is to engage in combat, while the former is expected to avoid combat.

While reconnaissance units act as the eyes and ears of a force on the march, other units provide protection for the main force. Protection is subdivided by area into front, flank, and rear and involves units which provide march security for the main force. The most important of these units is the advance guard which deploys forward in anticipation of a clash with the enemy.[4] The advance guard usually consists of a regiment (from a division) or a battalion (from a regiment). Its missions are to prevent an enemy surprise attack on the main force, forestall penetration by enemy reconnaissance into the vicinity of the main force, and create favorable conditions for the deployment of the main force and its introduction into battle. While performing its mission, the advance guard can engage and destroy enemy units, but only if that combat does not inhibit fulfillment of its primary task. The advance party (GPZ), a smaller version of the advance guard, is used in lieu of an advance guard by regiments marching along separate routes or by advance guards and forward detachments.[5] It normally consists of a motorized rifle or tank platoon or company which moves along the march route in advance of its parent unit. Its missions are similar to those of an advance guard.

Flank parties (BPZ) and rear parties (TPZ) complete the all-round security for a force on the march.[6] The flank party, of reinforced motorized rifle or tank company size, is sent out a distance of up to five kilometers by forward detachments, advance guards, and main force regiments on the march to protect against surprise enemy attack, to frustrate enemy reconnaissance, and to facilitate deployment of its parent force. In turn, the BPZ dispatches security and reconnaissance patrol vehicles a distance of two kilometers. The rear party, in reinforced platoon or company strength, serves the same purposes as the flank parties. These security forces protect both the forward detachment and main force column. In performing their functions they are subject to definite constraints, in particular regarding their involvement in any combat that would prevent accomplishment of their primary mission.

The Soviets employ other specialized elements during conduct of a march. These include movement support detachments, chemical reconnaissance patrols, and outpost detachments. The movement support detachment (OOD) is a temporary formation of variable size, tailored to the situation. It normally consists of engineers, motorized rifle, tank, and other subunits and is tasked with preparing and maintaining march routes during all march situations.[7] The OOD conducts route reconnaissance, builds and repairs

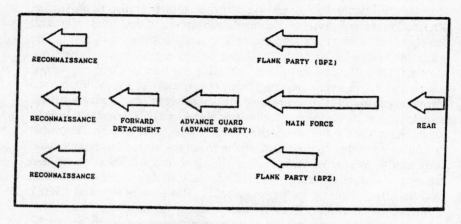

Fig. 16. Principal elements of a Soviet march formation

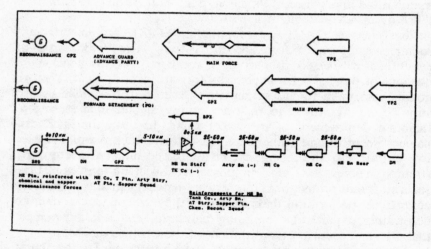

Fig. 17. March formations in anticipation of a meeting engagement (variants)

routes, and prepares passages across manmade and natural obstacles. When conducting its missions, the OOD forms sub-groups for reconnaissance, obstacle removal, road-bridge repairs, and combat security.

Chemical reconnaissance patrols (KhRD) supplement the action of regular reconnaissance units.[8] They operate independently or as part of a reconnaissance or security element, a forward detachment, a movement support detachment, or a subunit tasked with securing or destroying nuclear or chemical stores. The KhRD detects radio-active, chemical, and bacteriological contamination; determines the level and type of contamination; designates the contamination area; and finds and marks routes through or around the contamina-tion. The least specialized of special march security elements is the outpost detachment, which is used primarily during the positioning of forces – during halts or deployment in position.[9] Outpost detach-ments of from company to battalion strength provide security, conduct reconnaissance, and defend in designated sectors. They employ outpost parties, observation posts, and patrols to a distance of 1,500 meters to protect the main force from surprise attack.

The diverse functional elements of the Soviet march formations are arrayed spatially to accomplish their primary task of ensuring the main force success (see Figure 16). Reconnaissance elements lead, followed in turn by the forward detachment, an advance party and/or advance guard, the main force (usually organized in echelons), the rear party, and finally rear service units. The entire procession is flanked by security parties. Within this array the Soviets attempt to tailor and structure units and weaponry so that they can respond quickly in any direction and in any combat situation. Often the Soviets will also vary the overall array and structure of march formations to meet diverse needs (see Figure 17).

Soviet combat formations display less variety than their march formations but are no less significant. The Soviets have included in their combat formations all those elements required to produce offensive success. They define combat formation as "the disposition (formation) of subunits, units, and formations and their reinforcing means for the conduct of battle."[10] It is a combined arms concept whereby all types of forces fulfilling a common mission are united in a single combat formation. The combat formation "must reflect the concept of anticipated operations, provide for fulfillment of assigned combat missions, as well as firm, continuous cooperation and command and control."[11]

The elements of the combat formation include:

forward detachment
first echelon
second echelon or combined arms reserve
rocket subunits (groups)
artillery means (groups)
antiaircraft means (groups)
antitank reserves
engineer reserves
mobile obstacle detachment (*podvizhnyi otriad zagrazhdenii* – POZ)
specialized detachments, i.e. enveloping detachments (*obkhodiashchii otriad*)
tactical air assault landing group (party)

Virtually all elements of the combat formation are involved in combat or combat support tasks, including that of reconnaissance (see Figure 18). All first or second echelon (reserve) units engage in reconnaissance to some degree before and during battle. Certain of these elements are created solely to perform the function of tactical maneuver – specifically the forward detachment; the enveloping detachment; the tactical air assault force; and, to a lesser extent, the mobile obstacle detachment.

The premier tactical maneuver force, the forward detachment, leads the advance while relying on its own assets and those of its parent force to conduct reconnaissance. Its combat function is often pre-emptive in nature. An element closely associated with the forward detachment is the enveloping detachment, formed primarily for employment in mountainous terrain, but also used in deserts, forested-swampy regions, northern regions, and other unusual terrain.[12] The enveloping detachment usually consists of a motorized rifle subunit, reinforced by mobile antitank weapons, mortars, guns, engineer subunits, and specialized forces. Its mission is to envelop the defending enemy, strike his flank and rear, and seize and hold important objectives in the depths of his dispositions. The enveloping detachment operates in tactical coordination with forces advancing from the front and is generally supported by forces and means of the senior commander.

The tactical air assault group (party) consists of combined arms subunits from reinforced company to regimental strength.[13] Employed by formations (divisions) and large formations (armies) its missions include the seizure and destruction of important enemy

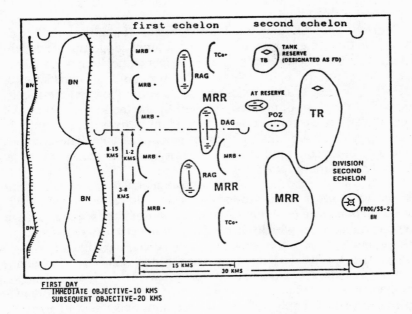

Fig. 18. A Soviet combat formation

objectives in the tactical and close operational depths (i.e. nuclear weapons, command and control points, communications centers) and seizure and destruction of tactically important positions and objectives (road junctions, bridges, river crossings, hydro-electrical facilities, mountain passes, passages, defiles, etc.). Tactical air assaults are tasked with "cooperation with attacking forces in rapidly overcoming natural obstacles, interdicting the maneuver of enemy forces, and ensuring high offensive tempos; and destroying rear bases, warehouses, and demolishing pipelines, etc."[14] Air assaults are conducted by helicopter or fixed wing aircraft at tactical depths so that attacking ground forces can link up with air assault forces within several hours. Recently, the Soviets have stressed the increased utility of independent air assaults, conducted as part of an air echelon, without immediate link-up with ground echelons.

The third functional tactical maneuver force, the mobile obstacle detachment (POZ), provides specialized engineer support to attacking or defending forces. This "temporary military formation [is] created in ground forces from subunits (units) of engineer forces

363

for construction of mine-explosive obstacles and execution of demolitions."[15]

Cooperating with combined arms forces (battalions and regiments) and antitank reserves, or sometimes operating independently, the POZ sows antitank and antipersonnel mines on likely enemy avenues of approach into the formation of attacking or defending forces. It also places obstacles in the gaps, on the flanks, and across the front of units as required by the tactical situation. All these battalion or smaller size tactical maneuver forces employ specially trained subunits to conduct reconnaissance. These reconnaissance units come either from organic assets or are provided by higher headquarters (divisions and regiments).

The Soviets field forces at the divisonal level specifically configured to conduct troop ground *razvedka*. These include the divisional reconnaissance battalion and the regimental reconnaissance company, each of which form the reconnaissance detachments, groups, and patrols at the tactical level to screen the advance of their parent forces. The divisional reconnaissance battalion, consisting of a headquarters and service company, two BMP reconnaissance companies, one scout car company, and a radio/radar reconnaissance company is equipped with six medium tanks and 30 armored combat or scout vehicles (BRDM/BRDM-2, BMP/BMP-1, and BTR-60 PA).[16] The battalion, less its radio/radar reconnaissance company, which remains in the rear area, forms a reconnaissance screen up to 50 kilometers (one to two hours) ahead of the division main body. The long-range reconnaissance (scout car) company may operate as far as 100 kilometers ahead of the division. As contact develops, the distance between the screen and the division's main force shrinks to 10–15 kilometers. Battalion subunits advance in six to eight groups along three or four axes of advance, with squad-size elements operating across frontages of up to three kilometers.

Divisional reconnaissance detachments, groups, and patrols have the mission of reconnoitering divisional march routes, locating enemy forces in the vicinity of those routes, and locating targets for engagement by divisional nuclear or conventional firing means. These forces conduct area (general) reconnaissance along march routes and, whenever possible, they bypass enemy forces after pinpointing their location. The presence of armor in the reconnaissance forces provides it with the capability of dealing with opposition when necessary and feasible. To the rear of divisional reconnaissance forces, operating at shallower depths, are reconnaissance groups and patrols from regimental reconnaissance companies. The reconnaissance company of motorized rifle or tank regiments consists of a headquarters company, a BMP scout platoon, a scout car platoon, and a motorcycle section equipped with eight armored combat or reconnaissance vehicles and three motorcycles.[17] These forces, arrayed in groups or patrols, normally numbering three squad-size groups per regiment, follow divisional reconnaissance elements and perform missions in support of the regiment analogous to the missions of divisional reconnaissance forces. Regimental reconnaissance normally extends to a depth of 25 kilometers ahead of the main force.

Recently, Soviet theorists have stressed the utility of forming a combined arms mix of forces at the battalion level, capable of conducting more flexible operations in warfare increasingly dominated by new high-technology, high-precision weaponry. The new battalion groups which emerge in response to this concern will likely possess, in addition to an improved weapons mix, a distinct reconnaissance capability in their own right, perhaps consisting of a battalion reconnaissance platoon, which will supplement reconnaissance forces at regiment and division level.

One of the most important types of troop *razvedka* is the reconnaissance in force (*razvedka boem*), a technique the Soviets extensively employed and refined during the Second World War. The Soviets conduct reconnaissance in force to obtain "reconnaissance information about the enemy by means of combat actions (offensives) of specially designated subunits," in particular, when intelligence collection by normal means has not provided necessary information about enemy dispositions and intentions.[18]

The Soviets routinely employed reconnaissance in force beginning in late 1942, when reinforced companies or battalions attacked days before a planned offensive to determine precise enemy dispositions. Since, at first, this *razvedka* occurred several days before the planned operation, and in the main offensive sectors, the technique became a prime attack indicator. To solve this problem, the Soviets then conducted reconnaissance in force across a broad front within 24 hours of the planned attack. Often, late in the war, the Soviets would deliberately employ reconnaissance in force as a diversionary measure, as an integral part of their deception planning. During the latter stages of the war, divisional reconnaissance battalions, often advance battalions from first echelon regiments, conducted reconnaissance in force in multiple sectors.

Today, the Soviets consider reconnaissance in force to be an important *razvedka* tool, especially in conventional operations.

Normally they conduct reconnaissance in force by employing a reinforced motorized rifle or tank battalion or company, depending on the terrain and enemy strength. These battalions or companies contain reconnaissance patrols and groups which are assigned the specific mission of seizing prisoners, documents, and enemy equipment. Attached artillerymen and sappers are tasked with conducting artillery and engineer *razvedka*. Reconnaissance in force subunits are supported by artillery fire and, on occasion, air strikes by fixed-wing aircraft or helicopters. Commanders of divisions and regiments control reconnaissance in force in their specific sectors, but such action is often planned by higher headquarters as an integral portion of its *razvedka* plan.

Thus on the march and during combat itself, the Soviets field an array of forces organized to perform specific functions which, if properly executed, contribute to overall combat success. While the combat function remains most critical, those of reconnaissance and protection are essential ingredients for successful operations. To deny the Soviets tactical and operational success, prospective opponents must be able to distinguish between the wide array of specialized Soviet units, operating separated from Soviet main forces. The identification and destruction of Soviet ground reconnaissance forces promises to blind the parent Soviet force. The identification and destruction of Soviet forward detachments may cripple a Soviet main effort by stripping the initiative from Soviet hands. Finally, the penetration of Soviet protective systems and forces may permit disabling of the Soviet main force. Since reconnaissance units operate farthest forward and tend to be the most fragile of these specialized forces, their identification, engagement, and destruction must be a high priority aim.

ARTILLERY *RAZVEDKA*

Closely associated with ground troop *razvedka* are artillery and engineer *razvedka*, which the Soviets conduct to determine the precise configuration of enemy dispositions, particularly regarding firing systems and engineer features such as defensive positions and obstacles. Both artillery and engineer *razvedka* have the principal goal of target identification, and both rely on a combination of direct observation, ground and air reconnaissance, and a variety of more technical collection means. The range of artillery and engineer *razvedka* extends up to 20 kilometers in the enemy rear. The main mission of artillery *razvedka* is "the acquisition and processing of data, necessary for the preparation of effective artillery fires and tactical rocket strikes."[19] It operates in close cooperation with other *razvedka* means. In order of priority, acquisition means concentrate on detecting enemy nuclear weapons systems, high-precision weapons, artillery positions, combat reserves, assembly areas, headquarters, logistical installations, and lines of communications.

The commanders and staffs of rocket and artillery forces are responsible for organizing artillery *razvedka*. To accomplish this task, they employ specially equipped reconnaissance artillery sub-units and optical, electro-optical, sound, radio-location means as well as radio-technical stations and helicopters for aerial target acquisition (in Russian, reconnaissance-corrective helicopters). Ground artillery *razvedka* exploits captured documents, interrogation of POWs and civilians, and seized enemy equipment.

Fronts, armies, and divisions conduct artillery instrumental *razvedka* using a dense network of command-observation and observation points (KNPs and NPs), mobile reconnaissance points (PRPs), sound and radio-technical reconnaissance posts, radio-location stations, and ground artillery reconnaissance groups. The Soviets further subdivide artillery instrumental *razvedka* into optical, sound, radio-location, radio-technical, and photographic reconnaissance, each of which is conducted by specialized artillery reconnaissance units and subunits. Optical reconnaissance relies on the variety of fixed and mobile observation points, often operating in combination (two or three in a common network). Sound *razvedka* subunits employ sound detection devices from a variety of specialized ground artillery *razvedka* stations to pinpoint enemy firing location. A similar network of ground reconnaissance stations (PRS) determines target locations by analysis of enemy radio traffic. Finally, helicopters and ground observation points engage in systematic photography, which, with other aerial photography, creates a mosaic of enemy positions for use in target identification. Intelligence subunits at each level provide photo interpretation support.[20]

Artillery *razvedka* units and subunits are deployed through every level of the artillery force structure. Within the artillery regiment of Soviet divisions, the target acquisition battery provides artillery *razvedka* capability. This battery consists of a headquarters, communications, sound ranging, reconnaissance, and topographic survey platoons, and radio and surveillance radar sections. Depending on their function, these subunits are equipped with mobile radar and sound, range, and radar-direction finders. The

BMP-mounted "Small Fred" radar operates with forward regiments while the MT-LB-mounted "Big Fred" radar, with a range of up to 15 kilometers, functions at division level. Within artillery and motorized rifle regiments, artillery battalions also field the "Small Fred" battlefield surveillance radar which forms the nucleus of an artillery mobile reconnaissance point, and a basic range-finding capability as well.[21] At army level, artillery units have a similar artillery *razvedka* capability supplemented by other intelligence collection means organic to the army. Similar assets also exist within the target acquisition battalion subordinate to *front* artillery divisions. Artillery *razvedka* at all levels is coordinated by artillery reconnaissance groups (ARG) formed in all artillery units and subunits. These groups, consisting of the artillery force commander, several staff officers, engineer forces, and communications means, plan and control all artillery *razvedka*.

Given the increased tempo of operations on the modern tactical battlefield, the Soviets are directing even greater attention to the necessity for rapid target identification. To solve this problem, they have devised a system for closer cooperation of reconnaissance means and artillery units through employment of a reconnaissance-fire artillery group (*razvedyvatel'naia-ognevaia gruppa* – ROG). The reconnaissance-fire group is created within a larger artillery group, and it contains, under a single command, several artillery battalions, an artillery reconnaissance subunit, and sometimes a helicopter for use in correcting fire. The ROG engages and suppresses "particularly important enemy targets," which threaten a friendly force, either on the offense or the defense.[22] Each reconnaissance-fire group operates in a specific assigned sector of fire, in which it engages targets. Target engagement priorities are determined either by the group commander or the senior artillery commander. The artillery reconnaissance subunit reconnoiters targets, determines their coordinates, and reports the targets to the reconnaissance-fire group commander and battalion fire control which then fires on the target. The artillery reconnaissance subunit controls the fire throughout its duration.

Soviet writings on this subject highlight the importance of the concept (as well as the difficulties), especially regarding communications. Creation of the reconnaissance artillery fire groups is analogous to similar Soviet efforts to tailor and task-organize forces to fight more effectively at the lowest level of command. The ROG is also a lower level equivalent of the more sophisticated concept of the reconnaissance-fire complex. The Soviets expect this elaborate system of artillery *razvedka* to be able to identify the majority of targets in enemy tactical depths. The current and future challenge will be to extend this detection capability into the shallow operational depths in order to counter enemy high-precision weaponry.

ENGINEER *RAZVEDKA*

The Soviets define engineer *razvedka* as "part of tactical *razvedka* intended for the acquisition of information about the terrain and its engineer preparation, and about the condition and capabilities of enemy engineer forces."[23] Specifically, engineer *razvedka* determines:

- the nature and degree of engineer preparations of enemy positions;
- enemy obstacle systems, especially those containing atomic demolitions;
- the trafficability of terrain for military forces and transport means;
- road and bridge conditions;
- the location and nature of obstacles (destroyed areas, obstructions, fires, flooded areas, etc.) created by nuclear fires;
- the nature of water obstacles and crossing capabilities;
- the location and condition of sources of water and local materials of use for engineer construction;
- cover and concealment and defensive characteristics of the terrain.

The chiefs of engineer forces, along with engineer commanders and staffs at all levels, are responsible for organizing engineer *razvedka* in accordance with the force commander's *razvedka* plan. All planned measures are implemented by engineer units and subunits, operating independently or as part of a larger reconnaissance force. The Soviets create engineer observation posts (INP), engineer photographic posts (IPF), engineer reconnaissance patrols (IRD), and engineer reconnaissance groups (IRG) to fulfill their assigned missions. These elements employ basic observation techniques, ground sweeps, photography, ambushes, map study, and interrogation of POWs and civilians to acquire necessary data. They are equipped with a variety of mine-detection, optical observation, photographic, and deciphering charts.

Engineer observation posts (INP) usually consist of two to three sappers equipped with optical devices, maps, journals, compasses, watches, and flashlights. Each post is located near the FLOT and is assigned a 1 to 2 kilometer sector of observation, from which it can observe 5 to 6 kilometers into the depth of enemy positions. Posts are usually created on the basis of one post per first echelon battalion. Engineer photographic posts (IPF) are similar in size, but are equipped with cameras to help construct photographic panoramas of enemy positions. Engineer reconnaissance groups (IRG) of engineer-reconnaissance subunits operate independently in front of the FLOT or as part of a troop *razvedka* group. Finally, engineer reconnaissance patrols (IRD) of squad to platoon strength, often with chemical reconnaissance personnel, operate independently forward of main forces or as part of a troop *razvedka* force. Parent units arrange communications with each engineer *razvedka* element. To an increasing extent, the Soviets are employing helicopter transported INP, IPF, and IRDs.

Engineer personnel routinely participate in ground reconnaissance as a part of reconnaissance detachments, groups, and patrols and provide personnel and equipment to man movement support detachments (OOD) which conduct engineer reconnaissance for moving forces. The OOD is a task-organized engineer unit in platoon to company strength which deploys forward, often accompanied by a combat reconnaissance patrol (BRD). Although it is not an engineer reconnaissance unit *per se*, the mobile obstacle detachment (POZ) incorporates reconnaissance in its mission of providing mobile engineer support on the battlefield. A distinct element in the force's combat formation, the POZ is made up of engineer obstacle-laying or obstacle-clearing subunits in about company strength, reinforced by antitank weapons and infantry and equipped with a variety of mines and mineclearing equipment. Mobile obstacle detachments are formed by both armies and divisions.

Engineer forces within a motorized rifle and tank division are the regimental engineer company and the divisional battalion. The former consists of a headquarters and mine warfare, bridge and technical (construction) platoons. The latter includes combat engineers, assault-river crossing, technical, road/bridge construction and pontoon bridge companies, and engineer reconnaissance, communications, maintenance, and service platoons.[24] Although some of the manpower of the regimental company can be used for engineer *razvedka* (normally in conjunction with other forces), the engineer reconnaissance platoon of the divisional engineer battalion provides basic *razvedka* capability. This specially trained reconnaissance force is often augmented by sappers and minelayers from the combat engineer company and equipment from other battalion elements. Engineer units at army and *front* level possess specialized engineer forces for deeper operational *razvedka*.

Engineer reconnaissance is performed in specialized and functional subunits as well. For example, the most likely candidate to serve as forward detachment in motorized rifle divisions, the separate tank battalion, has an engineer section which assists that force in accomplishing the unique combat mission, which requires a considerable degree of initiative. The engineer section tailored with other battalion combat forces performs engineer *razvedka*. Emerging combined arms battalions or battalion tactical groups are likely to contain improved engineer *razvedka* capability, perhaps relying more heavily on helicopter mounted engineer *razvedka* forces.

RADIOLOGICAL, CHEMICAL, AND BIOLOGICAL *RAZVEDKA*

Related to ground *razvedka* in the sense that they are essentially tactical, are radiological, chemical, and biological *razvedka*, all of which perform similar functions. Biological and chemical *razvedka* are conducted "to reveal the scale and degree of radioactive contamination of a locality, air space, water regions, and military objectives."[25] Reconnaissance, chemical reconnaissance, helicopter, and all types of conventional forces conduct it, employing specialized equipment or simple dosimeters. Specialized chemical forces perform more complicated missions along specifically designated routes or in specific combat sectors. Biological *razvedka* to detect potential or actual enemy use of toxic agents is conducted by the same range of forces.

To conduct this specialized *razvedka*, the Soviets use a system of coordinated chemical observation posts (KhNP) and chemical reconnaissance patrols (KhRD). Observation posts have the task of identifying the presence of radiological, chemical, or bacteriological contamination and issuing appropriate warnings to forces either while on the march or in combat. The observation posts operate from specialized chemical reconnaissance vehicles (BRDM-2), from trenches, or other positions near the force command post. It consists of two or three observers equipped with optical devices, maps, or graphics of the region, compasses, watches, chemical and radiological detecting equipment, and communications and warning apparatus. The observation post at all times maintains an observation journal.

Chemical reconnaissance patrols mounted on BRDM-2 vehicles operate independently or as part of reconnaissance and security forces, forward detachments, and movement support detachments. As such they are an extension of the more elaborate observation post system, but they perform the same basic missions. They are also formed in special subunits dispatched to secure or destroy enemy nuclear or chemical delivery systems or storage sites. Medical service units provide personnel for reconnaissance whenever there is a likelihood of biological weapons use. In that case, they function in similar fashion to radiological and chemical reconnaissance forces.

Specialized radiological and chemical defense forces are found within regiments and higher command levels. The two BMP reconnaissance companies of the divisional reconnaissance battalion each possess two BRDM-2 (rkh chemical) with which to establish chemical reconnaissance patrols. The division's regiments each field a chemical defense company with a reconnaissance platoon and decontamination platoon. Each reconnaissance platoon also has two BRDM-2rkh. The division's chemical defense battalion consists of two decontamination companies, a chemical reconnaissance platoon, and supporting subunits. The reconnaissance platoon possesses nine radio-equipped BRDM-2rkh. At higher levels, Soviet tank and combined arms armies contain chemical defense battalions, each with three chemical companies and a chemical reconnaissance company.[26] This broad array of specialized chemical forces possesses the capability of employing a significant network of chemical observation posts, and chemical reconnaissance patrols to provide warning of nuclear or chemical contamination.

Supplementing this ground-oriented network are Soviet helicopter-equipped units which have either the primary or secondary mission of detecting the presence of radiological and chemical contamination. The Soviets place helicopters at the disposal of chemical reconnaissance forces to extend the range of their detection capabilities.

AIR *RAZVEDKA*

Traditionally, air *razvedka* has been one of the most important sources of Soviet intelligence information. It has played a significant role in Soviet *razvedka* theory since the 1920s, and since late 1942 it has been one of the most productive means of intelligence collection. By definition air *razvedka* "is conducted by units (regiments) of reconnaissance aviation, by reconnaissance subunits [squadrons] of aviation formations [divisions], by all air crews fulfilling combat missions, as well as by pilotless flying apparatus (aircraft, automatic aerostatic equipment, etc.) with the aim of obtaining information concerning the enemy (objectives, forces and means, terrain, etc.) necessary for all elements and types of armed forces to conduct military operations successfully."[27] This definition also includes modern satellite collection platforms.

Air *razvedka* by satellite, piloted, and unpiloted aircraft encompasses the tactical, operational, and strategic depths in the enemy rear. Using radio, and sometimes computer link, intelligence information can be provided in timely manner, thus solving one of the most vexing problems of air *razvedka* in the past. Air *razvedka* at all depths coordinates closely with all other collection means. The principal missions of air *razvedka* are:

- detection and determination of the coordinates of enemy nuclear delivery means and high-precision weapons systems;
- establishment of the location and grouping of enemy forces, aircraft, ships, air defense forces and means, and their maneuver;
- revealing enemy command and control systems and means;
- reconnaissance of enemy communications lines;
- determining enemy air base networks, ship basing, naval bases, and rear service organizations;
- obtaining information about radiation and weather conditions.[28]

Strategic air *razvedka* has taken on preeminent importance in the nuclear age. It provides high-level commanders with necessary data concerning enemy strategic objectives located far to the rear. Most important, satellite and long-range reconnaissance aircraft are the principal means of locating enemy strategic nuclear weapons systems. Operational air *razvedka* serves *front* and army commanders by providing information required to plan and conduct *front* and army operations as well as operations conducted by fleets and air forces. In addition to detecting mid-range and long-range tactical nuclear weapons, operational air *razvedka* has the important new task of locating enemy long-range precision weapons systems. Tactical air *razvedka*, in support of division and regimental commanders, gathers information necessary to plan and fight the tactical battle.

Each level of air *razvedka* has its own parameters regarding range. These parameters change in accordance with prevailing conditions, but, in general, tactical *razvedka* extends to 50 kilometers, operational up to 600 kilometers, and strategic extends beyond. The *front* commander prepares the overall *razvedka* plan, which establishes detailed tasks for tactical aviation assets. These assets focus on *razvedka* in the tactical and operational depths.

Air *razvedka* relies on visual observation, aerial photography, and airborne radio-electronic collection equipment to obtain required intelligence data. When selecting collection means, commanders consider the mission, type of aerial platform and its equipment, the time of day, and weather conditions. Visual observation is conducted by the naked eye or by using optical devices. It is useful for rapidly surveying wide regions to obtain general information about enemy dispositions and movement and about objectives, weather, and terrain. Information obtained by visual reconnaissance is passed to controlling headquarters by radio.

Photographic *razvedka* occurs during the day and at night using systematic, perspective, or panoramic photography. It provides "full, reliable and exact information about enemy forces, objectives, and terrain."[29] Radio-electronic air *razvedka* employs radio, radio-technical, radio-location, and televisual techniques to acquire information. Radio reception (interception) aircraft conduct radio *razvedka* "to intercept enemy radio transmissions, to determine the composition and dislocation of his forces, and to obtain information about his activities and intentions."[30] Radio-technical *razvedka* uses radio-reception and radio-location devices (*priemo-pelengatsionnaia ustroistva*) to determine the technical parameters and disposition of enemy radio-location and radio-television command and control. It can be conducted in any weather condition, day or night. Radio-location uses aircraft (RIS) to discover and discriminate enemy objectives, to obtain photo representations of radio-location images (portrayals) of objectives and terrain and to uncover enemy radio-location and *maskirovka* (deception) measures.

Televisual *razvedka* employs airborne-mounted televisual collection systems to transmit real-time information to ground reception stations. This permits timely observation and monitoring of both enemy and friendly forces. Supplementing these aerial collection means are more technical collection methods involving use of heat sensors, lasers, etc. The Soviets transmit aerial reconnaissance data to ground force headquarters directly by radio or by "automatic on-board reconnaissance apparatus." After an aircraft or satellite returns to base, air crews or technical personnel prepare documented information and reports about enemy objectives from deciphered (integrated) photographs or films and from automatically recorded aircraft collection devices (photo, film, laser, heat sensing).

The Soviets employ reconnaissance aviation units (regiments) and separate subunits (squadrons) subordinate to *frontal*, long-range (TVD), and naval aviation to conduct air *razvedka* even more extensively than they have in the past. *Front* assets conduct tactical and operational missions, and theater aviation handles strategic and deep operational tasks. Both fixed-wing aircraft and helicopters participate, and the Soviets note that helicopters are especially well suited for radio-location and radiation reconnaissance as well as for visual reconnaissance. Reconnaissance helicopter subunits of squadron size provide air reconnaissance support within armies, while reconnaissance aviation regiments, with at least four squadrons each, provide the reconnaissance capability for each wartime *front*. Regiments are designated to conduct either operational or tactical reconnaissance, while helicopters limit themselves to tactical reconnaissance. Aviation divisions within *frontal* aviation also contain one reconnaissance squadron. In addition, long-range reconnaissance aviation squadrons are subordinate to the Soviet High Command (probably the GRU) and theater commands. These concentrate on long-range strategic *razvedka*. Each reconnaissance aviation squadron numbers 25 to 30 aircraft configured for various types of intelligence collection, including visual, photo, infrared, and radio missions.[31] At the tactical level, divisional helicopter squadrons contain a Hoplite flight with six Hoplite helicopters, which they use for observation tasks and for radiological and chemical reconnaissance. A similar capability may be found in the army general-purpose helicopter squadron.

The important and expanding Soviet satellite reconnaissance program is understandably shrouded in secrecy. It is clear, however, that information obtained by satellites, as well as that obtained by long-range strategic reconnaissance aircraft, is sent directly to the High Command. Within the General Staff of the High Command, the GRU assigns tasks to such *razvedka* assets and collects and analyzes obtained data.

AGENT/RECONNAISSANCE-DIVERSIONARY *RAZVEDKA*

One of the most ubiquitous yet shadowy aspects of Soviet *razvedka* relates to the use of agents and reconnaissance-diversionary forces operating in the enemy rear. In part, the obscurity surrounding this human *razvedka* results from Soviet reluctance to talk openly of these efforts, at least in a contemporary sense. Soviet theoretical writings on the subject are couched in terms of enemy use of "special" *razvedka* and agents. It is clear from these descriptions that such techniques are useful to the Soviets as well. Documentation and Soviet writings on the Second World War, moreover, reveal the degree to which the Soviets engaged in such activities. Soviet success with agent and reconnaissance-diversionary *razvedka* during that period makes it clear they will redouble their efforts in that regard today.

The Soviets define agent *razvedka* as the use of secret agents "to obtain information about the armed forces and the military-economic, and mobilization potential of governments." It is conducted in peacetime as well as wartime, and "it intensifies during periods of crisis and acquires an especially important meaning during the course of war."[32] Closely related to agent *razvedka* is special (*spetsial'naia*) *razvedka*, which is conducted to "undermine the political, economic, military, and morale potential of the probable or actual enemy." Its principal missions are "the acquisition of intelligence information about important economic and military objectives, the destruction or neutralization of these objectives, the organization of sabotage and diversionary-terrorist acts, ... the conduct of propaganda, the organization and training of insurgents, etc."[33]

Special *razvedka* is organized "by military organs and special services and is conducted by the forces of agent *razvedka* and forces of special designation (*voisk spetsial'nogo naznacheniia*) − often translated as 'special purpose forces.'" These forces employ special types of weapons, ammunition, and technical means including explosives and radios of various types. Forces of special designation are specialized units and subunits designated to conduct reconnaissance-diversionary activities. In wartime "subunits of these forces are thrown into the enemy rear to inflict damage on him by means of surprise strikes (raids, etc.), to seize and destroy important objectives, to destroy groups of enemy forces, to disrupt communications, to disorganize civilian life, to disrupt the work of organs of authority and control, to organize the escape of POWs, and to create underground organizations and groups." In short, these forces will replicate the activities which both reconnaissance-diversionary and partisan forces conducted during the Second World War. The Soviets add to these definitions the statement, "forces of special designation are used also in peacetime, especially in periods of strained international conditions." Although the Soviets label these definitions "foreign," they apply equally to practices the Soviets have employed in the past.[34]

Given the paucity of Soviet writings regarding contemporary use of agents and reconnaissance-diversionary forces, it is necessary to reflect upon the system the Soviets employed in the Second World War to understand the reconnaissance-diversionary system the Soviets would today attempt to replicate. During wartime reconnaissance-diversionary forces operated at virtually every level of command from national level down through army. At the lower levels, these forces gradually merged with reconnaissance groups and detachments subordinate to lower level operational (army) and tactical headquarters (corps and divisions). The chief difference between reconnaissance-diversionary and simple reconnaissance forces rested in the mission and manner of operations of each force. The former engaged in a variety of military and non-military missions at considerable depths in the enemy rear. They were specially trained for sabotage and intelligence collection tasks, they usually operated dressed in civilian clothes or enemy uniforms, and often spoke the enemy's language. The latter performed military missions of a tactical nature (intelligence collection, reconnaissance, and direct combat) dressed in Soviet military uniforms. Despite the distinction between the two, their efforts formed a continuum.

By 1944 an intricate web of agents and reconnaissance-diversionary forces had been institutionalized in support of the Soviet war effort. This web became a model for contemporary and future Soviet practices. Often the Soviets employed reconnaissance-diversionary teams on secondary axes to deceive the enemy regarding the location of the main attack. This reconnaissance-diversionary activity became one more facet of deception planning.

In peacetime and in wartime, today the Committee for State Security (*Komitet gosudarstvennoi bezopostnosti* – KGB) and GRU control an extensive agent network. The GRU, prospective TVD commands, and *fronts* control reconnaissance-diversionary forces in brigade and company configuration, which can be delivered by a variety of means (air, sea, land) into the enemy rear area. These forces can operate as detachments, groups, or parties of varying size, depending on their specific mission. Similarly trained forces of smaller size also operate either within airborne and naval infantry forces or subordinate to armies.

The reconnaissance-diversionary brigade organic to Soviet *fronts* and the long-range reconnaissance-diversionary company subordinate to army employ reconnaissance-diversionary forces in support of operations. Normal operations involve use of five to eight-man teams to depths of up to 1,000 kilometers in the enemy rear. Each team can cover an area of roughly 25–40 square kilometers. These forces overlap in function with divisional long-range reconnaissance assets whose activities extend up to 100 kilometers. *Front* reconnaissance-diversionary brigades can field more than 120 teams, while armies can field as many as 15 such teams. Larger detachments can be formed, if required.[35] Soviet fleets and naval infantry formations possess similar forces and capabilities. Other specialized Soviet forces can provide reconnaissance-diversionary forces for use by *front* commanders. These include traditional airborne and naval infantry elements and, to an increasing extent, helicopter-delivered reconnaissance-diversionary forces from Soviet air assault brigades. It is likely Soviet use of helicopter *desant* forces in a reconnaissance-diversionary role will increase. This imposing array of reconnaissance-diversionary forces represents, in its own right, an imposing intelligence collection and diversionary capability. It increases in importance when integrated into the overall Soviet *razvedka* effort.

RADIO-ELECTRONIC *RAZVEDKA*

The Soviets had developed theoretical concepts for the exploitation of radio *razvedka* in the 1930s and practical concepts for the conduct of radio *razvedka* during the Second World War. By war's end, they demonstrated a considerable capability for the use of radio to collect intelligence data. Those experiences underscored the importance of that technology and provided a basis for subsequent Soviet radio *razvedka* efforts.

The Soviets consider radio *razvedka* to be an integral and key element of radio-electronic struggle (*radioelektronnaia bor'ba* – REB) which they define as "a complex of measures conducted for the purposes of *razvedka* and subsequent radio-electronic neutralization of enemy radio-electronic means and systems, as well as radio-electronic defense of one's own radio-electronic means and systems."[36] Radio-electronic struggle is thoroughly integrated with other military measures.

Radio *razvedka* is conducted "with the purpose of obtaining information about the enemy by means of interception and analysis of his radio transmissions and radio direction finding of [his] operating radio stations."[37] Radio *razvedka* incorporates the subordinate fields of radio-technical (*radiotekhnicheskaia razvedka* – RTR) and radio-location *razvedka* (*radiolokatsionnaia razvedka* – RLR). Radio-technical *razvedka* involves the use of specialized radio-technical means to obtain data concerning "the type, designation, and location of enemy radio-electronic means."[38] These means include antenna and radio-reception apparatus designed to intercept and analyze enemy radio transmissions. Multiple reception stations use techniques like triangulation and other special analytical devices to determine the type of enemy radio, the nature and location of the transmitter, and the identity of transmitting units. Radio-location *razvedka* seeks to "disclose objectives (targets) and determine their coordinates or movement parameters" by use of radio waves reflected from them.[39]

"Radio-location *razvedka* is designed to accomplish the following:

- to discover the composition, location, and nature of the actions of objectives (targets) during the day and at night in any weather condition,
- to determine the flight parameters of aircraft and helicopters and the flight trajectory of mines, shells, and rockets and to establish the locations of enemy artillery firing positions and rocket launch positions,
- to determine the type and intensity of enemy radio-location systems,
- to correct artillery fire,
- to determine by interception the epicenter of nuclear explosives.[40]

Radio location can be conducted on the ground, from aircraft, on board ship, or from a variety of other mobile means. It is employed in close coordination with other collection assets and the Soviets feel it is particularly effective when integrated with air *razvedka*.

During the Second World War, the Soviets conducted radio *razvedka* by fielding and employing special purpose radio battalions (*radiodivisiony spetsial'nogo naznacheniia*) at *front* level in December 1942. By war's end, such battalions existed both at GRU and *front* level. In 1944 the Soviets also created communications equipment close reconnaissance teams (GBRSS) at army level to monitor enemy radio and telephone communications. The experience of these radio *razvedka* organs provided the basis for post-war and current Soviet radio *razvedka* organization.

Today Soviet radio *razvedka* forces and equipment are integrated into every level of command. They include a capability at the national level (within the GRU) and at the TVD, *front*, army, and divisional levels. Soviet *fronts* include, at a minimum, a radio and radar intercept regiment, which consists of a radio intercept battalion, a radio direction finding battalion, and a radar intercept and direction finding battalion. Additional *front*-level radio-electronic combat assets include a radio intercept regiment, radio and air defense jamming regiments, and an early warning regiment. These units are supported by the intelligence regiment, whose collection battalion and analysis and production company process received information.[41] The *front* radio intercept regiment focuses on enemy communications above corps level, while the radio and radar intercept regiment target enemy air forces as an adjunct to the work of the early warning regiments. In addition to its collection assets, *fronts* will field at least one radio jamming regiment to disrupt enemy communications.

Each Soviet army (tank and combined arms) contains a radio intercept battalion, targeted against enemy communications below corps, and a radio and radar intercept battalion, which targets enemy air power. These collection means supplement the ground radar locating systems of the army artillery regiment, which conducts artillery instrumental *razvedka*. Within divisions, the divisional reconnaissance battalion contains a radio and radar intercept company made up of a radio intercept and direction finding platoon, a radar intercept and direction finding platoon, and an air/air–ground intercept and direction finding platoon. In addition, the division fields another battlefield radar locating system within the artillery regiment. These divisional collection means focus on enemy tactical communications. Together with army intercept and direction finding posts, divisional posts are located from 3–30 kilometers from the FLOT. Posts deployed 3–6 kilometers from the FLOT intercept VHF communications, and posts located 10–30 kilometers from the *front* cover HF communications. Expected ranges of Soviet tactical intercept equipment are 25 kilometers for artillery ground radars, 40 kilometers for VHF, 80 kilometers for HF ground, and unlimited for HF air waves. Higher commands' HF radio equipment can intercept from ground stations to a range of up to 80 kilometers and from air collectors to a range of over 1,000 kilometers. Direction finding capabilities extend to similar ranges, with the exception of HF air direction finding, which is limited to about 200 kilometers.[42]

OTHER CATEGORIES OF *RAZVEDKA*

Within the overall function of protecting the rear area of forces, the Soviets conduct rear area *razvedka*. It is designed to gather data concerning "the stationing regions of rear service subunits, units, and installations and their working conditions." Data includes information regarding the location of the following:

- rear service subunits, units, and installations;
- supply and evacuation routes;
- water sources;
- the presence of local resources and possibilities for their use;
- medical conditions in the region;
- other considerations affecting the planning and conduct of rear service operations.[43]

Responsibilities for performing rear area *razvedka* rest with rear service subunits, units, and installations. Rear service staffs organize it at the operational level, and the assistant commander for rear services arranges it at the tactical level. Medical *razvedka*, a separate category of rear service *razvedka*, is organized by the chief of the medical service and implemented through a series of medical points and participation of medical personnel in reconnaissance groups and patrols.

Closely associated with tactical troop *razvedka* is the ubiquitous Soviet practice of personal reconnaissance (*rekognostsirovka*) which involves visual study of the enemy and terrain. Derived from the former Soviet concept of the "commander's reconnaissance," *rekognostsirovka* still involves the personal presence of the commander with his subordinates. Soviet commanders conduct it when organizing combat actions, movement and dislocation of forces, and when selecting the site of command posts and other key locations. They are usually accompanied by commanders of subordinate, attached, and supporting formations, units and subunits, chiefs of forces and special forces, and by staff officers. When time is short, *rekognostsirovka* covers only main directions (axes), while deputies and staff officers perform the function on secondary axes.

Personal *razvedka* can be conducted from selected fixed command points, from mobile command posts, or from helicopters. In all cases, commanders use a variety of optical and photographic equipment.

When sufficient time is available, *rekognostsirovka* is conducted according to a plan which designates the mission, the makeup of the group, march routes, means of movement, specific observation points, and what is to be accomplished at each point and during each period of time. The results of *rekognostsirovka* provide a basis for planning further topographical *razvedka*.

The Soviets note that *rekognostsirovka* is also conducted in peacetime. Here it involves use of "specially designated *rekognostsirovka* groups," which have the mission of "determining march routes for the departure of forces from their points of permanent station and from their concentration (disposition) regions and for determining the plan of exercises on terrain, etc."[44] While *rekognostsirovka* is routine in nature, it is also often organized to obtain additional information critical to decision making.

NEW *RAZVEDKA* CONCEPTS

In concert with the ongoing technological revolution in weaponry, the Soviets are studying and testing concepts for employing new weaponry or for responding to newly developed enemy weaponry. The reconnaissance-fire artillery group is but one of those new concepts. Even more complex in its design and farther reaching in its implications is the concept of the reconnaissance-strike complex (*razvedyvatel'no-udarnyi kompleks* – RUK). Although this concept is inherently Western (U.S.), and the Soviets refer to it as "foreign" it is likely they have begun development of an analogous system. In fact, the Soviets first referred to the concept by its proper name in their 1986 *Military Encyclopedic Dictionary*, where they described it as:

> long-range, high-precision weapons unified in a single automated system and [other] means for facilitating their combat use (intelligence [*razvedka*], target designation, guidance, navigation, process and representation of information and the working out of command communications).[45]

The Soviets describe two such systems, one operational in its scope and one operational-tactical. The former, typified by the U.S. PLSS (Precision Location Strike System), is tasked first with detecting and destroying enemy air defense and air reconnaissance means in a sector of 500 to 600 kilometers wide and deep, and, second, with combating enemy radio-electronic means and other non-radiating targets. This operational system employs aircraft, air platforms, and multiple ground stations unified by a sophisticated real-time communications and information processing system to detect and engage targets. Target engagement is by aircraft, ground-to-ground, and air-to-ground missiles, and by aerial bombs. The operational-tactical reconnaissance-strike complex is typified by the U.S. "assault breaker" system, which, the Soviets state, "is designated basically for combat with enemy second echelon tank groups at a distance of up to 200 kilometers from the line of contact of forces and provides guidance against moving or stationary groups of targets."[46] Strikes against targets at operational-tactical depths are made by aircraft and operational-tactical missiles.

The Soviets identify the following key elements of the reconnaissance-strike complex:

— aircraft for radio-location *razvedka* and guidance means for strikes, equipped with means for processing information and for command and control, and with communications apparatus;
— mobile ground transmission points for radio-location information and for selection of targets;
— guided air-to-ground and air-to-air rockets equipped with multiple warheads with homing ammunition.[47]

The key to success of the reconnaissance-strike system is effective automation and integration of acquisition and fire means. Soviet systems developed to match Western systems will be modified to reflect Soviet norms and capabilities. Operational complexes will extend to depths of up to 500 kilometers in the service of *front* commanders, while the operational-tactical systems will range from 100–300 kilometers deep.

Reconnaissance-fire concepts employing high-precision weapons or defending against those weapons have the potential of revolutionizing battle by drastically increasing force engagement ranges and the lethality of long-range engagement. Already the prospects for U.S. deployment of reconnaissance-strike complexes have affected Soviet offensive techniques by compelling them to re-emphasize tactical maneuver to avoid linear combat at the tactical level and by necessitating greater tailoring of battalion-level forces for independent operations. The concept has also rendered second echelons more vulnerable and hence less important to the outcome of battle than had been the case in the past (just as tactical nuclear weapons increased the vulnerability and lessened the importance of operational second echelons). In the future, when increased numbers of reconnaissance-strike systems are fielded, the concept of reconnaissance-strike may alter the traditional distinction between offense and defense by according to defenders a distinct initial advantage. This, in part, may be one of the motives for the recent Soviet proclamation of a defensive doctrine.

The Soviets will develop their own concepts for reconnaissance-fire and reconnaissance-strike. They will do so by building upon the already well-articulated *razvedka* systems they employ. While recognizing the importance of these new systems, they will remain convinced that efficient lower-level and human *razvedka* remains the key ingredient of achieving success in battle.

CONCLUSION

The comprehensive Soviet approach to *razvedka* responds to the Soviet belief that intelligence provides the essential basis upon which to conduct deception and, hence, achieve surprise. The increased importance of surprise in contemporary combat further accentuates the importance of *razvedka*. Although *razvedka* does not guarantee success in battle, its absence can contribute to failure.

The Soviets are convinced that the complexity and lethality of future combat requires that increased importance and attention be accorded to intelligence collection and processing. As in the past, they continue to place critical emphasis on the latter function. In future warfare, given the proliferation of technologically sophisticated collection means, the problem will not involve gathering data. Rather, there will be a problem of sorting and assessing data – of filtering through the noise of battle and the torrent of intelligence flowing from a multitude of collection means. This is made even more critical by the likelihood that at least some of the collected information will be deliberately deceptive in nature.

The Soviet answer to this perplexing problem is to continue to create a ubiquitous and comprehensive intelligence-gathering network, which cross-references data from numerous sources and relies on the brain and judgement of the trained analyst to distinguish patterns and meaning from the collected data. This demands sharply centralized control and direction over an articulated intelligence system, extending unbroken from *STAVKA* to battalion level. Analysis nodes at each level, staffed with well-trained analysts, must operate in tandem, in close cooperation with respective operations departments and sections if the resulting intelligence is to be of any relevance. Soviet analysts must employ automation to simplify analysis, and redundant communications are essential to provide timely processing and use of intelligence data. In short, the Soviets today stress the quality of intelligence rather than the quantity of information. They believe small amounts of accurate data, combined with sound human judgement, more than outweigh the value of vast quantities of raw information collected by numerous sophisticated systems but subject to weak analysis.

As we move into the twenty-first century and as weaponry develops to a point which we cannot now determine, the quality approach to intelligence operations will become ever more critical. Man and his judgement, however, will still be the key ingredient in the intelligence equation.

NOTES

CHAPTER TWO

1. R. G. Simonian, "Razvedka" (Intelligence – reconnaissance), *Sovetskaia voennaia entsiklopediia* (Soviet military encyclopedia), 8 vols. (Moscow: Voenizdat, 1976–80), 7:32. Hereafter cited as *SVE* with appropriate volume.
2. V. S. Prokhorov, I. V. Shcherbakov, "Obespechenie boevykh deistvii" (Protecting combat actions), *SVE*, 5:651.
3. Simonian, "Razvedka," 7:32.
4. R. G. Simonian, "Strategicheskaia razvedka" (Strategic *razvedka*), *SVE*, 7:552.
5. R. G. Simonian, "Operativnaia razvedka" (Operational *razvedka*), *SVE*, 6:52.
6. R. G. Simonian, "Takticheskaia razvedka" (Tactical *razvedka*), *SVE*, 7:640.
7. Simonian, "Razvedka," 7:32.
8. *Ibid.*
9. "Rekognostsirovka" (Reconnoitering), *SVE*, 7:602.
10. Raymond L. Garthoff, "The Soviet Intelligence Services," *The Soviet Army* (Suffolk, England: Richard Clay and Co. Ltd, 1956), pp.265–75; Victor Suvorov, *Inside the Red Army* (NY: Macmillan Publishing Co., Inc., 1982), pp.92–9. See also extensive wartime German documentation, including, "Die Organisation des Sowjet Nachrichtendienstes im Kriege, Oktober 1943" (The Organization of the Soviet Intelligence Service in the War, October 1943), *Abteilung Fremde Heere Ost, H 3/1850* NAM T–78, p.677, which provides details of the organization and structure of Soviet intelligence throughout the entire military structure and confirms both Garthoff's and Suvorov's general data.

CHAPTER THREE

1. L. Korzun, "Razvedka v Russkoi armii v pervoi mirovoi voine" (*Razvedka* in the Russian Army in the First World War), *Voenno-istoricheskii zhurnal* (Military-historical journal), No. 4 (April 1981), 60. Hereafter cited as *VIZh* with appropriate number and date.
2. *Ibid.*, 61.
3. I. Bol'shakov, "Russkaia razvedka v pervoi mirovoi voine 1914–1918 godov" (Russian *razvedka* in the First World War 1914–1918), *VIZh*, No. 5 (May 1964), 44–8.
4. Korzun, 61–3.
5. *Ibid.*, 64.
6. *Ibid.*
7. Bol'shakov, 47–8.
8. "Staff, Intelligence," *Combat Factor – Soviet Russia*, From M.O.B.2 Memorandum No. 96 dated 3 Sept. 1920 (Washington: Office of Chief of Staff, Intelligence Division, 18 Oct. 1920). Memorandum quotes from Bolshevik newspaper, *Voennoi Delo*, issue of 31 May 1920.
9. *Ibid.*
10. A. Pevnev, *Voiskovaia konnitsa i ee boevoe ispol'zovanie* (Troop cavalry and its

combat employment), (Moscow: Voenizdat, 1926), p.12.
11. *Ibid.*, p.25.
12. *Ibid.*
13. A. N. Lapchinsky, "Vozdushnaia razvedka" (Air *razvedka*), *Voprosy taktiki v sovetskikh voennykh trudakh (1917–1940 gg.)* (Questions of tactics in Soviet military works (1917–1940)), (Moscow: Voenizdat, 1970), p.321. Quoting from Lapchinsky's 1926 work, *Taktika aviatsii* (Tactics of aviation). Hereafter cited as *Voprosy taktiki* with appropriate author.
14. *Ibid.*, 323.
15. K. Monigetti, *Sovmestnye deistviia konnitsy i vozdushnogo flota* (Joint actions of cavalry and air fleets), (Leningrad: Gosudarstvennoe Izdatel'stvo otdel voennoi literatury, 1928), pp.7, 20.
16. *Ibid.*, p.20.
17. *Ibid.*, p.42.
18. *Polevoi ustav RKKA 1929* (Field service regulations of the Red Army, 1929), (Moscow: Voenizdat, 1929), p.20. Translation by JPRS–UMA–85–019, 13 March 1985.
19. *Ibid.*
20. *Ibid.*
21. *Ibid.*, p.24.
22. *Ibid.*
23. *Ibid.*
24. *Ibid.*, p.25.
25. *Polevoi ustav krasnoi armii (PU–1936), (vremennyi)* (Field service regulations of the Red Army (PU–1936) (provisional)), (Moscow: Voenizdat, 1936), p.9. Translated by Translation Section, The Army War College, Washington, D.C., 1937.
26. *Ibid.*
27. *Ibid.*, pp.10–11.
28. *Ibid.*, p.12.
29. *Ibid.*, p.14.
30. *Ibid.*
31. David M. Glantz, *Soviet Conduct of Tactical Maneuver: The Role of the Forward Detachment* (Ft. Leavenworth, KS: Soviet Army Studies Office, 1986), pp.132–6.
32. M. Lobanov, "K voprosu vozniknoveniia i razvitiia otechestvennoi radiolokatsii" (Concerning the question of the origin and development of native radio location), *VIZh*, No. 8 (Aug. 1962), 13–29.
33. V. Griankov, V. Zmievsky, "Iz istorii radioelektronnoi bor'by" (From the history of radio-electronic struggle), *VIZh*, No. 3 (March 1975), 83–4.
34. G.K. Zhukov, *Reminiscences and Reflections*, Vol. 1 (Moscow: Progress Publishers, 1985), pp.186–7. Translation of *Vospominaniia i razmyshleniia* (Moscow: Izdatel'stvo Agenstva Pechati Novosti, 1974).
35. N. I. Gapich, *Sluzhba sviazi v osnovnykh vidakh obshchevoiskovogo boia (sd i sk)* (The signal service in basic types of combined arms battle (rifle division – RD and rifle corps – RC)), (Moscow: Voenizdat, 1940), p.27.
36. *Ibid.*, p.28.
37. *Ibid.*, p.97.
38. *Ibid.*, p.220.
39. I. Kovalev, "Aviatsionnaia razvedka" (Aviation *razvedka*), *Voennaia Mysl'* (Military Thought), No. 9 (Sept. 1938), 57–81. Hereafter cited as *VM* with appropriate number and date.
40. *Ibid.*, 81.
41. *Ibid.*
42. B. L. Teplinsky, "Voprosy upravleniia boevymi deistviiami aviatsii i raboty aviatsionnykh shtabov" (Questions of the command and control of combat actions

of aviation and the work of aviation staffs), *Voprosy taktiki*, p.338.

43. M. D. Smirnov, *Voiskovaia aviatsiia* (Troop aviation), (Moscow: Voenizdat, 1940), p.27.
44. *Ibid.*, p.61.
45. A. Starunin, "Operativnaia razvedka" (Operational *razvedka*), *VM*, No. 11 (Nov. 1939), 78–86.
46. *Ibid.*, 78.
47. *Ibid.*
48. *Ibid.*, 79.
49. *Ibid.*, 81.
50. *Ibid.*
51. *Ibid.*, 82.
52. *Ibid.*, 83.
53. *Ibid.*, 84.
54. *Ibid.*, 86.
55. *Ibid.*
56. Among other articles, see A. I. Starunin, "Operatovnaia vnezapnost'" (Operational surprise), *VM*, No. 3 (March 1941), 27–35; A. Kononenko, "Boi v flandrii (Mai 1940 gg)" (The battle in Flanders (May 1940)), *VIZh*, No. 3 (March 1941), 3–20.

CHAPTER FOUR

1. S. Alferov, "Strategicheskoe razvertyvanie sovetskykh voisk na Zapadnom TVD v 1941 godu" (Strategic deployment of Soviet forces in the Western TVD in 1941), *VIZh*, No. 6 (June 1981), 26–33; V. A. Anfilov, *Proval Blitskriga* (The failure of Blitzkrieg), (Moscow: "Nauka," 1974); Iu. G. Perechnev, "O nekotorykh problemakh podgotovki strany i Vooruzhennykh Sil k otrazheniiu fashistkoi agressii" (Concerning some problems of preparing the country and Armed Forces for repelling Fascist aggression, *VIZh*, No. 6 (June 1988), 42–50; M. M. Kir'ian, "Nachal'nyi period Velikoi Otechestvennoi voiny" (The initial period of the Great Patriotic War), *VIZh*, No. 6 (June 1988), 11–17.
2. S. M. Shtemenko, *The Soviet General Staff at War, 1941–1945*, Book 1 (Moscow: Progress Publishers, 1985), pp.33–4. A translation of *Sovetskii general'nyi shtab v gody voiny* (Moscow: Voenizdat, 1981).
3. See *Lage der Roten Armee im europäischen Russland abgeschlossen am 20.VI.41*, Abteilung Fremde Heere Ost, H3/1346, NAM T-78, p.677, which shows all assessed Soviet unit locations in the border military districts. Records of German army groups and armies participating in Operation Barbarossa confirm this intelligence picture. Later intelligence documents of the same commands confirm the actual Soviet order of battle as described in a multitude of Soviet sources.
4. For contemporary Soviet views on deception (*maskirovka*), see David M. Glantz, *Soviet Military Deception in the Second World War* (London: Frank Cass, 1989).
5. A. M. Vasilevsky, *A Lifelong Cause* (Moscow: Progress Publishers, 1978), p.82. A translation of *Delo vsei zhizni* (Moscow: Izdatel'stvo politicheskoi literatury, 1973). Recent revelation of Soviet awareness of German military preparedness found in A. G. Khor'kov, "Nakanune groznykh sobytii" (On the eve of menacing events), *VIZh*, No. 6 (June 1988), 42–4; V. I. Beliaev, "Usilenie okhrany zapadnoi granitsy SSSR nakanune Velikoi Otechestvennoi voiny" (Strengthening of security of the USSR's borders on the eve of the Great Patriotic War), *VIZh*, No. 6 (June 1988), 50–5; V. D. Danilov, "Sovetskoe glavnoe komandovanie v preddverii Velikoi Otechestvennoi voiny" (The Soviet High Command on the threshold of the Great Patriotic War), *Novaia i noveishaia istoriia* (New and recent history), No. 6 (June 1988), 3–20. The latter quotes reports from Richard Sorge

(codenamed *Ramzaia*) to the GRU between November 1940 and June 1941, detailing plans for the German attack.

6. *Ibid.*, pp.84, 85.
7. Zhukov, p.273.
8. Vasilevsky, *A Lifelong Cause*, pp.84–5. Among other warnings of an impending attack were reports from agent networks abroad (particularly Switzerland). One key Swiss network operative reportedly warned the GRU in a message dated 17 June, which read:

> 17.6.1941 To Director About 100 infantry divisions are now positioned on the German–Soviet frontier. One third are motorized. Of the remainder, at least ten divisions are armoured. In Romania, German troops are concentrated at Galatz. Elite divisions with a special mission have been mobilized. The 5th and 10th divisions stationed in the General Government [the Nazi description of occupied Poland] are taking part. Dora.

Subsequent reports from the network are said to have set exact date and time of attack. However, even if this is accurate, Soviet skepticism and Stalin's political misjudgement discounted the veracity of the report.

9. Zhukov, p.283.
10. *Ibid.*, p.285.
11. *Ibid.*
12. Shtemenko, pp.39–40.
13. Zhukov, p.297.
14. *Ibid.*, p.312.
15. Anfilov, p.244.
16. I. Kh. Bagramian, *Tak nachinalas' voina* (How war began), (Kiev: Izdatel'stvo khudozhestvennoi literatury "Dnipro," 1975), p.89.
17. Zhukov, p.387.
18. *Ibid.*
19. Vasilevsky, *A Lifelong Cause*, p.108.
20. A. I. Eremenko, *V nachale voiny* (In the beginning of war), (Moscow: "Nauka," 1965), pp.300–6.
21. *Ibid.*, pp.308–9.
22. K. S. Moskalenko, *Na iugo-zapadnom napravlenii 1941–1943* (On the southwestern direction 1941–1943), (Moscow: "Nauka," 1973), p.82.
23. *Ibid.*, pp.82–3.
24. Anfilov, p.551.
25. Vasilevsky, *A Lifelong Cause*, p.113. See also Eremenko, p.388.
26. L. M. Sandalov, *Na moskovskom napravlenii* (On the Moscow direction), (Moscow: "Nauka," 1970), p.201.
27. *Ibid.*
28. G. Z. Zhukov, *Reminiscences and Reflections*, Vol. 2 (Moscow: Progress Publishers, 1985), p.44.
29. Zhukov, Vol. 1, p.323.
30. P. A. Kurochkin, *Obshchevoiskovaia armiia v nastuplenii* (The combined arms army on the offensive), (Moscow: Voenizdat, 1966), p.68.
31. Eremenko, p.404.
32. Moskalenko, p.107.
33. I. Kh. Bagramian, *Tak shli my k pobede* (Thus we marched to victory), (Moscow: Voenizdat, 1977), p.6.
34. "Kharakter oborony nemtsev na demianskom platsdarme" (The nature of German defenses on the Demiansk bridgehead), *Sbornik Materialov po izucheniiu opyta voiny No. 9 noiabr'-dekabr' 1943 g.* (Collection of materials for the study of war experience No. 9 November–December 1943), (Moscow: Voenizdat, 1944), pp.150–65, classified "secret." Hereafter cited as *Sbornik*

materialov No. 9 with appropriate pages.

35. "Nekotorye vyvody po desantnym operatsiiam za 1941 god" (Some conclusions regarding amphibious (*desant*) operations in 1941), *Sbornik materialov po izucheniiu opyta voiny No. 1 iiul'–avgust 1942 g.* (Collection of materials for the study of war experience No. 1 July–August 1942), (Moscow: Voenizdat, 1942), p.13, classified "secret." Hereafter cited as *Sbornik materialov No. 1* with appropriate pages.

36. "Operativno-takticheskie uroki zimnoi kampanii 1941/1942 g." (Operational-tactical lessons of the winter campaign 1941–1942), *Sbornik materialov po izucheniiu opyta voiny No. 2 sentiabr'–oktiabr' 1942 g.* (Collection of materials for the study of war experience No. 2 September–October 1942), (Moscow: Voenizdat, 1942), p.3, classified "secret." Hereafter cited as *Sbornik materialov No. 2* with appropriate pages.

37. *Ibid.*, pp.8–9.
38. "Osobennosti nastupatel'nykh deistvii zimoi" (The characteristics of offensive operations in winter), *Sbornik materialov No. 2*, p.24.
39. *Ibid.*, pp.32–4.
40. "Boevaia rabota artillerii zimoi 1942 g" (The combat work of artillery in the winter of 1942), *Sbornik materialov No. 2*, pp.35–6.
41. *Ibid.*, p.37.
42. V. P. Krikunov, "Iz opyta raboty komanduiushchikh i shtabov armii na mestnosti" (From the experience of the work of commanders and staff on the terrain), *VIZh*, No. 7 (July 1987), p.22.
43. Zhukov, Vol. 2, p.71.
44. Vasilevsky, *A Lifelong Cause*, p.156.
45. *Ibid.*, p.162.
46. Bagramian, *Tak shli*, p.51.
47. *Ibid.*, p.52.
48. *Ibid.*, p.53.
49. *Ibid.*, p.67.
50. *Ibid.*, p.69.
51. *Ibid.*, p.90.
52. *Ibid.*, pp.103–5.
53. *Ibid.*, p.107.
54. Zhukov, Vol. 2, p.77.
55. A. M. Vasilevsky, "Nezabyvaemye dni" (Unforgettable days), *VIZh*, No. 8 (Aug. 1965), 9.
56. Earl F. Ziemke, "Operation Kreml: Deception, Strategy, and the Fortunes of War," *Parameters*, Vol. 9, No. 1 (March 1979), 72–83.
57. Moskalenko, p.214.
58. *Ibid.*, p.215.
59. *Ibid.*
60. *Ibid.*, pp.244–5.
61. *Ibid.*, p.245.
62. Shtemenko, pp.76–7.
63. *Ibid.*, p.77.
64. Vasilevsky, *A Lifelong Cause*, p.165.
65. Shtemenko, pp.81–2.
66. *Ibid.*, p.85.
67. *Ibid.*, p.88.
68. *Ibid.*, p.98.
69. "Nekotorye vyvody po operatsiiam levogo kryla zapadnogo fronta" (Some conclusions concerning the operations of the left wing of the Western Front), *Sbornik materialov po izucheniu opyta voiny No. 5 mart 1943 g.* (Collection of materials for the study of war experience No. 5 March 1943), (Moscow: Voenizdat, 1943), p.67,

classified "secret." Hereafter cited as *Sbornik materialov No. 5* with appropriate pages.

70. *Ibid.*, p.65.
71. Kurochkin, p.68.
72. *Sbornik materialov No. 5*, pp.67–75.
73. "Nekotorye voprosy voiskovoi razvedki" (Some questions of troop *razvedka*), *Sbornik materialov No. 2*, p.47.
74. *Ibid.*
75. *Ibid.*
76. *Ibid.*, p.48.
77. *Ibid.*
78. *Ibid.*, p.49.
79. *Ibid.*
80. *Ibid.*, pp.57–8.
81. *Ibid.*, p.58.
82. *Ibid.*, p.60.
83. *Red Army Field Service Regulations 1942* (Moscow: Voenizdat, 1942). Translation by Chief of the General Staff, Canada, July 1944.
84. *Ibid.*, p.43.
85. *Ibid.*
86. *Ibid.*, p.46.
87. *Ibid.*
88. *Ibid.*
89. V. Chikin, "Razvedka v operatsiiakh 61–i armii" (*Razvedka* in 61st Army operations), *VIZh*, No. 10 (Oct. 1979), 53–4.
90. N. N. Popel', V. P. Savel'ev, P. V. Shemansky, *Upravlenie voiskami v gody Velikoi Otechestvennoi voiny* (Troop control in the Great Patriotic War), (Moscow: Voenizdat, 1974), pp.76–143.
91. S. I. Rudenko, ed., *Sovetskie voenno-vozdushnye sily v Velikoi Otechestvennoi voine 1941–1945 gg* (The Soviet Air Force in the Great Patriotic War), (Moscow: Voenizdat, 1968), p.125.
92. I. V. Timokhovich, *Operativnoe iskusstvo Sovetskikh VVS v Velikoi Otechestvennoi voine* (Operational art of the Soviet Air Force in the Great Patriotic War), (Moscow: Voenizdat, 1976), pp.124, 213, 221.
93. M. V. Zakharov, ed., *50 let vooruzhennykh sil SSSR* (50 years of the Soviet Armed Forces), (Moscow: Voenizdat, 1968), p.238.
94. N. I. Belousov, M. A. Boguslavsky, "Opyt ispol'zovaniia aviatsii dal'nego deistviia dliia narusheniia zheleznodorozhnykh perevozok protivnika" (Experience of the use of long-range aviation for the destruction of enemy railroad transportation), *VIZh*, No. 10 (Oct. 1987), 32–3.
95. Rudenko, *Sovetskie voenno-vozdushnye*, p.125.
96. "Topograficheskoi obespechenie voisk po opytu otechestvennoi voiny" (Topographic support of forces based on the experiences of the patriotic war), *Sbornik materialov No. 2*, pp.149–59; L. Safronov, "Iz opyta photorazvedki v Velikoi Otechestvennoi voine" (From the experience of photo *razvedka* in the Great Patriotic War), *VIZh*, No. 5 (May 1979), 20–3.
97. "Protivovozdushnaia oborona krupnogo punkta (po opyta goda voiny)" (Anti-aircraft defenses of a large point (according to war experience)), *Sbornik materialov No. 2*, p.133.
98. S. Ostriakov, *Voennye chekisty* (Military *Chekists*), (Moscow: Voenizdat, 1979), p.150.
99. A Soviet biography states Rado was:

An internationalist, scientist-cartographer, a doctor of geographical and economic science (1958). He was a member of the Hungarian Communist party from 1918. During the Second World War 1939–1945, he participated in the struggle against German and Italian fascism; he directed an intelligence group in Switzerland (acting as a cartographic agency), which reported to the Soviet leadership important information about the plans of the German-Fascist High Command, the dislocation of forces etc. which proved especially beneficial in the period of battle at Moscow, Stalingrad, and Kursk. ... Awarded the Order of the Patriotic War, 1st Degree and Friend of the People.

See *Velikaia Otechestvennaia Voina 1941–1945: Entsiklopediia* (The Great Patriotic War 1941–1945: Encyclopedia), (Moscow: "Sovetskaia entsiklopediia," 1985), p.604.

100. See F. H. Hinsley, *British Intelligence in the Second World War*, Vol. 2 (New York: Cambridge University Press, 1981), p.60, in which Hinsley writes:

There is no truth in the much-publicized claims that the British authorities made use of the "Lucy" ring, a Soviet espionage organization which operated in Switzerland, to forward intelligence to Moscow.

101. T. P. Mulligan, "Spies, Ciphers and Zitadelle: Intelligence and the Battle of Kursk, 1943," *Journal of Contemporary History*, Vol. 22 (1987), 237.
102. Hinsley, Vol. 2, pp.60–1.
103. *Ibid.*, p.70.
104. *Ibid*, p.73.
105. *Ibid.*, p.95.
106. *Ibid.*, pp.97–8.
107. *Ibid.*, p.98.
108. *Ibid.*, p.99.
109. *Ibid.*, pp.61–2.
110. *Ibid.*, p.69, which states:

To begin with, the intelligence (Enigma) was derived mainly from the GAF's general key (Red) and although other GAF and a number of Army keys were to contribute, this always remained the steadiest source of Enigma decrypts on the eastern front. Of the further GAF keys only one other was intercepted in 1941. This was the key of the GAF field Sigint service on the eastern front (named Mustard at GC and CS). This was broken on 12 days between June and September, but not again till April 1942. It was then broken with fair frequency and provided a comprehensive picture of the order of battle of the Soviet Army and Air Force. Of the Army Enigma keys the most important appeared at the beginning of the campaign. It was used for communications on a highly complex network between armies and army groups on the eastern front and the Army High Command (OKH). Called Vulture by GC and CS, it was broken a few times between June and September, but from October till mid-December with some regularity. From the end of 1941, however, largely owing to the introduction of land-lines, it was lost for over a year. It provided regular and detailed operational reports as well as occasional high-level appreciations, statements of intent and some supply information which came on no other key, and from no other source, until GC and CS regularly broke the German non-morse teleprinter traffic in 1943. Only two other Army keys were broken before 1943. One was an army/air co-operation key (Kestrel to GC and CS) which was read fairly frequently in the autumn of 1941 and then lapsed in March 1942. It yielded mostly air reconnaissance reports. The other (Kite to GC and CS) was concerned with army supply matters; it was read occasionally in the early part of 1942.

111. Ostriakov, p.168.
112. *Ibid.*, p.169.
113. F. L. Kurlat, L. A. Studnikov, "Brigada osobogo naznacheniia" (Special designa-

tion brigade), *Voprosy istorii* (Questions of history), No. 9 (Sept. 1982), 95.

114. *Ibid.*

115. S. V. Bulenko, *Na okhrane tyla strany: Istrebitel'nye batal'ony i polki v Velikoi Otechestvennoi voine 1941–1945* (In securing the country's rear area: Destroyer battalions and regiments in the Great Patriotic War 1941–1945), (Moscow: "Nauka," 1988), p.220.

116. *Ibid.*, pp.4, 214.

117. *Ibid.*, p.216.

118. *Ibid.*, p.215. Bulenko provides considerable detail about the strength, deployment, and operations of many of the detachments fielded by destroyer battalions and regiments.

119. David M. Glantz, *The Soviet Airborne Experience*, Research Survey No. 4 (Ft. Leavenworth, KS: Combat Studies Institute, 1984), pp.46–7, 121–6.

120. Zhukov, Vol. 2, p.170.

121. V. N. Andrianov, "Partisanskaia razvedka v gody Velikoi Otechestvoennoi voiny" (Partisan *razvedka* in the Great Patriotic War), *VIZh*, No. 8 (Aug. 1986), 44.

122. D. Z. Muriev, V. A. Perezhogin, "Partisanskoe dvizhenie v Velikoi Otechestvennoi voine 1941–1945" (The partisan movement in the Great Patriotic War), *SVE*, 6:230.

123. Andrianov, 22.

124. V. A. Perezhogin, "Sovmestnye deistviia partisan s voiskami v khode Rzhevsko-Viazemskoi operatsii" (Joint actions of partisans with forces during the Rzhev–Viaz'ma operation), *VIZh*, No. 2 (Feb. 1987), 26.

125. *Ibid.*, 28.

126. Andrianov, 25.

127. Kurochkin, p.68.

128. K. S. Kolganov, *Razvitie taktiki Sovietskoi armii v gody Velikoi Otechestvennoi voiny (1941–1945 gg.)* (The development of Soviet tactics in the Great Patriotic War (1941–1945)), (Moscow: Voenizdat, 1958), p.202.

129. I. Viazankin, "Sovershenstvovanie organizatsii i vedeniia razvedki boem" (Improvement in the organization and conduct of reconnaissance in force), *VIZh*, No. 11 (Nov. 1969), 26.

130. Kurochkin, p.68.

131. P. M. Simchenkov, "Opyt organizatsii i vedeniia razvedki boem" (Experience in the organization and conduct of reconnaissance in force), *VIZh*, No. 9 (Sept. 1985), 21.

132. *Ibid.*, 25.

133. *Razvedka v boevykh primerakh* (*Razvedka* by combat examples), (Moscow: Voenizdat, 1972), p.12.

134. Krikunov, pp.21–2.

135. *Ibid.*, p.22.

136. M. Sidorov, "Ognevoe porazhenie pri proryv oborony protivnika po opytu Velikoi Otechestvennoi voiny" (Fire destruction during the penetration of an enemy defense based on the experience of the Great Patriotic War), *VIZh*, No. 8 (August 1984), 18.

137. *Ibid.*

138. G. Peredel'sky, G. Khoroshilov, "Bor'ba s artilleriei protivnika" (Struggle with enemy artillery), *VIZh*, No. 6 (June 1978), 21.

139. Sidorov, 19.

140. The artillery offensive includes three phases: artillery preparation for the attack, artillery support of the attack, and artillery accompaniment for forces operating in the defensive depths.

141. G. E. Peredel'sky, A. I. Tokmakov, G. T. Khoroshilov, *Artilleriia v boiu i operatsii* (Artillery in battle and operations), (Moscow: Voenizdat, 1980), p.73.

142. E. Kolibernov, "Inzhenernoe obespechenie proryva oboroni protivnika po opytu voiny" (Engineer support of the penetration of an enemy defense according to war experience), *VIZh*, No. 8 (Aug. 1980), 46–7.
143. Glantz, *Soviet Military Deception*, pp.77–8.
144. Ia. Dashevsky, "Organizatsiia i provedenie operativnoi maskirovki" (Organization and conduct of operational *maskirovka*), *VIZh*, No. 4 (April 1980), 47.

CHAPTER FIVE

1. K. K. Rokossovsky, ed., *Velikaia pobeda na Volge* (Great victory on the Volga), (Moscow: Voenizdat, 1965), p.219.
2. *Ibid.*
3. A. M. Samsonov, ed., *Stalingradskaia epopeia* (Stalingrad epic), (Moscow: "Nauka," 1968), p.50.
4. A. M. Vasilevsky, "Nezabyvaemye dni" (Unforgettable days), *VIZh*, No. 10 (Oct. 1965), 8.
5. David M. Glantz, "The Nature and Legacy of Soviet Military Deception," *Strategic and Operational Deception in the Second World War* (London: Frank Cass, 1987), pp.201–13.
6. M. M. Kir'ian, ed., *Fronty nastupali: po opytu Vekiloi Otechestvennoi voiny* (The fronts have attacked: based on the experience of the Great Patriotic War), (Moscow: "Nauka," 1987), p.77.
7. *Ibid.*; see also a German appreciation of Soviet intelligence activity contained in "Die Organisation des Sowjet Nachrichtendienstes im Kriege" (The Organization of Soviet Intelligence Service in the War), *Abteilung Fremde Heere Ost*, Oct. 1943, NAM T–78, p.677.
8. Kir'ian, p.78.
9. *Ibid.*
10. *Ibid.*
11. Zhukov, Vol. 2, pp.116–17.
12. *Ibid.*, p.118.
13. N. N. Voronov, *Na sluzhbe voennoi* (In military service), (Moscow: Voenizdat, 1963), p.270.
14. M. M. Danilevsky, "Vozdushnaia razvedka" (Air *razvedka*), *SVE*, 2:282.
15. "Nekotorye voprosy operativnoi razvedki" (Some questions of operational *razvedka*), *Sbornik materialov po izucheniiu opyta voina No. 8 avgust–oktiabr' 1943 g* (Collection of materials for the study of war experience No. 8 August–October 1943), (Moscow: Voenizdat, 1943), p.115, classified "secret." Hereafter cited as *Sbornik materialov No. 8* with appropriate pages. Timokhovich, p.212, stated operational air *razvedka* was conducted at a depth of 300–350 kilometers and tactical air *razvedka* up to 100 kilometers.
16. Timokhovich, p.123.
17. *Ibid.*, pp.123–4.
18. Interview with Ilya Lechman, pilot in the 742d Special Air Reconnaissance Regiment subordinated to the High Command. According to Lechman, the regiment had four squadrons and was tasked with conducting strategic operational *razvedka*, using high altitude photography.
19. Safronov, pp.20–3.
20. "Topograficheskoe obespechenie voisk po opytu otechestvennoi voiny" (Topographic support of forces according to the experience of the patriotic war), *Sbornik materialov No. 2*, p.156.
21. G. K. Prussakov, ed., *16–ia vozdushnaia: Voenno-istoricheskii ocherk o boevom put 16-i vozdushnoi armii 1942–1945* (16th Air: military-political survey about the

combat path of 16th Air Army 1942–1945), (Moscow: Voenizdat, 1973).

22. K. A. Vershinin, *Chetvertaia vozdushnaia* (Fourth Air Army), (Moscow: Voenizdat, 1975), p.177.

23. *Ibid.*, p.194.

24. *17-ia vozdushnaia armiia v boiakh ot Stalingrada do Veny* (17th Air Army in battles from Stalingrad to Vienna), (Moscow: Voenizdat, 1977), p.9.

25. S. I. Rudenko, *Kryl'ia pobedy* (Wings of victory), (Moscow: 'Mezhdunarodnye otnosheniia, 1985), p.125.

26. *Sbornik materialov No. 8*, p.115.

27. *Ibid.*, p.117.

28. *Ibid.*, pp.119–20.

29. Ostriakov, p.168.

30. Kurlat, Studnikov, p.99.

31. "Planirovanie i podgotovka nastupatel'noi operatsii iugo-zapadnogo fronta v dekabre 1942 g" (Planning and preparation of the Southwestern Front offensive operation in Dec. 1942), *Sbornik materialov No. 8*, p.18.

32. *Sbornik materialov No. 8*, p.115.

33. *Ibid.*, pp.118–19.

34. Griankov, Zmievsky, p.84; A. Paly, "Radioelektronnaia bor'ba v khode voiny" (Radio-electronic struggle during war), *VIZh*, No. 5 (May 1977), 12.

35. Paly, 11.

36. *Sbornik materialov No. 8*, pp.118–19.

37. "Stalingradskaia gruppirovka nemtsev" (The German Stalingrad grouping), *Sbornik materialov po izucheniiu opyta voiny No. 6 aprel'–mai 1943 g.* (Collection of materials for the study of war experience No. 6 April–May 1943), (Moscow: Voenizdat, 1943), p.9, classified "secret." Hereafter cited as *Sbornik materialov No. 6* with appropriate pages.

38. Viazankin, p.28.

39. Kolganov, pp.202–3.

40. "Deistviia podvizhnoi-gruppy 5 tankovoi armii v proryve" (Actions of 5th Tank Army's mobile groups in the penetration), *Sbornik materialov No. 6*, pp.53–4.

41. *Ibid.*, pp.55–6.

42. B. S. Navysev, *Na sluzhbe shtabnoi* (In staff service), (Riga: Izdatel'stvo "Piesma," 1972), p.79.

43. *Ibid.*, p.80.

44. *Ibid.*

45. F. A. Samsonov, *Boevoi opyt artillerii v Otechestvennoi voine: Sbornik No. 1* (Combat experience of artillery in the Patriotic War: Collection No. 1), (Moscow: Voenizdat, 1943), p.64. Translated by USA General Staff G-2, No. F-9083, Nov. 1952.

46. Navyshev, p.81.

47. Samsonov, p.66. The 816th Separate Reconnaissance Artillery Battalion consisted of topographic and sound-ranging batteries and optical and meteorological reconnaissance platoons with a strength of 316 men. The 45th Separate Corrective-Reconnaissance Squadron contained five IL-2 and one U-2 aircraft. See A. S. Domank, S. P. Lazutkin, *Rezerva Verkhovnogo Glavno-komandovaniia* (The reserves of the High Command), (Moscow: Voenizdat, 1987), p.6.

48. K. P. Kazakov, *Vsegda s pekhotoi vsegda s tankami* (Always with the infantry, always with the tanks), (Moscow: Voenizdat, 1969), p.103.

49. "Artilleriia v nastupatel'nykh operatsiiakh pod Stalingradom" (Artillery in offensive operations at Stalingrad), *Sbornik materialov No. 6*, p.129.

50. *Ibid.*, p.130.

51. Samsonov, p.70.

52. *Ibid.*

53. *Ibid.*, p.66.

54. "Inzhenernoe obespechenie operatsii Stalingradskogo fronta" (Engineer protection of Stalingrad Front operations), *Sbornik materialov No. 6*, p.158.
55. Kolibernov, pp.44–5.
56. *Sbornik materialov No. 6*, p.164.
57. *Ibid.*
58. Zhukov, Vol. 2, pp.119–20.
59. Vasilevsky, *A Lifelong Cause*, p.193.
60. Voronov, p.273.
61. I. M. Chistiakov, *Sluzhim otchizne* (In service to the fatherland), (Moscow: Voenizdat, 1975), p.96.
62. P. I. Batov, *V pokhodakh i boiakh* (On marches and in battles), (Moscow: Izdatel'stvo DOSAAF SSSR, 1984), p.181.
63. *Sbornik materialov No. 8*, p.115.
64. *Ibid.*, p.119.
65. *Ibid.*
66. *Ibid.*, p.122.
67. *Ibid.*, p.123.
68. *Ibid.* The critique also added, "The purpose of this branch of intelligence may be served by extensive use of guards airborne demolition teams dropped in enemy rear areas to carry out the task of disrupting his communications."
69. *Ibid.*, p.124.
70. "Srazhenie za Stalingrad" (The battle for Stalingrad), *Sbornik materialov No. 6*, p.34.
71. "Flangovye udary Krasnoi armii v Stalingradskom srazhenii" (The flank blows of the Red Army in the Stalingrad battle), *Sbornik materialov No. 6*, p.47.
72. "Likvidatsiia okruzhennoi Stalingradskoi gruppirovki protivnika" (Liquidation of the surrounded enemy Stalingrad group), *Sbornik materialov No. 6*, pp.84–5.
73. *Sbornik materialov No. 6*, p.48.
74. *Ibid.*, p.49.
75. *Sbornik materialov No. 6*, p.54.
76. *Ibid.*
77. Samsonov, p.30.
78. *Ibid.*
79. *Ibid.*, p.64.
80. *Ibid.*, p.68.
81. *Ibid.*, p.71.
82. *Sbornik materialov No. 6*, p.60.
83. *Ibid.*
84. Vasilevsky, *A Lifelong Cause*, pp.197–8. Classified Soviet critiques set the strength of encircled German forces at 330,000.
85. *Ibid.*, p.207.
86. *Ibid.*, p.210.
87. Samsonov, p.71.
88. "Deistviia aviatsii v dekabr'skoi operatsii na srednom donu" (Aviation operations in the December operation along the Middle Don), *Sbornik materialov No. 9*, p.23; Rokossovsky, p.330.
89. *Sbornik materialov No. 9*, p.29.
90. *Ibid.*
91. *Ibid.*, p.30.
92. *Ibid.*
93. *Ibid.*, p.31.
94. *Sbornik materialov No. 8*, p.18.
95. "Artilleriia Iugo-Zapadnogo fronta v dekabr'skoi operatsii 1942 g." (Artillery of the Southwestern Front in the December operation 1942), *Sbornik materialov No. 8*, p.39.

96. *Ibid.*, pp.39–40.
97. *Ibid.*, p.46.
98. David M. Glantz, *From the Don to the Dnepr: Soviet Offensive Operations December 1942–August 1943* (London: Frank Cass, to be published 1990). Manuscript.
99. *Le Operationi della Unità Italiane Al Fronte Russo (1943–1944)* (Operation of the Italian Army on the Russian Front (1943–1944), (Roma: Ministero della Difensa, Stato Maggiore dell'Esercito, 1977), pp.343–58.
100. "Proryv voiskami Iugo-Zapadnogo fronta oborony protivnika na Donu i deistviia voist v operativnoi glubine" (Penetration of enemy defenses on the Don by forces of the Southwestern Front and operations of forces in the operational depth), *Sbornik materialov No. 9*, p.18.
101. *Sbornik materialov No. 9*, p.31.
102. *Ibid.*, pp.35–6.
103. Zhukov, Vol. 2, pp.134–5.
104. *Sbornik materialov No. 9*, p.36.
105. Voronov, p.294.
106. "Nekotorye vyvody po ispol'zovaniiu tankovykh i mekhanizirovannykh korpusov dlia razvitiia proryva" (Some conclusions concerning the use of tank and mechanized corps for the development of a penetration), *Sbornik materialov No. 8*, p.76.
107. *Ibid.*, p.53.
108. *Ibid.*, p.54.
109. *Ibid.*, p.77.
110. *Ibid.*, p.59.
111. *Sbornik materialov No. 9*, p.18.
112. *17-ia vozdushnaia armiia*, p.22.
113. "Deistviia VVS v bor'be za Stalingrad" (Air force operations in the struggle for Stalingrad), *Sbornik materialov No. 6*, p.154.
114. Vershinin, p.194.

CHAPTER SIX

1. A. G. Yershov, *Osvobozhdenie Donbassa* (The liberation of the Donbas), (Moscow: Voenizdat, 1973), p.32.
2. *Ibid.*, p.25.
3. V. Morozov, "Pochemu ne zavershilos' nastuplenie v Donbasse vesnoi 1943 goda" (Why was the offensive in the Donbas not completed in the spring of 1943?), *VIZh*, No. 3 (March 1963), 16.

  Reportedly the "Dora" spy ring operating in Switzerland passed to GRU "Centre" the following reports based on Swiss intelligence materials:

  11 Feb.: "German troops in the Donetz area are in full retreat."
  16 Feb.: "All German counter-attacks have failed. ... The Germans are being overtaken by a new disaster. Losses to be expected on the German side will greatly exceed their losses at Stalingrad."
  17 Feb.: "The object of German resistance ... is now confined to covering the German withdrawal from the Donetz bend."

  See, Anthony Read, David Fisher, *Operation Lucy* (London: Sphere, 1982), p.152. The authors claim virtually no Ultra material was passed through the "Lucy" ring during this period.
4. *Ibid.*, pp.16–17.
5. *Ibid.*, p.18.
6. *Ibid.*, p.23.

7. N. M. Skomorokhov, ed., *17-ia vozdushnaia armiia v boiakh ot Stalingrada do Veny* (17th Air Army in battles from Stalingrad to Vienna), (Moscow: Voenizdat, 1977), p.39.
8. Morozov, 17.
9. *Ibid.* Another "Dora" ring report dated 21 February read: "The consequence of the fall of Khar'kov and the collapse of the improvised German Donetz front are assessed as disasters at German high command. More than forty German divisions are in danger of being cut off." Read, Fisher, p.153.
10. For details in German planning, see E. Ziemke, *Stalingrad to Berlin* (Washington, D.C.: Center for Military History, 1968), pp.124–5.
11. *Ibid.*, p.127.
12. *Ibid.*, pp.131–2.
13. *Ibid.*, p.132.
14. "The Zitadelle Offensive," *MS #T–26*, Historical Division Headquarters, United States Army, Europe, Foreign Military Studies Branch Appendix, No. 4; J. Engelmann, *Zitadelle: Die grösste Panzerschlacht im Osten, 1943* (Citadel: The Greatest Tank Battle in the East, 1943), (Friedberg, FRG, Podzyn-Pallas-Verlag), pp.55–60.
15. Zhukov, *Reminiscences*, Vol. 2, pp.150–2.
16. *Ibid.*, pp.154–6.
17. *Ibid.*, pp.156–8.
18. S. M. Shtemenko, *The Soviet General Staff at War 1941–1945* (Moscow: Progress Publishers, 1970), pp.218–19.
19. Zhukov, *Reminiscences*, Vol. 2, pp.160–1.
20. Shtemenko, p.221.
21. *Ibid.*, pp.222–3.
22. Zhukov, *Reminiscences*, Vol. 2, p.166.
23. "Podgotovka k Kurskoi bitve" (Preparation for the battle of Kursk), *VIZh*, No. 6 (June 1983), 67.
24. Vasilevsky, pp.270–1.
25. *Ibid.*, p.271.
26. Zhukov, *Reminiscences*, Vol. 2, pp.170–2.
27. Vasilevsky, p.271.
28. G. Zhukov, "Na Kurskoi duge" (In the Kursk bulge), *VIZh*, No. 8 (Aug. 1967), 76.
29. *Ibid.*, 81.
30. Glantz, *Soviet Military Deception*, pp.146–60.
31. V. Matsulenko, *Operativnaia maskirovka voisk* (Operational *maskirovka* of forces), (Moscow: Voenizdat, 1975), pp.50–1. Hereafter cited as Matsulenko, *Operativnaia*.
32. Vasilevsky, pp.271–2.
33. Zhukov, *Reminiscences*, Vol. 2, p.176.
34. *Ibid.*, p.180.
35. Vasilevsky, p.273.
36. *Ibid.*
37. I. Konev, "The Great Battle at Kursk and Its Historic Significance," *The Battle of Kursk* (Moscow: Progress Publishers, 1974), p.17. Hereafter cited as *The Battle of Kursk* with respective section.
38. "Die Organisation des Sowjet Nachrichtendienstes im Kriege" (The Organization of Soviet Intelligence Service in the War), *Abteilung Fremde Heere Ost*, Oct. 1943, NAM T–78/677. Hereafter cited as "Die Organisation)." Appendices.
39. Ostriakov, p.179.
40. Kir'ian, p.78.
41. G. N. Pakilev, *Truzheniki neba* (Toilers of the Skies), (Moscow: Voenizdat, 1978), p.87.
42. *Sbornik materialov No. 8*, p.115; Timokhovich, p.212, stated operational air

razvedka was conducted at a depth of 300–350 kilometers and tactical air *razvedka* up to 100 kilometers.

43. A. Efimov, "Primenenie aviatsii v Kurskoi bitve – vazhnyi etap v razvitii operativnogo iskusstva Sovetskikh VVS" (The use of aviation in the battle of Kursk – an important step in the development of operational art of the Soviet air force), *VIZh*, No. 6 (June 1983), 46–7; Shtemenko, pp. 228–9.
44. Efimov, 47.
45. Timokhovich, p. 121.
46. *Ibid.*
47. *Ibid.*, p. 210.
48. *Ibid.*, pp. 123–4.
49. Interview with Ilya Lechman, pilot in the 742d Special Air Reconnaissance Regiment subordinated to the High Command. According to Lechman, the regiment had four squadrons and was tasked with conducting strategic and operational *razvedka* employing high altitude photography.
50. Timokhovich, p. 125.
51. *Ibid.*, p. 211.
52. E. Simakov, "Sovetskaia aviatsiia v bitve pod Kurskom" (Soviet aviation in the battle of Kursk), *VIZh*, No. 5 (May 1983), 42–3.
53. S. Rudenko, "The Gaining of Air Supremacy and Air Operations in the Battle of Kursk," *The Battle of Kursk*, pp. 189–90.
54. G. A. Koltunov, B. G. Solov'ev, *Kurskaia bitva* (The Battle of Kursk), (Moscow: Voenizdat, 1970), p. 197.
55. Kurlat, Studnikov, p. 101.
56. Koltunov, p. 39.
57. S. Kh. Aganov, *Inzhenernye voiska Sovetskoi armii 1918–1945* (Engineer forces of the Soviet Army 1918–1945), (Moscow: Voenizdat, 1985), p. 460.
58. *Ibid.*
59. *Ibid.*, p. 462.
60. Pakilev, pp. 67–88.
61. Koltunov, p. 25.
62. *Istoriia Velikoi Otechestvennoi voiny Sovetskogo Soiuza 1941–1945* T. 6 (History of the Great Patriotic War of the Soviet Union 1941–1945 Vol. 6), (Moscow: Voenizdat, 1965), p. 139.
63. *Ibid.*
64. Abteilung Fremde Heere Ost IIe, *Einzelnachrichten des Ic-Dienstes Ost* Nr. 6 H.Qu., den 30.12.1942., 2 NAM T–78/556.
65. *Ibid.*
66. *Ibid.*, pp. 3–4.
67. *Ibid.*, p. 4.
68. *Ibid.*, p. 5.
69. Mulligan, p. 251, which cites Abwehr Leitstelle III Ost, "Vorschlag zur Aktivierung der Irreführung des gegen die deutsche Ostfront gerichteten Sowjet-Aufklärungsdienstes," 8 Jan. 1945, NAM T78/488.
70. *Ibid.*, citing PzAOK 4/Ic, "Tätigkeitsbericht der Abt. Ic/A.O. für die Zeit vom 25.3 bis 31.5.1943 für den Monat Juni 1943", T313/371; and XLVIII Panzer-korps/Ic, "Tätigkeitsbericht der Abteilung Ic für die Zeit vom 1.5–30.6.43", 30 June 1943, NAM T–314/1167.
71. *Ibid.*
72. *Ibid.*, citing AOK 9/Ic, "Tätigkeitsbericht der Abt. Ic/A.O. für die Zeit vom 26.3–17.8.43, NAM T–312/318.
73. "Die Organisation."
74. See *Velikaia Otechestvennaia Voina 1941–1945: Entsiklopediia* (The Great Patriotic War 1941–1945: Encyclopedia), (Moscow: "Sovetskaia entsiklopediia," 1985), p. 604.

75. Mulligan, pp.236–7.
76. Hinsley, pp.619–20.
77. *Ibid.*, p.624. Meanwhile, "Dora" and "Lucy" reportedly supplied information which reflected German intent to attack but which conflicted regarding the attack timing. For example, on 8 April Rado reported, "The differences between the German High Command and the army command have been settled by the decision to postpone until the beginning of May ... the attack on Kursk." Subsequently, on 20 April, Rado informed the Soviets that "Citadel has been temporarily postponed." Nine days later another message set the attack date at 12 June. Subsequent Soviet requests for clarification produced a long assessment of German intentions which Rado sent on 9 May, probably reflecting the 30 April report of the British. Throughout the process, Soviet intelligence repeatedly sought to verify the veracity and nature of Rado's sources. Read, Fisher, pp.156–7.

On 25 April 1943 GC and CS decrypted a "Comprehensive Appreciation for Zitadelle," (CX/MSS/2499/T14), signed by Generalfeldmarschall von Weichs, C-in-C Army Group South, and addressed to the Supreme Command of the Army, Operations Section and Intelligence Section Foreign Armies East. It read as follows:

In the main, the appreciation of the enemy remains the same reported in Army Group South II No 0477/43 of 29 March [The 29 March appreciation never became available in SIGINT] and in the supplementary appreciation of 15 April. The main concentration, which was already then apparent on the north flank of the Army Group in the general area Kursk–Sudzha–Welchansk–Ostrogoisk, can now be clearly recognized: a further intensification of this concentration is to be expected as a result of the continuous heavy transport movements on the lines Yelets–Kastornoye–Kursk, Povorino–Svoboda, and Gryazi–Svoboda, with a probable [increase] in the area Valuiki–Novy Oskol–Kupyansk. At present, however, it is not apparent whether the object of this concentration is offensive or defensive. At present, in anticipation of a German offensive on both the Kursk and Mius–Donets fronts, the armored and mobile formations are still evenly distributed in various groups behind the front as strategic reserves.

There are no signs as yet of a merging of these formations or a transfer to the forward area (except for II Guards Armored Corps), but this could take place rapidly at any time.

According to information from a sure source [German SIGINT], the existence of the following groups of the strategic reserve can be presumed:

Two cavalry corps – III and V Guards – in the area north of Novocherkassk. It can also be presumed that one mechanized corps – V Guards – is being brought up to strength here.

One mechanized corps – III Guards – in the area [north] of Rovenki.

One armored corps, one cavalry corps and probably two mechanized corps – I Guards Armored, IV Cavalry, probably [I] Guards Mechanized and V Mechanized – in the area north of Voroshilovgrad.

Two cavalry corps – [IV] Guards and VII Guards – in the area west of Starobyelsk.

One mechanized corps, one cavalry corps and two armored corps – I Guards [Mechanized], I Guards Cavalry, II and XXIII Armored – in the area Kupyansk–Svyatovo.

Three armored corps, and one mechanized corps – II Armoured, V Guards Armored, [XXIX] Armored and V Guards Mechanized under the command of an army (perhaps 5 Armored Army) – in the area of Ostrogoisk.

Two armored and one cavalry corps – II Guards Armored, III Guards Armored and VI Guards Cavalry – under the command of an unidentified headquarters, in the area north of Novy Oskol.

In the event of Zitadelle, there are at present approximately ninety enemy formations west of the line Belgorod–Kursk–Malo Arkhangelsk. The attack of the Army Group will encounter stubborn enemy resistance in a deeply echeloned and well-developed main defense zone (with numerous dug-in tanks, strong artillery and local reserves), the main effort of the defence being in the key sector Belgorod–Tomarovka. In addition, strong counterattacks by the strategic reserves from east and southeast are to be expected. It is impossible to forecast whether the enemy will attempt to withdraw from a threatened encirclement by retiring eastwards, as soon as the key sectors of the bulge in the front line at Kursk, Belgorod and Malo Arkhangelsk have been broken through. If the enemy throws all strategic reserves on the Army Group front into the Kursk battle, the following may appear on the battlefield:

On day 1 and day 2 – two armored divisions and one cavalry corps;
On day 3 – two mechanized and four armored corps;
On day 4 – one armored and one cavalry corps;
On day 5 – three mechanized corps;
On day 6 and/or day 7 – two cavalry corps.

Summarizing, it can be stated that the balance of evidence still points to a defensive attitude on the part of the enemy, and this is in fact unmistakable in the frontal sectors of 6 Army [Sixth Army was reformed in the spring of 1943, after Stalingrad] and I Pz Army. If the bringing up of further forces in the area before the north wing of the Army Group persists and if a transfer forward and merging of the mobile and armoured formations then takes place, offensive intentions become more probable. In that case, it is improbable that the enemy can even then forestall our execution of Zitadelle in the required conditions. On the other hand, we probably must assume complete enemy preparations for defense, including the counter-attacks of his strong motorized and armored forces, which must be expected.

From: F. M. Hinsley, *British Intelligence in the Second World War*, Vol. 2 (New York: Cambridge University Press, 1981).

78. *Ibid.*, p.626. Subsequent reports from the Swiss rings in May and June cast light on German attack intentions but not the precise location. A 31 May Rado message to Moscow contained a 7 May "Werther" report that Germans were concentrating "at Kursk, Viazma (and) Velikiye–Louki" to launch preventative assaults in several sectors of the front. A 23 May "Werther" report claimed on 20 May German attack preparations were complete, and the attack could begin on 1 June. Moscow requested clarification of this imprecise data. Among the responses was a 23 June Rado message that muddied the waters further. It stated: "Since 1st June, the Soviets have concentrated ... such a quantity of troops that the Germans no longer talk of superiority. Hitler on the other hand wishes to attack." See Read, Fisher, pp.168–9.

These reports, undocumented in the work that provides them, cast doubt on the utility of the information. Obviously there was a severe time lag in transmission of the information. More important, they confirmed little except general German attack intentions, which the Soviets already knew. Their confusing content was reminiscent of similar reports during earlier periods; by now, the Soviet High Command was too experienced to place much faith in them. Instead the Soviets relied on the more accurate data provided by their own, more reliable sources of *razvedka* data. For further confirmation of this view, see also Mulligan, pp.239–43.

79. *Ibid.*, p.627.
80. Muriev, Perezhogin, p.231.
81. *Voina v tylu vraga I v.* (War in the enemy rear, Part 1), (Moscow: Izdatel'stvo politicheskoi literatury, 1974), p.115.
82. Andrianov, p.47.
83. Zhukov, *Reminiscences*, Vol 2, p.147.
84. Andrianov, p.47.
85. *Ibid.*, p.48.
86. I. D. Nazarenko, ed., *Ukrainskaia SSR v Velikoi Otechestvennoi voine Sovetskogo soiuza 1941–1945 gg T-3* (Ukrainian SSR in the Great Patriotic War of the Soviet Union 1941–1945 Vol. 3), (Kiev: Izdatel'stvo politicheskoi literatury Ukrainy, 1975), p.250.
87. An example of German records of partisan order of battle is found in Abteilung Fremde Heere Ost (I/BD), *Vermutliche Bandengliederung zur Bandenlage Ost*, Stand 16.6.43, NAM T78/589.
88. V. Fedorenko, "Deistviia sovetskikh partizan v bitve pod Kurskom" (Operations of Soviet partisans in the battle of Kursk), *VIZh*, No. 7 (July 1968), 111.
89. *Ibid.*
90. *Ibid.*, 112.
91. *Ibid.*, 113; V. K. Gogoliuk, "Partizany brianshchiny" (Partisans of Briansk), *Kurskaia bitva* (The battle of Kursk), (Voronezh: Tsentral'no-chernozemnoe knizhnoe izdatel'stvo, 1982), pp.316–23. For German data, see A.O.K.2 Ia *Chefkarten vom 1.4.43–30.5.43*, NAM T–313/71.
92. Vasilevsky, p.210.
93. K. Rokossovsky, *A Soldier's Duty* (Moscow: Progress Publishers, 1985), p.192.
94. Fedorenko, p.114.
95. Andrianov, p.46.
96. M. Absaliamov, V. Andrianov, "Taktika sovetskikh partizan" (Tactics of Soviet partisans), *VIZh*, No. 1 (Jan. 1968), 50.
97. Griankin, Zmievsky, 84; A. Paly, "Radioelektronnaia bor'ba v khode-voiny" (Radio-electronic struggle during war), *VIZh*, No. 5 (May 1977), 12.
98. Mulligan, p.250, citing 11. Panzerdivision/Abt. Ic, "Beutepapierauswertung," 14 July 1943, NAM T-314/1174; OKH/Chef des Generalstabes/Chef Heeresnachrichtenwesten (HNW) IV, "Funkdisziplin," 28 Sept. 1943, NAM T-311/84; OKH/Chef HNW 1, "Funkblatt Nr. 6," 15 Nov. 1943, T-78/204; and Oberbefehlshaber West/Ia, Ic, Nachr, Führer, "Sonderanordnung des OB West Nr. 20 für das Nachrichtenwesen: 'Die Abhörgefahr'," 29 Feb. 1944, in Wilhelm von Schramm, *Verrat im Zweiten Weltkrieg: Vom Kampf der Geheimdienste in Europa, Berichte und Dokumentation* (Düsseldorf/Vienna 1967).
99. Paly, p.13.
100. *Ibid.*, pp.13–4.
101. Hinsley, Vol. 2, p.65.
102. Mulligan, 249, citing XXX. AK/Korpsnachrichtenführer, "Geheimhaltung-Tarnung der Nachrichtenübermittlung," 18 Sept. 1942, NAM T-315/1530.
103. Viazankin, p.28.
104. Koltunov, Solov'ev, p.69.
105. K. S. Moskalenko, *Na iugo-zapadnom napravlenii 1943–1945* (On the south-western direction 1943–1945), (Moscow: "Nauka," 1972), p.38.
106. *Ibid.*
107. *Ibid.*, p.39.
108. *Ibid.*, p.40.
109. *Ibid.*
110. *Ibid.*
111. Batov, p.287.
112. *Razvedka v boevykh primerakh (Velikaia Otechestvennai voina 1941–1945 gg. i*

poslevoennyi period) (*Razvedka* in combat examples (The Great Patriotic War 1941–1945 and the post-war period)), (Moscow: Voenizdat, 1972), p.301. Hereafter cited as *Razvedka*.

113. "Organizatsiia i planirovanie kontrapodgotovki" (Organizing and planning a counterpreparation), *Sbornik materialov No. 9*, p.48.
114. *Razvedka*, p.187.
115. *Sbornik materialov No. 9*, p.47.
116. *Razvedka*, p.188.
117. *Sbornik materialov No. 9*, p.48.
118. Konev, p.18.
119. A. Domank, *Na ognevykh rubezhakh: Artilleristy v Kurskoi bitve* (On the firing lines: Artillerymen in the battle of Kursk), (Voronezh: Tsentral'nochernozemnoe knizhnoe izdatel'stvo, 1984), p.15.
120. *Ibid.*, pp.15–16.
121. A. S. Domank, S. P. Lazutkin, *Reserva Verkhovnogo Glavno-komandovaniia* (The Reserve of the Supreme High Command), (Moscow: Voenizdat, 1987), p.39.
122. Navysev, p.132; G. Peredel'skii, G. Khoroshilov, "Bor'ba s artilleriei protovnika" (Struggle with enemy artillery), *VIZh*, No. 6 (June 1978), 21.
123. Domank, Lazutkin, p.15.
124. Peredel'skii, G. Khoroshikov, p.21.
125. G. E. Peredel'skii, A. I. Tolmakov, G. T. Khoroshilov, *Artilleriia v boiu i operatsii* (Artillery in battle and operations), (Moscow: Voenizdat, 1980), p.75.
126. Navysev, p.133.
127. Domank, Lazutkin, p.40.
128. *Ibid.*, pp.45–6.
129. Domank, pp.15–16.
130. E. Kolibernov, "Inzhenernoe obespechenie proryva oborony protivnika po opytu voiny" (Engineer support in the penetration of an enemy defense based on war experience), *VIZh*, No. 8 (Aug. 1980), 44–5.
131. "Inzhenernoe obespechenie armeiskoi nastupatel'noi operatsii" (Engineer support of an army offensive operation), *Sbornik materialov No. 9*, p.125.
132. Aganov, p.322.
133. *Ibid.*, p.323.
134. *Ibid.*
135. *Ibid.*
136. *Ibid.*, p.325.
137. *Razvedka*, pp.188–9.
138. *Ibid.*, p.190.
139. *Ibid.*, p.191.
140. "Podgotovka k Kurskoi bitve," p.64.
141. Shtemenko, p.216.
142. "Podgotovka k Kurskoi bitve," pp.64–5.
143. *Ibid.*, pp.65–6.
144. *Ibid.*, p.67.
145. Mulligan, p.237.
146. Zhukov, *Reminiscences*, Vol. 2, p.166.
147. "Podgotovka k Kurskoi bitve," p.67.
148. Hinsley, Vol. 2, p.624.
149. German positions and movements on 27 April taken from PzAOK 2, Ia, *Anlagenband 38 zum KTB*, Lage am 27.4.43–30.4.43 abends. NAM T-313/171; Pz AOK4, Ia, *Lagenkarte 4.Pz. Armee*, Stand 27.4.43.2200 NAM T-313/369; PzAOK1, Ia *Lagenkarten*, Lage 27.4.43 NAM T-313/60.
150. German dispositions on 1 May derived from PzAOK 2, Ia, Anlagenband 38 zum KTB, Lage am 1.5.43–4.5.43 abends NAM T-313/171; PzAOK 1, Ia *Lagenkarten*,

Lage 1.5.43 NAM T-313/60; PzAOK 4, Ia, *Lagenkarte 4. Pz. Armee*, Stand 1.5.43, NAM T-313/369.

151. Shtemenko, p.232.
152. K. Moskalenko, "The Voronezh Front in the Battle of Kursk," *The Battle of Kursk*, p.99.
153. Shtemenko, p.231.
154. "Podgotovka k Kurskoi bitve," p.69.
155. Vasilevsky, p.271.
156. German situation on 24 May derived from PzAOK 2 Ia, Chefkarten, *Anlagenband 36 zum KTB*, Lage am 24.5.43–27.5.43 abends, NAM T-313/171; PzAOK 4, Ia, *Lagenkarte 4. Pz. Armee*, Stand 27.4.43 2200, NAM T-313/369; PzAOK 1, Ia, *Lagenkarten*, Lage 24.5.43, NAM T-313/60.
157. G. Zhukov, "In the Kursk bulge," *The Battle of Kursk*, pp.36–7.
158. Mulligan, p.239.
159. Shtemenko, p.232.
160. Mulligan, p.239.
161. Shtemenko, p.233.
162. German positions on 6 June taken from AOK 9, Ia, *Anlage zu KTB*, Lage vom 23.5.43–16:6.43 früh NAM T-312/295; PzAOK 4, Ia, *Lagenkarte 4. Pz. Armee*, Stand 6.6.43 2200 NAM T-313/369; Pz AOK 1, Ia, *Lagenkarten*, Lage 6.6.43 NAM T-313/60.
163. Vasilevsky, p.272.
164. German positions on 16 June taken from AOK 9, Ia, *Anlage zum KTB*, Lage vom 23.5.–16.6.43 früh NAM T-312/395; PzAOK 4, Ia, *Lagenkarte 4. Pz. Armee*, Stand. 16.6.43, 2200, NAM T-313/369; PzAOK 1, Ia, *Lagenkarten*, Lage 16.6.43, NAM T-313/60. Movement of 3d and 19th Panzer Divisions took at least four nights to complete. While they moved, 17th Panzer Division conducted daytime movements to confuse Soviet intelligence. See Panzerarmee-Oberkommando 1, *Abt, Ia Nr. 73/43 g. K.* Chefs, dated 5 June 1943 NAM T-313/60.
165. Mulligan, p.239.
166. *Ibid.*
167. German movements and dispositions from 29 June through 1 July taken from AOK 9, Ia, *Anlage zum KTB*, Lage vom 17.6–4.7.43 früh, NAM T-312/295/304; PzAOK 4, Ia, *Lagenkarte 4 Pz. Armee*, Stand 29.6.43–1.7.43 2200, NAM T-313/369; PzAOK 1, Ia, *Lagenkarten*, Lage 29.6.43–1.7.43, NAM T-313/60.
168. Zhukov, *Reminiscences*, Vol. 2, p.176.
169. German dispositions from 2–4 July taken from AOK 9, Ia, *Anlage zum KTB*, Lage vom 17.6–4.7.43, früh, NAM T-312/304; PzAOK 4, Ia, *Lagenkarte 4. Pz. Armee*, Stand 2–4.7.43 2200, NAM T-313/369; PzAOK 1, Ia, *Lagenkarte*, Lage 2–4.7.43, NAM T-313/60.
170. Moskalenko, *Na iugo-zapadnom*, pp.51–2.
171. A. Konenenko, "Voprosy voennogo iskusstva v bitve pod Kurskom" (Questions of military art in the battle of Kursk), *VIZh*, No. 4 (April 1964), 116.
172. M. E. Katukov, *Na ostrie glavnogo udara* (At the point of the main effort), (Moscow: Voenizdat, 1976), p.211.
173. From "Orders pertaining to the 'Zitadelle' offensive, 1 May–31 August 1943," PzAOK 1, 44652/6, *Chefsachenanlagen zum KTB Nr. 11. PzAOK 1. Ia*, NAM T-313/60.
174. *Ibid.*
175. For example, see S. P. Ivanov, "Zavershenie korennogo pereloma v voine" (Completion of a fundamental turning point in the war), *VIZh*, No. 6 (June 1983), 16.
176. Soviet unit locations based on Koltunov, Solov'ev, pp.55–6; Vasilevsky, pp.264, 267, 268; A. S. Zhadov, *Chetyre goda voiny* (Four years of war), (Moscow: Voenizdat, 1978), pp.84–91 (5th Guards Army); A. M. Zvartsev, *3-ia gvardeis-*

NOTES

kaia tankovaia (3d Guards Tank), (Moscow: Voenizdat, 1982), pp.61–69; P. A. Rotmistrov, *Stal'naia gvardiia* (Steel guards), (Moscow: Voenizdat, 1984), pp.171–81 (5th Guards Tank Army); I. M. Managarov, *V srazhenii za Khar'kov* (In the battle of Khar'kov), (Khar'kov: "Prapor," 1978), pp.50–5 (53d Army); I. F. Vorontsov, N. I. Biriukov, A. F. Smekalev, *Ot volzhskikh steppei do avstriiskikh al'p* (From the Volga steppes to the Austrian Alps), (Moscow: Voenizdat, 1971), pp.26–8 (4th Guards Army); V. P. Istomin, *Smolenskaia nastupatel'naia operatsiia* (The Smolensk offensive operation), (Moscow: Voenizdat, 1975), pp.6–18; V. I. Chuikov, *Gvardeitsy stalingrada idut na zapad* (Stalingrad guardsmen advance to the west), (Moscow: Izdatel'stvo "Sovetskaia rossiia," 1972), pp.52–62 (8th Guards Army); "Dvenadtsataia armiia" (12th Army), *SVE*, 2:112. These locations have been verified by ex post facto German intelligence maps. Soviet personnel strengths in various sectors taken from B. G. Solev'ev, ed., *Istoriia vtoroi mirovoi voiny 1939–1945 T-7* (History of the Second World War 1939–1945, Vol. 7), (Moscow: Voenizdat, 1976), pp.114, 120, 140, 159, 172, 194, 221, 241. Consideration has been made for armies which shifted sectors during the operations, e.g. 37th Army.

177. Field Marshal Erich von Manstein, *Lost Victories* (Chicago: Henry Regnery Co., 1958), p.444. For contemporary German order of battle assessments of Soviet forces, see Fremde Heere Ost (11c), *Übersicht über Streitkräfte, Fronten, Armeen und Korps der Roten Armee*. Gliederung am 4.4.43, 14.4.43, 24.4.43, 4.5.43, 14.5.43, 24.5.43, 3.6.43, 13.6.43, 23.6.43, 3.7.43, 13.7.43, 23.7.43. NAM T-78/588.
178. P. Ia. Egorov, I. V. Krivoborskii, I. K. Ivlev, A. I. Rogalevich, *Dorogami pobed: boevoi put' 5-i gvardeiskoi tankovoi armii* (Roads of victory: the combat path of 5th Guards Tank Army), (Moscow: Voenizdat, 1969), pp.23–6.
179. "Podgotovka k Kurskoi bitve," p.71.
180. V. I. Chuikov, *Ot Stalingrada do Berlina* (From Stalingrad to Berlin), (Moscow: Voenizdat, 1980), p.347.
181. Chuikov, *Gvardeitsy stalingrada*, p.66.
182. A. Kh. Babadzhanian, N. K. Popel', M. A. Shalin, I. M. Kravchenko, *Liuki otkryli v Berline: boevoi put' 1-i gvardeiskoi tankovoi armii* (They opened the hatchway to Berlin: the combat path of 1st Guards Tank Army), (Moscow: Voenizdat, 1973), pp.82–7.

CHAPTER SEVEN

1. Glantz, *Soviet Military Deception in the Second World War* (London: Frank Cass, 1989), pp.292–467.
2. *Polevoi ustav Krasnoi Armii* (Field regulation of the Red Army), (Moscow: Voenizdat, 1944). Translated by JPRS (JPRS-UMA-PS-006), 17 Jan. 1985. Hereafter cited as *Polevoi ustav 1944*.
3. *Ibid.*, p.34.
4. *Ibid.*, p.35.
5. *Ibid.*
6. *Ibid.*; information confirmed in *Auszug aus der Übersetzung der Dienstvorschrift über das Zusammenwirken der Fliegertruppe mit den Erdtruppen* (Extract from Translation of Soviet Service Regulation Concerning Cooperation Between Air and Ground Forces) from Detailed Report No. 34, 5 Sept. 44, of German *Fremde Heere Ost*. Translated by the Directorate of Military Intelligence, AHQ, Ottawa, Canada, 1952. See also, translation of captured German document on "Breakthrough and Pursuit" prepared in 1944 and translated in 1951 which critiqued Soviet air reconnaissance, stating:

405

Flawless air-photo-reconnaissance (1:5,000–1:10,000), supplemented by engineer and artillery reconnaissance, was required to permit map distribution 5 days before the attack. Observation was carried out according to a detailed army plan. Its mission was to detect last-minute changes in enemy positions in order to correct or supplement maps of the enemy defense system.

7. The 1944 Regulation sketched out the following *razvedka* forces, missions, and ranges:

105. Units (soyedineniye and chast') conduct ground reconnaissance with reconnaissance detachments, separate reconnaissance groups, separate reconnaissance patrols, separate mounted patrols and dismounted reconnaissance subunits.

106. A reconnaissance detachment is formed from reconnaissance, rifle (motorized rifle), ski and cavalry subunits from company (troop) to battalion (cavalry regiment) in strength, reinforced by artillery, tanks (armored cars), engineer subunits and chemical defense subunits.

The separate reconnaissance group is up to a company of tanks (armored cars) reinforced by motorized infantry subunits, motorcycles and other assets.

The separate reconnaissance patrol is from a squad to a platoon of infantry or, in the tanks troops, a platoon of tanks (armored cars), reinforced by motorized infantry and motorcycles.

The separate mounted patrol is from a cavalry platoon to a troop.

Dismounted reconnaissance subunits are dispatched when there is immediate contact with the enemy, primarily for raids, with a strength of from a squad to a company (one or two reinforced troops).

107. A reconnaissance detachment receives a zone for reconnaissance and conducts reconnaissance by sending out reconnaissance patrols (mounted patrols), with the strength of the patrol (mounted patrol) being from a squad (section) to a platoon. The width of a reconnaissance zone is determined by the mission, strength and composition of the detachment, the road network and nature of the terrain; it averages from 3 to 8km.

A separate reconnaissance group, patrols and mounted patrols receive axes and objectives for reconnaissance.

108. The distance of reconnaissance subunits from the unit (soyedineniye) main body is determined by the reconnaissance mission and by the strength and composition of the subunits being dispatched, and it can reach:

Up to 8–10km for a reconnaissance detachment and up to 25–30km for a motorized detachment;

Up to 10–15km for a separate reconnaissance group, separate mounted patrol and separate reconnaissance patrol (motorized);

Up to 1–3km for mounted reconnaissance patrols and reconnaissance patrols sent out from a reconnaissance detachment.

109. Reconnaissance subunits penetrate the enemy reconnaissance and security zone and gather information about his forces. They attempt to capture small enemy groups while avoiding combat with his large forces.

8. *Polevoi ustav–1944*, p.37.
9. *Ibid.*, p.38.
10. Popel, *et. al.*, p.84.
11. *Ibid.*, p.85.
12. Chikin, p.58.
13. E. Simakov, "Boevoi i chislennyi sostav VVS v tret'em periode voiny" (Combat and numerical composition of the Soviet Air Force in the third period of war), *VIZh*, No. 7 (July 1975), 75–7.

14. Timokhovich, p.122.
15. *Ibid.*, p.125.
16. "Schwerpunkte des Sowj. Agenteneinsatzes im Operationsgebiet Ost. Dezember 1943" (Centers of Gravity of Soviet Agent Operations in the Eastern Operational Area, December 1943), *Abteilung Fremde Heere Ost* (I) Amt Russland--Abwehr Abwehrabteilung III, Walli III, NAM T-78/582.
17. "The Role of the Partisans in Soviet Intelligence" HRRI Project "War Documentation Project" Research Study No. 6 Vol. 1 (Air Research and Development Command, Human Resources Research Institute, Maxwell Air Force Base, Alabama, Jan. 1954), confidential, declassified 1959, p.41.
18. T. Vorontsov, "Organizatsiia i vedenie razvedki v 4-i gvardeiskoi armii v Umansko-Botoshanskoi operatsii" (The organization and conduct of *razvedka* in 4th Guards Army in the Uman'-Botoshany operation), *VIZh*, No. 5 (May 1971), 22–30.
19. Chikin, p.56.
20. *Ibid.*
21. *The German G-2 Service in the Russia Campaign (IC Dienst Ost)* (Washington, D.C.: Military Intelligence Division, War Department, 22 July 1945), p.203.
22. Viazankin, 34.
23. G. K. Zhukov, *The Memoirs of Marshal Zhukov* (New York: Delacorte Press, 1971), p.556.
24. A. M. Shtemenko, *General'nyi shtab v gody voiny* (The General staff in the war years), (Moscow: Voenizdat, 1981), Vol. 1, p.379.
25. Zhukov, p.560.
26. Shtemenko, p.381.
27. Zhukov, p.558.
28. *Ibid.*, p.561; *front* missions delineated in N. A. Svetlishin, "Vislo-oderskaia operatsiia 1945" (The Vistula-Oder operation 1945), *SVE*, 2, 147–8.
29. Svetlishin, 148.
30. B. Petrov, "O nekotorykh tendentsiiakh v sozdanii i ispol'zovanii udarnykh gruppirovok po opytu frontovykh nastupatel'nykh operatsii Velikoi Otechestvennoi voiny" (Concerning some tendencies in the creation and use of shock groups based on the experience of *front* offensive operations of the Great Patriotic War), *VIZh*, No. 11 (Nov. 1983), 14.
31. For further details, see Glantz, *Soviet Military Deception.*
32. I. Konev, *Years of Victory* (Moscow: Progress Publishers, 1984), p.16. A good translation of *God pobedy* (Year of Victory), (Moscow: Voenizdat, 1966).
33. A. I. Radzievsky, ed., *Armeiskie operatsii* (Army operations), (Moscow: Voenizdat, 1977), pp.147–9.
34. V. A. Matsulenko, *Operativnaia maskirovka voisk* (Operational *maskirovka* of forces), (Moscow: Voenizdat, 1975), translation by U. S. Army Foreign Science and Technology Center, Charlottesville, VA., 1977, p.151.
35. Shtemenko, p.378.
36. *Ibid.*, p.382.
37. Popel', *et. al.*, p.81.
38. Shtemenko, pp.385–6.
39. R. Simonian, "Razvedka v interesakh podgotovki i vedeniia frontovoi nastupatel'noi operatsii" (*Razvedka* in the interests of preparing and conducting a *front* offensive operation), *VIZh*, No. 12 (Dec. 1977), 11.
40. *Ibid.*
41. *Ibid.*
42. *Ibid.*, p.12.
43. Zhukov, p.559.
44. K. S. Moskalenko, *Na iugo-zapadnom napravlenii 1943–1945* (On the southwestern direction 1943–1945), (Moscow: "Nauka," 1973), p.506.

45. I. A. Samchuk, P. G. Skachko, Iu. N. Babikov, I. L. Gnedoi, *Ot Volgi do El' by i Pragi* (From the Volga to the Elbe and Prague), (Moscow: Voenizdat, 1970), pp.216–17.

46. S. I. Blinov, *Ot Visly do Odera* (From the Vistula to the Oder), (Moscow: Voenizdat, 1962), p.37.

47. M. M. Kir'ian, *S sandomirskogo platsdarma* (From the Sandomierz bridgehead), (Moscow: Voenizdat, 1960), p.71.

48. *Ibid.*, p.72.

49. Timokhovich, p.123.

50. S. Krasovsky, "Sovetskaia aviatsiia v boiakh za osvobozhdenie Pol'shi" (Soviet aviation in battles for the liberation of Poland), *VIZh*, No. 1 (Jan. 1965), 15; Simakov, 77.

51. S. I. Rudenko, *Kryl' ia pobedy* (Wings of Victory), (Moscow: "Mezhdurnarodnye otnosheniia," 1985), p.254.

52. A. Efimov, "Primenenie aviatsii pri vedenii operatsii v vysokikh tempakh i na bol'shuiu glubinu" (The use of aviation in conducting an operation at high tempos and at great depths), *VIZh*, No. 1 (Jan. 1985), 23.

53. Simonian, "Razvedka v interesakh," 12–13.

54. Efimov, 244; Rudenko, p.255.

55. Rudenko, p.255.

56. *Ibid.*

57. *Ibid.*

58. *Ibid.*, p.256.

59. I. Korotchenko, *Razvedka* (Intelligence), *VIZh*, No. 3 (March 1982), 30.

60. *Ibid.*

61. Efimov, 34; Kir'ian, *S sandomirskogo platsdarma*, p.47.

62. A. S. Zhadov, *Chetyre goda voiny* (Four years of war), (Moscow: Voenizdat, 1978), p.220.

63. V. I. Chuikov, *Ot Stalingrada do Berlina* (From Stalingrad to Berlin), (Moscow: Voenizdat, 1980), p.503.

64. *Ibid.*, p.504.

65. F. L Kurlat, L. A. Studnikov, "Brigada osobogo naznacheniia" (Special designation brigade), *Voprosy istorii* (Questions of history), No. 9 (Sept. 1982), 103.

66. *Ibid.*

67. *Tätigkeitsbericht des General des Transportwesens*, H.Gr.A. Vom 1. Nov. bis 31 Dez. 1944. NAM T-311/274.

68. *Einsatz sowj. Kundschaftergruppen nach s. Qu 1.11.–20.11.44* Anlage 2 zu Abt. Frd. H. Ost (I) Nr. 4404/44 GKdos v. 5.12.44. NAM T-78/582.

69. *Tätigkeitsbericht des General des Transportwesens*, ObKdo. Heeresgruppe Mitte Abt III. für die Zeit vom 1.–31.12.1944..28.1.1945. NAM T-78/582.

70. *Ansatz sowj. kundschaftergruppen 1.12.44–4.1.45*. Anlage 3 zu Abt. Frd. H. Ost (I) Nr. 81/45 gKdos v 5.1.45. NAM T-78/582.

71. Palyi, p.16.

72. Simonian, "Razvedka v interesahk," 13.

73. Popel', *et al.*, p.81.

74. Simonian, "Razvedka v interesakh," 13.

75. G. I. Khetagurov, *Ispolnenie dolga* (Fulfillment of duties), (Moscow: Voenizdat, 1977), p.157.

76. V. A. Beliavsky, *Strely skrestilis' na shpree* (Arrows cross the Spree), (Moscow: Voenizdat, 1973), p.228.

77. Kir'ian, *S sandomirskogo platsdarma*, p.93.

78. A. I. Radzievsky, ed., *Taktika v boevykh primerakh (diviziia)* (Tactics in combat examples (division)), (Moscow: Voenizdat, 1976), p.46.

79. *Ibid.*

80. *Ibid.*, p.57.

NOTES

81. Korotchenko, p.30.
82. V. S. Antonov, *Put' k Berlinu* (The path to Berlin), (Moscow: "Nauka," 1975), p.193.
83. S. Alferov, "Iz opyta proryva oborony strelkovym korpusom" (From the experience of penetrating defenses by a rifle corps), *VIZh*, No. 3 (March 1983), 51.
84. A. F. Malenkov, *Ot Rigi do Berlina* (From Riga to Berlin), (Riga: "Avots," 1985), p.36.
85. For details on commanders' personal reconnaissance, see V. P. Krukunov, "Iz opyta raboty komanduiushchikh i shtabov armii na mestnosti" (From the experience of work of army commanders and staffs on the terrain), *VIZh*, No. 7 (July 1987), 21–8.
86. Konev, p.9.
87. Radzievsky, *Taktika*, p.36.
88. Antonov, p.197.
89. *Ibid.*, pp.192–3.
90. Chikin, pp.55–6.
91. Viazankin, p.34.
92. *Ibid.*
93. *Ibid.*, pp.36–7.
94. Konev, pp.17–18.
95. Viazankin, p.35; Chuikov, p.510.
96. Alferov, p.54.
97. I. P. Roslyi, *Poslednii prival – v Berline* (The last halt – in Berlin), (Moscow: Voenizdat, 1983), p.239.
98. M. Sidorov, "Ognevoe porazhenie pri proryve oborony protivnika po opytu Velikoi Otechestvennoi voiny" (Fire strikes during the penetration of an enemy defense based on the experience of the Great Patriotic War), *VIZh*, No. 8 (Aug. 1984), 19.
99. Chikin, pp.56–7.
100. A. S. Domank, S. P. Lazutkin, *Rezerva Verkhovnogo Glavno-komandovaniia* (Of the reserve of the Supreme High Command), (Moscow: Voenizdat, 1987), p.131; G. F. Biriukov, "Opyt upravleniia ognem artilleriiskikh grupp v nastupatel'nykh operatsiiakh Velikoi Otechestvennoi voiny" (Experience in control of fires of artillery groups in offensive operations of the Great Patriotic War), *VIZh*, No. 5 (May 1986), 41.
101. Kir'ian, *S sandomerskogo platsdarma*, p.46.
102. Malenkov, p.46.
103. Simonian, "Razvedka v interesakh," 12, states that 1st Belorussian Front possessed 11 artillery instrumental *razvedka* (AIR) battalions.
104. Kolibernov, "Inzhenernoe obespechenie," 45.
105. Aganov, p.387.
106. A. Tsirlin, "Nekotorye voprosy inzhenernogo obespecheniia armeiskoi nastupatel'noi" (Some questions concerning engineer protection of an army offensive operation), *VIZh*, No. 12 (Dec. 1976), 36.
107. V. Kharchenko, "Inzhenernye voiska" (Engineer forces), *VIZh*, No. 4 (April 1975), 72.
108. Kir'ian, *S sandomirskogo platsdarma*, p.59.
109. Blinev, pp.37–8.
110. Tsirlin, "Nekotorye voprosy," 36.
111. A. D. Tsirlin, P. I. Buriukov, V. P. Istomin, E. N. Fedoseev, *Inzhenernye voiska v boiakh za sovetskuiu rodinu* (Engineer forces in battles for the Soviet homeland), (Moscow: Voenizdat, 1970), p.291.
112. *Ibid.*
113. E. Kolibernov, "Kharakternye osobennosti inzhenernogo obespecheniia voisk frontov v Vislo–Oderskoi operatsii" (Characteristic features of engineer support

of front forces in the Vistula–Oder operation), *VIZh*, No. 1 (Jan. 1985), 40.

114. Simonian, "Razvedka v interesakh," 12.
115. Rudenko, p.257.
116. Chuikov, p.505.
117. Efimov, 24.
118. M. N. Kozhevnikov, *Komandovanie i shtab VVS Sovetskoi Armii v Velikoi Otechestvennoi voine 1941–1945 gg.* (The command and staff of the Soviet Army Air Force in the Great Patriotic War 1941–1945), (Moscow: "Nauka," 1977), p.195.
119. Simonian, "Razvedka v interesakh," 13.
120. Popel' *et al.*, p.81.
121. Korotchenko, p.31.
122. *The German G-2 Service in the Russian Campaign*, p.38.
123. Simonian, "Razvedka v interesakh," 13.
124. Moskalenko, p.512.
125. Alferov, p.51.
126. M. Kh. Kalashik, *Ispytanie ognem* (Ordeal by Fire), (Moscow: "Mysl," 1985), p.327.
127. Viazankin, p.33.
128. Simonian, "Razvedka v interesakh," 13.
129. *Ibid.*, 14.
130. Kir'ian, *S sandomirskogo platsdarma*, p.73.
131. Blinov, p.38.
132. Kolibernov, "Inzhenernoe obespechenie," 45–6.
133. Shtemenko, p.382.
134. Antonov, pp.182–3. Confirmed by copy of original order in author's possession.
135. Alferov, pp.51–2.
136. Zhadov, 227; Samchuk, *et al.*, p.217.
137. Simonian, "Razvedka v interesakh," 14.
138. *Ibid.*
139. *Razvedka v boevykh primerakh (Velikaia Otechestvennaia voina 1941–1945 gg. i poslevoennyi period)* (*Razvedka* in combat examples (The Great Patriotic War 1941–1945 and the postwar period)), (Moscow: Voenizdat, 1972), p.73.
140. *Ibid.*, p.74.
141. *Ibid.*, p.76.
142. N. Kireev, "Presledovanie protivnika soedineniiami i ob'edineniiami bronetankovykh voisk" (Pursuit of the enemy by formations and large formations of armored forces), *VIZh*, No. 6 (June 1977), 83.
143. Kolibernov, "Inzhenernoe obespechenie," 41.
144. Simonian, "Razvedka v interesakh," 15.
145. *Ibid.*
146. *Ibid.*
147. *Ibid.*
148. *Ibid.*
149. *Ibid.*, 16.
150. *Ibid.*, 17.
151. *Ibid.*
152. M. Radugin, "Initsiativnye deistviia v razvedke" (Initiative actions in reconnaissance), *VIZh*, No. 2 (Feb. 1976), 61–4.
153. Simonian, "Razvedka v interesakh," 15–16.
154. *Ibid.*, 16.
155. Rudenko, p.258.
156. Krasovsky, p.21.
157. Rudenko, p.259.
158. V. Fedorenko, "Opyt presledovaniia protivnika soedineniiami bronetankovykh

voisk" (Experience in the pursuit of the enemy by formations of armored forces), *VIZh*, No. 8 (Aug. 1963), 33.

159. *Sovetskie voenno-vozdushnye sily v Velikoi Otechestvennoi voine 1941–1945 gg.* (The Soviet Air Force in the Great Patriotic War 1941–1945), (Moscow: Voenizdat, 1968), pp.369–70.

160. *Ibid.*, p.374.

161. *Ibid.*, p.375.

162. Fedorov, p.92.

163. *Ibid.*

164. *Sovetskie voenno-vozdushnye*, p.378.

165. Konev, p.34.

166. Zhukov, pp.565–6.

167. Rudenko, p.300.

168. *Ibid.*, p.301.

169. *Sovetskie voenno-vozdushnye*, p.382.

170. Antonov, pp.182–3.

171. OKH *Lage Ost*, Stand. 11–12.1.45 abds. (original).

172. *Ibid.*

173. "Fremde Heere Ost (I) No. 81/45 SECRET, Estimate of the Overall Enemy Situation: 5 Jan. 1945," *The German G-2 Service in the Russian Campaign* (Ic-Dienst Ost) (United States Army, 22 July 1945), Appendix A, p.181. Hereafter cited as Fremde Heere Ost (I) No. 81/45.

174. *Ibid.*

175. *Ibid.*, H. van Nes, "German Intelligence Appreciation – The Vistula–Oder Operation," *A Transcript of Proceedings 1986 Art of War Symposium, From the Vistula to the Oder: Soviet Offensive Operations – October 1944–March 1945* (Carlisle Barracks, PA: Center for Land Warfare, 1986), p.492.

176. *Ibid.*

177. Fremde Heere Ost (I) No. 81/45, pp.182–3.

178. O.K.H. *Lage Ost*, Stand:11–12.1.45 abds; Hgr A, *Gen StdH/Op Abt 111b.* Stand:11–12.1.45 abds. (original).

179. *Ibid.*

180. Simonian, "Razvedka v interesakh," 18.

181. *Ibid.*

182. *Ibid.*

CHAPTER EIGHT

1. V. A. Kiselev, "Pokhodnyi poriadok" (March formation), *SVE*, 6:482.

2. N. N. Znobin, E. V. Ivanov, "Razvedyvatel'nyi otriad" (Reconnaissance detachment), *SVE*, 7:39.

3. "Razvedyvatel'nyi dozor" (Reconnaissance patrol), *SVE*, 7:38–9.

4. V. I. Beliakov, "Avangard" (Advance guard), *SVE*, 1:12–13.

5. "Golovnaia pokhodnaia zastava" (Advance party), *SVE*, 2:592–3.

6. "Bokovaia pokhodnaia zastava" (Flank party), *SVE*, 1:548; "Tylovaia pokhodnaia zastava" (Rear party), *SVE*, 8:158.

7. "Otriad obespecheniia dvizheniia" (Movement support detachment), *SVE*, 6:169–70.

8. "Khimicheskii razvedyvatel'nyi dozor" (Chemical reconnaissance patrol), *SVE*, 8:374.

9. "Storozhevoi otriad" (Outpost detachment), *SVE*, 7:547.

10. V. G. Reznichenko, G. D. Ionin, N. K. Grishkov, A. N. Tiunaev, "Boevoi poriadok" (Combat formation), *SVE*, 1:530.

11. *Ibid.*

12. "Obkhodiashchii otriad" (Enveloping detachment), *SVE*, 6:676.
13. V. A. Bulatnikov, E. D. Grebish, N. N. Fomin, M. M. Kholodov, "Desant" (Desant), *SVE*, 3:152.
14. *Ibid.*
15. "Podvizhnyi otriad zagrazhdenii" (Mobile obstacle detachment), *SVE*, 6:374.
16. *FM 100–2–3, Soviet Army Troops Organization and Equipment* (Washington, D.C.: Headquarters, Department of the Army, 16 July 1984), 4–67. Hereafter cited as *FM 100–2–3*.
17. *Ibid.*, 4–15. Depth of troop *razvedka* at division and regimental level varies with a number of circumstances. Soviet sources underscore the increased reach of artillery and depth of battle and state: "Therefore the forces of *razvedka* now must be directed at revealing important enemy objectives throughout the entire tactical and close operational depth of the defense in the sector of the forthcoming offense." By definition, this means from 40 to about 100 kilometers deep. See O. Kulishev, "Sovershenstvovanie sposobov vedeniia voiskovoi razvedki" (Perfecting the means for conducting troop *razvedka*), *VIZh*, No. 6 (June 1980), 33.
18. R. G. Simonian, "Razvedka boem" (Reconnaissance in force), *SVE*, 7:30–4.
19. "Artilleriiskaia razvedka" (Artillery *razvedka*), *SVE*, 1:267.
20. *Ibid.*, 268. See also "Artilleriiskaia instrumental'naia razvedka" (Artillery instrumental *razvedka*), *SVE*, 1:265. The Soviets employed artillery instrumental *razvedka* extensively beginning in late 1942. By that time, they were able to detect accurately well over 50 percent of existing targets in the depth of enemy tactical defenses. See D. M. Glantz, *Soviet Operational Intelligence (Razvedka) to 1943* (Ft. Leavenworth, KS: Soviet Army Studies Office, 1988).
21. *FM 100–2–3*, 4–47, 4–55.
22. Z. Czarnotta, "Integration of Reconnaissance and Fire," *Przeglad Wojsk Ladomwych* (Ground Forces Review), No. 5 (May 1987), 16–26. Translated by Dr. Harry Orenstein, SASO.
23. "Inzhenernaia razvedka" (Engineer *razvedka*), *SVE*, 4:536. See also E. S. Kolibernov, V. I. Kornev, A. A. Soskov, *Inzhenernoe obespechenie boia* (Engineer protection of combat), (Moscow: Voenizdat, 1988), 49–55, for an expanded version of the missions of engineer *razvedka* and for the details which follow on the nature, composition, and missions of engineer *razvedka* organs.
24. *FM 100–2–3*, 4–70, 4–15, 4–17.
25. "Radiatsionnaia i khimicheskaia razvedka" (Radiation and chemical *razvedka*), *SVE*, 6:663.
26. *FM 100–2–3*, 4–67, 4–19, 4–118.
27. M. M. Danilevsky, "Vozdushnaia razvedka" (Air *razvedka*), *SVE*, 2:282.
28. M. M. Danilevsky, "Razvedyvatel'naia aviatsiia (RA)F" (Reconnaissance aviation (RA)), *SVE*, 7:35.
29. Danilevsky, "Vozdushnaia," 283. For Soviet success with aerial photography and the systems they employed, see D. M. Glantz, *Soviet Operational Intelligence (Razvedka) to 1943*.
30. Danilevsky, "Vozdushnaia," 283.
31. *FM 100–2–3*, 4–124. Numbers of aircraft based upon wartime figures and data in Contact 2 I Br Corps Intelligence Training Coordination Coll (CITCC), 7th Intelligence Company, Intelligence and Security Group (Germany), 1984, p. 13.
32. "Agenturnaia razvedka" (Agent *razvedka*), *SVE*, 1:95.
33. "Spetsial'naia razvedka" (Special *razvedka*), *SVE*, 7:493.
34. "Voiska spetsial'nogo naznacheniia" (Special purpose forces), *SVE*, 2:326.
35. *Contact 2*, p. 16; *Soviet Military Power 1987* (Washington, D.C.: Superintendent of Documents, U.S. Government Printing Office, 1987), p. 89; V. Suvorov, "Spetsnaz, The Soviet Union's Special Forces," *International Defense Review*, No. 9 (Sept. 1983), 1,208–16. Suvorov's description tracks well with Soviet experience and appears thoroughly credible.

36. A. I. Paly, "Radioelektronnaia bor'ba (REB)" (Radio-electronic struggle (REB)), *SVE*, 7:29.
37. V. M. Zmievsky, "Radiorazvedka" (Radio *razvedka*), *SVE*, 7:18.
38. "Radiotekhnicheskaia razvedka (RTR)" (Radio-technical *razvedka* (RTR)), *SVE*, 7:24.
39. V. Ia. Grankin, "Radiolokatsionnaia razvedka (RLR)" (Radio-location *razvedka* (RLR)), *SVE*, 7:6.
40. *Ibid.*
41. *FM 100–2–3*, 4–123, 4–130, 4–133.
42. *Contact 2*, p.14; *FM 100–2–1, The Soviet Army Operations and Tactics* (Washington, D.C.: Headquarters, Department of the Army, 16 July 1984), 15–2.
43. "Tylovaia razvedka" (Rear area *razvedka*), *SVE*, 8:156.
44. "Rekognostsirovka" (Personal reconnaissance), *SVE*, 7:102.
45. "Razvedyvatel'no-udarnyi kompleks (RUK)" (Reconnaissance-strike complex), *Voennyi-entsiklopedicheskii slovar* (Military encyclopedic dictionary), (Moscow: Voenizdat, 1986), pp.616–17. The terminology RUK did not appear in the 1984 version of this dictionary.
46. *Ibid.*, p.617.
47. *Ibid.* For more details of reconnaissance-strike complexes, see M. Vego, "Soviet Ground-Based and Air-Based Recce-Strike: Theory and Practice" (Ft. Leavenworth: SASO, 1989), draft manuscript.

INDEX